PROSPECTS
FOR GROWTH

edited by
Kenneth D. Wilson

The Praeger Special Studies program, through a selective world-wide distribution network, makes available to the academic, government, and business communities significant and timely research in U.S. and international economic, social, and political issues.

PROSPECTS FOR GROWTH

Changing Expectations for the Future

Praeger Publishers   New York   London

Library of Congress Cataloguing in Publication Data

Main entry under title:

The Prospects for growth.

    (Praeger special studies in U.S. economic, social,
and political issues)
    Includes index.
    1. Economic development—Social aspects—Addresses,
essays, lectures. 2. Natural resources—Addresses,
essays, lectures. 3. Energy policy—Social aspects—
United States—Addresses, essays, lectures. I. Wilson,
Kenneth D.
HD82.P74   330.9   77-14567
ISBN 0-03-041446-6 Hardback
ISBN 0-03-041441-5 Paperback

PRAEGER SPECIAL STUDIES
200 Park Avenue, New York, N.Y., 10017, U.S.A.

Published in the United States of America in 1977
by Praeger Publishers,
A Division of Holt, Rinehart and Winston, CBS, Inc.

9 038 98765432

To Jack K. Horton,
for his leadership,
guidance, and support

| Preface |

The chapters in this volume were commissioned by the Edison Electric Institute (EEI), the principal association of America's investor-owned electric utility companies. The project was an outgrowth of the Institute's major study of the growth issue published in 1976 as *Economic Growth in the Future: The Growth Debate in National and Global Perspective* (New York: McGraw-Hill).

The original two-year study was directed at analyzing the arguments for and against growth and projecting what growth patterns would be under different pro-growth and no-growth economic policies. The project was supervised by a special committee made up of chief executives of EEI companies. The committee chairman was Jack K. Horton, chairman and chief executive officer of Southern California Edison Company. Jack Horton was the moving force in the industry for the conduct of a wide-ranging analysis of all aspects of economic growth including, but not limited to, energy growth.

A large number of independent experts and consultants representing many different points of view contributed to the original report. About half the authors of articles contained in this volume were consultants on the original project. Both the original study and this book reflect a commitment on the part of EEI to participate in a constructive way in the ongoing dialog about growth policies.

The contributors to this volume represent a wide range of views on what the future of growth should and will be. The articles deal with many different facets of growth policy. It should be noted that although EEI commissioned the articles it does not endorse the analyses or proposals they contain. Indeed, the Institute would disagree with some of the positions being advanced. However, the policy formulation process works best when all the different points of view and proposed alternative courses of action are heard. EEI sponsored this effort in the spirit of constructive dialog and mutual concern about the future of economic growth.

Kenneth D. Wilson
November 1977

| Contents |

| Tables |

| Figures |

| Introduction |

Kenneth D. Wilson

> Remember that the future is neither ours nor wholly
> not ours, so that we may neither count on it as sure
> to come, nor abandon hope of it as certain not to be.

This cautionary observation was made by the Greek philosopher Epicurus in 300 B.C., and it expresses well the problems of modern policy analysis and futures forecasting. Analysts, planners, and policy makers—using the best of tools and techniques—cannot promise an intended future. They can at most influence the general outlines. The specific shapes of things to come are determined by the unforeseeable and by chance.

To the extent that the general outlines of the future of economic growth *are* intentional, they are influenced by human expectations. The 1950s and 1960s, decades of rising expectations, were decades of rising economic growth. The 1970s, a time of lowered expectations, is a time of slackened growth rates. We now stand at a point in time when growth patterns are mainly cross currents, and when the most definite thing that can be said about expectations is that they are changing.

This book, then, reflects the pattern of changing expectations and represents the growth debate in its third and most productive phase. As Ian Wilson suggests in Chapter 8, this is the synthesis phase of the growth issue dialectic.

The first phase was launched, in the early 1970s, with attacks on growth which challenged traditional values of growth and progress. Most prominent among these attacks were the ideas set forth by E. J. Mishan, Meadows et al./The Club of Rome, and E. F. Schumacher.

In *Technology and Growth* (1970),[1] Mishan decried the side-effects of growth, spelling out the human costs of our technology-driven lifestyle. *The Limits to Growth* (1972)[2] the landmark report by Meadows et al./The Club of Rome, forecast that modern society would collapse if growth trends in population, industrialization, food production, resource consumption, and pollution continued. Schumacher, in *Small is Beautiful* (1973),[3] critiqued the fundamental premises of Western economic thought and the ways it is applied to developing countries. His "Buddhist Economics" has proven increasingly popular over time, and similar themes and additional challenges to the conventional wisdom of growth have been sounded by other critics during this time period.[4]

The second phase of the debate took shape with the responses to the challenges. These include a whole body of literature devoted to rebutting

The Limits to Growth report alone. Some of the almost immediate reactions were "The Computer that Printed Out W*O*L*F" by Karl Kaysen in *Foreign Affairs* (1972);[5] "How to Live with Economic Growth" by Henry Wallich in *Fortune* (1972);[6] and "The Future of Economic Activity" by Anthony Wiener in *The Annals* (1973).[7] Additional responses that followed along the same lines were "Growth and Its Enemies" by Rudolph Klein in the British Journal *Commentary* (1972)[8] and *The Retreat from Riches* by Passell and Ross (1973).[9] The most complete rebuttal was *Models of Doom,* edited by H. S. D. Cole et al. (1973).[10]

Although the *Limits* report was quickly critiqued and discounted by the scientific community, it had struck a resonant chord with a concerned public. The challenges to growth, far from attenuating, have resounded in a continuing stream of writings and actions.

The intellectual give-and-take was preceded and paralleled by actions taken at the community level. Practice in this case, as in others, has led theory. People in different areas all over the country have proceeded to control and stop growth in many different ways. The variety of grass-roots actions and the issues they raised have been reported in *Managed Growth,* edited by Carolyn Turner;[11] *The Use of Land: A Citizens' Policy Guide to Urban Growth,* edited by William K. Reilly;[12] and *The Taking Issue* by Fred Bosselman, David Callies, and John Banta.[13]

As growth-curtailing actions have proliferated at the local level, the federal government has studied and discussed the question from the standpoint of national policy. Examples of policy deliberations at the federal level are contained in a variety of government documents, including *U.S. Economic Growth from 1976 to 1986: Prospects Problems, and Patterns,* a 12-volume set of studies prepared in 1976 for the use of the Joint Economic Committee, U.S. Congress.[14] To date, this review and consideration has been of a study nature. It has not resulted in any concerted growth management actions by the Congress or the executive branch, despite the fact that the growth question underlies today's most important and difficult national policy issues. Indeed, it is at the base of the policy struggles revolving around the environment, energy, population, food, land use, income distribution and social equity, employment, civil order, technical development, capital formation, government regulation, and relations with other countries in regard to trade and national defense. The federal government pattern of deliberation on growth-related issues with minimal and fragmented action has been most clearly observed in the arena of energy policy.

As indicated in the sources cited above on local initiatives, *action* on growth and development policy has been at the grass-roots level. More and more communities have moved to halt specific projects and to manage and regulate growth in general. The cumulative effect of these actions across the country begins to be a de facto national policy of slow growth.

Meanwhile the intellectual exchange has continued.[15] Lacking in most cases, however, are concrete recommendations for operational courses of action. Policy formulation on the growth question has tended to be ad hoc, de facto, and by default.

The 16 chapters in this volume are organized in four parts. Part I contains three chapters that primarily describe the nature of the controversy, its origins, and how it is manifest in real case examples. Daniel Bell describes the political phenomenon of the "the issue attention cycle" in analyzing the dynamics of the growth debate. He traces the emergence and decline of the idea of physical limits before shifting to his central topic: the question of social limits. Speaking as a sociologist, Bell diagnoses social limits as deriving from a change in scale and as being resolvable through political means. He suggests that management of scale is one of the major problems of modern society. The reasons for the difficulties, he believes, are largely political. The scales of the functional problems (that is, social system breakdowns) are not matched by the scales of administrative operation (that is, government structure). This is not a technological or organizational question but rather a political one that involves the conflict between participation and efficiency. Within this context Bell counters the argument that technology is dehumanizing. He concludes that the problems of human organization are resolvable through such existing social mechanisms as open debate and the rule of law.

Luther Gerlach's chapter shifts the focus from the macro to the micro level. In the nonnormative descriptive style of the anthropologist, Gerlach relates in three case studies how the growth question is being dealt with by people in different communities and another culture. He notes that people at the local level have adopted the conceptual and theoretical propositions from the intellectual debate for their own purposes. The cases—which shift attention from the abstract to actual events—deal with water supply as the basis for further development in Florida; resource extraction in Northeastern Minnesota; and the impact of Western growth values on a nongrowth-oriented African culture. The cases serve to illustrate Gerlach's own analysis of the dynamics of the growth controversy. Included is a discussion of the ways different cultures historically have dealt with the problem of distribution of wealth.

Anthony Wiener introduces the theme of the central role of expectations as he explores the cultural origins of the growth controversy. He points out that opinions and arguments are derived as much by values and ideologies as by given facts and data. Sounding the psychological and social depths of those positioned on the growth issue, Wiener emphasizes the importance of motives, underlying beliefs, and the resistance of such beliefs to change. In diagnosing the "functions of the debate" he applies several conceptual tools including the sociology of knowledge. The discussion ranges over history and the evolution of thought to provide a deeper understanding of where the growth question comes from and where it may lead.

Part II contains four chapters presenting qualitative analyses with different approaches and suggestions on how to proceed. As a transition from the descriptive material in Part I, Robert Theobald critically reviews the shifts and changes which have occurred over time in the growth and no-growth positions. He faults both sides for their pessimism about the capacity of human beings to manage their own world. In what amounts to a "human potential manifesto," Theobald says that the key issue of our time is our view of people. In our present view, people who do not fit into American and world society should have their characters adjusted. On the contrary, says Theobald, the problem is that such people lack a world in which they can realize their legitimate goals. The task then becomes one of restructuring economic and social arrangements to accomplish a shift from what Theobald terms the "industrial era" to the "communications era." Included in the adjustments needed to accomplish this are instilling the capacity to live with "enoughness," an acceptance of diversity versus equality, the realization that changes in social behavior cannot be forced, and the recognition that religious and intellectual thought no longer clash. Theobald identifies four central policy issues in the areas of economics and employment, health, justice, and education. In these areas he proposes radical changes in the tax system; he suggests methods to produce a model for health maintenance organizations rather than national health insurance; he suggests new orientations and points of emphasis for the justice system; and, among other reforms in the field of education, he urges educational measures to support greater citizen participation. Theobald concludes with a description of a course of action to reach the "communications era."

The focus on human considerations is continued by Willis Harman and Richard Carlson who emphasize the primacy of social issues and social decision making over both economic and energy issues. Discounting the need for high economic growth, Harman and Carlson conclude that a variety of political and social pressures make slower growth more likely in any case. The determining factor will be human attitudes and perceptions, and Harman and Carlson attempt to outline "the new consensus." This is marked by a growing challenge to the "legitimacy of present social systems of the industrialized world—particularly to its economic, political, technological, corporate, and scientific aspects." The challenge is on three points, that is, whether the social system and its power concentrations are duly constituted, adhering to moral principles, and effective in achieving agreed-upon goals. Harman and Carlson point out that a challenge at such a fundamental level "could well end in dramatic domestic and international upheaval. It is more than the issue of economic growth. It is what lies behind the issue of economic growth."

Kenneth Boulding looks at the energy part of the overall growth question and contemplates the difficulty of solutions. The problem is compounded by what he terms the "anxieties of uncertainty." Boulding believes that the conditions prevailing in recent decades have been exceptionally favorable and cannot be counted on to continue. What conditions will mark the future, however, are entirely uncertain.

In his characteristically positive style, Boulding suggests that uncertainties can be viewed as a source of hope. "If all the certainties lead to anxiety, then perhaps we should cultivate the uncertainties." Boulding suggests the need for "policies for certainty and uncertainty" including the institution of a technological lottery. He concludes that it is by hopes and dreams, as well as sober plans that the sources of today's anxieties will be relieved.

Drawing comparisons between the United States and Great Britain, English economic writer Norman Macrae takes critical aim at the no-growth view and its reliance on computer models. Macrae argues that economic and energy growth are more likely to accelerate than to decline. Moreover, the United States is in a position to continue its world leadership—if it chooses to. Macrae worries about the parallels to be drawn between a receding Great Britain in the late 1800s and the United States today. He takes stock of a set of bizarre dangers that could alter the course of history. These include the use of thermonuclear weapons and the choices over life and death made possible by medical technology.

Looking at the potential impacts of the technology of telecommuting, Macrae anticipates profound changes in the modes of operations of organizations and the whole social fabric. These new modes will be more decentralized and more entrepreneurial. "Rich countries will have to reprivatize, recompetition, and denationalize a lot of present public sector activities over the next few decades." Macrae finds himself becoming more optimistic over time about whether the United States will regain its dynamism and world leadership.

The five chapters in Part III are forecasts and economic analyses. Ian Wilson looks at the structural factors of labor input and productivity and concludes that the United States will be "passing through an inflection point on the growth curves, almost regardless of the outcome of any specific public debate about national growth policies." The altered relationships within the economy, such as the ratio of energy to GNP, are described as "the changing metabolism of growth."

Wilson grapples with a new definition of growth and expects that, by the old definitions, growth rates will be lower. To Wilson, as suggested earlier, the evolution of the growth issues is an example of Hegel's dialectic process. The most probable future, he suggests, will be defined in terms of some synthesis of growth, restraint, and ecological consciousness. He concludes with prescriptions for public policy action in the areas of population, land use, and recycling. He also sees a role for public policy in the fostering of values which would result in more ecological/holistic/systemic/futuristic thinking.

Barry Hughes and Mihajlo Mesarovic present a computer-based modeling analysis. Using the Case Western Reserve Regionalized Multilevel World System Model, they have postulated U.S. energy policy options as influenced by the world energy and economic system. Forecasts are through the year 2000. The results are presented in three forms: alternative energy demand scenarios and their impacts on energy and economic variables; the effects of possible shocks to the energy system and their potential impact on the U.S. economic system; and alternative energy supply strategies that might be pursued by the economy and by energy planners.

The energy demand scenarios are derived from strategies of no change, moderate conservation, and accelerated conservation. The "shocks" examined have to do with changes in the pace of nuclear development, a second oil embargo, the effect of a nuclear accident, and the influence of energy independence policies. The energy supply scenarios flow from the three alternatives examined for energy demand.

The results of the Hughes and Mesarovic analysis show decided advantages in the "accelerated conservation" strategy. "Economic growth in the 'no-change' and 'moderate conservation' demand scenarios proved to be not only lower, but much more heavily toward energy production." Likewise, the resilience of the system to shocks was considerably greater with the accelerated conservation strategy. Thus, the central conclusion that energy demand policies to be pursued over the next 25 years are critically important.

William Nordhaus takes a fresh look at the question of the feasibility of sustained growth. In his view this is more central to the recent debate and logically prior to the desirability question in the growth issue. To Nordhaus, the feasibility of continued growth depends on "the metering problem" or whether current economic institutions are adequate to efficiently allocate normal goods and environmental goods: "economic growth is misdirected because we are either unwilling or unable to meter the different goods and bads of economic growth and to price these goods or bads appropriately." Nordhaus illustrates this point with examples from the energy sector. By charting a specific energy flow through the economy he identifies external economies and diseconomies. An examination of these leads to the conclusion that the cost of metering negative effluents or externalities may be critical along future growth paths. Carbon dioxide and nuclear power are presented as two "global" examples of unmetered growth.

Fred Singer examines the price system as it works to provide an adjustment mechanism. To this subject he brings a different perspective: that of geophysicist and professor of environmental sciences. Singer scrutinizes the operation and effectiveness of the price system (or free market) in seven areas: the formation and growth of capital; the management of the physical environment; the control of catastrophes, both natural and man-made; the continued growth of science and technology, and the consequences flowing therefrom; natural resources, their finiteness, now and in the future; population, its continued growth and distribution; and government and the growth of complexity.

Overall, Singer concludes that the growth versus no-growth controversy is a red herring. "The real issue is whether the price system can do the job of guiding the necessary adjustments or whether centralized decision making is called for." On this question Singer finds no instance where centralized decision making is superior to the dispersed decision making of a free market.

In the most detailed and sharply focused article in this collection, Gerard K. O'Neill presents the technical and economic bases for constructing satellite solar power stations in space. In its own way, O'Neill's plan is a positive response to attacks on growth. It points to a constructive and environmentally advantageous direction for economic growth and technological advance. The proposal calls for using materials from the moon and placing satellites in geosynchronous orbit above the earth. They would supply "clean, full-time, reliable solar energy in electrical form."

Part IV concludes with three chapters that argue the need for a steady state and the futility of growth. The final chapter is a response to the entropy argument against growth. Herman Daly consolidates his position as the leading proponent of "the steady-state economy(SSE)." He suggests policies for making the transition from growth to a SSE, and points out that the recommended mechanisms build on the existing institutions of private property and the price system. To Daly, the kinds of institutions needed follow straight from the definition of a steady-state economy, that is, "constant stocks of people and artifacts maintained at chosen levels that are sufficient for a good life sustainable for a long future, by the lowest feasible rate of throughput." The mechanisms proposed are the transferrable birth license plan, the depletion quota auction, and a distributist institution. The birth license plan has been discussed by Daly elsewhere, and he concentrates on elaborating the mechanism of the depletion quota auction. The suggested distributist institution would limit the range of inequality in income distribution. The combination of the three mechanisms, Daly argues, would provide the necessary macro controls with the least sacrifice of micro freedoms. Without such measures Daly believes that the real facts of life will push the growth paradigm into ever-greater anomalies, contradictions, and practical failures.

E. J. Mishan presents what amounts to a meta-level critique of growth. He has as his specific target the Edison Electric Institute report, *Economic Growth in the Future.* His chapter concentrates on the problems of growth rather than means of dealing with the problems. It is a further, and possibly ultimate, extension of the first phase of the growth debate. Focusing primarily on social limits, Mishan sees the world moving into increasing conflict and hazard as a result of the unforeseen by-products of scientific and technical progress: "Men will come reluctantly but inevitably to surrender to governments far greater powers of surveillance, control, and repression than are compatible with contemporary notions of personal liberty."

Nicholas Georgescu-Roegen is concerned with the physical laws of thermodynamics as related to economics. His theoretical work in applying the entropy law to economics is well established, and in his chapter he advances this abstract analysis even further to develop a critique of the steady-state economy. To Georgescu-Roegen the operation of entropic processes makes economic and physical decline inescapable, thus precluding the maintenance of even a steady state. "The picture is now clear. Terrestrial available matter-energy, as well as solar radiation reaching earth, would gradually degrade, whether life were present or not. But the presence of consumer species speeds up this degradation." He feels that prices do not serve as reliable entropic indexes.

To sharpen his analysis and make it more instructive, Georgescu-Roegen constructs a general flow matrix of the circulation of matter and energy. This general diagram illustrates the inflows of environmental energy and matter and the outflows of dissipated matter and waste. What is needed, he concludes, is a quantitative expression of the general flow matrix.

Peter Auer's chapter is the first response from a physical scientist to Georgescu-Roegen's theories on entropy and economics. Auer, a physicist, and professor of engineering at Cornell University, critically considers the economic implications of entropic processes. Georgescu-Roegen bases much of his argument on conflicting concepts of reversibility in classical physics and thermodynamics. On this Auer says he is "just plain wrong." Further excursions into the laws of thermodynamics lead Auer to conclude that although valuable lessons can be drawn from applying the principle of entropy production to economic theory, it provides little really useful guidance. "Resorting to more standard methods of analysis, one can infer that there are possible paths along which humankind could sustain a high level of economic activity for indefinite periods of time."

NOTES

1. E. J. Mishan, *Technology and Growth* (New York: Praeger, 1970).

2. Donella H. Meadows, Dennis L. Meadows, Jorgen Randers, and William W. Behrens III, *The Limits to Growth* (New York: Universe Books, 1972).

3. E. F. Schumacher, *Small is Beautiful: Economics as if People Mattered* (New York: Harper, 1973).

4. These include "A Blueprint for Survival," *The Ecologist* 2, no. 2 (January 1972): 1–44; and Herman E. Daly, ed., *Toward a Steady-State Economy* (San Francisco: Freeman, 1973).

5. Karl Kaysen, "The Computer that Printed Out W*O*L*F," *Foreign Affairs*, July 1972, pp. 660–68.

6. Henry Wallich, "How to Live with Economic Growth," *Fortune*, October 1972, pp. 114–22.

7. Anthony J. Wiener, "The Future of Economic Activity," *The Annals of the American Academy of Political and Social Science—The Future Society: Aspects of America in the Year 2000* 408 (July 1973): 47–61.

8. Rudolph Klein, "Growth and Its Enemies," *Commentary*, June 1972, pp. 37–44.

9. Peter Passell, and Leonard Ross, *The Retreat From Riches—Affluence and Its Enemies* (New York: Viking, 1973).

10. H. S. D. Cole, Christopher Freeman, Marie Jahoda, and K. L. R. Pavitt, eds. *Models of Doom: A Critique of the Limits to Growth* (New York: Universe Books, 1973).

11. Carolyn Turner, ed., *Managed Growth* (Chicago: Urban Research Corporation, 1973).

12. William K. Reilly, ed., *The Use of Land: A Citizens' Policy Guide to Urban Growth* (New York: Crowell, 1973).

13. Fred Bosselman, David Callies, and John Banta, *The Taking Issue* (A Study of the Constitutional Limits of Governmental Authority to Regulate the Use of Privately-Owned Land Without Paying Compensation to the Owners) (Washington, D.C.: U. S. Government Printing Office, 1973).

14. Joint Economic Committee, *U.S. Economic Growth From 1975 to 1986: Prospect, Problems and Patterns*, 94th Cong. 2d sess. (Washington, D.C.: U.S. Government Printing Office, 1976), 12 volumes. Other examples of policy deliberations at the federal level are Domestic Council Committee on National Growth, *Report on National Growth 1972* (First Biennial Report on National Growth as Required by Section 703(a) of the Housing and Urban Development Act of 1970) (Washington, D.C.: U.S. Government Printing Office, February 1972); U.S. Congress, House, *Growth and Its Implications for the Future, Part 1* (Hearing with Appendix before the Subcommittee on Fisheries and Wildlife Conservation and the Environment of the Committee on Merchant Marine and Fisheries) 93rd Cong., 1st sess. (Washington, D.C.: U.S. Government Printing Office, May 1973); and Congressional Research Service, Library of Congress, *Toward a National Growth and Development Policy: Legislative and Executive Actions in 1970 and 1971* 92d Cong., 2d sess. (Washington, D.C.: U.S. Government Printing Office, September 1972).

15. Examples of this literature are Mihajlo Mesarovic and Eduard Pestel, *Mankind at the Turning Point* (New York: Dutton/Reader's Digest Press, 1974); Barry Commoner, *The Poverty of Power: Energy and the Economic Crisis* (New York: Knopf, 1976); *Critical Choices for Americans: Values of Growth* (Lexington, Mass.: Lexington Books, 1976), Vol. VI; Herman Kahn, William Brown, Leon Martel et al, *The Next 200 Years: A Scenario for America and the World* (New York: Morrow, 1976); Lewis J. Perelman, *The Global Mind: Beyond the Limits to Growth* (New York; Mason/Charter, 1976); and William Ophuls, *Ecology and the Politics of Scarcity* (San Francisco: Freeman, 1977).

PART ONE
Descriptive Analyses

1 | Are There "Social Limits" to Growth?
Daniel Bell

THE ISSUE-ATTENTION CYCLE
AND THE GROWTH DEBATE

One of the more remarkable aspects of public policy debate in the United States, as Anthony Downs pointed out several years ago, is that "American public attention rarely remains sharply focused upon any one domestic issue for very long—even if it involves a continuing problem of crucial importance to society." Instead, as Downs continues, "a systematic 'issue-attention cycle' seems strongly to influence public attitudes and behavior concerning most key domestic problems. Each of the problems suddenly leaps into prominence, remains there for a short time, and then—though still largely unresolved—gradually fades from the center of public attention."[1]

The *Limits to Growth*[2] controversy is a prime example of the issue-attention cycle and its deleterious effects on public policy debate. There were three elements that conjoined to give this study, and the issue, an undue attention. First, it was sponsored by a group of international businessmen, organized under the ambiguous name of the Club of Rome. Second, the results were presented as deriving from a presumably sophisticated computer simulation model that was developed by young colleagues of Jay Forrester at MIT. And third, its calamitous and apocalyptic warnings of the impending exhaustion of resources, or the drowning of the world in pollution and wastes, came fortuitously close in time with a worldwide Arab oil embargo. This development shut down gasoline stations, reduced available fuel oil, and limited oil for energy and industrial power. Events became a Hollywood scenario of what the end of the industrial world might face *if*—it was quickly assumed *when*—the resources were depleted. The simple warning was evident: The world, particularly the advanced industrial countries, would have to cut back on economic growth if it was to survive, let alone provide an unspoiled environment.

Two crucial changes have made many of the recent issues quite different from similar policy problems of the past, even when the same issues
reappear in a new guise (for example, the conservation issue, the Pinchot-
Ballinger controversy of the Theodore Roosevelt period, reappearing as
the ecology issue). These changes are in the modes of presentation and
the nature of the involvements. The first is the impact of intensive media
exposure. We now have, because of the revolutions in transportation and
communication, a national society, and every issue now receives redou-
bled and national attention. National television networks seek out issues
they can dramatize. The national newsweeklies seek to encourage public
focus on policy problems. The difficulty is that the very nature of the
media—the two-to-three-minute intensive set of photoflashes, or the an-
ecdotal and human-interest stories—tend to simplify, overdramatize, ex-
aggerate (and usually seek to pin a question on good guys and bad guys).
This increases the alarms and anxieties of the listeners and readers. It
also provokes other individuals who want public attention to think up
media events (such as burying an automobile to dramatize the ecology
issue). In the end, the effect is to distort the complexity of the problem
and inhibit solutions.

The second difference is that these issues now mix economic and social
questions with symbolic and expressive emotions that are derived from
conflicting values. And while values underlie all public policy questions,
what often happens is that the issues become dominated by heavy emotional charges that tend to absolutize the question and make it more
difficult to attempt mediation and compromise. Any attempt at a trade-off
is seen by one or another faction that is emotionally involved as a betrayal
of principle, and thus the resolution of the issue is often more difficult
than in the past.

The *Limits to Growth* issue has now become largely exhausted. I don't
mean that it has disappeared, as a public policy issue; but it has run its
course through the issue-attention cycle, and is now in a very different
stage. On one level, a fickle public and a fickle media have found new
issues. (And that is a problem, largely, for the "sociology of mass communications.") But on the more serious level, a debate was provoked that
sought to disentangle the issues and to assess the consequences of one
or another alternative course. Under severe criticism from the academic
community, most of the assumptions and the logic of analysis of the Club
of Rome study was found to be faulty.[3] The comprehensive, scholarly,
and fair-minded assessments of the Edison Electric Institute study, *Economic Growth in the Future,* has provided a basis for the establishment of
relevant facts and the clarification of values.[4] And, in a meeting in Philadelphia in April 1976, the Club of Rome reversed itself almost completely. It virtually abandoned the argument regarding the extent of
physical resources. It stated that its aim had been, primarily, to alert the

worldwide public to environmental and resources problems, and that its chief concern was with the gap between rich and poor nations, a gap that, if widened, would lead to extended famines, social disturbances, and war.

Yet the logic of its reversal was clear. If one is to make the question of reducing the disparities between nations the central question for the world polity, then it is obvious that economic growth is a necessity in order to expand the wealth of the world and make it available for rising standards of living for the peoples of the world.

Two other, different questions then arise. One is how to assure that economic growth is possible, both within resource constraints (principally rising costs of energy) and the maintenance of a livable environment. The other is the new question that the limits to growth are not physical resources or economic, but social. In recent years the issue of economic growth has become an umbrella for a wide range of social discontents: for those who have become antitechnology and want a return to nature; for those who believe that size, bigness, and complexity dwarf the human being and reduce the human scale; for those who have turned against materialism on the grounds that the possession of goods leads to alienation or dissolute ways, and so on.

If we are to deal with these two questions, first we have to review the way the growth issue arose, and to sort out the different assumptions (and misleading notions) that were entangled together. And then, on the social limits issue, we have to sort out the factual questions and the value assumptions and test both against a set of standards.

THE IDEA OF PHYSICAL LIMITS

In its emergence, and in the debates that swirled around it, the economic growth issue was more complicated than the usual single-dimension issue, because mixed up within it were three very different issues, different in their causal sources and sequences, and different in their policy consequences. These were the pollution issue, the environmental spoilation issue, and the depletion of physical resources issue.

The pollution issue arose because alarmed observers pointed out that economic growth simply increased industrial wastes that were propelled into the air or tossed into the waters, thus creating smog and foul air or dirty lakes or rivers where fish could not survive or men and women swim. There was an obvious point to all this. As C. B. McCoy, then the president of duPont, once remarked wryly: "We used to have a mural in the duPont auditorium which showed our smokestacks belching smoke, and we all took that as a symbol of industrial prosperity. But now we have had to erase that picture from our wall."

Yet what was less obvious were three other factors. First was the lack of historical actuality in the alarm over the issue. Nineteenth-century American cities were probably more polluted and the air worse to breath than the present, largely because of the heavy use of coal as a fuel. In London in the late nineteenth century there was a serious proposal to put large tubes hundreds of feet into the air with suction pumps below to draw in fresh air from the skies, because of the heavy smogs created by the coal-burning stoves. When, in the late 1950s, the London municipality barred all coal-burning within the metropolitan areas, the famous pea-soup fogs, which had been so distinctive a feature of London winter life (and the marvelous setting for so many great detective stories) virtually disappeared. The disappearance of coal-burning locomotives and their replacement by diesels, and the control of emissions from the great steel mills in Pittsburgh and Chicago, certainly made those cities cleaner and more livable. History does not point to the elimination of a social problem, but it does provide a better perspective on the nature of change.

The second fact was that a large part of the pollution was a trade-off for other gains. In the case of the automobile, this was the increase in personal mobility. But more important, and much less well known, was the fact that much of the pollution of the rivers and streams of the country resulted from the runoff of nitrates from fertilizers applied to the farms, and that it was this technological revolution on the farm that had resulted in the extraordinary increases in productivity which, before World War II, was about 1 to 2 percent a year, and in the quarter of a century after was averaging 6 to 8 percent a year. As a result of this productivity, about 4 percent of the labor force could feed the entire population of the United States and a large part of the world besides. The restriction of such fertilizers, in order to reduce water pollution, inevitably would mean some reduction in the supply of food.

The third fact, however, was the very belated realization that the reasons for the pollution lay less in the greed of industry, or the indifference of municipalities about the disposal of wastes, or the casual approach of the motorist to car emissions—though there was a basis of truth in all of this—than the simple fact that the market principle had never been applied to the use of air and water. In most economic textbooks, until recently, air and water were given as the illustrations of a free good, that is, a good that had no cost because of the very abundance of the resource. All other resources had costs—because of the costs of extraction, such as oil or minerals, the costs of machinery, the costs of capital and labor to transform the resources into goods and services, and so on. Air and water had no cost.

Now there is a simple economic principle that if something has no cost, it will be used recklessly and heedlessly. If you have some wastes, toss them into the water and let them be washed away or pumped into the air where they would be blown away. In effect, pollution increased because there were few costs. Or, to put it more precisely, the costs that did arise were externalized since the individuals generating these costs did not have to pay for them. But if air and water are treated as scarce resources, one puts a price on their use, and the existence of a price forces a user to economize on the resource.

To that extent, the problem of pollution was a failure of economic imagination. And to the extent that a price becomes put on a resource, and has to be internalized by the person generating the costs, it becomes, like safety in the factory, a force for the reduction of pollution.

The issue of environmental spoilation was raised primarily in relation to unregulated patterns of growth, particularly in regard to land use. There was fear that the widespread strip mining of coal would scar large sections of the landscape, the speed-up in the cutting of timber lay bare large sections of forests, and the rapid spread of "ticky-tacky" houses led to an ugly suburban sprawl that would disfigure the countryside, especially in coastal regions, and reduce the amenities (picturesque views, recreational facilities, and so on) available to the population as a whole.

Many of these fears were justified. But the fact was that by the time of alarmed discovery, regulative steps, both legislative and judicial, had been taken to control the reckless use of land, while the slowdown in population growth, as well as rising costs and inflation, had reduced the number of housing starts and, for many communities, had provided a breather to do more intelligent land use planning.

The resources issue has probably played the heaviest role in the attack on the idea of economic growth. In large measure this was because of the extraordinary publicity of the Club of Rome's *Limits to Growth* study, a publicity that was accentuated by the sudden embargo on oil by OPEC (Organization of Petroleum Exporting Countries) as a result of Arab initiatives. The sight of gas stations shut down, the fear of little fuel for winter heating, the alarms by utilities and government exhorting people to save on energy use all reinforced the belief that somehow a resource limitation, or even the threat of exhaustion, was responsible for that situation. Of course it was not. The OPEC action was entirely political, the result of a cartel action, rather than a response by the market to the fear of declining resources. But in the popular view the resources issue had become salient.

In quiet retrospect it is clear that the resources issue is as good an example as one can find on the mishandling and misdirection of a public policy issue, and that the Club of Rome study is as fearful an example as one would ever dread of how badly social science can be misused to push a particular point of view.

The first and most obvious fact is that no matter how elegant or complicated or abstruse or dominating a computer model may be, its conclusions, in the working out of the interrelations of resources, population growth, and intensities of use, are only as good as the reliability of the initial data and the assumptions used. Yet in instance after instance the assumptions were questionable. For example, the estimates of ultimately recoverable crude oil in the United States published within the past ten years range *nine times* from the lowest to the highest estimate, and such a range renders useless any notion of national policy if one or the other of the estimates is to be used as the basis for a national energy policy.[5]

The second, less obvious, fact is that few resources command a monopoly use, and once one puts price into a model (and more specifically in the real world) then the level of price will determine alternative patterns of use and substitutions.

A recent UN analysis, "The Long-Term Supply of Copper" is a central case in point.[6] The analysis begins with the statement that in the *Limits to Growth* study "the authors singled out copper as one of the natural resources the world will have used up within a generation." With this prediction of a physical shortage of copper, and the energy crisis, a rush to build stocks sent copper to an all-time high of $1.50 per pound in April 1974. By the end of the year, however, the price had broken badly and since then has been between $.50 and $.60 per pound.

The reason is simple. Copper normally was found in veins that contained other metals such as lead and zinc, and the output of copper in the past was determined, in part, by the price of other minerals in mixed or complex ores. But with the price of copper itself so high, it becomes feasible to exploit a different source of copper, porphyry copper, which in the past had been considered too low grade as it had less than nine pounds per ton of rock. With the increase in the price of copper, nations possessing massive deposits began mining the copper and selling it on the world market. At the same time, with the price so high, users began to substitute other items for copper, so with a new supply and a change in the patterns of demand the price broke.

As the authors of the UN analysis conclude:

> The long-term prospects for copper, however, are quite different from what was described in *The Limits to Growth*. From the resource viewpoint, therefore, there are no reasons to assume that natural supplies of copper will run out in the foreseeable future. On the demand side, however, the prospects are more difficult to assess, given the increase in competition from aluminum, steel, plastic, and also now glass. There are very few applications for which copper is the only possible choice. Thus, a sharp increase in copper prices, always leads to substitution.[7]

If one thinks only in physical terms, then it is likely that one does not need to worry about ever running out of resources. Reserves are almost infinitely greater than the 250-year supply that is assumed in the *Limits to Growth* model. As Bent Sorenson has noted:

> By classifying resources according to their properties, for example, as met-
> als, semi-conductors, and insulators one can obtain broad groups of sub-
> stitutable materials that are present in the earth's crust, including the water
> of the oceans, in quantities that probably exceed any foreseeable require-
> ment of man. If one can assume that the use of a resource will rarely result
> in its being removed from the earth into space, then the term usage will at
> worst imply dilution to the average concentration of the resource in the
> earth's crust. Thus, the absolute degree of resource depletion is of minor
> relevance; rather one must expect to spend an increased effort, related to
> cost, in order to recover the resources from still lower grade deposits. If used
> raw materials were returned at maximum dilution, the cost of recovering
> new raw materials would increase as a function of the integrated usage over
> the past.[8]

But the crucial point is that economic development, while it does depend upon technology, has a wide range of alternative methods, each one
being characterized by a different mix of capital, labor, and resource
inputs. Society tends to adopt technologies, as Glenn Hueckel has observed, that are compatible with existing resource endowments. When
the resource pattern changes, new techniques are introduced, either for
extraction and exploration, or by the introduction of substitutes, that
provide a different pattern of organization. As Hueckel points out:

> This proposition has implications for both an understanding of past techno-
> logical change and an assessment of future advance. It undermines the
> hypothesis that technological advance is of necessity pollution-creating or
> resource-depleting and thus makes it impossible to argue that the level of
> pollution in modern society is solely the result of past technological advance.
> Yet, this is precisely the view implied by the Meadows team when they take
> "pollution generation" and "per capita resource usage" as functions only of
> the level of "per capita industrial output." In the case of pollution, the
> function is simply assumed to be linear; and in the case of resource usage,
> the functional form employed in the model assumes that as economic growth
> raises per capita incomes in the rest of the world to the 1970 level in the
> United States, world resource usage will approach the corresponding U.S.
> rate. Such an event is very unlikely, however, because other countries do not
> possess the same mix of resource endowments and thus will not develop the
> same structure of relative input prices as that which characterized the U.S.
> experience.[9]

In the public policy debate on economic growth there is, however, a
far different issue, and a paradox: The challenge to the idea of economic
growth (often from upper-middle-class liberals) has come at the very time

when there has been an unprecedented sociological revolution, what I have called the "revolution of rising entitlements."[10] Over the past 25 years we have seen the expansion of the welfare state and the spread of the normative social policy. Central governments in all societies, but in particular the industrial democracies, have made an irreversible commitment to redress economic and social inequalities and to provide for a range of services and support for large sections of the society, particularly the disadvantaged. This takes the form of social security, unemployment insurance, medical care (Medicare and Medicaid), housing subsidies, educational subventions, welfare payments, social services, legal aid, and dozens of other modes of help. In the United States, federal spending for what is defined as "social welfare purposes," rose from $14 billion in 1950 to $180 billion in 1975, or from less than one-fifth of the federal budget to more than one-half. The sociological revolution has been more, though, than the expenditure of money. It has taken the form— a basic shift in the values of the society—that what was once considered to be an individual effort is now a claim on the government, a claim for protection against societal hazards and, in effect, an entitlement, something that a person is entitled to by virtue of being a citizen of that society.

Now these large new expenditures can be financed only in two ways: either out of economic growth or by direct redistribution of incomes. In the 1960s the philosophy of government was to finance the expansion of these services out of the rising revenues created by economic growth. The simple fact is that economic growth is a political "solvent." While growth invariably raises expectations, the means for financing social welfare expenditures have come essentially from economic growth. In a trillion-dollar economy, an increase in the economic growth rate of 1 percent means a net addition of $100 billion by the end of a decade. And as the Kennedy and Johnson administrations found out (until Vietnam war expenditures began to escalate), the Congress was more willing to vote for the social welfare costs of the New Frontier or the Great Society, so long as economic growth provided additional fiscal revenues, than to reform the tax structure or shift the weight of taxes in the society.[11]

Given the continuing demand for social expenditures, the only other means of financing these, other than economic growth, would be through direct income redistribution—a political fact that invites not only obvious social conflicts but special dysfunctions as well. As Harvey Brooks points out,

> a large part of the housing stock would probably have to be converted to higher density occupancy. Many consumer durables, such as automobiles and home appliances, would have to be standardized to achieve a more universal distribution . . . mass transportation would have to be substituted

for the automobile on a considerable scale, and the resulting redistribution of population would make many dwelling structures obsolete or useless and create new demands for new structures in new locations[12]

THE IDEA OF SOCIAL LIMITS

Considering the EEI report *Economic Growth in the Future,*[13] I think that conclusions on the resources and economic questions are persuasive. Economic growth is desirable, possible, and necessary. It is necessary to meet the social demands on the society. It is necessary, as the report points out, "to increase extractive and processing capacity, to develop new, more efficient technologies, and to develop fuels and processes which are more consistent with the stringent environmental standards being set for the nation."

What, then, of the question of social limits to growth. Here the report concludes: "On the question of psychological and organizational limits to growth, it is concluded that there are *no inherent limits* to man's capacity to adapt and cope with complexity. Given the will to do so, man can devise evermore intricate organization forms and make them work. It is a matter of social choice whether this will be done."[14] Such a sweeping and unqualified statement reflects a lack of appreciation for the complexity of the problem. It does not allow us to even consider in what way there may or may not be social limits. Therefore, I would like to reformulate the argument as a means of identifying the relevant problems, avoiding the rhetoric that accompanies so much of the issue.

It is a fundamental sociological theorem that growth involves a change in scale. But a change in scale is not simply a linear extension in size of any existing organization. No institution that undergoes a change in size does so, *if it is to survive and adapt,* without changing its form and shape. It was Galileo, more than 350 years ago, who laid down this principle. As the great biologist D'Arcy Wentworth Thompson described the problem in his classic volumes, *On Growth and Form:*

> [Galileo] said that if we tried building ships, palaces or temples of enormous size, yards beams and bolts would cease to hold together; nor can Nature grow a tree or construct an animal beyond a certain size while retaining the proportions and employing the materials which suffice in the case of smaller structures. The thing will fall to pieces of its own weight unless we . . . change the relative proportions.[15]

For Galileo, changes in proportion followed a mathematical principle, defined in normal spatial geometry as the square-cube law: as volume increases by cubic function, the surface enclosing it only increases by a square. A change in volume, or size, therefore, necessarily is a change in shape.

Every organization theorist knows this, and the corollary principle is that a change in size necessitates a change in structure—if the organization, or the society, is to continue functioning. To put it less abstractly, the continued growth of an organization, or a society, involves a necessary decentralization of structure and operations, as the scope and scale of the enterprise or the society itself, which involve more centralization of control and policy, continue to expand.

The management of scale is one of the major difficulties besetting a modern society—and the reasons for these difficulties are largely political. Let me revert to an earlier point. We have become in the past 30 years, because of the revolutions in transportation and communication, a national society. Yet we do not have the institutions to match the new scales. The American polity is divided into 50 states, 3,000 counties, and more than 50,000 municipalities of varying scope. The boundaries of the 50 states follow no rational boundaries and range from small principalities such as Delaware, Rhode Island, and Connecticut, to large, outlandish empires such as Texas and Montana. In the Midwest, the counties were laid out on the principle of how long it would take a person to go from any part of the county to the county seat in one day, by horse and buggy. In the New York metropolitan region there are 1,400 local governments: water districts, recreation districts, sewerage districts, police districts, and so on, each with their own sovereignties. This is not decentralization, but disarray.

The scales of function and administrative operation simply do not match. And as a result we get escalating costs of state and local government and fewer and fewer services as some tax bases shrink and others exempt themselves from the costs of government. In short, we have here a structure of vested interests that are resistant to change and that, increasingly, levies more and more of a charge on the society.

The point has to be expanded. The question of social limits is not a technological or organizational question, but a political one. And those who raise it, rhetorically, as an argument against economic growth rarely face up to the problems they themselves create. Thus, for example, there *is* an inherent conflict between participation and efficiency. One of the more important facts about American life in the last two decades has been the enormous expansion of citizen involvement in all aspects of public policy debate. Yet while much of this is highly desirable, it also has a cost. For the multiplication of citizen groups also leads to the multiplication of veto groups, and to a politics of stymie. One can no longer take into account purely economic factors in locating a jet airport, or siting a utility plant, or planning a road, without encountering some citizen group that will find itself unsettled and, because the locus of decision is the political arena, can go into the courts or the legislatures to block action. Yet this, too, creates a further curious paradox. Many persons claim today that government has grown too large and that they are unable to have a voice in its decisions. And they believe, therefore, that political apathy is on the rise. Yet the converse is true. There is much more participation than ever before, but because, in the clash of multiple interests, each group may not get its way, it feels helpless and alienated.

The answer to these situations is not a technocratic solution of ever-more intricate organization forms, but the simpler recognition by every segment of the society that no single group can ever wholly have its way, that one cannot absolutize a position, and that bargaining and trade-offs are necessary. Any solution to a political issue involves differential costs; and that is the principle of public government that has to be recognized and accepted. An increase in public services for the disadvantaged means an increase in taxes and a reduction of personal consumption. Tightened environmental restrictions may lead to plant shutdowns and loss of jobs for communities. These are, inevitably, differences in values and, short of war, they have to be mediated.

One other point needs to be confronted: the argument that technology is dehumanizing and reduces the human scale. The facts are simply quite different. There are two characteristics to technology that have to be established. The first is that, basically, technology is instrumental. It is a machine, or a design, or a technique that can be used in many different ways, according to the social purposes or the social system in which it is embedded. Take the automobile. One can have a system of complete private ownership, allowing for a wide degree of personal mobility, yet the use of more land for garages, parking, and so on. Or one can have a system that bars the use of private automobiles and restricts all uses to taxis, leased cars, or shared pooling arrangements. It is the same technology, the same instrument, but used differently in different social settings. Which system one prefers is a political choice.

The second fact is that technology tends to become more simplified rather than more complicated in design, in the ability to use it and to understand it. The use of a telephone, a radio, a television set, a camera, or an automobile requires fewer skills in the operation of present-day push-button products than at the start. A computer, which for many persons is a mystery, is constantly being simplified so that, in a few years, one will talk to a computer in natural language (for example, English), rather than a special computer language. And, in all these instances, as products become simplified (regard only the hand-held electronic calculator), the price goes down with the advance in technology.

The idea, then, that there are social limits to growth does not derive from technology, or even organizational size—if it is adaptive to the requirements of new functions and scale—but to the differing fears, vested interests, and value conflicts of individuals and groups. But this is the oldest of all problems of human organization and is resolvable if one accepts the "rules of the game," that is, the procedures of open debate, of compromise, and of the acceptance of the rule of law.

CONCLUSION

The issue-attention cycle, as I have suggested implicitly, has its negative and positive features. The negative ones have tended to dominate. Issues flare up, are posed in striking rhetoric, gain emotional adherents, receive exaggerated attention, are resolved often by "fiat," that is, legislation is passed and an agency is created to "do something" about the problem, and then attention fades. Yet there are obvious positive values as well which are illustrated by the report of the Edison Electric Institute. An industry shows that it is willing to face an issue squarely, rather than back off and engage in propaganda or rhetorical debate. There is an emphasis on factual inquiry. The different points of view are weighed and tested, and there is an emphasis on both the different values involved as well as the costs and trade-offs of the different policies that are proposed.

One of the dangers of the issue-attention cycle is that because the issues are often symbolic, as well as economic, there is a tendency to ideologize the question and for contrary positions to harden. If there has been a strength to the American approach to social policy it has been that its emphasis has been on what is primarily instrumental (that is, possible) though this has, at times, neglected the underlying values at stake in an issue.

What does emerge from all this is the implicit acceptance by all parties of the legitimate right of government to raise issues of public interest and to demand a public accounting from all interested parties. What has been less evident is the willingness of the parties to break away from "prejudged" or stereotyped conceptions that often have an ideological flavor. Thus, for the liberal, the first reaction to an issue is to call for public intervention and government "regulation" of an industry. And government regulation usually has meant the multiplication of another administrative agency, with the right to set standards, enforce compliance, and levy penalties. For industry, the cry has usually been, "let the free market take care of the problem," and reject any government intervention. Yet both positions simply bypass each other. There is a legitimacy to the governmental concern, on the level of values and policy, and there is a utility to the market as an instrumentality. What I am saying is that the

market *is* a useful instrument for regulation because the price mechanism
is impersonal and forces compliance by an individual on himself, since a
rising price usually will force him to economize, and in such instances the
market is clearly preferable to bureaucratic intervention. Yet the point is
that the market can be used for social purposes as well, by government.
In the case of pollution, for example, rather than an administrative intervention with detailed engineering standards, one could levy effluent
charges and seek compliance through the price mechanism. If there need
be rationing, then rationing by purse is preferable to rationing by cou-
pon, and if injustices occur among particular segments of the population,
those injustices could be remedied by rebates through the tax mechanism.

Whatever the opinion on this specific argument, what is at stake is the
need to think creatively and clearly on public policy questions and, on a
factual basis and within the values that are consensually accepted, come
to agreements that allow us to meet these questions in an open and
democratic way. And this is what we are doing.

NOTES

1. Anthony Downs, "Up and Down With Ecology—The 'Issue Attention Cycle,' " *The Public Interest*, no. 28 (Summer 1972): 38. The number and rapidity of these issues, in just the last decade, is remarkable: automation, nuclear testing, student protests, black power, women's lib, abortion, legalization of marijuana, crime, urban decay, civil rights, poverty, educational equality, pollution, ecology, environment, prison reform, medical care, busing, social responsibility of business, alienation in work, consumerism, redistribu-tion of income, quotas for minorities, zero population growth, economic growth, and so on.
2. Donella H. Meadows et al., *The Limits To Growth* (New York: Universe Books, 1972).
3. Mention should especially be made of a detailed study and replication of the *Limits to Growth* study by a work group at the University of Sussex, England, that demolished the factual underpinnings and the logic of the Forrester-Meadows model, a work that regretta-bly received insufficient attention in this country. See H. S. D. Cole, Christopher Freeman, Marie Johoda, and K. L. R. Pavitt, eds., *Models of Doom: A Critique of the Limits to Growth*, (New York: Universe Books, 1973).
4. Edison Electric Institute, *Economic Growth in the Future: The Growth Debate in National and Global Perspective* (New York: McGraw-Hill, 1976).
5. Earl Cook, "The Depletion of Geologic Resources," *Technology Review*, June 1975, pp. 23–25. If a 1944 forecast of minerals had proved correct, the United States would by now have exhausted its reserves of tin, nickel, lead, zinc, and some 17 other minerals. Instead, in the following decade, there were new discoveries of deposits of these materials contain-ing a greater estimated quantity than discovered in the previous 25 years. See W. Page, "The non-renewable resources sub-system," in *Models of Doom*, pp. 33–42.
6. "The Long-Term Supply of Copper," in *Important for the Future*, publication of UNI-TAR (United Nations Institute for Training and Research), from their "Special Project on the Future," 1, no. 3 (April 1976):3–4. (Emphasis in the original). The political conclusions reached by this analysis themselves are interesting, for as the analysis points out, the rise in the price of copper encouraged a number of countries, such as Panama, to make heavy

investment in porphyry copper mining, only to find themselves with heavy financial losses when the market price began to drop. What may be needed, concludes the analysis, is a commodity agreement between the "copper exporting developing countries and the industrial countries" to cover *"not only present but also future producers of copper and the copper recycling capacity as well as a price structure that would discourage large-scale substitution of copper by other materials."* (Emphasis in the original.)

7. *Ibid* (Emphasis in the original).

8. Bent Sorenson, "Energy and Resources," *Science* 189, no. 4199 (July 25, 1975):255.

9. Glenn Hueckel, "A Historical Approach to Future Economic Growth," *Science* 189, no. 4195 (March 14, 1975):926.

10. See Daniel Bell, "Revolution of Rising Entitlements," *Fortune*, February 1975.

11. Otto Eckstein, "The Economics of the 1960's—A Backward Look," *The Public Interest*, no. 19 (Spring 1970): 86–97. Eckstein was a member of the Council of Economic Advisors in the Johnson administration.

12. Harvey Brooks, "The Technology of Zero Growth," *Daedalus*, Fall 1973, pp. 139–52. For those who think that mass transportation provides cheaper and more efficient transportation than the private automobile, I recommend to them the account told by David Wilson, a columnist for the Boston *Globe*, of his adventures one Christmas week last year. Wilson, who lives in a Boston suburb took himself, his wife, and three children in his car to his wife's relatives in a Long Island suburb, a trip by car that took about four and a half hours and cost about $9 for gasoline and tolls. On Long Island, however, the car broke down and had to be left for repairs. Consequently, he was driven by his in-laws to the suburban train station to take the train into Penn Station in New York. After a long wait, he and his family boarded the train to Boston. At Boston, he took a bus to his suburban town and from the bus station took a taxi to his house. In all, the trip home took about nine hours and cost about $25 in fares.

13. EEI, *Economic Growth in the Future.*

14. This is the formulation in the Executive Summary, p. 6. A slightly different formulation is in Chapter 4, p. 63, where the words "psychological and organization limits" are dropped, but the words "no absolute" are substituted for "no inherent" limits.

15. D'Arcy Wentworth Thompson, *On Growth and Form*, Vol. 1 (Cambridge: University Press, 1963). p. 27.

2 | The Growth Debate: Cosmic Concepts and Grass-Roots Adaptations

Luther P. Gerlach

"MOVING ON UP"

Ask middle- or upper-income Americans how they justify their having more money and higher position than many others in their society, and what do they say? Their first response is likely to be that the question is rather strange or meaningless and the answer obvious: "We worked for it, anyone can. Anyway, others are doing even better than we." It seems that most have never really given such a question deep thought. The American system of allocating economic rewards and of ranking people along some sort of scale of success seems in the very nature of things. But as people think about the question, they usually realize that it *is* provocative and wonder what is the catch and what is the motive of the questioner. On reflection, they know that the legitimacy of the American system of allocating rewards and social position is being challenged by some people within the United States and across much of the less-affluent world. But as discussion of this subject continues, those questioned usually return to their initial premise: that since just about anyone can move up in the American system, anyone who is up usually deserves being there. Recent civil rights, black power, women's liberation, and other protest movements have pointed out that some people have been systematically prevented from moving up. But it seems that most Americans think that the country is now overcoming this exception to the American dream. "We are not perfect, but we are trying. People can get ahead." For example, just as television played an important role in driving home the injustice of racism and sexism, as well as the power of the protest against it, it now plays an important role showing how those who have been down are indeed "moving on up."

To accept that everyone has a right to move on up and to believe that in time most everyone will be able to make such a stride if he or she tries hard enough depends upon popular acceptance of another powerful principle, the principle of growth: growth in economy, and thus growth in jobs, opportunities, chances for advancement and individual progress. Business and community leaders interpreted the black power movement and women's liberation as demands not only for liberation of the spirit but also for economic advancement. Thus, Detroit's key answer to inner-city rioting was to provide more jobs for black Americans in the auto industry. One answer to unrest in Minneapolis and St. Paul was to help deprived minorities learn skills and get jobs through a special "Opportunities and Industrial" training program.

But if the moving on up of minorities into these jobs would have necessarily meant the moving down or out of the whites who had them, would the whites have permitted this, or the community leaders have advocated it? If people thought about it at all, presumably they just assumed that in most cases the number of available jobs would be increased. After all, Detroit can always make more cars. There would be economic growth. Yes, there has been some talk about the rightness of reversing past wrongs even if it means reverse discrimination Yes, some whites and some males have protested that they have lost ground because of the advancement of blacks, chicanos, or women through "affirmative hiring." But, generally, both those who are up and those who are moving there still seem to share a belief in what might best be called the "principle of the expanding good." The good life, the opportunities, and the jobs can keep on expanding so that anyone can get more without anyone necessarily getting less. Often people express this by using the analogy of the pie of possibilities, income, and the good life. They say that it is logical that have-nots want to get a larger slice of the possibility pie. And they seem to assume that this can be gotten not by slicing the pie into smaller pieces, but by making it bigger. This is, of course, a stablizing concept. It means that those who are up are not threatened by the upward striving of others. It legitimates the basic system of allocation and stratification even as it accepts the right of people to mobilize in interest groups or special movements to strive for advancement.

It is economic growth which supports this system of beliefs. It has been economic growth as well as an expanding frontier which has made the possibility pie keep growing, and which has seemed to fulfill the image of the constantly expanding good. But the system is cybernetic; effects tend to feed back and become causes. Thus, it is this image of ever-expanding opportunity that has made it seem that growth is in the very nature of things, and that has recently enabled developers of every type to push ahead on almost any project with the cry "you can't stop progress." Almost anyone who tried to stop a development project was considered a misfit. To gain public support, he or she would have to protest the project by showing that its proponents were devious, dishonest, or that it would not really contribute as much to growth and progress as other courses of action. The project could not be challenged on the grounds that the growth it was generating was itself undesirable. Yet, by the late 1960s that is exactly what did happen on an ever-increasing scale. People were challenging and even blocking development projects on the grounds that expansion was no longer good, that resources to power growth were finite and that growth itself was, as some put it "the ideology of the cancer cell." It is difficult to say which came first: the cultural shift, with its challenging of the ideas of growth and the expanding good, or the social activist shift, with its mobilization of people against specific development projects. They interwove complexly, cybernetically, with each being cause and effect of each other. This is the way culture and society change. And where does that leave those other movements of social and cultural change; the black power, chicano, and women's liberation movements? If the possibility pie does not keep growing, how do they get larger slices unless, indeed, someone gets less? And what about the middle Americans who have made it and now worry that their gains are slipping away in the face of inflation, recession, give-away welfare programs, and reverse discrimination? Some experts say that the answer for everyone lies in new ways of growing. Some claim that growth in providing more labor-intensive services and communicating and advancing knowledge can proceed without endangering finite material resources, while growth requiring materials consumption must slow down. But who is it who gets "laid off" when funds run low? Is it not those in service jobs? Who is going to do the labor-intensive work? Is it not likely that those who most advocate such labor expansion will themselves not perform it? Who is going to be generating and communicating knowledge? Will workers who lose their jobs in resource and energy-intensive industry be likely candidates for these positions? What kind of growth is going to be acceptable and how will it be powered and controlled? Again, this is part of what is being worked out as various people, communities, and interest groups act and interact not only to seek to move on up or to seek new modes of redistributing slices from a more stable pie but also to determine the fate of various development projects. In the process they are dealing with the growth issue and are using and in turn influencing major concepts about growth and no-growth by scholars, specialists, and officials. For example, the opponents of large-scale energy and mineral development or irrigation projects find it useful to say that "small is beautiful," there must be "limits to growth," the fragile ecosystem can only take so much abuse, or that our society is becoming dangerously overconnected. The proponents of such development projects find it logical to say that the projects are needed to prevent further decline of rural America, to help prevent shortage, to achieve energy independence, or to play our part in meeting the realities of global interdependence.

Growth is being questioned as a general cultural principle and as a pragmatic process which involves specific social, political, technological, and economic decisions, actions, and impacts. As this volume helps show, the principle and the process of growth is being debated by scholars and opinion leaders on the macrocosmic level, focusing on the nation and the world as units of analysis, forecasting over long range using abstract and mathematical models of ecosystem function and broad-based growth patterns. One example of this type of analysis is *Economic Growth in the Future.*[1] Growth is also being debated by specialists and leaders on the moral-ethical level, in terms of what should be or should not be, often according to utopian or doomsday scenarios. And the principle and process of growth is also being debated and worked out by ordinary people at the relatively microcosmic level of their local communities in cases of conflict over specific development projects that affect their lives and sense of well-being. All three levels of debate are important, and all three interweave to generate change and strategies of adaptation. The microcosmic is often given shorter shrift in written accounts than the other two. Thus, let us now examine two case studies about action at the grass roots and in the process note how this microcosmic debate is informed by ideas from the macrocosmic and moral-ethical levels.

CASE STUDY 1: POPULATION GROWTH IN THE FLORIDA KEYS

The Florida Keys are islands curving south and west form the tip of the Florida mainland. They are linked to each other and the mainland by bridges and causeways and the central spine of a highway. Running down the length of this highway is a large water pipe or aqueduct that carries water for the fresh water needs of the inhabitants of the Keys. A desalinization plant on Key West also contributes water to the system.

There was a time before World War II when the few people who lived in the Keys caught rainwater on their roofs and stored it in cisterns. And this provided their basic supplies. But the old homes with the sloping roofs and the cisterns are mostly gone. Population has grown steadily and almost all the homes built since the 1940s rely upon water from the pipe. The life style of the new residents is water-intensive, just as it is energy-intensive. Unlike the mainland, little fresh water can be obtained through wells. The aqueduct and the overextended and aging desalinization plant provided just enough water to meet needs as the Keys entered the 1970s.

By 1973 developers pressing south from Miami collaborated with development interests in the Keys. These interests sought ways to move the Keys to a whole new level of growth and expansion. They aimed to open the area to many new people by building, on a major scale, new apartments and condominiums. They also sought to bring in new business and to carve out new waterways by dredging canals up to the new buildings. The highway was widened to four lanes, new permits for multiple dwellings and high-rise structures were allowed, and plans were made by the county commissioners and the Florida Keys Aqueduct Authority (FKAA) to increase fresh water supplies. The authorities made plans to increase the diameter of the aqueduct, to add new pipes, and to bring in the water from wells on the mainland at a place called Florida City. These wells were fed by the Biscayne Aquifer, which in turn links it to the Everglades. The old pipeline was built and is owned by the U.S. Navy. The navy built it originally to provide fresh water for the Naval Base at Key West. Private individuals contracted for a share of this water through the Aqueduct Authority.

The aim of the commissioners in the FKAA was now to get control of the line by buying it from the navy, and then to increase supply by enlarging the system. The FKAA expected to finance this by new loans to be paid by increasing water rates charged to private users. Anticipating this development, zoning and planning had already approved plans for increased density and new construction.

Simple enough? It seemed like a logical sequence of developments. After all, as the boosters explained, lots of people want to move to the Keys to make use of its wonderful climate and waters: "You can't put up a fence to keep them out."

When some Keys began growing as fast as the other boom areas in Florida, citizens started organizing groups to block increased development. For many, it was at first mostly defense against specific growth projects that threatened to change the character of their neighborhoods and to force them to pay more for water and other services. As groups formed and "talked it up," participants came to fear fundamental change in their life styles and to see the projected growth as an enemy. Participants began to perceive their islands as small entities having limited space, limited resources, limited access to clean ocean, to good fishing, good swimming, and to open vistas. They saw themselves as established residents threatened by hordes of newcomers because a few outside developers wanted to make money even if it was at the expense of the established residents. Increasingly, reinforcing each other by repeated discussion, participants in such groups suspected that local politicians and administrators had been bought out by the developers.

Anti-growth groups sprang up independently throughout the Keys, following the typical segmentary pattern of social movements. Each did its own thing: Some attacked specific high-rise construction; others attacked trailer-court projects; some fought proposed new dredging or land-fill operations designed to provide new water fronts for the new developments; some opposed the pipeline expansion or rezoning for high density; many challenged members of the water authority, or the zoning board, or the county commissioners and other local politicians. Each group recruited locally to increase membership and get petitions signed. Soon the groups began to interact in networks and developed a common thrust. Strategically they sought to block expansion of the pipeline and to hold population within the limits of their present water supply. Also, they sought to establish zoning that would prevent further construction of high-density high-rises.

They established links with groups across Florida and the United States who were speaking or acting against growth. They began to use such terms as "steady state." Some of their spokesmen developed an ideology of no growth, which emphasized a "sufficiency" ethic. They stressed the concept of living within limits and of protecting the environment by maintaining balanced ecology.

The pro-growth forces explained that the development would increase property values. They said that it would be possible to design the new buildings so that the environment would be protected. In any case, they said, you really could not stop the inevitable development because people wanted to live in the sun, near the water. They implied that some of the anti-growth leaders were acting only in self-interest, seeking fame and perhaps political fortune. One developer suggested that some of the anti-growth people were in effect saying "Stop the world, let the strangers get off." Other pro-growthers said that those who opposed the new development were seeking to be exclusive; now that they had their spot in the sun they wanted to change the rules which let them in and now prevent others from enjoying the same benefits.

To the pro-growth interests it was obvious that the Keys should get more water. To get the "more" water that everyone wants and needs, it was only necessary to enlarge the pipeline to the "unlimited" supply of the Biscayne Aquifer.

The anti-growth forces responded by saying that the Aquifer really has a limited supply of water and that these limits have been reached and cannot be expanded simply by bringing in a larger pipe to the supply. They warned that Miami draws upon the Aquifer for its ever-growing needs and that in times of cyclical drought there simply would not be enough to meet all demands, especially if the growth forces made these keep rising. They formed alliances with environmental groups in Miami who also worried about water supply and the limits to growth. The Miami groups felt that years of canal building, draining of the Everglades, over-building, and overpopulating threatened the fresh water systems of South Florida. They said that the main problem in South Florida was not how to drain off water through canals, but rather how to conserve this very limited good. They agreed with the Keys anti-growth groups that it was foolhardy to increase growth in the Keys and to seek to pull ever more water from the Florida City wells. Instead, they said that every effort must be made to control growth and reduce water use to keep up the water table and prevent salt water from intruding into the system.

Some pro-growthers found alliances with labor in the construction industry. They pointed to the need for more growth in construction in order to provide needed jobs and to fight the "extremes to which environmentalism has gone." Some pro-growthers met with various minority organizations to discuss the possibility that if new construction were blocked, minorities would not have a chance to move to the Keys.

Continuing their offensive, the anti-growth forces sought to enlist the aid of various state and federal agencies and offices that related directly or indirectly to environmental control. For example, the head of one major anti-growth group on Key Marathon worked with the Coastal Co-ordinating Council of Florida. He helped encourage them to conduct extensive studies on such aspects as the "carrying capacity of the Keys under existing conditions" and to survey public opinion about growth. He was certain that such a study would prove the futility of major new growth. Also, he and others urged a moratorium on further construction until the studies had been conducted and statewide, long-range planning established.

As events progressed, each side continued to develop overarching ideologies either to curb or encourage growth. While at first the respective ideologies were simply tools and rationales for the more pragmatic aims of self-interested people, later they became forces in and of themselves. At least one leader in the fight against the high-rise development and the water pipeline construction eventually spoke generally, conceptually, about the limits to growth at environmental symposia. He used the book *The Limits to Growth* almost as an evangelical text.[2]

The anti-growth forces apparently won a brief victory when they helped force zoning and planning to impose a moratorium on further construction and dredging operations until it could be demonstrated that enough water would be available. But an alternative premise is that the pro-growthers approved of the moratorium to force people to fear water shortage and to support the pipeline expansion project. In any event, the pro-growth forces moved ahead by obtaining variances for specific construction, including that for high rises, and by persuading local zoning and planning to approve specific requests for high-density construction.

The anti-growth forces also used the energy crisis, and especially the gasoline shortage, to argue that they were right in their warnings: There are limits to growth and it is insane to push construction on the Keys since more sprawl means more gas consumption and more people traveling vast distances along the Keys.

The struggle goes on, but it appears that the development in the Keys is also continuing. The anti-growth people feel that their only chance lies in "throwing the rascals out" of local government and putting in their own candidates on a no-growth or slow-growth platform. It also appears that the anti-growth people really do not believe that fundamental change is required in the system, if only they can get better men, their men, in government. Essentially, they believe that the only thing that needs to be changed in the system is the officials. With the right officials, new buildings will not be built, population will hold steady, the way of life as they know it will be stabilized. Most expect that the jobs or investments which support their way of life will continue to support them.

Perhaps all of this discussion of limited water supply, and limited energy supply, has sensitized people on the Keys to the problem of conservation and living within limits. Perhaps some people are conserving use of these resources because of this sensitivity. Maybe some builders are designing new homes to make them more energy and water efficient. But preliminary indications suggest that more people, including some of those in the anti-growth movement on the Keys, are seeking to install their own emergency electricity generators, to build larger water tanks, and to restore or build cisterns to collect rainwater where roof construction makes this feasible. In short, they seek a hedge against shortage by increasing their own supply through technology.

CASE STUDY 2: RESOURCE DEVELOPMENT IN NORTHEASTERN MINNESOTA

A favorite argument of those who warn of limits to growth is that we are running short of the key resources of energy fuels and minerals that power growth. Pro-growthers reject this proposition. They admit that we may be running short of resources that are easy and cheap to extract by old technology or inexpensive to buy through old trading arrangements. But they say that industrial society can and will move ahead to develop technology and pay the costs to get the still-very-plentiful low-grade or hard-to-recover fuels and ores, to substitute scarce for more plentiful minerals, and to synthesize and concentrate high-grade and desired fuels and materials from the low-grade, dispersed stuff. Furthermore, they believe that as prices rise, people will learn to conserve such material and resources and industry will pay the sharply ascending price of controlling environmental damages associated with the question of hard-to-get and/ or low-grade resources.

This aspect of the growth debate is illustrated by controversies over resource development in Northeastern Minnesota, especially over the development of low-grade iron and copper-nickel ores, the future of wood products and forest industries, and the relative roles of state and federal government and local people in deciding these matters. Northeastern Minnesota is a land of many lakes, often linked by rivers and streams, an area of pine forests and striking rock formations carved by the glaciers. Three major economic enterprises have developed in this region: mining of iron and taconite; production of lumber, pulp, and other wood products; and tourism.

As is well known, until the early 1950s this area exported iron ores of high quality, that is, of about 60 percent iron. These are called direct shipping ores, referring to the fact that they do not need to be refined or concentrated to make it economic to ship them. But as these ores played out and the iron industry found it could get iron cheaper from foreign sources, it began to close down its mines in Northeastern Minnesota. The area, particularly that part called the Iron Range, experienced a depression. The economy was revitalized in the early 1960s with the development of the taconite industry, which mines low-grade or 24–28 percent iron ores called taconite and processes these in the form of 60–62 percent pellets for shipping. Growth of this industry has generated prosperity and almost full employment on the Iron Range, with considerable economic spinoff elsewhere in the region. However, the industry is capital- and energy-intensive rather than labor-intensive; it requires large chunks of land, which are dug, ground, and sifted with huge machines. And it requires vast quantities of water to process the ores and to separate and flush the tailings left over from these processes. It recycles much of its water, and is now beginning to reclaim some of the land whose face it changed through dumping of the tailings from its conversion process. Six of the seven taconite companies in Minnesota dispose of their tailings on land. The exception dumps its tailings into Lake Superior.

Since the mid-1960s this dumping has been under strong opposition from citizen groups and state officials. Very reluctantly, and following years of legal battle, the company has agreed to the expensive process of changing to an on-land disposal site, and this had led to new controversy about where this site should be. It took hard, skillful, and persistent effort by various environmental groups to mobilize public and government opinion against such dumping into the lake. These groups contributed to, and in turn were aided by, the growth of the ecology movement across the state and country. In the process they both used and contributed to the development of concepts that became part of the ideology of the movement. For example, they spoke of the lake as an ecosystem and warned of the way seemingly insignificant changes in one part led to maladaptive changes throughout the system. Further, they found the ideas of limits to growth and impending resource shortage useful to explain why Minnesota should not be despoiled simply to provide Americans temporarily with more iron to waste in its throwaway economy. Just as environmental groups militantly opposed this taconite company, other interest groups have organized to assure that the company does not simply close down operations and thus end the jobs and economic spin-off on which some North Shore communities depend.

The Gabbro Rock Formation of Northeastern Minnesota also holds copper-nickel ores, but in concentrations reportedly less than 1 percent. Changing world conditions have led at least eight companies to explore development of these ores. One company actually wanted to initiate open-pit mining near the famous Boundary Waters Canoe Area (BWCA), which is a unique area of interconnected lakes and wilderness. The company asserted that its mining project would not have a negative impact on this wilderness area but would provide important economic growth and jobs for the region. While some people in the region endorsed the project, chiefly for economic reasons, sufficient numbers across the state mobilized to resist it as an environmental risk. Faced with this resistance and declining copper prices, the company withdrew its proposal. Another company is now digging a 1,700-foot exploratory shaft into the Gabbro Rock some 20 miles from the BWCA, thus to investigate the feasibility and impacts of a mining project which would be chiefly underground. Environmental groups mobilized to resist even this exploratory operation, but state environmental protection and resource agencies felt that the benefits for this investigation outweighed the risks, and that the company—collaborating with the state—would carefully monitor and control any risks. While much of the dispute over whether copper-nickel mining should be permitted relates to environmental concerns, much also relates to the general question of the growth this mining could bring. With this in mind, it is useful to consider some of the ways people in the region speak about and deal with ideas and actions which affect the present state and future of growth in the area.

Some people in the area of Northeastern Minnesota like the area the way it is and seem content with their level of opportunity and income and their life styles. They do not want the additional growth the new copper-nickel development or even the extension of taconite mining can bring. They have an ethic of sufficiency. As one said, "We know when enough is enough." Some perceive that access to lakes, woods, fish, and game is a limited good, so that they will lose their accustomed share if more people come in and if mining expands, consumes more land, and has other environmental impacts. They are not persuaded to the contrary proposition that the mines will offer new jobs. Many people who have this ethic of sufficiency are satisfied to work only seasonally or as they from time to time need money. For example, some work summer and fall in the resort business and keep winter free for ice fishing, hunting, snowshoeing, skiing, snowmobiling, and just plain relaxing, thinking, and reading. Others might want to do a bit of logging or "cutting pulp" when this work is available and when they need cash for specific purposes. In short, they like to live in Northern Minnesota because of its outdoor environment, low population density, and relative freedom from the middle-class work and growth ethic. Some work just enough to support this life style. Many will resist or at least speak out against development which they view as threats of new controls, more people with different ideas, or changes in their environment.

Those with this sufficiency ethic have varying backgrounds. Some grew up in the region. Getting by proudly on little was the way their families lived. They learned to exchange goods and services with others in similar situations, so that all would make it. Some are newcomers, a few escaping from affluence or the urban rat race to seek life with more meaning. They want to get a piece of land and solitude in the forest and along the lakes and rivers. A young lawyer and his wife illustrate this pattern. They left his budding career in Minneapolis to live in the north woods with their two children. They had spent summers "up North," always to return, but with increasing reluctance, to straight city life in the fall. "Why not just stay?" they asked themselves, and they decided to settle permanently in their cabin on a remote lake island. They did this for one year, but then, to give their children formal school education, they moved to an 80-acre abandoned farmstead close to a town on Lake Superior. To be able to afford to buy the land and build their home, the man has returned to law practice. At first he did so only part time. But the demand and need for his services is so great that he has gotten a partner and is now county attorney. He is greatly troubled that this is pulling him right back into the rat race he left and vows he will find some way to keep free. He and his family point out that while their needs remain small, they have found that nature does not easily provide even the essentials. They haul their water from a well that can go dry in drought. They cut their own wood as fuel and conserve what they use since they see not only how much work this is, but also how quickly wood is depleted and how difficult it is to grow trees. They also find it hard to raise enough food in so short a growing season. Fish and game are scarce. They raise goats for milk, chickens for eggs and sale, but this consumes feed. They now consider their two horses to be a luxury. As a family, they are seeking to work out an adaptive pattern to living within limits. They do not seek to missionize others or to pass judgment on any other life styles. They hope they can find their own answers. But their story has been reported in the urban press and does influence others.

There are some environmental groups and activists who live year around in Northeastern Minnesota, but many of the environmentalists who have organized to fight threats to the environment in Northeastern Minnesota are based in the Minneapolis-St. Paul area. Many may vacation in Northeastern Minnesota and some have second homes there, but for most of the year they work and live miles away from the area they have organized to defend. Many were spurred to action on specific issues. Some have the complete banning of copper-nickel development as their objective, others are content to slow it up, hopefully for many years, while yet others seem to feel that eventually copper-nickel mining should be permitted if it is done with strong environmental controls. These environmentalists vary in their general attitude toward growth. It seems fair to say that most of them profit from growth in the Twin Cities area and indeed may not be opposed to continued growth in such urban sectors. But they do tend to resist growth in Northeastern Minnesota. Some use or at least mention the idea of limits to growth as a rationale or ideological base to support their opposition to mining. Some adopt the premise that the country would not need to mine copper-nickel in Northern Minnesota if Americans cut down in their wasteful use of such metals, or if big industry were not so committed to profits.

There are also those in Northeastern Minnesota who strongly believe that their area must have more growth. One leader of a regional development association explained that while he supports tourist and recreational use of the area, this does not provide the kinds of jobs that really give most people pride and opportunity. He described the new kind of technologically advanced mining and related industry as being necessary in the region to help people fulfill their ambitions for satisfying work. Many other Northeastern Minnesotans express similar views, but even as they do so, they often show that they worry that mining, be it for copper-nickel or iron and taconite, will not really help the area grow that much. Some worry that since the new mining is capital intensive, rather than labor intensive, it will provide relatively few jobs for local people. A few worry that the mining companies will bring in skilled labor as well as heavy equipment from the outside, but most say that the people of the area are quite skilled in the most advanced technology of mining. Some say that if Northeastern Minnesota is to grow, and to get adequate return from mining copper-nickel, it must also smelt the ores in Minnesota and develop this industry. The idea of a smelter frightens the environmentalists even more than mining, since they have images of the environmental destruction that old-time smelting, with its sulfur fallout, brought in Canada and Michigan. Those who favor a smelting industry to generate real growth point out that new smelting technology reduces pollution almost to zero. But specialists then say that this new method is energy-intensive and would require new power plants or new transmission lines. And this, of course, raises yet other questions.

A leader of another Northeastern Minnesota development organization seeking to bring in diverse new industry while protecting established mineral and wood products firms explains how jobs in mining and lumbering gave many immigrants the opportunity to get ahead. Describing his own family history as an example, he explains that through these jobs and their hard work and intense saving, hundreds of once-poor families put their children through school and college and marched to fulfill the American dream. "The only trouble is that if we don't build new opportunities, the people we educated so well leave the area. You can find them across the country. We need growth to hold them."

Some pro-growth advocates in Northeastern Minnesota argue that since their resources are needed by people and industry across the country, their political leaders should act as have the Arabs with oil and seek to obtain maximum gain from such resources. They explain that Northeastern Minnesota has been like a colony of the industrial states to the east. They point out that Easterners have grown wealthy by mining and using Minnesota iron ore and have used this wealth and ore to promote continued growth in the Eastern industrial states. They explain that the mining industry has provided at most a few jobs which end when the mines play out in the typical boom-bust cycle. They argue that Northeastern Minnesota should have a new policy in which that state obtains enough revenue from the ores to invest in new development other than mining that will provide steady growth and diverse employment and opportunities. And they also say the revenue should be set aside to reclaim the land despoiled by mining.

There are those who say that the state must continue to encourage the mining industry even if it means continuing to give major tax breaks and reducing environmental controls. But their voices are growing weaker in the face of attack by both the antigrowth and environmental forces and the forces that want more broad-based growth and environmental protection financed by greater revenues from mining. New mining, such as of copper-nickel, will probably obtain broad public support only if the prospective companies positively respond to these latter forces. One, in particular, has expressed a willingness to do so.

Many Northeastern Minnesotans of both growth and no-growth persuasion also complain that interest groups in the Twin Cities try to run the affairs of the Northeastern area, as if the people there cannot manage.

They explain that Twin Citians want to keep Northern Minnesota from developing so that city people can use it as an unspoiled, rustic vacationland. When a coalition of 32 environmental groups, most of them based in the Twin Cities area, organized to protest development of copper-nickel in the BWCA region, some Northeastern Minnesotans saw this as but further evidence of this policy. They argue that Twin Citians want growth and its benefits in the "Cities" but do not want to extend this to Northeastern Minnesota if it seems to change the environment. "We can live poor just so they have a place to get away and fish a few weeks," said one northerner who works in the taconite company that is under fire for dumping in Lake Superior. "They tell us we can't run a few motor boats into the BWCA, but it's not the people who grew up here who crowd up and litter the place. They would rather let the old trees die and rot than have us cut them, where do they think their paper comes from?" Many agree with such statements. They admit that they made some mistakes in the way they treated the environment. But it is their land and more than anyone else they love it, and know how to save it. They want to preserve its outdoor beauty and recreation. Growth and environmental protection can go together. Some say that a handful of outsider environmentalists and St. Paul officials should not be allowed to stop everything and interfere without really knowing the people and area. Some Northeastern Minnesotans have organized in a group to resist what they consider to be unwarranted attempts by state and federal government to control their use of lakeshore and forest resources. Some are relatively affluent landowners and businesspersons, some are people who have retired to this region. They differ in their views about growth and about how much or what kind or resource development is appropriate for the area. But they agree that it should be chiefly up to area people to determine the pattern of development.

Some Northeastern Minnesotans who seem to manifest the sufficiency ethic explain that while they really do not want to see more mining and growth, they will support copper-nickel mining just because "the environmentalists in the Cities" don't want it to come in. Others explain that while they do not want more people carving up their fishing and hunting, their lakes and woods, they are for more growth if it is the only way people can get jobs they need.

To get the resources they need for growth, people are innovating. For example, the wood-products industry has faced the depletion of various types of high-grade pine not only by planting new stands of these, but also by using the wood of the "popple" or poplar, until recently considered a kind of waste tree, good for little but pulp. This substitution is facilitated by the way the wood-products industry is using new technology to cut whole trees into chips and use these to make a variety of composition boards for home building. This greatly reduces the amount of a tree that is discarded as waste, and it also helps insure that the region will continue to support wood industry.

Several of the small and medium-sized wood-industry firms are owned and managed by second- and third-generation descendants of the founders. They remember the old days when they or their fathers used waste wood, bar, twigs, and sawdust to fire steam boilers for heating buildings, lumber kilns, and driving equipment. They converted to fuel oil and natural gas when these were promoted after pipelines from Canada came through. They then disposed of their wood wastes simply by dumping or burning in teepee burners. Now, pollution-control measures restrict such practice, and supplies of oil and natural gas are expensive and uncertain. The people who grew up running these family firms take pride in their ability to keep their equipment operating and to recycle old gear and put it to new uses. Thus a group of brothers who run one such family firm found it logical to convert a furnace again to burn their wood wastes, fire their boilers, and heat their kilns. They modified a farm silo to store the wastes. One of them then helped the brothers running another family lumber firm in the region to locate and carry home a boiler system from a defunct creamery in Wisconsin, and to convert it to similar purpose. This latter family then improved this kiln heating system by adapting a grain auger to take the wood wastes from the silo into the furnace. These two families continue to experiment with ways to use such waste as fuel to generate steam or electricity to power equipment. One brother is investigating ways to use waste wood from several area firms to generate steam heat or electricity for a local town.

Native Americans of the Grand Portage Chippewa band worked together with a growing international hotel corporation and the federal government to build a resort hotel on their reservation, along the Lake Superior shore. It is a beautiful, rugged-looking, but environmentally sensitive area. At first, environmentalists from Northeastern Minnesota and the Twin Cities opposed this, but reluctantly agreed to it when the Chippewa explained that they wanted a chance to grow free from economic dependence and poverty, and when they and their consultants presented an environmentally sound architectural plan. The hotel continues to have financial trouble because it attracts sufficient guests only during the very short summer tourist season, but the Chippewa are exploring ways to build a winter recreation center, with ski runs and snowmobile trails. They worry that environmentalists will object to the snowmobiling but feel they can also work this out.

In sum, Northeastern Minnesotans are involved in continuing discussions, actions, and decision making about the way their land and its resources should be used or controlled to meet their varying opinions about what constitutes the good and adaptive life. Such debates and decisions reflect the history of the area and the whole range of local adaptations and interactions. All of these grass-roots factors will influence outcomes as much as the opinions and exhortations of experts about whether or not the country is reaching limits to growth or can override these by using technology and capital to secure necessary resources. But since Northeastern Minnesota, like Southwestern Florida, is tied into the rest of the country and the world, these local, microcosmic actions are ultimately affected by and influence the macrocosm.

HOW OTHER CULTURES HAVE DEALT WITH THE DISTRIBUTION OF WEALTH

Of course, it is not only in America that growth is being debated and developmental processes are being worked out. Scholars and opinion leaders in Western Europe and Japan have been dealing with the issue much as have their counterparts in the United States. They interweave in various informal networks of specialists and colleagues as well as formal organizations such as the Club of Rome and participate in international gatherings like the various global conferences on ecology, poverty, food and hunger, energy, and habitat. And it is in such interactions that they think through and work out major concepts about growth, help popularize the subject, influence opinion, and contribute to policy making. Scholarly, managerial, and policy-making elites from the developing lands also interweave in this global network of growth and resource specialists. But it seems that most of these leaders in the developing lands are both ideologically and pragmatically committed to move their peoples from traditional conditions of underdevelopment and no growth to technological modernization, economic development and growth. Their concern is not that their peoples and lands suffer from too much growth, but that they have for generations been stymied by cultural principles, social structures, colonial exploitation, and resource deficiencies that systematically prevent their economic development. Attempts have been made at least since the end of World War II to promote development in these Asian, African, Pacific, and Latin American lands. Western specialists encouraged and teamed up with indigenous modernizing elites to do this and have from time to time mobilized considerable financial and technological aid to such purpose. But these modernizers and developers discovered, often painfully, that the belief systems of the peoples they wished to push ahead were hostile to Western ideas of economic growth, and/or that the social, political, and economic structures of these societies prevented the rise of entrepreneurs siphoned away capital, contravened the working of supply and demand, prevented land or livestock from being used most economically, at least according to Western models. The literature of economic development and social change is filled with horror stories about how well-meaning but culture-bound Western specialists blundered time and again in attempts to promote growth because they did not understand non-Western systems; and the literature is filled with theories about how growth can be promoted only by adapting to or changing these traditional beliefs and structures.

It appears that many such traditional systems are fundamentally different from the American system in that they rested on and reinforced the cultural principle that resources and opportunities are limited or fixed and could not be expanded except by taking it from other peoples. Thus, if someone got more, someone else must get less. And they acted upon and then reinforced this belief by the particular way they sliced up this fixed pie, distributed the slices, and legitimated the cut.

Egalitarian Societies

Some traditional non-Western systems have been relatively egalitarian. The most obvious examples are hunting-gathering societies such as the Eskimo or the Bushmen, with their very small populations, subsisting from day to day on what they catch or forage. But many other examples are to be found in various African pastoral and horticultural societies, such as the Digo of Kenya, who will be discussed in detail as a case study, below. They usually herd or grow enough to meet their basic needs but they do not build up or siphon off a surplus to support a class of managers or religious experts. They develop various institutions, rituals, and beliefs to insure that whatever success anyone has, he or she shares it with others, so that no one rises while someone falls, and so that no one lays permanent claim to larger shares of the community product. If some of their number do begin to get more property, more food, more cattle, more crops to be converted into cash or wives or other forms of power then they are persuaded to redistribute this, often by providing food or money for community or family curing ceremonies or religious rituals. This curbs entrepreneurship and innovation and prevents the accumulation of capital which might be devoted to spurring on growth. But it thus also prevents some people from dominating others economically. Beliefs that growth is not possible are reinforced by the reality that no one can grow.

Frozen Stratified Societies

Some societies are highly stratified into layers of economic position by social custom, religious belief, and political power. The clearest example is classical India, even though medieval Europe showed some aspects of this. Such frozen stratified societies divided wealth, power, and role or work assignment quite unequally and then froze these amounts and positions in endogamous or inmarrying families or castes. At least in theory and often in fact, families were locked into one kind of work and one narrow role across generations.

While this usually prevented people in lowly status from moving up, at least in theory it assured that their specialized roles would be needed by the upper status. That is, if priests, warriors, and merchants can't themselves do any sweeping, then at least the sweepers always have a job. In India if people rebelled against this system and tried to rise to a higher level this would break their karma or fate and cause them to be reincarnated at lower levels in the future. But if they accepted karma, they would rise through successive reincarnations. The system was hence legitimated by the idea of interdependence among specializations and by religious principle.

Cyclical Stratified Societies

Other societies are stratified but permit cyclical mobility of families. Families rise as others fall—indeed because others fall. Over generations they repeat the cycle time and again. The number of opportunities and amount of wealth to be distributed does not really grow, but positions on the cycle change. The classical Chinese are the prototypical example of this system. It parallels their traditional world view that life is not the upward march of progress but rather the balance of opposites and the swing of cycles. Dark and light, yin and yang, a swing up and a swing down —they complement each other so that one cannot be without the other. A dynasty rises to rule only to fall and be replaced by another, which then repeats the pattern. A family rises only to fall and rise again. The pattern is cause and effect of their life style.

Wealthy Chinese were expected to have large families, live in luxury, spend much, work little, study the classics, contribute to the running of the state, be a patron of the arts, and finance religious rituals and lavish displays to honor their ancestors. Their many sons inherited equally, thus chopping their estates into ever smaller and more uneconomic units. When they could no longer squeeze more income from their tenants or borrow more, they had to sell land to maintian this lavish life style and in time to pay off their debts. It was a life style that would pull them down in something like a generation or two. In contrast, the poor Chinese usually had small families, worked very hard, spent very little, and bit by bit tried to save to buy land from the declining rich until in about two generations they would rise to control land and establish their wealth. Then, once up, they would behave like the wealthy did and start their inevitable slide down. Ideally, those on the bottom of the cycle would accept being there as a temporary misfortune that they or their children's children could change. And those on top could legitimate their good fortune as being the result of their hard work and virtuous life, but then also say that in time this too will pass. Chinese were not barred from rising or falling by simple accidents of birth, but openness and mobility came not from growth but from cyclical exchange of the big slices. From time to time some elites and rulers did beat the system and retained their power and money for many generations. But if rulers and landlords became too oppressive and did not play the game in ways that contributed to cyclical mobility, then the masses of people rebelled and overturned those on top in a giant all-encompassing swing of redistribution. Some Chinese in treaty ports and Chinese merchant families living and working in other lands also found ways to beat this system. They could invest their wealth and avoid spending it in traditional displays and duties since they were strangers in alien cultures. But as strangers they had to worry about being wiped out by taxes from these alien governments or looted by envious or angry natives.

It will be recognized that terms like egalitarian, frozen stratified, and cyclical stratified are convenient abstractions that do some violence to the enormous diversity in real life. They are the terms the analyst imposes upon this diversity to lump it into categories that can be compared and that illustrate propositions. In real life people do not always fit into these categories and for some purposes it is this variation that attracts the most attention. But for the purposes of this chapter it is useful to identify these as three of the basic ways people have adapted to and then helped perpetuate a steady-state or no-growth system. For these purposes it is also important to compare these ways with those in the United States, where the fact or theory of growth has enabled people not to worry about how to divide a fixed pie. These comparisons help demonstrate that Americans have created a new kind of system, one in which growth is both cause and effect of the belief that everyone can keep moving up in a stratified system—without anyone moving down. It is difficult to know what to call this apparent anomaly, but for want of a better term, open stratified seems acceptable.

Learning about types of no-growth societies brings home the point that the idea of growth and of everyone moving up is unique and new. It is a social invention rather than being in the very nature of things. These no-growth societies and their adaptations demonstrate that it is the concept of limits to growth that is old and common. Many societies had what today is called a "spaceship" ethic in that they regarded their opportunities and resources as fixed, their environments as bounded and externally hostile. Many tried to control population within their systems, for example, by establishing norms and taboos that restricted sexual intercourse and that told women to space their children over three- or four-year intervals. And population was also controlled by higher rates of death among those least able to care for their offspring.

It is clear that no growth and the idea of living within fixed limits was not simply tacked onto these societies. It penetrated all aspects of the way their peoples lived and thought. It interwove closely with the fabric of their social, political, economic, and religious patterns. It had its costs as well as benefits. From a conventional Western standpoint, these systems characteristically curtailed entrepreneurship as a threat to their stability, and they developed complex institutions to absorb and redistribute capital that might otherwise have gone to finance economic ventures that could lead to the rise of such entrepreneurs. People in such systems spend considerable time and wealth in ritual activities designed to maintain stability and to share their fixed assets. These limitations or control upon entrepreneurship and growth became especially noticeable during the 1950s and 1960s as barriers to the economic development projects generated by Western aid officials and modernizing elites. But it now appears that these projects and the ideas and examples of growth demonstrated by the West have generally been powerful and pervasive enough to override traditional ideas of the need to live within limits. It seems that people and leaders in the developing world accept that they should move up. Expectations have been raised, usually well beyond the ability of the resource and technological base to respond. This is seen, for example, in the way various African pastoral and agricultural peoples have expanded production into areas they would have considered marginal in the past. They overgrazed and overcultivated these areas and then were devastated when periodic drought struck.

Perhaps egalitarian, frozen and cyclical, and open stratified models now have relevance for debates on the world level about the furture of countries. If global opinion leaders admit that growth is not possible for all peoples of the world, or indeed that we are now entering a period of worldwide shortage, how then do they envisage various countries dividing up this fixed pie? Do they anticipate an egalitarian world, in which the pie is redistributed so that all peoples have about the same shares? Is it even remotely possible that the rich nations would agree to this, or that the poor could successfully promote it? Or will the world freeze in its present stratified mode, with the relative positions of rich and poor locked into place by convention and force of arms? Or will the world assume a cyclical stratified shape, in which those who are now up slide down to be replaced, for example, by some of those who have jumped from colonial and underdeveloped status to being in control of vast amounts of oil? Some OPEC leaders have said that this is what is already happening. But will the Western systems accept such a reversal of fortune? Or can the have-nots accept a global society in which they remain frozen at the bottom?

Presumably the most tolerable vision of the future is that it will be one in which there will be a constant expansion of the good life for ever more people, and that growth will enable those on top to stay there while others also move on up. These concepts and approaches at the global level will continue to impact the microcosm of small communities and ordinary lives.

It is thus important to examine one such microcosm in which ordinary people had long adapted to living within the tight limits they perceived, but then became involved in a process that eroded these adaptations and began to push them to growth. The microcosm to be examined in this case study is a community along the East African coast in Kenya. The people are the Digo, particularly those living in the sprawling village of Lunga Lunga. Their example will help show how all of their cultural beliefs and social practices fit together to maintain an effective no-growth, egalitarian society. And it will show how change from such no-growth patterns to a growth mode comes about because of and requires fundamental social and cultural change. By extrapolation, this case may also help to show what is meant by the seemingly simple proposition that to shift from growth to no growth it is necessary that people make life style changes. It suggests that changing from one mode to another may require a transformation far more fundamental and more difficult than proponents realize if they do not understand that a way of life is an integrated system.

CASE STUDY 3: NO GROWTH TO GROWTH AMONG THE DIGO IN KENYA

In the late 1960s, the Digo people of the Kenya coast of East Africa typified an egalitarian no-growth society in the process of shifting to the growth mode. The Digo people are farmers. Their main food crops are corn, cassava, and bananas. For sale in the markets they raise coconuts and chili peppers. Digo believe that community resources—the land, soil, water, and opportunities—are limited, so that if one person in the community gets too big a share, others will get too little.

Enterprising Digo do strive to become more productive and more successful farmers and traders. But, according to Digo custom, they must be very generous in sharing their good fortune, even if this means redistributing their profits among their fellows. If they do not share, their neighbors and kin will gossip angrily about them; maybe even accuse them of being witches or in league with evil spirits. Digo also explain their failures as being a result of the success of others. A man looks at his poor crop of cassava root. He confides that his neighbor has a much better crop because the neighbor made magic to pull the cassava of others to his fields, under the ground. There is only so much cassava to go around; so if one gets a lot, others must get little. The successful neighbor denies that he made such magic, but he does share his large crop and is not particularly interested in expanding his planting next year. He knows when enough is enough. Left alone, he might have sold part of his crop or used profits to buy new tools, more seed, and to hire labor to expand production even more.

The religion of the Digo centers on a belief in the spirit forces, spirits that live all around them and in them. Spirits can hurt, or protect, humans, depending on how successfully people can learn to control them through coaxing, bribery, or special rituals. Spirits are known to be especially fond of residing in the minds and bodies of married women. A spirit becomes very unhappy when the person in whom it resides has trouble —trouble, for example, with relatives, especially husbands who appear to think only of their own pleasures or personal profits. In short, spirits reflect the dominant attitudes of conventional culture. They are the idiom by which this is expressed. They do not like people to use profits for personal pleasure or for reinvestment in growth enterprise. When a typical spirit is crossed, it troubles the woman with headaches, an angry disposition, unwillingness to have sexual relations, and sometimes, the inability to bear children. Naturally enough the husbands, fathers, brothers, and uncles of such spirit-troubled women seek to avoid this trouble and do what they can to restore well-being. For help, they go to the spirit doctor, called a Muganga. The Muganga is a specialist in dealing with the spirit troubles of people in his community. He uses medicine, magical gourds, amulets, special songs, and rituals to treat his patients. He calls upon the spirits in his own body to use his voice and to speak with the spirit of the troubled person. Sometimes the spirits in the patient speak clearly in the Digo language, so all can easily understand. But often they speak in a babble, or in a kind of rhyming nonsense language, which only the Muganga can understand and interpret.

When a Muganga is not busy with patients and spirits, he keeps active as a salesman, particularly of tobacco. This keeps him mixing with people, in tune with the community grapevine, and well aware of everyone's affairs. Thus, when the Muganga treats a patient, he already knows much of the patient's life history, problems, and prospects. And he knows the economic state of the family. Treatments follow a prescribed pattern that restores social and psychological balance and redistributes any windfall profits.

A typical case illustrates: There is a gathering of the neighbors and relatives; the women join in dancing and singing, the men help the Muganga play the drums, rattles, bells—music to please the various spirits. The driving rhythmic music will draw the spirit up into the head of the patient, where it can speak through her voice for all to hear. The music drives on and on. The patient sits draped under a cloth, swinging and swaying while her neighbors and kin dance round and round her to call up the spirit. Then the spirit takes over and leads her forward. Suddenly, she spins and collapses. And the Muganga rushes to speak with the spirit.

Through the woman's voice, the spirit tells of the family problems besetting her, problems that anger the spirit, causing it to lose sleep and become nasty. The spirit says what the woman herself would not dare to say—and everyone listens. It explains that the woman's husband has been successful planting, harvesting, and selling red chili peppers. But what has he done with his money? He has not shared it with others. He is hoarding it for his own use.

The spirit explains that the woman's father and her brothers were so busy with their own affairs that they did nothing to bring the husband to his senses. The spirit and the Muganga urge them to join with them in making the husband change. He must put a new roof on his wife's house and they will help him. He must buy her new clothing. Reluctantly, he agrees, pointing out, however, that this will cut into his pepper profits and prevent him from investing in a new business. The woman and her relatives are satisfied, and they agree to help pay for the ritual just held, and for a follow-up feast. Thus, they also reduce their savings and potential capital for investment in new growth. If they don't help, they will be victimized by gossip.

As long as belief in the spirits holds strong, Digo are sure to be concerned with their neighbors' problems and to contribute food and money when necessary. Not only is community solidarity maintained, but the economic resources of the community are spread around, creating a general well-being in which everyone shares, a system the Digo like.

From the Western point of view, economic growth is stifled. The workings of the spirit system direct that any extra produce or profit be distributed around the community rather than saved or reinvested. An enterprising Digo finds it difficult to become too big or too rich. Digo soon learn that the more successful they are in growing food or making money, the more likely it is that their wives or kinswomen will be bothered by spirits that demand expensive attention.

Thus, the spirit system reinforces the conventional Digo view that community resources are limited and that if one man begins to rise above his fellows, he will gain too large a share of these resources and upset the community.

What happens when this system is exposed to forces of change—forces originating outside of the community? First of all, the system already reflects the impact of Islam, the religious cultural system brought to East Africa by the Arabs. For centuries Digo traded with the Arabs and many converted to Islam. Islam did not upset the spirit system; instead, the Digo selected and added elements of Islam to their traditional religion, to enhance, rather than alter, the old ways. By Western definition, this is developmental change. As Digo show in their ceremonies, Islamic spirits joined the company of Digo spirits without displacing them.

In the last century there was yet another force of change: the Christian missionaries who wanted to convert and remake the cultures of many African people, who they classified as pagan. But The British, who ruled East Africa from the end of the nineteenth century to 1963, had an agreement with the Arabs to discourage Christian missionaries from working among Africans who had converted to Islam. The British wanted to avoid a holy war in their many Islamic possessions. So the Digo were off-limits to Christian missionaries, and therefore, by converting to Islam, Digo were able to insulate themselves against more fundamental change.

In time, however, the Islamic shield was pushed aside by waves of Western experts who had come to help prepare Africa for self-govern-ment and economic development. A chief target of the modernizers was the Muganga and the spirit-possession system, which they regarded as superstition. Western education taught children to question and disre-gard the beliefs held by their elders. For example, children in schools were directed by their British-trained Digo teacher to take part in skits mocking the Muganga and ridiculing belief in the spirit ritual system. Children became quick with answers about the superiority of new, mod-ern ways and the deficiency of the old religious ways. As these children have matured and spread the word, a counterculture has grown. More and more Digo refuse to take part in Muganga rituals, or to contribute to their cost, or to meet the demands of the spirits. They find that the government will support and even encourage them in their rejection of the old ways. The striving entrepreneur has more freedom to push ahead, accumulate wealth, and use it as he pleases, while the old patterns of community sharing and distribution fall apart, or change, bringing both the gains and costs of growth.

Such changes among the Digo have also led to rejection of other traditional ideas and practices of population control. Digo used to believe that if a family grew too fast, if a woman had too many children in rapid sequence, they would take energy from each other since the mother could not breast feed them adequately. Thus, women tried to space births at intervals of three to four years. If a Digo saw a child suffering with what Westerners would term protein malnutrition, they traditionally explained it as the consequence of its mother breaking taboos against vaginal intercourse. Digo identified the symptoms of protein malnutrition as *chirwa*, and said about an afflicted child: *Amerchirwa na ndugu yake,* that is, "It (the weak child) had had this *chirwa* inflicted on it by the birth of its new brother or sister," (whom its mother must now feed and thus neglect the first born). Since a primary nourishment for an infant was the milk of its mother, and since a woman would only nurse one child, this made sense. It is not surprising that the Digo, like many other peoples, regarded the birth of twins as a misfortune brought on by angry spirits. It was best to let both twins die, rather than have both grow up to be weak or one survive to be envied by the ghost of its dead sibling. Now, Western medicine has helped the Digo define *chirwa* as protein malnutrition and to believe that even if the local environment cannot always produce necessary food, outside aid agencies can bring in nutritious supplements. Old taboos are discarded as superstition. Population can grow, and why not?

In the 1970s the Kenya coast began to flourish as a mecca for tourists who are attracted to its beaches, coral reefs, and colorful peoples. The Digo village of Lunga Lunga is now a Safari Center through which tourists pass on travels to and from Tanzania. Kenyan and world development officials feel that such tourism is necessary to provide jobs and the money which expanding population and aspirations require. The Digo can share in the benefits, and costs, of this development. It will help them change even more.

It took fundamental system change to generate the practice and ethic of growth among the Digo, but now that it has been generated and constantly reinforced, it might require a whole new transformation, or a catastrophe, to establish a no-growth ethic.

The Digo case is repeated in varying form across the developing world. While some Western experts may see this as the opening of the proverbial Pandora's box, it is unlikely that the West will now be able to close it. It is more likely that Westerners will be pressured to help the developing peoples grow to meet their now-rising expectations and to help provide their entrepreneurs with opportunities.

CONCLUSION

Thus it is seen that a shift in a developing society from no growth to growth is cause and effect of spiraling systemic change. Similarly, the generation in the United States of a challenge to the growth mode is part of a broad movement of sociocultural system change.

It is not possible simply to add the growth principle to a society that otherwise continues to be organized to maintain a steady state and to retain its sufficiency ethic. Organization and values change in order for the growth principle to develop *and* because the principle develops. Similarly, it seems unlikely that a society long organized to achieve and depend upon growth can simply add on the no-growth principle and otherwise hold its structures and values constant. To make a revolutionary economic change to no growth, a society will need to make revolutionary change in its social, political, religious, and ethical life. This chapter has shown how people, elites, and institutions interact to bring this issue to fundamental question.

NOTES

1. Edison Electric Institute, *Economic Growth in the Future: The Growth Debate in National and Global Perspective* (New York: McGraw-Hill, 1976).

2. Donella H. Meadows et al., *The Limits to Growth* (New York: Universe Books, 1972).

3 | Some Functions of Attitudes Toward Economic Growth

Anthony J. Wiener

In any disagreement there are always two levels of interest: what is being said on each side, and why it is being said. The concern with what is being said is related to determining who is right and what is the truth, while the concern with why each adversary makes certain statements is related to a desire to understand and predict what kinds of people are likely to agree with one side or the other. In regard to the question of economic growth, a good example of the first level of discussion is provided by the Edison Electric Institute's report, *Economic Growth in the Future: The Growth Debate in National and Global Perspective.* [1] The volume is a careful and judicious statement of the pro-growth view, the no-growth view, and the electric utility industry's view of the issues and the future of growth. It also contains the results of two in-depth modeling efforts to forecast future patterns of growth in the United States and the world.

The industry position, as one would expect, strikes a reasonable balance between the two views. The risk such a report takes, especially in a consensus document that has been worked over by many hands, is that of striking too reasonable a balance in an attempt to offend as few people as possible.

If the debate is one among reasonable men trying to find common ground, the Edison Electric Institute's middle road may succeed. Moreover, it may gain attention for its most original and useful section, Part III "Growth and the Electric Utility Industry." It is here that the troublesome implications of even moderate growth for electric power pricing are addressed and, most seriously, the problems of financing the capital requirements of the electric utility industry are set forth. Part III is surely the Message and it deserves a public hearing, well in advance of regulatory decisions.

To the extent the no-growth and pro-growth positions are ideological, the attempt in the report to split the difference will offend both sides. The comments of reviewers and others may be revealing in this respect. My purpose in this chapter is not to contribute additional arguments to the growth debate as such, although I consider such contributions (if there is anything new to be added) of obvious value. I have made clear my own views on the merits of the question elsewhere.[2]

On the whole, I am sympathetic to the Edison Electric Institute's position that economic growth can and should continue, but with some changes in directions and priorities.[3] I think more could have been done in the report to explore the implications of substituting goals of betterment for goals of increase in the exchange value of goods and services produced. Another promising avenue, not developed in the report, involves a partial substitution of a goal in favor of growth in what might be termed real wealth (consisting of physical capital; the educational and skill levels of the population; the accumulation of art, architecture, recreation facilities, landscapes, and other amenities; the level of technology and managerial skills; and the current value of the stock of consumable goods and services, depreciated according to realistic lifetimes—that is, durables valued much more highly than quickly consumed items—and the current value of both proven reserves and probable additional resources). This is as distinguished from an exclusive concentration on growth in an annual production of primarily "throughput" items. These essentially accounting changes might not change many of the activities that would continue to take place, but they would help to make marginal shifts in national (and international) directions. They would also facilitate the discussion of changes in priorities and assumptions of economists, managers, and policy makers that will inevitably take place in any case.

When it came to postulating a growth rate in GNP (even in the decreasingly useful current definition) and electric output, I felt the Edison Electric Institute report conceded too much to the opponents of growth and estimated rates of growth that are probably too pessimistic and, in my view, certainly lower than desirable. For example, the problem of unemployment in the U.S. economy during periods of low growth might have been given greater attention.

These are minor criticisms of what is an extremely, even excessively, temperate report, which also succeeds in being comprehensive, lucid, intelligent, and interesting. My point of departure (rather than dissatisfaction) is that the Edison Electric Institute report follows too closely the structure of presenting the pro-growth view, the no-growth view, the industry's compromise view, and the problems confronting the industry, given its view. This leaves two major issues relatively unexposed. One is new directions for growth and a related potential restructuring of economic thought to improve its capacity to treat changing economic preferences as endogenous variables. Second is an analysis of the sociological substructure of the controversy. It is this second issue that provides the primary focus of this chapter. I leave it to others to continue the debate on the manifest and explicit level. I will instead comment briefly on what might be termed the latent functions of the debate.

THE SOCIOLOGICAL STRUCTURE OF
THE GROWTH CONTROVERSY

It is clear that there are sociological, economic, political, and psychological determinants, or at least correlates, of opinions, especially on complex and ambiguous matters. One may notice that opinions follow patterns without at all losing interest in determining the truth of the issue being debated. Not only is "which side is right" likely to be an important question, if it can be answered, but correct opinions will be found to be as patterned as incorrect opinions. Information and understanding are distributed through society neither uniformly nor randomly; they tend to be acquired by various kinds of people, under certain circumstances, and for certain reasons, and therefore "correct" as well as "incorrect" opinions are distributed in certain patterns, which vary, of course, depending on what is being discussed.

The debate on the future of economic growth is well-suited to analysis of the functions (as well as the validity) of opinions. The issues are extremely complex and the real situation is extremely ambiguous. We are dealing for the most part with speculations about the future—a period of time about which few beliefs should be held with high confidence. Since the future hasn't happened yet, it presents us with no data for study; in fact, it does not exist, except as expectations in our minds. These expectations may be well-informed and valid with respect to moderately well-understood phenomena such as tomorrow's weather; but when it comes to the future of economic growth—the very long-term destiny of mankind, embracing his aspirations and goals, his concepts of progress, his character and view of the world, his relationship to the spiritual and physical universe, his capacity to satisfy his needs and wants, and including his prospect for survival—even the best-informed expectations may turn out to be wrong, if for no other reason than that human beings may change their minds and behave in significantly different ways in the future.

The ambiguity is compounded by the fact that much of the debate is inevitably carried on by people who are at best well-informed about only a small part of the problem on which they propound their views. They may understand some ecology, but no economics (or vice versa), or they may understand a method for modeling complex systems, but pitifully little about the system they are attempting to model—the whole world, in effect, and all its future. At the opposite extreme, they may be extremely knowledgeable, wise, and sophisticated about current political, economic, and social realities, but they may tend to regard them as relatively fixed and have little capacity to imagine problems potentially posed by continued exponential change in the scale of human activities.

Under these circumstances it is clear that values, ideologies, philosophies, even religions, in both the broadest and narrowest senses of that word, play some role in determining positions in the debate. This is not to deny that information and rational understanding also play a significant role—obviously they do, and some people are even capable of changing their minds on receiving new information or hearing a new argument. But how many of those already concerned with these issues change their minds as they learn? How many more read and listen primarily in order to bolster their previously formed opinions, or to strengthen their competence to debate anyone who disagrees? People tend to seek or be receptive to new information and understanding only selectively, only as the new perceptions seem consonant with their previous opinions. And most people are willing to discuss controversial matters only after they have assured themselves they are talking with people who share their views. After all, disagreements lead to irritation and mutual hostility, unpleasant feelings most people try to avoid. Agreement, by contrast, is not only reassuring about one's own views but also conducive to mutual respect and friendship. Minds once made up tend to protect themselves from having to change.

While I am emphasizing here the importance of motives underlying beliefs, and the resistance of such beliefs to change, it should be noted that many, even most, people can be influenced by an idea, especially when it is new to them and there are no preformed defenses, and especially when they hear it on good authority. Thus school children, including college students, listening to their teachers, and ordinary citizens reading newspapers, magazines, or popular books can certainly be swayed by hearing a strongly held opinion. What needs to be analyzed is the motivations of the teachers, the journalists (an editorial writer for the New York *Times* actually wrote an article about *The Limits to Growth* which started, "This story is about the end of the world") or the scientists who set out to influence the public with subjective opinions dressed up as scientific conclusions.

TOWARD AN IDEOLOGICAL MAP

Considering this phenomenon it seems both useful and feasible to find out in some detail who the anti-growth people are, and who the pro-growth people are, in socioeconomic, political, or psychological terms. If an ideological map or chart could be prepared, it would do much to illuminate the controversy.

Let us begin by reviewing the controversy as it might have appeared to a superficial observer, more interested in the political history than in analysis of substantive arguments. Many such observers perceived the beginnings of the opposition to growth as part of the radical student movements of the 1960s and the counterculture. Earth Day was, in this view, merely another left-wing attack on the establishment. But shortly thereafter it became clear that conservation was also a concern of conservatives, many of them hunters and fishermen who resented the encroachments of growth on the forests and streams, others well-to-do believers in the status quo who were offended by the vulgarity of the postwar suburban sprawl and who felt their own amenities (such as relatively uncrowded highways, beaches, sailing waters, and hiking trails) being reduced as too many vulgar and brash newcomers crowded into them.

Soon the picture became still more complex as spokesmen for various communist countries made it clear that Marxism required continued, if possible accelerated, economic growth. Western European social democrats, who in some cases considered themselves Marxist, were attracted to the antigrowth attitudes (perhaps because of the pessimism of these attitudes and their implied permission for passivity to social problems).

The Club of Rome appeared with its set of convictions, centering around overcrowding, about *la problematique.* Many people agreed, and Jay Forrester and his assistant Dennis Meadows and colleagues produced almost identical books that elaborated on the antigrowth assumptions using a systems dynamics model.[4] The astonishing popular success of the Meadows book, deliberately addressed to a popular audience, made clear how many were already disposed to agree. Unlike most simulation studies, *The Limits to Growth* was introduced at a press conference, at the Smithsonian Institution, in which Meadows emphasized that there was no time for the customary professional debate since immediate action was needed to reach "zero net capital investment." (Why not "constant industrial output" or some other surrogate for near zero growth? The answers lay buried in the assumptions of the model-makers.)

After the professional reaction there was, predictably, little left of *World Dynamics* or *The Limits to Growth.* The Club of Rome, which had sponsored the books, went on to second- and third-stage studies and withdrew its support for the systems dynamics books, calling them methodological experiments and valuable as warnings. Warnings about what? The dangers the Club of Rome assumed, or at least judged, to be present before the models were constructed. The belief preceded, temporarily and logically, the models; and the belief outlived them too. Moreover, to argue that the Forrester and Meadows models proved no more than they assumed, as most reviewers quite properly did, was not to demonstrate that their assumptions were not valid. Continued growth might be impossible even if Forrester and Meadows were wrong. And it might also be undesirable, even if possible, for the kinds of reasons that Ezra Mishan and others had argued eloquently for years before there was a Club of Rome.

Then authoritarian talk was heard from parts of the anti-growth camp about what stern measures would be needed to force the world to change course. Attempts to help poor people were denounced as yielding counterintuitive and counterproductive results, and tough talk was heard about triage and the need to throw some countries out of the lifeboat—as though Bangladesh would sink beneath the ocean, its epidemics safely quarantined and its scenes of starvation and squalor safely banned from the TV screens of countries that had made a rational decision that to save lives now is to lose more lives later.

The pro-growth advocates provided complexities too. Not only did business want to expand GNP in order to expand earnings (and, if possible, market share too), but government and labor needed economic growth to reduce unemployment, and advocates of increased government spending on welfare, health insurance, and other redistributive programs understood that these programs would have to be financed from increased revenues from GNP growth, if they were not to be inflationary or to increase the tax burden excessively.

This history could be elaborated further, of course, but that would only add to the impression of confusion. How can the various attitudes be organized and their roots or functions be analyzed?

THE AWKWARDNESS OF FUNCTIONAL ANALYSIS

One approach might be to try to identify the primary concern or main theme of each of the writers in the debate, and then to seek its cause. This approach (which I have tried) fails for two main reasons. The first is that many of the contributors to the debate, having chosen their positions, then adduce every argument they can think of in support of their choices. It becomes difficult to identify which theme is principal, and even if one thinks he knows which it is, it would be difficult to demonstrate it to others. If one happens to know personally many of those who have participated in the debate (as I do), he could say what they told him they cared about most when he asked them in private conversation. But that would not be cricket.

The problem of fairness and propriety seems even more serious to me when it comes to diagnosing the cause of a particular writer's ideas. The ethical problems are like those involved in writing a psychohistory or psychoanalytic biography. It is justifiable for psychoanalysts like William Langer to try to produce a better understanding of Hitler, during World War II, for the OSS, or for Erik Erikson to try to shed new light on the historic figure of Martin Luther, who can no longer tell us his dreams or free associations. But to apply such techniques to participants in a debate, to colleagues, is to risk seeming to argue *ad hominem* and to be speculating with hypotheses that are not well-supported by evidence and that are in any case rude and ill-mannered suggestions, precisely because they attribute motivations, not necessarily laudable ones, and do not take the argument literally and at face value. It would be better, therefore, to construct ideal types—simplified and hypothetical types representing each variation in its purest form.

THE SOCIOLOGY OF KNOWLEDGE

Since it is impossible to exhaust the subject in a short chapter, let me merely sketch a few of the possibilities. That there are many approaches is amply demonstrated by Robert K. Merton, in his classic article on "The Sociology of Knowledge."[5] In that article on the social functions of mental productions, Merton outlines (pp. 460–61) a paradigm or list of crucial issues, which is well worth quoting in its entirety.

PARADIGM FOR THE SOCIOLOGY OF KNOWLEDGE

1. Where *is the existential basis of mental productions located?*

a. *social bases:* social position, class, generation, occupational role, mode of production, group structures (university, bureaucracy, academies, sects, political parties), "historical situation," interests, society, ethnic affiliation, social mobility, power structure, social processes (competition, conflict, etc.).

b. *cultural bases:* values, ethos, climate of opinion, *Volksgeist, Zeitgeist,* type of culture, culture mentality, *Weltanschauungen,* etc.

2. What *mental productions are being sociologically analyzed?*

a. *Spheres of:* moral beliefs, ideologies, ideas, the categories of thought, philosophy, religious beliefs, social norms, positive science, technology, etc.

b. *which aspects are analyzed:* their selection (foci of attention), level of abstraction, presuppositions (what is taken as data and what is problematical), conceptual content, models of verification, objectives of intellectual activity, etc.

3. How *are mental productions related to the existential basis?*

a. *causal or functional relations:* determination, cause, correspondence, necessary condition, conditioning, functional interdependence, interaction, dependence, etc.

b. *symbolic or organismic or meaningful relations:* consistency, harmony, coherence, unity, congruence, compatibility (and antonyms); expression, realization, symbolic expression, *Strukturzusammenhang,* structural identities, inner connection, stylistic analogies, logicomeaningful integration, identity of meaning, etc.

c. *ambiguous terms to designate relations:* correspondence, reflection, bound up with, in close connection with, etc.

4. Why? *manifest and latent functions imputed to these existentially conditioned mental productions.*

a. To maintain power, promote stability, orientation, exploitation, obscure actual social relationships, provide motivation, canalize behavior, divert criticism, deflect hostility, provide reassurance, control nature, coordinate social relationships, etc.

5. When *do the imputed relations of the existential base and knowledge obtain?*

a. historicist theories (confined to particular societies or cultures).

b. general analytical theories.

Clearly there is a monumental job to be done if only a small percentage of Merton's very pertinent questions are to be answered with respect to the growth debate. The reader is invited to carry out the attempt; I shall give up after suggesting a few possibilities and failing to answer some critical questions.

IDEAL TYPES

Let us inquire, for example, into the self-interest of partisans in the debate. To avoid naming names and dealing with too many complexities we may use some simplified ideal types (that is, simplified prototypes). By distinguishing various kinds of self-interest, or various ideological or value orientations, we can see how partisans might be aligned on either side of the controversy. All these types are recognizable, I believe, although some are far more numerous and/or vociferous than others. Lest anyone feel maligned, let me repeat Merton's important point, that "the 'Copernican revolution' in [the sociology of knowledge] consisted in the hypothesis that not only error or illusion or unauthenticated belief but also the discovery of truth was socially (historically) conditioned."[6] If we add some autonomous psychological conditioning for the disposition to acquire true or false beliefs, we have an even more complete statement. Table 3.1 is illustrative.

In the table, some form of self-interest, whether or not recognized by its holder, and generally accompanied by an ample supply of self-righteousness and moral indignation, is a characteristic motive (among other

TABLE 3.1: Partisans in the Debate

Forms of Self-Interest	Ideal Types	
	Pro-Growth	Anti-Growth
Economic and social self-interest	Business and governments	Elitists, preserving privileges against encroachment by the multitudes
Technocrats (who have political self-interest)	Most economists, scientists, engineers	Doomsday ecologists and systems modelers
Romantics or Aesthetes	Space buffs, some architects, some planners, cornucopian utopians	Keep Mother Nature a virgin, back to the wilderness (or at least to pastoral landscapes)
Self-righteousness and moralistic contempt (emotional self-interest)	Contempt for crackpots, fools who don't understand the system and will wreck it	Contempt for the destructive system; we are the only moral people—we stand outside the system and condemn it

Source: Compiled by the author.

motives, of course) of participants in the growth debate. In general, those who are most self-righteous are least aware that they are pressing for their own self-interest.

For example, the anti-growth advocate who wishes to preserve wilderness areas for his solitary contemplation generally believes (honestly) that to do so is in the general interest of mankind; he rarely recognizes at the same time that he is arguing, as a practical matter, to preclude access to these areas by those who do not *now* share his own very unusual affluence, leisure, education, and opportunities for travel. Similarly, the conventional government official or businessman who hopes each new quarterly report will show a greater increase in the GNP growth rate believes himself (honestly) to be motivated by a concern to see inflation abated, unemployment reduced, and an economic recovery leading to an improvement in national economic health. His scorn for the no-growth advocates is rarely troubled by the reflection that he has a personal stake in increased profitability or tax revenues for the corporate division or government bureau in which he has responsibilities and for the performance of which he is rewarded. Similarly, the technocrats on either side of the debate who are most scornful of the ignorance of their opponents, which they believe in either case constitutes a real and present danger to society, are the least likely to perceive that they are arguing for a situation in which members of their own profession, holding their own opinions, would be the *only* people capable of guiding the world away from the precipices to which any other advice would lead.

There are other ways of diagnosing the "functions" of the debate. Let me suggest two having to do with attitudes toward related, but not identical, issues: the idea of progress, and the idea of distributive justice.

THE IDEA OF PROGRESS AND
MANIPULATIVE RATIONALITY

The idea of progress is closely bound up with attitudes toward good and evil that emerged early in the Christian era. As Dostoevsky argued so persuasively in *The Brothers Karamazov,* the fact that evil exists in this world requires a theological explanation. ("Why do children suffer?") The nature of this explanation affects—or even determines—the question whether man and society are perfectible.

We can identify three attitudes toward good and evil that competed with one another during the third, fourth, and fifth centuries after Christ. The earliest and most pessimistic was preached by Mani in Persia until his execution about 276 A.D. His Manichaean religion was based on the idea that the world is a mixture of good and evil, that there is a constant struggle between the powers of Darkness and Light. Evil has a separate existence apart from God, and Primal Man has been permanently infected by envy, greed, and hatred. This gloomy creed was challenged by an Irish monk named Pelagius who came to Rome in the fifth century. Although devout and indeed saintly, Pelagius rejected the idea of original sin and preached that salvation and the good life were attainable without divine intervention. This optimistic view was denounced as heretical by Augustine on the fully justified grounds that Pelagius was devaluing the importance of divine grace.

Augustine had, however, himself been a Manichaean before embracing Christianity. Although he developed a more acceptable Christian explanation to the effect that evil existed as a distortion of good, Augustine, in his great work, the *City of God,* saw the heavenly and earthly cities as inextricably intertwined. Nevertheless, Augustine rejected the cyclical conception of history, holding instead that the story of mankind is part of the divine plan and therefore reflects the presence of divine reason. Augustine's tempered view of life is represented in secularized versions of the idea of progress and social utopias that emerged in Europe more than a thousand years after his death.[7]

The Augustinian concept dominated medieval thought until Aquinas. It was not until much later, with Fontenelle and Descartes in seventeenth-century France, that the modern idea of progress began to emerge. Essentially a French conception, it was formulated most fully by the Abbe de St. Pierre and the Marquis de Condorcet in the eighteenth century. During the last months of his life, spent under the menace of the guillotine, Condorcet produced the following paean to progress: "Nature has set no term to the perfection of human faculties . . . the perfectibility of man is truly infinite; and the progress of this perfectibility, from now on independent of any power that might wish to halt it, has no other limit than the duration of the globe upon which nature has cast us."[8]

The idea of progress readily crossed the channel in the late eighteenth century. Adam Smith's *Wealth of Nations* was much more than a treatise on economic principles; it contains a history of the gradual economic progress of human society, suggesting that an indefinite augmentation of wealth and well-being is to be expected. The nineteenth century saw the concept reach its fullest fruition. Robert Owen in England and the Comte de Saint-Simon in France used the idea as a gospel for political and social reform. August Comte founded the study of sociology upon a systematic search for the laws of progress. The final argument that seemed to put the concept of progress beyond dispute was made in the *Origin of Species* in 1859. Charles Darwin concluded his work with these words:

> As all the living forms of life are the lineal descendants of those which lived long before the Cambrian epoch, we may feel certain that the ordinary succession by generation has never once been broken, and that no cataclysm has desolated the whole world. Hence, we may look with some confidence to a secure future of inappreciable length. And as natural selection works solely by and for the good of each being, all corporeal and mental environments will tend to progress toward perfection.[9]

Herbert Spencer extended the theory of evolution to sociology and ethics, interpreting progress in the most optimistic light possible. He considered evil to be a temporary phenomenon that perpetually tends to disappear:

> Always towards perfection is the mighty movement—toward a complete development and a more unmixed good; subordinating in its universality all

petty irregularities and fallings back, as the curvature of the earth subordinates mountains and valleys. Even in evils the student learns to recognize only a struggling beneficence. But above all he is struck with the inherent sufficingness of things.[10]

By the end of the nineteenth century the dogma of an inevitable trend toward greater perfection in human history had become an article of faith in Europe and the United States. Only nihilists or skeptics like Nietzsche and Schopenhauer doubted the truth of what had become the consensus. In general, a typical well-educated gentleman of this era was confident that the whole history of mankind up to that point had culminated in him; he expected his children to go on to do even better.

This belief sustained a profound shock when Europe came close to committing a kind of suicide in World War I. Many millions of men were thrown into a gigantic slaughtering system that, in retrospect, made very little sense to anyone. Statesmen and generals had shown an utter incapacity to stop the mutual destruction before an incredible amount of damage had occurred. In many ways, Europe has not yet recovered from this cataclysm, or is only recovering now.

Writing in Germany during the war, Oswald Spengler forecast the *Decline of the West.* Aldous Huxley created his dystopian *Brave New World* in 1932. The world depression of the 1930s was the economic counterpart of World War I. Although Arnold Toynbee became less rigid in his later writings, his renowned *Study of History,* published between 1934 and 1954, confidently predicted the imminent demise of Western civilization. Even such an inveterate optimist as H. G. Wells found his *Mind at the End of Its Tether* in his last book:

> The writer sees the world as a jaded world devoid of recuperative power. In the past he has liked to think that man could pull out of his entanglements and start a new creative phase of human living. In the face of our universal inadequacy that optimism has given place to a stoical cynicism. The old men behave for the most part meanly and disgustingly, and the young are spasmodic, foolish and all too easily misled. Man must go steeply up or down and the odds seem all in favor of his going down and out.[11]

Just as World War II was ending with the defeat of the combined forces of aggressive fascism, the horrors perpetrated in Nazi concentration camps and the numbing reality of atomic weaponry revived manifestations of despair. More hortatory than dogmatic, George Orwell took a deeply pessimistic view of human nature and modern technology in his *1984,* published soon after World War II. The vogue of existentialism during the 1940s and 1950s can be seen as the response of disappointed rationalists to a world they saw yielding no meaningful patterns, least of all an eternal movement onward and upward throughout history.

Nevertheless, the dynamic sweep of postwar experience revived faith in an endless vista of human progress. Europe and America reached new heights of affluence and vigor, the communist world grew in economic and military strength, and a new Third World of liberated Asian and African nations emerged as a force on the international scene. Buddhists and pagans joined with Christians and Muslims in accepting Western development, Russian or American, as its prototype.

This new period of unprecedented prosperity was accompanied, on a worldwide basis, by unprecedented peace. The world death rate as a result of organized violence in the period since World War II (that is, deaths as a proportion of the population) probably is considerably lower than it has been in any comparable period of 25 years, in spite of the fact that we have had quite a few serious local wars, such as the Korean war, the Vietnam war, the Congo, the Nigerian Civil war, the slaughter in Indonesia, and the series of wars in the Middle East. Until there was the minor clash between El Salvador and Honduras in 1969, this was the only period in which 25 years had gone by without a serious war between some pair of Latin American countries. In many ways the postwar period has been comparable to that between the Franco-Prussian War and World War I, a period that was known as *La Belle Epoque,* the "fine period."

As Herman Kahn has pointed out, the world has recently been going through another *belle epoque.* Yet a very curious thing has happened: Previously, during fine periods, there was an almost unanimous belief in progress. Yet, in spite of the great successes of the current period, in terms of technological development, economic growth, and the spread of affluence, not only in this country, but throughout the world, it is easy to find many expressions of pessimism. If we have been living in a golden age, many people have difficulty in recognizing it, or believe it is about to come to an end for any one of a number of reasons.

But at no time until the present have philosophies of despair held much charm for Americans. Writing during the depth of the depression, even such a hardheaded realist as Charles Beard saw technology as mightily strengthening the idea of progress: "What appears to be impossible may be surmounted. The ancient theory that mankind revolves in a vicious circle is destroyed by patent facts. The medieval notion of a static society is swept into the discard by events."[12]

As recently as 1968 a noted British professor of Economic History was able to write that

> The idea of progress is, in this modern age, one of the most important ideas by which men live, not least because most hold it unconsciously and there-fore unquestioningly. It has been called the modern religion, and not un-justly so. Its character, and its assumptions, have changed with time, and so has the influence exerted by it, but at present it is riding high, affecting the social attitudes and social actions of all of us.[13]

But in 1974 the British sociologist Julius Gould could refer to "a general feeling (now converted to a near certainty) that endless economic growth is neither feasible nor desirable."[14]

Today the idea of a static economy—zero economic growth—is being actively promoted in advanced industrial countries. Technology has been transformed from a hero into a whipping boy. The lead editorial in a recent issue of the New York *Times* tells us that "uncontrolled technology is the gravest menace to the future of people and the survival of a habitable planet."[15] All faith in progress is not, of course, about to be discarded. The U.S. social philosopher Daniel Callahan strikes a more reasonable note: "If the idea of progress is not likely to be abandoned, it cannot go on the way it has manifested itself in the past, wildly, recklessly, heedlessly throwing up a profusion of uncontrolled goods and evils."[16]

It seems abundantly clear that the idea of progress is undergoing a new period of questioning, tension, and perhaps even crisis. If we search for a single process or principle that has underlain, and provided a motor for, progress in the modern era, it is undoubtedly the force of secular, humanistic manipulative rationality—the problem-solving mentality of the Western, industrial manager.

PELAGIAN VERSUS AUGUSTINIAN PERSPECTIVES

On one level the current debate is primarily one between two utopian, or Pelagian, perspectives. The pro-growth utopian believes in infinite material progress for all, with increasing equality and justice. The neo-Malthusian believes that a transition to economic equality and social justice can be made at a very low general standard of living, constrained by scarcities, or even romanticizes the benefits that general poverty or at least austerity will bring. These positions are summarized in Table 3.2.

The more realistic choices are likely to be of the Augustinian school indicated in Table 3.2. The pro-growth utopian Augustinian believes that some gaps are likely to increase; economic and technological growth will continue; there will be an increasing need for adjustment, planning, technology assessments, and other forms of stratified, stabilized, centrally governed economies and societies. As a result of these, there will be an increasing dominance of the requirements for order—such as worldwide zoning ordinances—over the requirements for justice, as the world grows more complex, technologically developed, and dependent on maintenance of technological growth. This will be necessary, in order to avoid limits imposed by resource or environmental constraints, or

TABLE 3.2:   Religious Assumptions (or Heresies) Underlying The
"Two Views"—Some Additional Distinctions

	Pro-Growth	Neo-Malthusian
Pelagian utopias	1. Infinite material progress for all, with increasing equality and justice on a business-as-usual basis (utopian view of the Enlightenment and Industrial Revolution)	2. "Equilibrium with economic equality and social justice and stability at low general standard of living (Club of Rome's utopia—or dystopia)
Augustinian (the real choices?)	4. Some progress but increasing gaps; much economic and technological growth; stratified, stabilized, centrally governed societies; order over justice; 1985 technological crises and Faustian choices (Most Likely?)	3. Prometheus Bound; man forever constrained by greed, scarcity, and catastrophic natural limits; totalitarian rule or Hobbesian state of nature (Manichean extreme) (Most Dangerous)

Comment: Many intellectuals oscillate on the Pelagian-Manichean Heretical Axis—No. 1 to No. 3, with occasional excursions to No. 2.

Source: Compiled by the author.

unintended consequences of new technology itself. This possibility recognizes that there are both true and false barrel bottoms.

The other possibility may be described as the Augustinian or, better, Manichean/neo-Malthusian case: Where there are inadequate adjustment mechanisms, man will be constrained forever by his greed and natural limits. Of course, this implies a wide range of unpleasant possibilities. At the extreme, man would be forced to live, because of overshoot and collapse, in a Hobbesian state of nature until the end of his history.

We ought to take these less-optimistic choices seriously. The postindustrial Augustinian case does permit very real, though limited, improvements of the kind that wealth and science make possible: freedom from starvation and disease, if not from boredom or unhappiness, for billions of people; increasing access to information, communication, goods and services—though certainly not to utopia, nor to freedom from extraordinarily difficult problems of management.

PROGRESS IN PRODUCTION AND DISTRIBUTION

Another way of seeing the consequences of the continued increase in affluence, and the accompanying hostility to economic rationality, is to examine the questions it has raised about the values of progress in production, as contrasted with the values of progress in distribution. Progress in production has meant technological and economic advance, a rising standard of living for all, but with "gaps" continuing. Progress in distribution has meant progress in terms of increasing equality and reduction of gaps, a change that is seen as moral rather than technical. The more affluent a society becomes, the more likely it is to raise issues of distribution. Similarly, the poorer the society, the more it needs to emphasize the values of production, so that there will be some material progress to be distributed. Nevertheless, the ideological landscape contains people who are for both of these sets of values, for one and not the other, or for neither.

There are many people who are for the values of production and the values of distribution simultaneously. However, this group is now dwindling. It consists primarily of the old left, old socialists, most traditional liberals, and many economists and businessmen who accept the conventional wisdom concerning the value of the free market and entrepreneurial activity. Whatever the differences among these people, they have in common that they believe the best way to increase everyone's share of the pie is to enlarge the pie.

A second group is for production but against distribution—or at least not for progress in distribution. These people are elitists; many of them are technocrats. It is worth noting that many revolutionists who may be opposed to such an ideological stance in theory and in public statements nevertheless institute proproduction and antidistribution programs once they have come to power. As is well-known, communist countries and dictatorships (with the possible exception of communist China) are much more unequal in their internal distribution of wealth, in spite of their ideological pretensions, than are the more affluent capitalist democracies.

A third group may be so preoccupied with issues of distribution as to deny the virtues of production. *The Limits to Growth,* and many other early statements associated with the Club of Rome, seem to have this characteristic. Much of the now old New Left holds this position, which is also that of the counterculture; its antecedents include Mohandas K. Gandhi.

Logically, there is a fourth possibility, which is to reject the values of both production and distribution. There are very few people who are seriously opposed to both, but it is possible to find here and there a feudalist, and perhaps more frequently an anthropologist, who would prefer to see no progress made in either direction, in order to preserve a traditional society.

CONCLUSION

A final comment on the controversy may be in order. Let me abandon the role of "sociologist of knowledge"—to which I have been unfaithful at many points in this chapter—and take a position on the manifest debate that seems to emerge from a diagnosis of the functions of the debate.

The principal problem of the advocate of economic growth may be to make the point persuasively that what is required for social progress in the face of changing values is not self-righteousness and moralistic ideology but the management of complexity in the service of the values of civilization. Freud's central point in *Civilization and Its Discontents* was that the greatest destructiveness in human affairs results when the superego or conscience is enlisted in destructiveness. The only thing worse than ordinary barbarism is moralistic barbarism—the kind of self-righteousness that often accompanies utopian ideologies. Civilization, therefore, is an elusive goal. It requires reason, and the balancing of objectives. In spite of ideological change, civilization requires economic progress as well as an increasingly equitable distribution of the results of progress.

As we advance in the coming decades into a world in which the objectives of economic growth have been fulfilled for some, and have hardly begun to be achieved for others, we will find that the meaning and purpose of economic activity are increasingly called into question, and that the rational and manipulative managers of economic activity in business and government are increasingly the object of hostility from several mutually exclusive positions. The attack on economic growth may be, most fundamentally, an attack upon both the objectives and the means of progress since the Industrial Revolution.

If we ask whether manipulative rationality must remain the key to economic progress, the answer is, perhaps unfortunately, yes. The goals of economic activity are changing as values change, and there will be continued erosion of the traditional meaning of progress. The current malaise springs from confusion about objectives; such confusion is likely to persist as long as our course continues to change. The economic growth controversy suggests that avoiding future catastrophe may be largely a matter of applying new technology and prudent management to emerging problems before it is too late. Again, the controversial answer seems to be more, not less, manipulative rationality. What I have called the pro-growth Augustinian position combines realism about hazards with hope for further, though cautious, progress.

NOTES

1. Edison Electric Institute, *Economic Growth in the Future: The Growth Debate in National and Global Perspective* (New York: McGraw-Hill, 1976).

2. Anthony J. Wiener, "The Future of Economic Activity," *The Annals of the American Academy of Political and Social Science* 408 (July 1973):47–61; and G. M. Dalen and C. R. Tipton, eds., "The Economic Growth Viewpoint," *The Dilemma Facing Humanity* (International Symposium at Expo '74, sponsored by EPA and CEQ) (Columbus, Ohio: Battelle Memorial Institute, 1974).

3. EEI, *Economic Growth in the Future.*

4. Jay W. Forrester, *World Dynamics* (Cambridge, Mass.: Wright-Allen Press, 1971); Donella H. Meadows et al., *The Limits to Growth* (New York: Universe Books, 1972).

5. Robert K. Merton, *Social Theory and Social Structure* (New York: Free Press, Macmillan, 1949, rev. ed. 1957), pp. 456–88.

6. Ibid., p. 459.

7. John A. Mourant, "Augustinianism"; R. McL. Wilson, "Pelaguis and Pelagianism"; R. A. Markus, "St Augustine" *The Encyclopedia of Philosophy* (New York: Crowell, Collier and Macmillan, 1967).

8. Marie-Jean-Antione-Nicolas Caritat, and Marquis de Condorcet, *Sketch for a Historical Picture of the Progress of the Human Mind* (1795) Trans. June Barraclough (London: Weidenfeld and Nicolson, 1955), p. 4.

9. Charles Darwin, *The Origin of Species by Means of Natural Selection: or, The Preservation of Favored Races in the Struggle for Life* (New York: A. L. Burt, n.d), p. 504. (Originally published in 1859.)

10. Herbert Spencer in J. B. Bury, *The Idea of Progress: An Inquiry Into Its Origin and Growth* (New York: Macmillan, 1932), p. 340. (Reprinted by Dover Publications, New York, 1955.)

11. H. G. Wells, *Mind at the End of Its Tether* (New York: Didier Publishers, 1946).

12. Charles Beard, in Bury, *The Idea of Progress,* p. xxiii.

13. Sidney Pollard, *The Idea of Progress* (New York: Basic Books, 1968).

14. Julius Gould, "Shape of Things to Come," *Encounter,* May 1974, p. 37.

15. New York *Times,* June 4, 1974.

16. Daniel Callahan, *The Tyranny of Survival* (New York: Macmillan, 1973), p. 158.

PART TWO
Qualitative Analyses

4 | Managing the Quality of Life

Robert Theobald

It seems appropriate to start this chapter by quoting some of the central conclusions of the Edison Electric Institute report, *Economic Growth in the Future.*

> Having considered the specific questions and issues, it is concluded that the significance of the growth debate does not lie in any real choice to be made between "maximum growth" and "no growth." Some form of economic growth will continue, and its composition will be different from the past. A "new concept of economic growth" is evolving as the economy adjusts to the constraints and problems which gave rise to the growth controversy. Indeed these factors already are resulting in slower rates of growth. In the United States and some other advanced countries there is increasing reluctance to commit energies and potentials singlemindedly to growth. The transformation of the economy is observable in trends toward expansion of the service and information sectors over production. . . .
>
> The full implications of the present change process are difficult to foresee. A hopeful view is that current trends point to a natural evolution toward a form of economic expansion that could be described as "clean growth," "quality growth," or "optimal growth."
>
> Patterns of growth depend as much on cultural attitudes as on economic factors. Neither the present pro-growth view nor the no-growth view is descriptive of or adequate to our times. . . .
>
> It is imperative that the processes of policy consideration and decision-making remain open and democratic. Decisions on economic growth must always be subordinate to the maintenance of a free society which maximizes individual choice.[1]

I shall attempt to show that these conclusions are indeed central to our capacity to deal with the questions that confront us today. The hope for an open and democratic society is not a left-over dream, as is all too often assumed, but the central necessity of our time if we are to deal with the rate of change that now exists around us. We must find ways to concentrate on the type of questions raised by the Edison Electric Institute rather than being distracted by simplistic growth issues.

Regrettably, there is little sign of this shift in societal attention. Rather we are caught up in a dizzying set of changes in the positions of the primary protagonists in the growth debate. We are spending more time arguing about the need for, and the possibility of, growth than we are thinking about the ways in which we can learn about and then manage the alterations that are necessary if we are to improve the quality of life in America, in the rich countries, and throughout the world.

THE HISTORICAL BACKDROP

In order to understand these issues, it seems appropriate to go back in intellectual history. The Club of Rome study entitled *The Limits To Growth* was an impetus for the growth debate.[2] This volume argued that continued growth for even 100 years would produce insoluble problems from excessive population, excessive pollution, lack of raw materials, energy shortages, or some combination of these. The report caught the imagination of a large part of the idea-moving community and became dominant in many academic decisions.

The pessimistic conclusions of much thinking in recent years can be traced, at least indirectly, to this volume. Malthus had been updated and placed in modern dress using computers. This style of thinking had proved both compelling and, in a strange way, attractive. In a sense, the report provided an excuse for many of the failures of the 1960s, and a large number of people were ready to pick up the reasoning.

The counterpoint to the Club of Rome's viewpoint was provided by a large number of thinkers, notable among them was the Hudson Institute led by Herman Kahn, which created a set of arguments against the Malthusian point of view. The Hudson Institute argued that the Club of Rome report was simplistic, that there was every reason to believe that new resources would be discovered as old resources were used up, and that it would be possible to provide everybody on earth with a good standard of living if world governments committed themselves to this task.

But this was only part of the intellectual discussion of the first half of the 1970s. While academics were concentrating on the growth/no-growth question, other groups were trying to raise the question of the appropriate style for society in the communications era. The book that is now seen as central to this question is *Small is Beautiful* by E. F. Schumacher.[3] He argues that the way we think about our society is itself wrong and that our only hope is to bring not only our technological systems but also our institutions down to a more human scale.

Seen in an oversimplified way, then, at the time the Edison Electric Institute report was being prepared, there were three primary views in the culture. First, there were people who had gathered under the banner of the Club of Rome. These people were trying to slow down and redirect growth: Some of the supporters of this view argued essentially for a no-growth position. Second, there were those who argued that if only we would recommit ourselves to the directions that had developed during the industrial era, then our recent problems would begin to dissipate. Third, there were people who argued that the central problem was that society saw all issues in economic growth terms but that, on the contrary, we needed to return to a simpler life.

RECENT ADJUSTMENTS IN POSITIONS

In 1976 there were some significant, indeed dramatic, changes in the views of all these groups. First, at a meeting in Philadelphia the Club of Rome made it clear that it no longer was pushing the tough conclusions of the *Limits To Growth* report. Those who were present at the meeting seemed to be saying that the purpose of the report had been to shock world thinkers and lead them to recognize that we had significant problems ahead. Given the fact that this recognition had been achieved, they argued that it was now appropriate to talk about a lessening of the growth rate rather than a fundamental shift in priorities as had been implied by the *Limits to Growth* document.

This fundamental change in the position of the pessimistic thinkers was paralleled by a significant alteration in the position of the Hudson Institute, which was crystalized in the book *The Next Two Hundred Years,* published in May 1976 by Herman Kahn.[4] The volume argues that both population and production rates can be expected to decline and should continue to do so over the long run. However, it is stated that there is no urgency to the shift. The Hudson Institute would prefer, indeed, to see an increase in the growth rate in immediately coming years.

In effect, then, the debate between the Club of Rome and the Hudson Institute largely evaporated in the first half of 1976, leading one to wonder what all the sound and fury had been about. Both sides of this particular debate were now prepared to agree that a transition was needed, that it was beginning to take place, that considerable economic growth was still required, that the gap between the rich and the poor countries was significant but that it was perhaps inevitable because it was this gap that provided the engine for continued economic growth. In effect, both groups have adopted an international trickle-down theory to go along with the national trickle-down theory—it is argued that the way to deal with the problems of both poor countries and poor people is to

ensure that the rich continue to do well. This, of course, contrasts with
the stance of many other thinkers who believe that only a shift in power
relationships can significantly improve income distribution patterns.

Just as nature abhors a vacuum, however, so does academic debate.
The growth/no-growth debate has now mutated into a more violent form
and is increasingly concentrating on a single policy issue: the question of
nuclear power plants. Should we permit and encourage growth if the only
way to do so is to build a large number of nuclear power plants? Are there
alternate energy sources that could be effective?

What is disturbing about this new debate is the distressing and continuing oversimplification of the issues on both sides. The California referen-
dum that would have closed down nuclear power plants in the state
started in many people's minds as a way to challenge citizens to think
about their priorities. It ended up, however, as a no-holds-barred fight.

The growth/no-growth debate between the Club of Rome and the
Hudson Institute took place between people who shared some fundamental assumptions and were willing to discuss in similar terms. The new
growth/no-growth debate starts from mutually incompatible positions
and the degree of tension between those on the various sides is increasingly high. We are seeing two nondebatable ideologies grow up. It is
urgent for us to revise the terms of the debate so that we can examine
questions that can be effectively discussed and eventually resolved.

In my opinion, both the growth and no-growth stances lead to prepos-
terous results. The proponents of growth admit that it will inevitably lead
to new knowledge and technological capacities that will create major
dilemmas for the society. For example, the capacity to determine the sex
of a fetus coupled with legal abortion would probably create a significant
imbalance between the sex of children who are actually born. This problem would be greatly enhanced if we achieve the capacity to actually
choose a male or female birth at the moment of conception. Another
example is the certainty of nuclear proliferation given present dynamics.
Nowhere in the work of growth proponents is there any suggestion as to
how society can deal with these new dilemmas without bringing on the
conditions so well described in *Brave New World* and *1984*.

The no-growth proponents, on the other hand, want to stop some of
the new technologies, particularly nuclear energy. Many of them believe
that the human race is incompetent to deal with the complex problems
it has created through its transnational transportation and communications web and wishes to decrease the interdependence that is the overwhelming new characteristic of our time. In effect, there is an argument
for a sharp turn away from technological competence into a radically
simpler life style.

Both sides of the new growth/no-growth debate share a deep belief:

a cynicism about the capacity of human beings to manage their own world. The growth advocates are largely committed to a simplistic "invisible hand" thesis arguing that if everybody follows their own narrowest self-interest, the needs of the world will be effectively met. They believe that society will somehow muddle through the problems that are inevitable as we develop more and more power over our world.

The no-growth advocates move to the opposite end of the spectrum. Despairing of the capacity of the human race to control the technological abilities it has created, they opt for abolishing them. They believe it is possible to put the genie back into the bottle, and they hope to scare people into believing that modern technologies are too dangerous to develop and use.

I believe both of these proposals are naive, indeed impossible. The human race must always struggle to achieve understanding and in so doing gains power over decisions that were previously out of its control. We cannot reject this drive toward understanding, and therefore increased power, without destroying those characteristics that make us distinctively human. However, as we achieve this power, it is ridiculous to believe that we can avoid reexamining our value base and our social policies to discover whether they accord with the new realities we have ourselves brought into existence.

A TURNING POINT

It is my conviction, therefore, that we need to make visible a stand that is increasingly adopted by a wide range of thinkers and the general public but that gets very little attention from those who presently determine the flow of ideas in our culture. This new school of thinkers believes that we have reached the central turning point in humanity's history and that we must change from doing the things to which we have become accustomed during the industrial era and learn how to manage the world in accordance with the realities of a complex and finite universe.

Our present policies are based on our present central assumption about human nature. The patterns of the industrial era developed from our belief that human beings are naturally lazy and that they will be idle unless they are promised rewards or threatened with punishment. There is today a new school of thinkers that believes that the drive toward self-understanding is built into every human being. If this is the case, then we need to set up a system that provides people with the maximum possibility of developing themselves and the society of which they form part.

The key issue of our time is our view of people. If people are incapable of understanding themselves and their society, then we are indeed caught in the dilemmas advanced by those who propose growth and no-growth policies. If, on the other hand, people are willing and able to make decisions about their own lives and help run the society, then we need to provide them with more opportunity to be involved in effective decision making.

Both the growth and no-growth proponents deny, in effect, that it is possible to manage "the world in accordance with the realities of a complex and finite universe." From my point of view, this implies that the human race will certainly destroy itself during the remainder of this century.

Economic Growth in the Future correctly states that, "Neither the present pro-growth view nor the no-growth view is descriptive of or adequate to our times.[5] So long as we agreed on the need for maximum rates of economic growth and accepted large increases in population, then we did need a culture that was efficiently designed to force economic growth. We created this sort of culture and its accompanying socioeconomic and political systems during the industrial era. Today this system is obsolete. A society that has to operate within the concept of limits and on the basis of highly complex interactions requires a very different set of institutional arrangements. It is therefore our obligation first to understand our new needs and then to create the form of society that can be effective in our changed conditions.

At the present time society assumes that current socioeconomic and political institutions are largely viable and that all we need to do is to make limited changes. I believe we are faced with the need for totally different patterns of thinking and action. Society also assumes that people who find difficulty in fitting into present social systems need to adapt their behavior patterns: from my persepctive the growing breakdown in the world results from the fact that it is not appropriately organized for people to be able to reach legitimate goals for a high quality of life.

A CURE FOR "AMONDIE"

Emile Durkheim, the eminent French sociologist, coined a word several decades ago, which was meant to describe the mental state of those who found difficulty in fitting into the industrial society: he argued that they were suffering from *anomie:* They lacked a name or character that would enable them to be effective. Because we still perceive people in this way, we believe that those who do not fit into the present American and world society should have their characters adjusted. I believe, on the contrary, that in today's conditions, people are suffering from "amondie," which means that they lack a world in which they can realize their legitimate goals. I am therefore convinced that we confront a very difficult set of tasks from those which are normally assumed.

What can be said about the basic shifts in ideas and values that are necessary if we are to accomplish successfully a shift from the industrial era to the communications era? First, we must recognize that it is impossible to act to create an ever-greater supply of goods and services within a finite universe. There can be many arguments about the population size and the amount of production that is feasible on this planet: The dangers of excessive population and excessive load on the carrying capacity of the earth are now both so clear that there is an immediate case for reducing the rate of increase in population *as rapidly as possible* and only increasing production to meet real needs.

In other words, we need to move away from our Western preoccupation with the creation of "more" to an understanding of the idea of enough. One of the ironies of the last 30 years is the extent to which the rich countries of the world have tried to move the poor countries of the world into a socioeconomic system whose viability depends on the creation of new wants, however peripheral they may be. (This pattern is common to both capitalism and communism: both require people to want new goods and services.) The capacity to live with "enoughness" has existed in many cultures. It can be part of human nature: The quesion we must face is whether it is possible to reintroduce this idea to societies which now effectively force most of us to spend all that we make and often more.

Second, we must recognize the inadequacy of the idea of equality, at least as it is presently expressed. Inevitably, the idea of equality leads us to the belief that while "all of us are equal, some of us are more equal than others." This statement of George Orwell in his book *Animal Farm* reminds us that an attempt to create an impossible goal must inevitably lead to social pathologies. We cannot be equal to each other. Indeed, surely, none of us would want to be equal with each other. Rather we must recognize the inevitability of diversity and learn to glorify in it. We must learn to respect our differences and to recognize that a range of views is as essential for the development of a viable society as a range of organisms is for a viable ecology.

In the past we have seen differences of opinion as threatening because we have believed that there was a single appropriate way to look at the world and that those who did not share our view of reality were necessarily wrong. Today we are coming to understand that there is no single correct perception: that the way we see reality emerges from our past experiences, our genetic inheritance, our sex and age, and so on. Once we recognize that this is true, we begin to perceive that it is highly desirable to be able to learn from people who hold a different view from our own because they may be able to provide us with ideas we have not previously managed to express.

The third requirement for change is that we understand that attempts to control the behavior of other organisms are usually ineffective. There is a classic story of a man who had a cat that insisted on clawing the curtains. This made the man angry and every time it happened he threw the cat out. It did not take long for the cat to realize that the way to get out was to claw the curtains.

As we look at the history of the 1960s, we find that all too often the people who have tried to control social systems have taught others to behave in antisocial ways to achieve the goals they wanted. There is hard evidence that ghetto dwellers and people in prison have learned to provide sociologists and other researchers with exactly the evidence they want while quietly laughing at them behind their backs.

Effective alterations in action patterns will only occur when people are involved in the decision-making process. Attempts to force change will often backfire. Even when they do not, the desired alteration will be maintained only as long as control can be maintained. Recent years are littered with experiments that worked so long as the people who started them stayed around but that ceased to be effective the moment they left.

The fourth requirement for change is to recognize that the destruction of our basic value systems, which has continued throughout the industrial era, is now making it impossible for societies to function effectively. When I was growing up in the 1940s, I was told that people lived by religious values if they were weak people but they would abandon them when they knew what they were doing. It was only when I was learning systems theory that I discovered that the classic religious values of honesty, responsibility, humility, love, and a respect for mystery are basic necessities for the effective functioning of *any* system. Depending on one's prejudices, therefore, it is valid to say that religions are primitive system theory or modern system theory is primitive religion.

The critical conclusion that we must draw at this time is that the clash between religious and intellectual thinking that has been assumed in the recent past does not exist. Religious thinking and intellectual work should reinforce each other rather than cut across each other. If we could get this idea into our heads, we should already have made major strides toward developing a viable international order.

This set of changes has been described only very briefly. It is impossible in this short chapter to provide a full picture of the implications of a model which argues that we are moving out of the industrial era into the communications era. Rather, I can only hope to open up some of the issues we must consider if we are to have any effective way of bringing about changes.

CENTRAL POLICY ISSUES

There are four central policy issues in the areas of economics and employment, health, justice, and education involved in moving from an industrial-era preoccupation with the standard of living to a communications era concerned with the quality of life. The proposals I shall make here are drawn from my book *Beyond Despair*.[6] It is, of course, impossible to provide all of the background for the reasoning here.

The first reality we must understand is that there are no real options in policy making so long as we persist with our present institutional arrangements. We have a socioeconomy that operates on the basis that the appropriate way to provide resources for people is for most of those between the ages of 20 and 60 to hold jobs. Given this reality, we must promote economic growth because this is the only way we can ensure the necessary increase in jobs and thus the availability of income to those who need it.

Economics and Employment

The question we urgently need to face is whether the best way to get our crucial work done is to structure it into jobs. J. M. Scott, an anthropologist, has raised the relevant issue well when she states that in today's conditions "most people are so busy doing their jobs that they have no time to work." Let me be clear. There is obviously enough work to go around. The question we must answer is why we are unable to create ways in which unemployed people could engage in valuable and urgent work. Given the fact that our socioeconomic system has failed to meet the work needs of individuals and society over an extended period of time, we need to think about the reasons and the options.

There is today widespread agreement that the operation of the job market is no longer satisfactory and that some significant change is required. The position held by most of those in Congress is that we should ensure that everybody would be guaranteed a job if the normal operation of the economic system does not provide enough jobs for those who require them. It is this position that was incorporated in the Humphrey-Hawkins bill. The measures in this bill are potentially highly destructive of American society. The likely long-run results were set out in a remarkable book by Kurt Vonnegut called *Player Piano*.[7] In this book, written several years ago, the author demonstrates the danger of trying to control both the consumption patterns and the job activities of citizens. The Humphrey-Hawkins Bill would inevitably lead to such a result, for it can only work through ensuring increasing control of the whole socioeconomic system.

We are trapped in our present patterns of thinking that demand more, that demand that people be controlled, that reject the idea that people can be responsible. It is extraordinarily unfortunate that we continue to listen to Keynes' disciples rather than returning to Keynes' own work. He knew that as we reached our present ability to produce we should "be able to rid ourselves of many of the pseudomoral principles which have hag-ridden us for two hundred years, by which we have exalted some of the most distasteful of human qualities into the position of the highest virtues.... All kinds of social customs and economic practices affecting the distribution of wealth and of economic rewards and penalties, which we now maintain at all costs, ... we shall then be free to discard."[8]

Our socioeconomic system is obsolete because it does not provide the individual, who is prepared to work to deal with the personal and social needs of our time, a fair opportunity to do so. We are still caught up in believing that the only true wealth is that produced in the form of goods and tangible services. In today's world when people are crying for more effective learning experiences through interpersonal relationships we need to shift our methods of distributing resources.

What should be the first steps in this direction:

First, we should provide basic economic security (a guaranteed income) to all. This should be sufficiently large that it would permit people to work in ways that are important to them without having to be part of the industrial-era economic system. Such an income would not be lavish and those who chose to work outside the industrial-era system would only be able to do so through sacrifice.

Second, we should provide an income base for the middle class so that when they lose their jobs they do not fall immediately and directly into poverty. I have called this proposal "committed spending" and believe that its urgency increases as we come to recognize the degree to which many of our institutions are overstaffed.

Third, we need to simplify radically the tax system. All exemptions and deductions except for necessary business deductions should be removed and capital gains and incomes should be taxed at the same rate.

The normal objection to such measures as these is that they cut into the rates of growth. They will therefore be automatically rejected if we are still committed to a culture that demands more. In the context of an "enough" culture they are clearly relevant. I would stress, however, the fact that the pace at which these innovations are achieved is one of the most critical questions that must always be considered. Almost all of the measures I shall suggest need a phase-in period.

Health

Turning now to health, the general opinion is that the only forward option now available is to move toward national health insurance. I would argue that this will have very little favorable effect because while we hope everybody can have quality health care, the hard reality is that we cannot provide the best health care to everybody.

It is, indeed, incorrect to argue that we have a health system in this country. Rather we have a system that is centered on sickness and that will pay extraordinary amounts of money to cure people when they are sick and very little to keep them well or to help them to keep themselves well. We need to move away from a curative health system to a promotive health system that will spend its time and money to help develop skills to keep people healthy. We need, in effect, to ensure the development of an intelligent model for health maintenance organizations rather than national health insurance. National health insurance will lock us into a health delivery system that ensures endless increases in costs and no end to the present problems. A movement toward promotive health care would permit us to rethink the issues of health in ways that will minimize the burdens of sickness on the society.

In developing health maintenance organizations, however, we shall be confronted with the issue of defining death in terms that recognize the potentials of our modern technologies. We now know it is possible to keep people alive even though there is no real chance of them operating again as full human beings. We also know that this power will be increased in coming years and decades. There is an increasing cry for a right to death, a recognition that there may come a time in anybody's life when they can no longer function. The Quinlan case brought home this set of issues to us: We have been extremely fortunate as a society to have a couple of parents with the dignity and patience to force us to look at the issues involved.[9]

I am convinced that the limitations of resources we are encountering will force us to introduce a right to death. The question we need to confront now is whether we shall introduce this right in a way that provides the individual, family, and friends with the information and capacity to make intelligent decisions in this area or whether we shall place it within the responsibility of the professional because of our fear that people are not competent to make decisions for themselves.

Justice

Many people have become deeply conscious in recent years that there is indeed one law for the rich and another for the poor. We invoke the statement that "people have suffered enough" when we are talking about the powerful but never use it for those who survive in the ghetto or the poor areas of the country and have suffered all their lives. We have not been prepared to recognize up to the present time, however, the fundamental factors that lie behind our differential patterns of justice. We sometimes talk in terms of the need for punishment: an eye for an eye and a tooth for a tooth. This model is predominantly used in our patterns of sentencing when we work with the poor and the powerless. The second thread that runs through our justice system is the possibility of rehabilitation. When the rich and the powerful get caught up in the justice system it is this theme that we tend to emphasize.

Which of these views is correct, in light of the new requirements I set out for the operation of the communications era? If we opt for the punishment model it increases the frustration of all those involved in the system. There are studies which show that the prison system is radically dehumanizing for all those involved in the system, whether prisoners or guards. Nevertheless, if there is any consensus at the present time it is that the rehabilitation system has failed and we must move toward punishment. But there is clear-cut evidence that rehabilitation, like religion, has never been tried. We have swung from a naive belief that prisoners will reform themselves to an equally naive belief that punishment will deter. We have spent only a minuscule amount of our effort trying to change the perceptions of prisoners about the world in which they live, thus enabling them to survive outside the criminal culture. Indeed, there is presently little chance that we can convince people that crime does not pay when it so obviously does. The very fact that it is the "successful"— that is, rich and powerful—criminal who usually obtains the short sentence makes any education in this area very difficult.

Where should we concentrate our attention?

We need to find ways to prevent young people from committing criminal acts by ensuring that there is enough legitimate challenge in their lives. We have not tried as a society to provide ways for young people to test themselves as they grow up in our more and more interdependent world. If young people do get into trouble for the first time, a maximum effort needs to be made to keep them out of contact with others who have significant police records.

We need to ensure the possibility of redemption. For the first time in human history, a police record gained through one error or risk can follow one all one's life and make many forms of activity impossible. We should develop routes to wipe out police records if any individual ceases to be involved in criminal activities.

We need a legal system that is more designed to discover the truth and less controlled by forensic ability. To provide "batting" averages for defending and prosecuting attorneys shows that we see a trial as a "sports contest" rather than as a way to decide whether or not a person is guilty of a certain crime.

We need to face the issue of what we should do with the hardened criminal. While it is true that his or her criminal characteristics are, at least in part, the result of the failures of the society, we must become more realistic about the need to protect the society. If this is true, we must ask ourselves whether the death penalty is necessarily a more cruel and unusual punishment than imprisonment for all of the rest of a person's life.

Education

We are thus led through our consideration of the legal system to examine our educational system and to ask ourselves why so many young people are destructive today. Why do we fail to provide people with the skills and desires to work within the framework of the society? If my argument is correct, people fail to be positively involved because of the problem of "amondie": the lack of a world in which they can meet their true needs for dignity and a chance to develop themselves to the fullest.

Instead of today's conventional argument, therefore, which suggests that people are inherently lazy and only work when forced to do so, I am suggesting that there is a drive to growth in all of us that is frustrated by the organization of society. I believe the reason our schools are doing so badly is that they underestimate very seriously the competence, drive, and concern of the students within them. I am convinced that most of our school problems emerge from the sheer boredom of young people who are very seldom challenged in the classroom. A Marshall McLuhan story tells it all. Two kindergarten children are walking down the streets and identifying the planes as they fly overhead. As they come to the school-room door, one turns to the other and says: "Now, lets go in and string those darn beads." How many of the activities in schools and colleges are equivalent to stringing those darn beads?

The conventional wisdom in federal and state educational organizations now appears to be that we should concentrate our declining financial potentials on the traditional four-year college and also on vocational education so that everybody can have some skills to get a job. Despite the rhetoric about life-long education, the trend is clearly away from providing significant funding for people to learn those skills they need throughout their lives. This reality is particularly clear in prevailing attitudes toward community colleges.

I do not believe we will make significant progress in dealing with our educational problems unless we recognize that nothing less than a fundamental change in our thinking about the life cycle of the individual will enable us to come to grips with present challenges. In other words, I believe that the idea of continuing schooling through 16 or 18 or 20 or 22 ignores a reality that Plato brought to our attention over two millenia ago. Young people are not particularly interested in formal education in their teens or early twenties. They want to get out and test themselves, to discover who they are and what they can do.

If this is the case, then we need to rethink fundamentally what people should do throughout their life span. Instead of preparing for school, for a job, for retirement, and for death as is the case at the present time, we need to create a new life pattern in which people learn and work in individually chosen and developed patterns. We need to permit wide diversity in styles and patterns. Fortunately, the new communication technologies give us the capacity to coordinate such differing models of behavior.

What types of changes should we begin to make? First, we should cut back on the laws that compel attendance at school and try to limit child labor abuses. The costs of these laws in preventing individual development are now higher than the benefits. There are laws that do prohibit young people from being abused or exploited in the labor market, but these laws don't prohibit them from handling many kinds of jobs.

Second, we should give a far higher priority to funding continuing citizen education. Despite our rhetoric, there is little large-scale funding for the education of adults. And yet, without it, there is little chance that the drive toward citizen involvement and participation can be effective. It requires an act of faith to believe that democracy is possible at all. It requires total stupidity to argue that democracy is possible with an ill-informed citizenry. Unless we can find better ways to inform people about the changes in our world that are developing as a result of the coming of the communications era, there is no possible way in which effective governance will be possible.

THE PARTICIPATORY MODE

Citizen participation, neighborhood power, community development are all words for one of the most significant, most ignored, and least understood movements. More and more organizations are putting ever greater time into the development of these patterns of activity. If we are to understand what is going on, however, we must recognize that there are three very different models for citizen participation activities and that there is little understanding of the critical differences.

Citizen participation can be simply a way to get agreement with ideas that have already been developed by the existing decision makers. Citizens are provided with a set of questions and an overall pattern of participation that provide them with little opportunity to raise new questions. No systems are set up to deal with those people who break out of the boundaries of the study and they are therefore effectively ignored. Many of the best known of the citizen participation and futurist models are heavily flawed by this approach.

At the other extreme it is often argued that there is no need for a decision-making group at all. It is suggested that modern technologies provide the opportunity for all decisions to be made on the basis of instant referenda: Each person should cast his or her ballot on all questions of importance. This proposal falls down because it is naive to believe that people can provide the right answers to questions they do not understand.

The central position between these two is that all decisions should be made by the most competent group that can be assembled. There will then be at any moment in time a group that is in charge of making decisions on a particular subject, but the members of the group should be the most knowledgeable that can be assembled at a particular time and should always be on the lookout for new people who can be brought into the system to help with the decision-making process. As opposed to the present time when people try to cling to power, there should be a willingness to move out of the decision-making process and to try to find younger people who can take over the load. The reality behind this statement can be discovered by examining the work of those people who are developing new leadership models and those who are working in new styles of leadership roles. This question is examined further in *Teg's 1994* by J. M. Scott and myself.[10]

The central dilemma that is going to emerge as new, effective decision-making groups develop locally is they will challenge existing federal, regional, and state laws that limit the ability of local groups to choose their own patterns of behavior. There are, of course, some laws and regulations that do require to be national, regional, or statewide in scope; there are many other laws, however, that were passed before we understood the importance of diversity in styles of behavior in various communities. It is my conviction that one of the primary concerns of the next few years will be to deal imaginatively and creatively with the growing desire of local groups to regain power.

The types of difficulties that will emerge are demonstrated by the busing and pornography questions. In the first case, the decision has been made to enforce a set of federal standards; in the second, local option has been held to prevail but First Amendment rights have also been held to apply. From my point of view, the consequences in both cases have been close to disastrous.

CHARTING A COURSE FOR TRANSITION

I have suggested in this chapter the changes in values and some of the alterations in policy if we are to deal with the shift from the industrial era to the communications era. I have argued that many of the sacred cows of Congress and the country—full employment, national health insurance, stiffer justice, back to the basics in education—are based on the belief that it is still possible to make the industrial-era system work. I have suggested that the passage of legislation designed to attain these ends would in fact make it impossible to achieve the quality of life that is now feasible.

The issue that faces us all at this time is whether it is feasible to consider such changes or whether the lock-ins of our present system make such thinking irrelevant. If we look back at history, it is clear from the work of such historians as Spengler and Toynbee that cultures have often collapsed from their own contradictions. There is no reason, therefore, to be overly optimistic about our plight and to believe that change will occur easily, let alone automatically.

But there are, on the other hand, reasons to believe that our situation is not hopeless. First, there are many people who have the time to think —on their own or through various styles of formal or informal education. Second, we do know a great deal about the ways in which we must behave if we are to make the transition from the industrial era to the communications era successfully. Third, we have the communications media that make it possible for us to bring new ideas to people's attention rapidly if we are willing to use them for this purpose.

What are the steps we must take if we are to have any chance of making the necessary changes before we lose our options? First, we must recognize that there is no single objective truth in any policy area. Different people perceive different necessities and these arise from their experience. We need to set up a communication process that allows people to perceive the reasons for the difference in perception rather than to continue to work within debate formats that exacerbate differences. In effect, we need to operate out of a different view of the world. At the present time we are taught to be right and we work toward this desired goal by trying to put other people in the wrong. If we are to survive in our complex, interdependent, and finite world we must learn that everyone is partially right and we need to stress agreements and to build from them. However, we cannot move in this direction unless we break out of the analytical style of the industrial era. We were all taught to analyze reality apart; we are now finding that we need to learn how to think the world together. Our decision making is almost always fragmented: We concentrate on one aspect of the situation rather than on the various interrelationships.

Perhaps the most effective way to discuss this is to consider the triangle of forces: economic growth, ecological balance, and energy conservation. We usually argue that we should try to achieve all three at once, but we should know it is impossible to maximize more than one factor at a time: We are presently finding out how true that is.

I shall examine the results of the consequent confusion at only two levels, although the results are developing at the international, national, regional, and state levels. From the point of view of the individual, the problem is symbolized by the fact that he or she is asked: to buy a car to stimulate the economy; not to run the car because this wastes gas; and if the car is run to use a catalytic converter to save the environment even though this reduces gas mileage. This example may appear too slick at first sight, but in reality it does reflect the fundamental failure of our decision-making systems. We can see this clearly if we look at the situation in Congress that possesses different committees that have different responsibilities. For ease of analysis we shall suggest that there are some that promote economic growth, others that are concerned with ecological balance, and still others that are concerned with energy conservation. Each of these sets of committees does its best to pass policy that is relevant to the concerns that it is meant to handle.

Unfortunately, however, given present attitudes, there is no way in which it is possible for economic growth to take place without using more energy and having some undesirable effects on the environment. The results of the work of each group of committees, therefore, have large-scale, but largely unconsidered, impacts on the activities of the others. Because our primary commitment is to achieve growth, in order to provide jobs, there can be no truly effective work in ensuring ecological balance and energy conservation.

There is absolutely no way out of this dilemma with our present patterns of thinking and commitments. So long as we live within a job-based society we are locked into maximizing economic growth and we cannot pay concentrated attention to the quality of life. We are controlled, therefore, by the need to increase consumption in order to provide jobs for all and there can be no change in this situation until we develop an alternative indicator for the success of our societies.

It is now possible to state the implications of the title of this article with some clarity. Acceptance of the idea of growth as the central issue of our time leads us into discussion at levels and in styles that prevent us from looking at today's central issue. We remain trapped in an idea-set that is obsolete. To break out of this situation we need a new direction; we need to concentrate on the quality of life rather than just its quantity. We need to recognize also that the term "quality of life" is more than just another cute way of discussing economic growth. We must remember that there are many times when economic growth does impact unfavorably on the quality of life.

Once we have taken this step—and it is far larger than we normally realize—than we are ready to look at the ways in which we can achieve a higher "quality of life." We are failing to be effective in this task because we do not know how to make good decisions. This failure results primarily from the distortion of information. Our survival depends on our ability to set up new systems for information creation and movement. Over the past few years I have been working on the development of problem/possibility focusers and networks that are designed to create and distribute knowledge about disagreements, agreements, and directions in various critical areas.

A commitment to strive for growth and control was appropriate in the industrial era. Today, only effective communication will permit us to deal with the questions of our time. This was the theme of a remarkable speech by Sir Geoffrey Vickers at the Third International Meeting of the Environmental Symposium Series held in Spokane, Washington, in October 1974:

> 1. The world we live in demands and depends on skill in communication and in knowledge relevant to communication to an extent far beyond anything previously known. The essential skills are those skills in appreciation which I have briefly described. The essential knowledge includes knowledge not only of the subject matter but also of the other communicating parties and of the process to which all are part. These skills, even more than the knowledge on which they are based, can and should be taught to a degree far exceeding what is now conceived by any education system known to me.
>
> 2. Communication depends on trust, as I have described it, and imposes on communicators a duty to sustain the level of communication, not only by their skill and knowledge but by being trustworthy communicators.

3. This is more important because there is a "law" of communication similar to "Gresham's law" in economics. Bad communication drives out good communication. A small minority with a few bombs and a lot of self-righteousness can soon reduce the level of communication in a whole society to the basic level of mutual threat.

4. Thus, the duty I have described assumes an importance, as well as a difficulty, which can hardly be exaggerated. It seems to me a trans-cultural human duty to sustain the level of communication, to resist its debasement and to cooperate in raising it.

5. The direction in which this duty points seems to me to be the direction of the more human, rather than the less human; a vector which can recognize as trans-cultural and which claims the allegiance of the whole species. It may be the only dimension in which any kind of progress is possible. It is surely a precondition for progress of any other kind.

NOTES

1. Edison Electric Institute, *Economic Growth in the Future; The Growth Debate in National and Global Perspective* (New York: McGraw-Hill, 1976), p. 7, see also pp. 73–74.

2. Donella H. Meadows et al., *The Limits to Growth* (New York: Universe Books, 1972).

3. E. F. Schumacher, *Small is Beautiful* (New York: Harper and Row, 1973).

4. Herman Kahn, William Brown, and Leon Martel, *The Next Two Hundred Years* (New York: Morrow, 1976).

5. EEI, *Economic Growth in the Future.*

6. Robert Theobald, *Beyond Despair* (Washington, D.C.: New Republic Book Company, 1976).

7. Kurt Vonnegut, *Player Piano* (New York: Delacorte, 1971).

8. John Maynard Keynes, *Essays in Persuasion* (New York: Harcourt, Brace, 1932), pp. 369–70.

9. The Quinlan case involves a young woman who has been in a coma for several months, her life prolonged by life-sustaining equipment. Doctors and her parents were in disagreement concerning the use of this equipment, since the prognosis was that she would be a "vegetable" were she to live at all. Wishing her to be allowed to die normally, the parents finally petitioned a court to this end. The court ruled in favor of the parents and the machines were turned off. The young woman is still alive and continues in a comatose state.

10. J. M. Scott, and Robert Theobald, *Teg's 1994* (Chicago: Swallow Press, 1971).

5 | Society, the Economy, and Energy

Willis W. Harman and Richard Carlson

Our title deliberately attempts to emphasize the primacy of social issues and social decision making over both economic and energy issues. Of course, there is some feedback between all three sets of issues, but this feedback loop is too often discussed as if it were a one-way chain of causality: energy → economy → society. Much of the credit (or blame) for this view of causality goes to a segment of the "no-growth party" who tend to take a relatively mechanistic, physical-science-oriented approach to energy and economic issues. Their approach can be summarized as follows:

The environment presents physical limits to continued growth in the use of energy and other physical resources.

Therefore, continued growth in energy supply, materials usage, and product of the economy is not possible.

Therefore, the economy must be dramatically changed.

Therefore, society must be dramatically altered.

It is interesting to note that a similar mechanistic view of causality is taken by an extreme wing of the pro-growth school. This group often simply projects past rates of growth of energy use and then states the problem as one of changing the economy and society to meet the projected energy demand. Typical examples of the pro-growth view and the no-growth view are contained in *Economic Growth in the Future*, authored by the Edison Electric Institute.[1] This report goes on to draw conclusions in favor of a "moderate growth scenario." The report is well done and the arguments are impressive. However, the basic statement of the issue is faulty, and as a result the report is less illuminating than it might otherwise be.

In this chapter we argue that a still more penetrating look is necessary. We challenge both of these simplistic views of economic and energy problems. The correlation between energy use and economic growth is significant, but it is not unalterable. Economic growth is important to society, but society has other vital goals as well. Broad social and sociopolitical constraints will limit economic and energy growth long before the United States reaches physical limits to growth. Fundamental issues are involved, and the future of industralized civilization is at stake; neither growth as usual nor stopping growth provides a viable resolution. Thus we have deliberately chosen the word order of the title to emphasize the primacy of social issues and social decision making over both economic and energy issues.

Our general conclusions, which will be explored in order in the remainder of the chapter are as follows:

Somewhat slower economic growth and much slower energy growth are desirable.

Continued high economic and energy growth would be difficult to achieve.

Lower economic and energy growth are feasible and no more difficult than achieving high growth.

A variety of political and social pressures make slower growth more likely than continued high growth.

Behind the limits-to-growth issue lies a far more fundamental challenge to industrialized society that we have yet to perceive clearly, let alone meet successfully.

DO WE NEED HIGH ECONOMIC GROWTH?

Economic growth and growth in energy consumption are too often discussed as if they were both basically desirable. Energy use itself is not intrinsically desirable. Energy is a means of producing a variety of goods and services, of achieving individual and societal goals, but energy use is not an end in itself. If the same or an equally desirable set of goods and services could be produced with less energy input, then society as a whole would be better off.

Economic goods and services, on the other hand, have some intrinsic desirability. This intrinsic desirability of economic goods is extended in the pro-growth arguments to the following assumptions:

The benefits of a high-consumption society as compared with any feasible alternative are obvious and generally agreed to.

The high-consumption, high-growth society is also the best hope for raising the nation's poor (and the poor of the world) to a higher state of material and social well-being.

The truth of these assumptions is no longer obvious. Circumstances have changed to such a degree that economic growth as currently defined is less important and society needs a different kind of growth. The year 2000 economy will not be the 1975 economy expanded by some constant. Several factors will change the desirability and direction of future economic growth. These factors include market saturation effects, demographic changes, changing relation between growth and poverty relief, changing relations between growth and inflation, and Third World political pressures.

Saturation

Over 90 percent of U. S. households wired for electricity now have a washer, a refrigerator, and a television set, and over 82 percent of U. S. households have an automobile.[2] By the year 2000 population will grow only 17 to 20 percent, but in a typical moderate-growth scenario the economy would expand to 250 percent of its present size. We simply don't need the quantity of physical goods that such an economy could produce.

Population Growth and Age Structure

The baby boom is over and the average age of the population will steadily increase. This has a wide variety of impacts on the need for economic growth:

Education: Economic growth was needed to finance the education of the baby boom. Education was the largest factor in the growth of government expenditure since World War II.[3] The peak of the baby boom is now in college, and between now and 2000 we will need fewer teachers, fewer school buildings, fewer professors, and fewer colleges.

Housing: Past growth was needed to house a growing population. It will take another decade to complete housing the baby boom, but after 1985 housing demand will decline until by 2000 new housing will be needed primarily for replacement and population redistribution.

Jobs: We are experiencing a period of difficulty in absorbing an unusually fast rate of growth of the labor force—nearly 2 percent per year. By 1990 the labor force will be growing at less than 1 percent per year.[4] Since the labor force will be growing more slowly, it will be possible to grow more slowly and still keep unemployment at acceptable levels.

Poverty

In 1959, when 28 million, or 72 percent, of the people living below the poverty level were in families with two parents of working age, it made sense to speak of economic growth as a great engine of social improvement. The most successful part of the "War on Poverty" was putting millions of these people to work. Now, with only 12 million (or less than 50 percent) of poor individuals in families with two parents of employable age (and many of these sick or disabled), providing more jobs through faster economic growth will have little impact on improving the economic circumstances of the poor.[5] We are near the irreducible minimum where the only way to fight poverty is to give money to poor people. In 1973 the aggregate gap between private income of poor families and the minimum low-income level was $18 billion.[6] In that same year our total welfare expenditures already exceeded $27 billion, excluding $56 billion for Social Security and $4 billion for unemployment;[7] this amount should be enough to solve the poverty problem. In reality, the poverty issue is enmeshed in a bureaucratic and political nightmare of hundreds of uncoordinated and often ineffective programs. Boosting economic growth is no substitute for a direct attack on the poverty problems remaining in 1976.

Inflation and Modest Income

Even if one uses a broader definition of low income, there is no guarantee that faster economic growth will produce relative gains or any gain for the lower-income segments of the population. The average worker in private industry lost in after-tax income adjusted for inflation between 1965 and 1974 in spite of substantial economic growth during that time period.[8] Gains in per capita income came from smaller families, more two-income families, and higher real wages in the public sector. Furthermore, one can make a psychological case that an erratic boom/bust growth pattern, even at a high average growth rate, is less desirable than a slow but steady pattern of economic growth.

U. S. Growth and the Third World

This issue involves complex tradeoffs among different classes of Third World countries and between different views of development. Individual countries plead for more exports to the United States and higher prices, while groups of countries demand slower growth of the industrialized nations. Venzuela cannot eat her oil and must export to grow, but that same oil could be used to speed South American development in the future.

Some images are as important as reality. Reducing the opulence of the U. S. society might provide a psychological boost to the Third World, but through reduced U. S. imports it would also reduce the economic growth of the Third World. Whether U. S. economic growth helps or hinders Third World growth is an argument that will continue for many years.

WHAT ARE THE PROBLEMS OF ECONOMIC GROWTH?

Economic growth is most often criticized primarily in terms of its effect on the environment. Much of this criticism is justified, but environmental problems are determined more by the composition of growth than by its magnitude. Classic environmental problems—air and water pollution— are associated with the production and use of durable goods, such as automobiles and appliances. These same durable goods are the chief causes of our growing appetite for energy. This part of the problem is partially solving itself as we reach saturation in the consumption of durable goods, and durable goods have shown a declining share of GNP for many years.[9]

Study of the prospects of air pollution over the next half century leads to the surprising conclusion that national air emissions are likely to *improve* or stay the same between now and 2000 and only particulates and oxides of nitrogen will worsen by 2020. This result depends on two assumptions: much higher gasoline prices and maintaining present emission standards. The result of these assumptions should be a dramatic shift to less polluting diesel and gas/methanol engines.[10]

This is not to say that environmental problems will disappear—there will be a variety of regional problems—but deterioration of the physical environment is unlikely to be the primary limit on economic growth in the United States in the next half century.

We are beginning to look more closely at the social limits to growth and the social costs of growth. Obviously, the United States is in a period of social upheaval with rising crime rates, vandalism, divorce, mental illness, drug abuse, and so on. Some of this is due to overall social change, such as the weakening of traditional values, defeat in Vietnam, and other noneconomic problems. However, most of these social problems are present in all industrialized nations and can be directly attributed largely to the fact that material wealth has become a goal in itself rather than a means. High economic growth does place pressure on the family. It is economically efficient to uproot and move a family every few years, to change jobs, and to have both parents work. The mental pressure brought on by this economic pressure has produced similar problems of family breakup in both the United States and the Soviet Union. Dreams of material prosperity always can outpace reality. Material satisfaction is unreachable as a primary goal.

A high-growth society becomes overspecialized and vulnerable to the smallest disruption. Small groups of individuals, from bus drivers to terrorists, can totally disrupt a modern city.

Increased economic growth can solve only economic problems. Families will fight over money no matter what their income, if they are continually induced to expand their material desires. If economic success is the only success, then the majority of a population will always feel unsuccessful compared to a conspicuous, opulent minority.

IS CONTINUED HIGH ECONOMIC GROWTH FEASIBLE?

A GNP growth rate of 3.5 percent through the year 2000 requires a rate of growth of productivity of nearly 3 percent per year, since the labor force will be growing at less than 1 percent per year by the 1990s. Productivity grew at only 1.6 percent per year from 1970 through 1975. (Note that this is a comparison between the troughs of two recessions, so it is not a misleading comparison.)

Accelerating the rate of growth of productivity would require most of the following:

Increase the relative share of high-productivity durable manufacturing. The economy has steadily shifted toward lower-productivity service industries. Higher prices for energy and materials, and saturation of many segments of the market for durable goods make it likely that this trend will accelerate rather than reverse.

Decrease government regulation of the economy. Growing government regulation has created an investment climate of such uncertainty that the most important factor in many investment decisions is guessing future government regulations. Governmental regulation of every phase of economic activity shows no sign of reversing. Slower investment can only worsen economic problems leading to more regulation, which will slow investment even more.

Slow the growth of government. Government activity slows the growth of productivity in two ways—a relative growth of government employment is a shift to a lower productivity industry, and government deficits can "push out" productive private investment. The growth of government employment—federal, state, and local—is slowing down, but overall government spending and borrowing at all levels continue to grow. The general consensus of a number of studies of capital shortages is that the key factor is the size of government deficits. If the government does not move back to balance, we will have a capital shortage.

Speed technological progress. We have been able to work from an inventory of basic scientific discoveries that came from the nineteenth and early twentieth centuries. It is likely that diminishing returns apply to science in the same way that they apply to so many other activities. It will be difficult to maintain, much less accelerate, the rate of technological progress.

Return to domestic and international tranquility. Domestic and international terrorism and crime continue to grow. Our political and legal systems have been unable to deal with these problems. This only worsens a difficult investment climate, requires unproductive investment in security systems and guards, and creates a general climate of fear.

Drop environmental standards. This would shift investment back to improving labor productivity, but who would support it?

The only other way the "desirable ... moderate" growth rate of 3.5 percent (commended in the EEI report) could be achieved is through an expansion of the labor force. However, this would require such socially controversial actions as reversing the trend to early retirement, allowing increased migration, and providing free day care to allow more mothers of preschool children to work.

IS CONTINUED HIGH ENERGY GROWTH FEASIBLE?

Even if the United States maintains projected economic growth in the 3.5 percent range, it will be particularly difficult, as well as undesirable, to reach the projected energy use of over 150 quads* per year by 2000, which is implied by past energy-GNP correlations. This projection rests on the following assumptions about energy supply and demand:

We really need the energy.
There are ample alternative energy sources that await development.

---

*This is roughly the equivalent of 75 million barrels of oil *per day*. A quad is one quadrillion BTUs; total energy usage in the United States is presently just over 70 quads per year.

The public has faith in, and will support, a technological approach.

The public will subsidize industry's development costs and risk protection where necessary to assure new energy supplies.

Environmental costs of large energy projects will be chosen in preference to the economic costs of not having enough energy.

Regional sacrifice (for example, in the Western states) will be accepted to further the nation's overall interest.

Economic and growth goals provide adequate cultural bonds to ensure concerted efforts to resolve difficult trade-offs (for example, land use, water rights) and take necessary actions to solve energy and environmental problems.

There would not be adequate public support to adopt a policy of voluntary frugality and austerity while awaiting clarification of the energy situation.

As has been pointed out by many experts, a variety of natural economic forces are operating to discourage energy use. The saturation of consumer durables will slow the growth of our most energy-intensive industries. Energy use per dollar of GNP has declined since 1970 and this has been in spite of government policies that have operated (press releases to the contrary) to encourage energy use. One price increase is worth a million exhortations. Price ceilings and regulations will hold back the tide of energy prices for only a short time.

Our energy-intensive economy developed during a period of declining relative cost of energy. The relative cost of energy is already increasing and will increase even faster once price ceilings finally fail. Industry is by far the largest and fastest growing user of energy and can be expected to react quickly to these cost changes. Consumers react more slowly, and advertising can induce large numbers of consumers to behave irrationally, but a new frugal ethic could lead to much faster consumer change.

While there are ample energy sources that await development, especially Western coal and nuclear power, it is not at all clear that the public will support the measures necessary for the development of these energy sources.

Nuclear power faces continuing problems of public acceptance. While two-thirds of California voters supported nuclear power in general, how many of those same voters would support nuclear power adjacent to their town? By the year 2000 we need sites for about six hundred 1,000-megawatt nuclear power plants. That means 600 battles with the courts, city councils, and state legislatures. Under existing state and federal laws, any well-organized group can hire a clever lawyer and have a good chance of delaying nuclear power plant construction for years. Even if the plant is eventually built, the certainty of delay and the chance of a permanent stoppage of a half-completed plant is enough to change nuclear economics significantly. In terms of the economics of nuclear power, the facts of nuclear safety are not nearly as important as public perceptions. Recently, a dam burst and caused damage and loss of life comparable to a small nuclear power plant accident, but we will still build more dams. If a similar nuclear accident had happened, it takes little imagination to think of the wave of antinuclear laws that would sweep through the Congress and state legislatures.

To continue beyond 2000, nuclear power must soon move to breeder reactors and the plutonium cycle. Also, the problem of permanent storage of high-level wastes has still not been solved. Again, public perceptions are more important than facts. Which congressman will risk his seat to put a breeder or a waste disposal facility in his district? To supply power economically, the breeder must be fairly close to a major city, and the high-level waste storage facilities most probably need to be in stable salt domes that underlie populated parts of the Midwest and South. In neither case is there the choice to put the facilities in the middle of a Nevada desert.

With increasing concern about nuclear power as we move toward the breeder, more restrictive state and federal laws are likely that will make it even easier for antinuclear advocates to delay nuclear power to death. One of the compromises that helped defeat the California antinuclear initiative is a law that requires the legislature to vote to affirm nuclear safety standards before further nuclear development takes place. Similar laws are pending in other states.

If the United States really needs 600 nuclear power plants by 2000, nuclear power will have to be exempted from most existing state and federal legal procedures. This would involve federalization of most public utility regulation. Such a solution is impossible without an overwhelming social consensus favoring nuclear power. No such consensus is on the horizon.

To reach 150 quads by 2000, coal is several times more important than nuclear power. Coal production would have to increase from approximately 650 million tons a year today to more than 2 billion tons a year by 2000. Most of this coal must come from Wyoming, Montana, and North Dakota. Such development involves political, social, and legal conflict over water rights, the environment, and states rights. Development on the required scale and pace means taking *all* unused water rights in the area (stopping all noncoal development); relaxing federal air pollution laws; mining on Indian reservations; obtaining exemption from the National Environmental Policy Act and state environmental legislation; granting powers of eminent domain to railroads, power companies, and coal slurry pipelines; and moving at least 500,000 if not a few million people to the area. Development at such a pace may not be perceived to be in the best interests of Wyoming, Montana, and North Dakota. These states may very well see their interests lying in slow and orderly development, with high reclamation standards and high severance taxes on coal. These states could easily finance their entire budgets from coal revenues.

Again we are left with a question of social consensus. Will there be sufficient national political consensus to enact federal laws to force a dramatic pace of coal development on the West? Note that this does not assume serious local support for *no* development, but local support limiting coal development to growing "only" by a factor of, say, 10, that is, 500 million tons a year from the West, when the nation would need a billion tons a year.

The remaining sources of domestic energy are even less likely to contribute significantly in the year 2000 time frame. Even the optimistic advocates of fusion power are talking about 2020 and beyond. We could be mining some oil shale, but massive oil shale development involves expensive underground mining, vast quantities of waste, and difficult water supply problems. Overall, the problems of oil shale make Western coal development look easy. Oil and natural gas in quantities sufficient even to maintain present rates of production through 2000 simply do not exist—even if we are lucky offshore and in Alaska.

Finally, we must look at solar and other "renewable" sources of energy. If one honestly looks at costs, solar energy can at best make only modest contributions to reaching a 150-quad energy supply. A recent investigation of the potential for solar energy reached the following conclusions:

> Solar energy has real potential for space heating, but this is our slowest-growing market where insulation would be less costly than using solar energy.
> Solar has some potential for providing intermediate electric power in the Southwest.
> If we assume solar electric capacity at an optimistic $.40 per peak watt by 1990, solar power must be subsidized by over $30 billion per year (70 percent) to substitute for nuclear power.
> Unless we nearly give away solar electricity, we cannot avoid the difficulties inherent in Western coal development.[11]

Does anyone seriously expect subsidies of $30 billion a year for solar power?

Of course, there is the alternative of importing more oil. Even optimistic scenarios of 20 quads of nuclear power and 2 billion tons a year of coal require a doubling of oil imports by 2000. In a world of growing political instability, do we dare depend on that level of imports? Relying on Middle Eastern oil means relying on one of the most politically unstable regions in the world. A coup in Saudi Arabia or one of the other oil-exporting countries could upset the whole oil situation. Among other problems, increased reliance on Middle Eastern oil could easily lead to a choice between oil and Israel. Who will take on that political battle?

Even if the basic energy sources are available, who will finance the development and energy conversion facilities? Investors in the energy sector face problems that are even worse than the problems facing investors in other sectors. Most importantly, government regulation is greater in the energy sector than in other areas. This means greater uncertainty, which leads rational investors to demand higher rates of return, which leads to high prices, which angers consumers who demand more regulations, and so on. Of course, we could move to government-guaranteed rates of return for all energy investments, but this would mean greater and more detailed governmental control of the entire energy sector. Since the political and legal processes are peculiarly will suited to magnifying the power of any small but well-organized groups whose goals involve delay, increased governmental involvement can only slow energy development. The problem of competition from OPEC oil almost mandates governmental involvement in energy investment. Imagine building a $1 billion oil shale facility and watching OPEC cut the price of oil enough to bankrupt you the day after construction is completed.

Through short-term price cuts, OPEC could easily destroy large-scale domestic competition. Investors must demand protection against OPEC, but this requires sufficient political trust in private business to support such investment guarantees on a large scale—over a trillion dollars between now and 2000.

THE LOW-GROWTH ALTERNATIVE

Thus it appears that continued high economic and energy growth is neither automatically desirable or feasible. No invisible hand will move us toward high growth. A deliberate, social decision is necessary to enact all the new laws we will need to achieve high growth.

This fact alone makes low growth both more appealing and more likely, for it means that taking no further federal action will certainly result in not meeting the 150-quad goal. That is not to say that present policies are in any way proconservation policies. Federal policy is a strange concoction designed to hide our energy problems from the electorate until Congress can get through another election. Present policies are clearly untenable in the long run. Price ceilings on interstate natural gas mean no new interstate gas. This would result in natural gas rationing, which would leave the Northern states a choice among freezing, losing their industry, and voting for a price hike. Price ceilings on domestic crude mean less drilling and little new oil. Nuclear would continue to be delayed, and without large-scale federal support for the breeder, nuclear power would be on the decline by the 1990s. Synthetic fuel plants will not be built on a large scale without federal guarantees, and the Western states are likely to limit coal development by themselves. OPEC would gladly supply the increased U. S. demand and continue to raise their prices. For another five to ten years people could continue to build uninsulated homes and commute with one person in a car. This high-energy-use wonderland could not continue forever. With such short-sighted national policies, we would increasingly rely on imported oil and ultimately U.S. prices would rise to the OPEC level. Conservation would come slowly as prices rose.

It should be apparent that a continuation of present shortsighted policies only delays and makes more difficult the transition to a high-energy-cost world. Such a transition will involve changes in the whole structure of U. S. society. Literally every capital asset in the United States—houses, factories, machines, automobiles, and appliances—has been designed on the basis of cheap energy. Our whole spatial structure—housing location, factory location, regional specialization—is also based on cheap energy. It takes 30 to 40 years to turn over these assets, so time is of the essence.

IS LOW GROWTH FEASIBLE?

If society finally decides to adopt a low-energy-growth policy, many implementation measures are available.

Stop subsidizing energy. Energy prices are kept low through a variety of policies. Nuclear power is subsidized through below-cost uranium enrichment and massive federal research and development. Hydropower is kept cheap by below-market-rate federal interest charges to federal power projects. Oil still has much of its depletion allowance and other tax benefits. Electric utilities receive special investment tax credits and public electric power utilities use their tax-exempt status to gain low-interest loans. More fundamentally, we persist in the faulty logic that irreplaceable fossil fuels are worth only what it costs to get them out of the ground. All these existing policies help keep energy prices low.

Use marginal cost pricing for energy. New energy sources are more expensive than old energy sources. Regulation of gas and electric utilities and price ceilings on oil keep energy costs down to the average of cheap old energy and expensive new. Since all consumers share in the new energy, all energy should be priced at the cost of the new energy. If this results in improperly high profits to energy companies, that can be handled as a separate problem.

Tax imports. Increased reliance on oil imports does create difficulties for U. S. foreign policy, and oil importers (that is, consumers) should pay for this cost. The simplest solution would be an import tax to finance a six-month to one-year oil inventory.

Subsidize conservation. This could include dropping sales and property taxes on insulation, and subsidizing solar heating in homes.

Reduce transportation. This should emphasize discouraging energy-intensive air travel through dropping airline and airport subsidies and charging private pilots their fair share of air traffic control costs. Another way to make transportation more energy efficient is to allow unlimited jitney, taxi, and bus service.

Reduce energy consumed in travel to work. This would include reducing zoning restrictions on multifamily dwellings, taxing parking, raising bridge tolls, and taxing horsepower or automobile weight.

Slowing down economic growth and shifting it away from material goods might require a few additional policies, such as the following:

Reduce advertising. Limit the tax deduction on advertising to a small percent of sales.

Reduce conspicuous consumption. This is centered in our entertainment industry and could be slowed dramatically by dropping tax deductions for business entertainment, professional sports investments, and corporate perquisites.

Lengthen useful product life. Make style changes not tax deductible, set mandatory guarantee levels, drop sales taxes on used items, and finance repair schools.

Shift taxation from income to consumption. In essence, what this adds to is that low growth is a social, not an economic, decision. It could be made by the society without excessive economic hardship. A variety of measures are available to implement the decision and to distribute any hardship equitably.

WHAT ARE THE PROBLEMS OF LOW GROWTH?

There *are* many problems in moving to slower energy and economic growth but they are primarily social and political rather than economic. The most significant economic problem is the difficulty inherent in shifting demand away from energy-intensive consumer durables toward labor-intensive, lower productivity industries. This involves high unemployment (at least temporarily) in many industries and regions that depend on those industries. A slow transition would be relatively easier, but any sudden change would produce dramatic unemployment in many areas of the country, particularly the industrial Midwest. The change also means lower productivity, slower growth in wages, and temporarily more inflation as high energy prices are passed through to the consumer.

This shift creates more important political problems because it shifts demand away from the high-productivity, high-wage, heavily unionized, concentrated durable manufacturing sector. These unions and corporations are the best organized and most influential political groups in the United States. The greatest relative impact would be on basic materials —steel, copper, aluminum, and chemicals. The United Auto Workers and General Motors (GM) would have relatively minor problems, since it takes little less labor to make a small energy-efficient car, and GM could maintain its profits if it plans well. However, this energy-efficient car means much less steel, aluminum, and plastics, and the labor and corporate impacts of that change are unavoidable.

Low growth also creates difficult problems for the government sector in that government expenditures (particularly local, state, and transfers) are growing far faster than GNP. Government share of GNP increased from 21.7 percent in 1946 to 35 percent in 1975. Government expenditure has proved difficult to control in a high-growth environment, and both the necessity for control and the difficulty of control would increase in a low-growth environment. High growth plus inflation have given the government sector the best of two worlds: Congress reduces income tax *rates* every year or two, but both the absolute amount of taxes and the government share of GNP continue to increase.

Another problem of moving to low energy growth is the problem of raising prices. The best possible solution would be to tax away much of the higher profits going to utilities and energy companies under the high-energy-price approach and then returning the tax revenue to the people as general income tax cuts. This requires that the public believes it will get its money back. The public is justifiably skeptical about the government's willingness to fill its part of the bargain and return the money to the public. Technically this proposal would work, but a stronger social consensus is needed before it could be implemented.

Utility regulation will be particularly difficult if the goal is energy conservation. Present-day utility regulation is an efficient mechanism to provide all the power society might conceivably need. With appropriately regulated rates, the utilities can afford to take the risks inherent in nuclear power, coal gasification, the Trans-Canada gas pipeline, or imported liquefied natural gas. If there is difficulty, the Federal Power Commission or a state utility commission simply raises gas or electric rates. If consumers balk at the higher rates, then the government steps in with tax subsidies or buys a few power plants and leases them back as New York did to save Consolidated Edison.

There is a fundamental conflict between conservation and consumerism. Conservation demands less energy while consumerism wants cheaper and therefore more energy. Consumer distrust of private energy companies and dislike of higher energy prices could easily result in changing the entire energy sector to a regulated public utility and using a variety of subterfuges to subsidize the industry. Recent action to provide federal loan guarantees for new energy sources is a move exactly in this direction. If the antiprivate utility movement went further to increased government ownership of the energy sector financed by tax-free bonds, we would have created an uncontrollable energy producer.

From the conservation viewpoint, the issue is how do we reintroduce risk into the utility's decision criteria? Under present regulations, utilities are making important gambles on the economic and social impacts of moving to nuclear power and synthetic fuels. If conservation is the goal, utilities should be discouraged from making these investments by being forced to accept part of the economic risk. A firm guarantee of 12 to 15 percent rate of return could produce too much energy production. (Present utility capital shortages are a function of investor distrust of the regulator's willingness and ability to meet such a guarantee.) One alternative is to decrease the rate of change of utility rates. Rates could be set for periods of five years or more with no change allowed during that period. Utilities that operate more efficiently than expected should be allowed to keep their profits, and utilities that miscalculate should have the right to lose money. Such a policy is likely to be opposed by both utilities and consumers.

WHAT WILL BE THE NEW CONSENSUS?

Energy and economic issues cannot be separated from larger social issues. The choice between high growth and low growth presents only modest economic problems but confronts the most pressing sociopolitical issues of today. Environmental problems relate intimately to energy supply and use. Resource depletion affects not only energy itself but also the entire mineral resource industry. Decisions relating to energy development are related to issues of land use, water rights, political decisions, status rights, the place of private enterprise in American society, and the place of the United States in the world.

The energy and economic decisions will be influenced by economic and technological trends, but they are likely to be even more a consequence of human attitudes, fears, aspirations, loyalties, virtues, and self deceptions.

Time and again changes in these "soft" dimensions have resulted in confounding careful forecasts made with the best quantitative data. Recent examples include changes in attitude with regard to

Family size, unexpectedly bringing U. S. population growth below replacement fertility rates in the mid-1970s;

Quality of the physical environment, which, reflected in legislation and public actions, delayed large construction projects and increased the risk of capital investments, and hence affected both energy supply and economic forecasts;

Consumer rights, with regard to safety of products, imposition of manipulative or misleading advertising, and so on, having significant effect on business forecasts;

Desirability of urban/suburban life, resulting in a net outmigration from the urban areas for the first time this century, completely contrary to demographic forecasts;

U. S. world responsibilities, with regard to resisting by armed force the spread of communism, the change resulting in the halting of the Vietnam war, and in serious doubts as to the conditions under which the United States might mount any similar future action overseas;

Reasonable returns in wages, interest, court settlements, and so on, contributing to inflation which, despite numerous attempts at economic explanations, is in its origins largely a function of cultural attitudes and expectations;

Science and technology, resulting in major departures from past trends in federal funding of basic research and introducing a significant perturbation in all post-supersonic transport technology forecasts.

Thus, to usefully assess future options, the system must be viewed as a whole, with the soft aspects emphasized as well as the harder demographic, economic, and technical data. A central task in such work is the search for an interpretive pattern that fits the data of the present and the recent past and that provides illumination for delineating the options ahead.

For example, consider three fundamentally different viewpoints— worldviews, Gestalts—about where we are going. One viewpoint, of course, is that all our present problems are minor alterations in a longterm trend that only needs modification by raising energy prices slightly. A second viewpoint is that of a new frugality, that slower growth is desirable for a more satisfying life and to meet our responsibilities to future generations, both in the United States and abroad. The final worldview perceives a growing and fundamental challenge to the legitimacy of the dominant industrial-scientific paradigm. All three of these views are currently held, and all three have some kind of validity.

The first of these worldviews assumes the desirability of continued high economic growth. For several decades the standard long-term economic projection for the United States, and indeed for nearly all the developed nations of the world, has been for around 4 percent real growth. Daniel Bell assumes such high growth as we move into a postindustrial age in which material want is forever banished.[12] Herman Kahn assumes another century or so of continued high growth and of other components of the "basic long-term multifold trend" of Western civilization, during which time society diverges still further from preindustrial societies in its unprecedented affluence, extraordinary development of technology, and institutionalization of secular, humanistic, and manipulative rationality.[13] This view demands continued high energy growth and assumes this will come from advanced technology.

There are a number of indications that the attitudinal assumptions supporting this "continued growth" view do not fit America of the mid-1970s. An alternative set of attitudes can be discerned, having been apparent since the late 1960s at least; these are characterized by

Search for meaning and commitment, for more adequate guiding values and goals;

Misgivings over present tendencies to put human affairs and even lofty goals in economic terms, to assume that the wisest decisions are made on an economic basis, and to elevate means—production and consumption of goods and services—to the position of ends;

Renewed appreciation of simple virtues, relationships to other persons and to nature, pleasure in such activities as handcrafts and gardening;

Strong ecological ethic;

Recognition of a "new scarcity"—of physical resources, waste-absorbing capacity of the environment, resilience of planetary life-support systems—qualitatively different from the scarcity problems "solved" by modern industrial production;

Recognition of the rising demands of developing nations for more equitable distribution of the earth's resources;

Appreciation of the virtues of voluntary frugality, doing more with less, particularly if it is made fair by equitable laws and regulations.

Numerous indicators attest to the existence of such a pattern of attitudes. Daniel Yankelovich gives survey evidence of what he terms a "new naturalism," including emphasis on harmony and relationship with nature, on the search for sacredness, on the nonrational—the intuitive, aesthetic, and mystical—and on community.[14] The strength and actions of the environmentalist movement, the "human potential" movement, the "appropriate technology" movement (for example, as indicated in rising popularity of E. F. Schumacher's *Small is Beautiful*), and similar public-interest groups provide another sort of indication.[15] Daniel Bell notes as an essential characteristic of postindustrial society a shift from an "economizing mode" to a "sociologizing mode": "The 'economizing mode' is oriented to functional efficiency and the management of things (and man treated as things). The 'sociologizing mode' establishes broader social criteria, but it necessarily involves the loss of efficiency, the reduction of production, and other costs that follow the introduction of noneconomic values."[16]

In the second worldview the above sorts of attitudes are perceived as strong and growing. This Gestalt involves a set of assumptions about energy and the future something like the following:

The supply of fossil fuels is limited by attitudes regarding the social and environmental consequences of their extraction and utilization (and ultimately, of course, by the finite supply that can be extracted with a net energy advantage.) Nuclear power, both of the conventional and breeder types, involves problems of public acceptance that are far from solution. Fusion is only a faint light on the horizon. Dependence on foreign oil import for a significant fraction of the nation's energy supply involves serious economic and political problems.

Thus, it is prudent to shift as far and as rapidly as possible in the direction of (1) husbanding energy resources through energy conservation, use of low-energy materials and processes, and altering consumption habits; and (2) developing renewable energy sources, mainly solar and geothermal. This course will buy important time, even if some satisfactory way is ultimately found to provide essentially unlimited power from fusion processes. And in the event of a fusion disappointment, we will not have committed future generations to an unsustainable course and the developing societies to permanent energy poverty.

Hence, the roles of coal and imported oil are essentially to sustain the economy through a period of transition from fossil fuels to renewable energy sources. The role of conservation is to minimize the difficulty of this transition.

Large energy projects are likely to be subject to delays, increasing costs, and cancellations because of protests over safety, environmental and social impacts, to increasing problems with legal liabilities, and to difficulties in obtaining investment capital. This is an additional reason conservation should be a dominant theme in the nation's economic policy.

The determination of the developing countries to accelerate industrialization and to raise their share of the world's production, and thus to bring about a redistribution in use of the earth's resources, provides yet another reason for reduction of energy demand by the industrialized nations, and for development of energy-frugal and materials-frugal technologies.

A GROWING LEGITIMACY CHALLENGE

There is a third worldview that perceives a massive and still-growing challenge, emerging over the past ten or fifteen years, to the legitimacy of the present social system of the industrialized world—particularly to its economic, political, technological, industrial, corporate, and scientific aspects.

Signs of this legitimacy challenge are identifiable in

Third World insistence on a "new international economic order";
The new "legitimacy of domestic and international obstructionism and terrorism";
Indications of disenchantment with the assumption that scientific and technological advances are necessarily good;
Consumerism, minority rights, women's lib, aging, youth protest movements;
General distrust in institutions of business and government;
Growing sense that old answers no longer work;
Increasing signs of alienation from work, from the communities, and from families;
Criticisms of industrial products, business practices, and advertising; ing;
Survey data showing values and attitudes calling for change in the old order;
Evidence of widespread search for transcendental meanings.

Some historical comparisons are illuminating. In some cases, legitimacy challenges (for example, that expressed in the Declaration of Independence[17]) have been linked with and followed by drastic system change. Causes of these major historical whole-system transformations seem (sometimes at least, according to some authorities) to stem from values and beliefs changing at a different pace from, and getting out of step with, changes in the political-social structure.[18]

Legitimacy of a social system and its power concentrations is fundamentally based on its being duly constituted, adherence to adequate guiding moral principles, and effectiveness in achieving agreed-upon goals. The contemporary challenge is with regard to all three bases.

The governments of the industrialized democracies are clearly duly constituted. However, there exist other concentrations of power that are not so constituted. First is the tremendous power inherent in the large multinational corporations and the world economic system. Because of their widespread impact these gigantic organizations are quasi public. As the largest corporations begin to wield influences over human lives that are comparable to those of governments, similar demands are being made of them that have historically been made of government: that they assume responsibility for the welfare of those over whom they wield power. Those who feel themselves to be disfranchised include members of nonindustrialized cultures, minorities, consumers, youth, the aging, and women. A separate challenge is to the intellectual power of the scientific-technological establishment, in terms of its assumed position as ultimate arbiter of truth while being dominated by the prediction-and-control values of industrialism and promoting an image of man and social goals that serve industrialism.

Second, the challenge is put forth that the system is not guided by adequate moral principles, particularly with regard to equity of distribution of the earth's resources. With regard particularly to food, energy, and economic resources, the poor continue to get relatively poorer and there is no effective ethic or mechanism of redistribution. Economic incentives predominate over all. There is no effective ecological ethic. Consumers feel manipulated, defrauded, and injured. The sense of pride in striving toward noble goals seems clearly to be dwindling; there are no adequate goals to enlist the deepest loyalties and commitments of citizens.

And third, the charge is made that the system is proving ineffective in achieving its own declared goals. The successes of technology and industrialization appear themselves to be main contributors to contemporary problems. The labor of the poor and unskilled is rendered worthless and there is a lack of satisfying work roles. The progress of the system does not foster preservation of habitability and enhancement of the total environment to promote the total health of individuals. System incentive structures fail to insure the welfare of future generations—especially in terms of their need for fossil and mineral resources, arable land, natural fresh water, and a fruitful ocean. The system does not promote socially responsible management of the impacts of new technological applications.

BEYOND ECONOMIC GROWTH

The first worldview is equivalent to saying the new consensus is the old one. This would imply retreating on the environmental movement; reestablishing faith in business, government, and science; and changing the whole legal system so that a determined minority can no longer obstruct the wheels of progress. This is the only social scenario that gets us to 150 quads, and its likelihood appears to be extremely questionable.

The second worldview implies a rational approach and resolution. Desirable as it may seem, there is scant encouragement from history that such a reasoning together, and deliberate reordering of priorities in society, will come about.

The third worldview more and more seems to fit our observations of where the world is going. It perceives that the challenge of basic legitimacy could well end in dramatic domestic and international upheaval. As nuclear weapons and other "high" technologies of mass destruction spread, the cost of such upheaval grows. Modern civilization cannot survive in a world of multiplying Lebanons, Libyas, and Northern Irelands. Does the challenge to the existing legitimacy contain the seeds of a new legitimacy; is a nondisruptive transformation possible? Will there be an attempt to suppress rather than respond to the challenge, and is this likely to lead toward worldwide totalitarianism? Is there any other way out for the most impoverished segments of the "Fourth World"?

More than any other single thing, the world of the future will be shaped by how this challenge is resolved. It is more than the issue of economic growth. It is what lies behind the issue of economic growth.

NOTES

1. Edison Electric Institute, *Economic Growth in the Future: The Growth Debate in National and Global Perspective* (New York: McGraw-Hill, 1976), Chapters 2 and 3.

2. U. S. Bureau of the Census, *Statistical Abstract of the United States: 1975*, 96th ed. (Washington, D. C.: U. S. Government Printing Office, 1975), pp. 723 and 718.

3. Ibid., p. 253.

4. U. S. Water Resources Council, *1972 OBERS Projections, Series E Population*, Vol. 1 (Washington, D.C.: U.S. Government Printing Office, September 1972), p. 12.

5. U. S. Bureau of the Census, *Statistical Abstract: 1975*, p. 399.

6. Ibid., pp. 902 and 903.

7. Ibid., p. 253.

8. Ibid., p. 265.

9. *Economic Report of the President*, Transmitted to the Congress January 1976 together with The Annual Report of the Council of Economic Advisers (Washington, D. C.: U. S. Government Printing Office, 1976).

10. John Reuyl et al., *Solar Energy in America's Future—A Preliminary Assessment*, (Menlo Park, Calif.: Stanford Research Institute, January 1977).

11. Ibid.

12. Daniel Bell, *The Coming of Post Industrial Society* (New York: Basic Books, 1973).

13. Herman Kahn, *The Next 200 Years* (New York: Morrow, 1976).

14. Daniel Yankelovich, *Changing Values on Campus*, (New York: Washington Square Press, 1972)

15. E. F. Schumacher, *Small is Beautiful*, (New York: Harper and Row, 1973).

16. Bell, *The Coming of Post Industrial Society*, pp. 42 and 43.

17. See, for example, the discussion of "dissynchronization" in Chalmers Johnson's study of *Revolutionary Change* (Boston: Little, Brown, 1966).

18. Other examples are slavery, workers rights (leading to labor unions being legitimated in the 1930s), and delegitimating of political colonialism after World War II.

6 | The Anxieties of Uncertainty in the Energy Problem

Kenneth E. Boulding

Energy policy is haunted by two goblins: anxiety and uncertainty. The anxiety stems from the fact that the one thing we are certain about is that we are going to run out of petroleum and natural gas in a relatively short time as human history measures it. The most sober estimate now suggests about 50 years as the world lifetime of petroleum and natural gas and, even on the most optimistic assumptions about new discoveries, it would be hard to push this beyond 100 years. Furthermore, no substitute for petroleum or natural gas seems to be in sight that is as cheap, convenient, transportable, storable, or even as nonpolluting. The other great fossil fuel, coal, is dirty, hard to handle, awkward to extract, inconvenient, and polluting. It already kills far more people in a year per unit of energy than the nuclear industry, either through mining accidents or the shortening of human life due to pollution. Even coal will not last more than 300 to 500 hundred years and, if it has to be substituted for oil and gas, it will of course be consumed all the faster.

The only other energy stock is nuclear fuel, whether for fission or fusion. Existing nuclear technology using uranium 235 relies on a fuel that may be exhausted almost as soon as oil and gas. Uranium is a scarce element and uranium 235 is less than 1 percent of the total, so that with existing nuclear technology we are likely to run out of nuclear fuel about the same time we run out of gas and oil. The breeder reactor, if successful, would expand the nuclear fuel supply, perhaps by 100 times, with a horizon of thousands of years rather than of decades. Breeder reactors, however, seem to be both very expensive and potentially dangerous. By contrast, with the small but certain disasters that we have with coal, breeder reactors face us with low probabilities of very large disasters, a probability that is much more dramatically present in people's minds than the steady flow of mine accidents or emphysema death due to coal. Even small probabilities accumulate, however, as time goes on, so that even though the probability of failure in any particular reactor is low, given enough time and enough reactors there will be one.

Fusion, which would provide fuel for perhaps half a million years if we can master the deuterium reaction, presents engineering problems of enormous difficulty. We still seem to be a long way from it, although there is always the possibility of unexpected breakthroughs. The problem of containing material at 50 million degrees, however, looks to the casual observer as involving a technology that might be both expensive and dangerous.

CAPITAL AND INCOME ENERGY

We must distinguish between energy capital and energy income. Energy capital is the accumulated chemical and nuclear energy present in the earth. For all practical purposes it can be assumed to be a fixed stock. There is a certain short-run capital in wood, the energy of which represents solar energy of the recent past. The energy income of the earth is entirely from the sun. It is very large in quantity, but also very diffuse and relatively low in quality for many uses, though not for all. The last few centuries have seen steadily rising use of energy capital, with a spectacular rise in the last 100 years since the discovery of petroleum and natural gas in 1859. Before the eighteenth century it is safe to say that all human societies, both primitive and civilized, relied almost 100 percent on the energy income from the sun, through agriculture, forests, animals, human muscles, or wind power and water power, which are derivatives of solar energy. Even in this period the energy capital problem presented itself occasionally in the form of deforestation, and periods of economic decline have sometimes been associated in the past with societies that used up their energy capital of wood. This is a subject that needs much further historical research. One has a suspicion that it is a much-neglected aspect of the decline and fall of early civilizations. It would not be surprising to find that deforestation played a major role in the decline of ancient Greece, Rome, the Mayan society, and the various Chinese empires.

The great anxiety of our day is whether we may not be facing a similar period of exhaustion of the known stock of energy capital, forcing us to fall back on energy income from the sun, which may be much more expensive and much less convenient. The expression "energy capital" may be misleading, for capital suggests something that is productive and constantly renewing itself, whereas what the fossil fuels represent is an energy stock or hoard—it cannot be renewed and when it is gone, it is gone, like a miser's hoard. When we discovered how to use petroleum in 1859 it was as if we had found a great chest full of golden guineas in the basement and we have been spending these with great enjoyment. When they are all gone, we will have to go back to living on our income again, which will not be as pleasant.

All of this of course is a central concern in the broad-ranging debate about the future of economic growth. The many dimensions of the growth question have been carefully detailed in the report, *Economic Growth in the Future,* by the Edison Electric Institute.[1]

THE FUNCTIONS AND VALUES OF ENERGY

"So what if we have to change energy sources?" some skeptics may reply. "What is so great about energy anyway? If great civilizations of the past have been based on solar energy, why cannot we simply go back to it and not worry ourselves about the exhaustion of our energy stocks?" It is true that the exhaustion of energy stock will not represent the end of the world, or even the end of civilization. It will represent, however, a very different order of things from what we have been accustomed to in the last 100 years. Energy has two major functions in economic life. One is to keep us, and other things, at a temperature at which we are comfortable and at which the life processes work well. This is by no means a negligible use. Some 25 percent of energy use in the United States is for space heating and cooling, and a great deal of the energy of food is devoted to keeping animal bodies at their most efficient temperature, whether this is above or below the temperature around them. This goes for livestock as it does for humans. One of the reasons why the animal foods like meat and milk require a large amount of vegetable production to sustain them is that these animals have to be kept at a temperature usually above that of their environment. Industrial processes like smelting metals or firing pottery likewise require energy for temperature maintenance.

The other economic use for energy is to push things around. All processes of production involve the selection, transportation, transformation, and rearrangement of materials into improbable shapes, whether this is a chicken, a human person, an automobile, or a pair of spectacles. The high correlation between the energy input into a particular economy and its GNP is a reflection of the fact that the GNP consists mainly of improbable structures and arrangements of materials which have to be put together by work, that is, by moving materials against gravity, friction or inertia, and rearranging them into the shapes of products. In these rearrangements energy may also be needed for chemical transformations, for instance, of ores into metals, petroleum into plastics, and of course food into the muscles, bones, and brains of our bodies.

It is important to realize, however, that from an economic point of view energy is not homogeneous. It does not consist just of ergs, for in human valuation one erg may have a very different value from another. The first law of thermodynamics states that if there is a fixed quantity of energy, it can only be pushed around. That is, the total stock of energy can only be moved around from one form or place to another. For any bounded segment of the universe, like a steam engine, the increase in the stock of energy (plus or minus) is equal to energy in minus energy out. If the energy stock is constant, any segment or process will have as much energy output as it does input if we count everything that goes in and everything that comes out in the way of energy. Energy exists in many forms, however, some of which we regard as being more significant and useful than others. But even this, it should be emphasized, is a human value. The concept of the energy efficiency of a process always assumes that the output can be divided into two parts: a significant and a nonsignificant part. The efficiency then is the ratio of the significant output to the total output or the total input, which is the same thing if the energy stock is constant, because of the law of conservation.

What is significant to the engineer, however, may not be significant to the accountant, private or social. Ultimately the energy that is significant is that which is significant for the satisfaction of human wants. First-law efficiencies may not correspond to this at all. A process that is more inefficient than another in terms of first-law efficiency may be much more efficient in terms of directing energy toward something that is highly valued by human beings. The second-law efficiencies, which Barry Commoner makes such a fuss about, are really not much more significant than first-law efficiencies.[2] A process that is inefficient on the second-law definition, that is, that increases thermodynamic entropy more than another, may be quite efficient again in terms of production of human values. It may even be worthwhile from the human point of view to utilize processes that involve a net energy loss, that is, in which the output of usable energy is less than what goes into it, if this output is particularly convenient in changing the state of the world toward a condition that is valued more highly by human beings.

There is a certain tendency for engineers and physical scientists to hanker for an energy theory of value or even an entropy theory of value. These, however, are delusions, for value is derived from human valuation in human interaction with human environments and from nothing else. This is not to say, of course, that political and biological limitations of systems are not extremely important in determining what we can have. The ultimate decision about whether one thing we can have is better than another thing we can have is by a human valuation of some sort and not by any physical process.

SOURCES OF ANXIETY

The anxiety about energy, therefore, arises from a highly legitimate fear that the exhaustion of energy stock will lead to a state of the world which by human valuations is much worse than what we have now. There is a snag, of course, in talking about human valuations in that my valuations may not be the same as yours, and the problem of reconciling the different valuations of different humans is a very severe one in society. This is the major problem of political life. It is worked out, however, imperfectly no doubt, in the complex interactions of human decisions, both on the part of the powerful and on the part of the nonpowerful, in that vast dynamic process that gets us from today to tomorrow. I may think that state of the world A is better than B; you may think that B is better than A, but these differences will be resolved in the melee of social life; and, furthermore, we are all likely to agree that there is a condition C which is worse for everybody. It is one of the peculiar virtues of economics, incidentally, that it has been the one social science that has been interested in those states of the world that are worse for everybody. This is indeed the theory of the Paretian optimum.

We can perhaps visualize the anxiety about energy if we ask ourselves what the world would be like today if there had not been any petroleum and natural gas to be discovered in 1859. Oil and gas are in a sense an accident of the geological history of the planet. We are still not sure of the details, but in the course of plate tectonics at various times there have been large, warm seas suitable for the proliferation of sunlight-capturing organisms, whose remains, subsequently covered by various deposits, turned into oil and gas. There may well be other planets in the universe rather like this one, but without oil and gas. If there had not been any oil and gas, of course, we could not have discovered it, for it is a very fundamental principle that we cannot discover what is not there. The history of the subsequent 100 years or so would then certainly have been very different. It is very doubtful whether we would have had automobiles, except rather primitive, coal-burning or very expensive, liquified coal machines. It is extremely doubtful whether we would have had airplanes without the extraordinary transportability and convenience of petroleum products. It is hard to visualize a coal-burning airplane, and a very large effort which the United States put into the attempt to develop a nuclear airplane completely failed.

Certainly without the oil and gas deposits of the world, both the automobile and the airplane, if they had come into existence at all, would be very small in quantity and would be the luxuries of the very, very rich. (The limitations of electric automobiles are discussed below.) The use of natural gas and oil for industrial production would also not have been possible and production would certainly have been less than it is today if we had had to rely on coal. We probably would have had electricity, which was waiting in the wings in 1859, with coal-burning power stations, and we probably would have had radio and television and all the things that come with electricity. We would still be relying on public transportation for the poor and either horses and carriages or very expensive automobiles for the rich, and the whole look and structure of our cities would be much more like 1860. There would be no sprawling suburbs, there would be very large slums, and there would be a much higher degree of inequality in real income than we have now. The extent to which the rise of the middle class to absorb a large proportion of the population, which is perhaps one of the most striking social phenomena of the last 100 years, would have taken place without oil and gas is a nice subject for the cliometricians, which has not so far been much researched.

If there had been no coal as well as no oil and gas, the modern world as we know it today would not have come into existence at all, and the world would look much more like the world, let us say, of 1600. We would have had a rise of science and a tremendous increase in human knowledge, but without energy stocks to work with, the application of science to economic life would have been very meager, as indeed before 1859 it was. It is perhaps no accident that the great impact of science on technology only took place after 1859, with the development of the chemical industry, the petroleum industry, the electrical industry, and now the nuclear industry.

Before the middle of the nineteenth century science contributed very little to productive technology or capacity. The inventions of the eighteenth century, which are sometimes quite misleadingly called the "industrial revolution," such as the steam engine, the spinning jenny, the power loom, and so on, owed very little to science. They came out of what might be called the "folk technology" of the European Middle Ages and beyond. Neither the spinning jenny nor the steam engine were much more complicated than the medieval clock or embodied any new principles. The steam engine indeed owed nothing to thermodynamics; it preceded thermodynamics by 100 years. Thermodynamics obviously owed a great deal to the steam engine. The electrical industry, however, would not have been possible without Faraday and Clerk-Maxwell. Nor would the chemical industry have been possible without Dalton, Mendeleev, and Kekulé. All the knowledge in the world, however, would not have given us the petroleum industry if there had not been any petroleum.

The enormous expansion of production and increase in per capita world income of the last 100 or 200 years has been the result of three things. First, there has been a tremendous rise in human knowledge and know-how both in prescientific technology, in the growth of science itself, and in science-based technology. Second, this new knowledge was able to unlock new sources of energy that were there waiting to be discovered. In the third place, also, this new knowledge created new sources of materials, such as aluminum, plastics, artificial fertilizers and the like, which also had a major impact on the growth of output. If there had been no petroleum, however, and still more if there had been no fossil fuels of any kind, the applications of science would have been very modest and the technology of the world and its standard of living would not be very different from that before the scientific revolution.

The anxiety, therefore, can be summed up perhaps by the reflection that in the last 100 or 200 years we have been extraordinarily lucky in finding these new and convenient sources of energy and materials. We know they are a limited stock and that the known stocks at present will be used up in a relatively short time. Then the question arises: How likely are we to be that lucky twice and so find new and unsuspected sources of energy and materials, at present unknown or perhaps even unguessed at?

The present anxiety about the exhaustion of petroleum and its associated natural gas is particularly acute, simply because nothing on the horizon looks like a substitute for it, not only in terms of cheapness (for what could be cheaper than simply getting oil or gas out of a well?), but also in terms of convenience, storability, and transportability. The only alternatives on the horizon all appear as sources of electric power. Electric power has many virtues, but it seems likely to become increasingly expensive, with more complex and difficult fuel technologies. Further-more, it is costly and inconvenient to transport by wires, with a great loss of efficiency. It is also virtually nonstorable in any large-scale, cheap, and convenient form.

THE DIFFICULTY OF SOLUTIONS

Energy, as emphasized above, is not just ergs. It is ergs when and where and in the form that we want them. The when is particularly important. We do not want space heating in the summer, or artificial light in the daytime, or transportation when we are at home in bed, or even factory production around the clock if it can be avoided, for the social consequences of continuous production are quite severe in terms of night shifts, the disruption of family life, and so on. Consequently, if the production of energy is localized and centralized, as it is in electric power, the problem of both storing it and transporting it becomes very acute. We have had electric power now for 90 years and in all that period the payoffs for a cheap and efficient method of storing electricity have been very large, yet the problem has not been solved. Storage batteries are heavy, expensive, inconvenient, and tend to use rather scarce and expensive materials. Electric power companies have been forced to use nonelectric devices like pumped storage, at a very substantial cost in power, in order to provide continuous service in quantities that were demanded. The persistence of the "peak load" problem, which could have been solved very easily had there been any cheap and convenient methods of storing electricity, suggests that the electricity storage problem is certainly extraordinarily difficult, though of course we can never be sure that any problem is insoluble. When there have been large payoffs for a solution for a long time, however, and the solution has not been found, it is hard to avoid a rising suspicion that the solution does not exist, or at least is highly elusive.

The fact that up to now electricity in large quantities can only be transported by wires, whatever the future may hold for microwaves and lasers, and can hardly be stored at all means that it is no substitute whatever for the automobile. Battery-driven electric automobiles, of course, have existed almost as long as gasoline engines, but they are slow, expensive, inefficient, and have very short range. Such being the case, the extinction of the cheap gasoline-powered automobile, which seems a distinct possibility within the lifetime of babies now being born, would creat a crisis, especially for the rich countries of the temperate zone, of absolutely first magnitude. The sprawling suburbs would have to be abandoned, people would be crowded into congested cities with public transportation, the distribution of income would change markedly for the worse, and there would be a strong sense of a golden age of freedom and mobility having come to an end.

What is even more ominous is that developed agriculture, especially in the United States, is extremely dependent on gasoline, not only for its energy input in the form of tractors, dryers, and agricultural machinery of all kinds, but also for artificial fertilizers, all of which virtually is derived from fossil fuels of some kind, and a great deal directly from petroleum. If this is threatened, we may be in for an even more spectacular crisis. Largely because of the application of energy from fossil fuels, especially petroleum, the United States is now able to produce all the food that it needs and have a surplus for export, with less than 4 percent of its labor force. Even as late as 1890, agriculture absorbed 50 percent of the labor force in the United States, and at the time of the Revolution, perhaps as much as 90 percent. Without petroleum and petroleum products, particularly if we have to go back to horses as an energy source, not only will the labor requirements be substantially increased, so that we might have to go to 20 percent or more of the labor force in agriculture, but the food available for humans would sharply diminish. In 1890 horses ate something like a quarter of the U.S. food production.

There is furthermore a reasonable anxiety about the possibility of ecological instability in U.S. agriculture, which is getting close to a three-crop economy based on wheat, corn, and soybeans. One could visualize some time within the next 50 or more years a wheat rust, a corn blight, a soy beetle, and a drought the same year, coupled with tractors idle for want of gasoline and fertilizer not available, and we might find ourselves in a situation perilously close to that of Ireland in 1846. This, of course, is the worst case, but even on more optimistic assumptions the disappearance of the U.S. agricultural surplus seems a high probability. When we add to this the worry of the meteorologists about long cycles of drought and weather change, the causes for anxiety mount even further. We have had 25 years of extraordinarily good weather over most of the world, especially in the great agricultural breadbaskets of the Great Plains, the Middle West, and so on. The development of long-term weather records, however, from tree rings and other deposits, suggests that the present periods have been quite unusual in the last 2,000 years and that we may reasonably expect much worse periods in the future.

All this doom and gloom perhaps is decades away. The next few decades, for the United States especially, look pretty good. There is widespread consensus among the experts that "Project Independence" is humbug, that the United States will be dependent on imports of oil and of natural gas for a substantial part of the energy requirements of the U.S. economy over the next two or three decades. It will be able to pay for these, however, by exports of food, a commodity the demand for which is just about as inelastic as the demand for oil. Of course, this is putting the matter very crudely. The United States exports many other things besides food, but its remarkable comparative advantage in food certainly suggests that the overall terms of trade are not likely to turn against it, as they almost certainly will turn against both Western Europe and Japan, who are much more vulnerable, with their higher populations, food deficiencies, and strong needs for energy imports. The exhaustion of world oil supplies, however, which is inevitable at some time, will also mean sharp decline in North American agricultural production with existing technology. Not being able to pay for the oil that is not there may seem rather an unreal problem, but the probability of a general decline in per capita world output and income, which would be particularly severe in the presently rich countries, is an anxiety that cannot be laughed off.

There are those, of course, who put their faith in oil shale, oil sands, coal liquefaction, and so on. It is certainly true that as the price of oil rises it will be increasingly profitable to exploit these, and of these the oil sands, such as those of Northern Canada, are perhaps the best bet. There must be a lot of other similar deposits elsewhere in the world. Oil shale is much more dubious. The environmental problems are severe simply because the muck that is produced has a substantially larger volume than the original rock and seems to be good for absolutely nothing. Also, the water requirements seem to be beyond what the arid regions, where most of the oil shale seems to be, can produce. Again, with existing technology the prospects for oil shale do not look very good and do not do very much to assuage the anxieties.

UNCERTAINTIES AS A SOURCE OF HOPE

The certainties of the future are mechanical, like the principle that if we go on using up a fixed stock, such as fossil fuel, the time will come when it will be all gone. The uncertainties all relate to the sphere of knowledge, pure and applied. One of the great difficulties in projecting the future in regard to something like energy is that it depends on two processes that move in opposite directions, and it is very hard to predict which of these will be the larger and will predominate. There are first the "entropic" processes, which involve the using up of potential of some sort, whether this is the stock of fossil fuels or even the evolutionary potential of a culture. Counteracting this, however, are the processes by which potential is re-created, particularly through increased knowledge and discovery. These re-creations of potential are extraordinarily hard to predict, and though we may have a certain confidence that they will continue, nobody really knows at what rate. Jevons wrote an early Club of Rome-type of report, published in 1865, on the coal question, in which he pointed out that coal was an exhaustible resource and would eventually be exhausted, he thought perhaps by the end of the twentieth century. Even as he was writing this, oil was discovered, something he did not anticipate, and it completely altered the situation in that it re-created great potential for development.

There is, however, a nonexistence theorem about the prediction of the future of knowledge and discovery: that if we could predict it, we would know it now, we would have discovered it now, and we would not have to wait. All genuinely new information or knowledge has to be in some degree surprising; otherwise, it is not new knowledge. There is, therefore, an irreducible uncertainty about the future, particularly in social systems and particularly in times like these when the future of knowledge and technology is of such enormous importance for the future welfare of mankind.

This does not mean, of course, that we should simply not think about the future of knowledge and technology, for even though we cannot predict the future in detail, we may be able to detect certain broad outlines. We might indeed divide our expectations of the future into a broad spectrum of uncertainties, with the reasonably certain at one end, the rather dubious in the middle, and the totally unexpected at the other end. From the course of past research and development, certain things could reasonably be expected, especially in the moderately near future, though even here the history of technological prediction has not been much better than that of demographic prediction, which is very dismal. Just as nobody predicted either the great baby boom of the 1950s or the great trough of the 1960s and 1970s, so nobody really predicted things like antibiotics, or the transistor, or computer technology. There is a principle, of course, that if you put a lot into something, you are likely to get something out. One wonders whether the enormous effort put into cancer research or into high-energy physics has really paid off in terms either of increasing knowledge or technology. The space enterprise is marvelous as a circus and as drama. I am personally very grateful for having lived in a period that has produced the moon landings and the Mars pictures for the sheer joy of expanding knowledge, but the earthly applications have been meager, at least up to now.

One thing that might reduce the uncertainty a little would be more research on research itself and on the whole organizational and economic matrix within which research takes place. The establishment of the Office of Technology Assessment by Congress is perhaps a small step in this direction and may turn out to be an important social invention insofar as it organizes the role of critic of the research enterprise, with a little more influence on budgets than critics have had in the past. The great difficulty here is that research and development almost inevitably have to be financed mainly out of grants or transfers, not through an exchange market. This is true whether the grants are in the government or from the budget of a private corporation. The grant system, unfortunately, has a pathology of its own that is not well understood. Grants tend to go to the persuasive, who are not always the deserving, but how one makes the persuasive deserving and the deserving persuasive is a very tricky problem I cannot claim to have solved.

A somewhat related problem is the growth of support of large-scale versus small-scale operations. There is a tendency for grants to be made by large organizations and people in large organizations tend to think big. Sometimes this is fine, but sometimes the answer lies in thinking small and in small-scale operations that are somehow beyond the agenda of those who operate mainly on a large scale. It may be, for instance, that the more efficient utilization of solar energy, which seems to be such an enormously high priority for the twenty-first century, will be solved at the level of household units rather than at the large-scale power stations. The technical problems of central stations at the moment seem very large, and it is hard to visualize the kind of process of increased efficiency that went on in the fossil fuel power stations. How does one interest people who think big to take an interest in the people who think small? I have sometimes thought the answer here is a system of prizes rather than of grants, which at least would simulate the lottery elements that are so important in the market and that enabled Henry Ford, for instance, to pick a winner in the field of technology, whereas 200 of his competitors picked losers. The great danger of large organizations is that there is not enough tolerance of failure, yet we all know that in evolutionary processes only one mutation out of thousands or millions may be a success.

Here we are edging toward the policy implications of these reflections, which certainly do not escape the general aura of uncertainty that governs the whole subject. The frank recognition of the uncertainties as well as the anxieties, however, may be an important guide in the formation of policy. It has been said with some justification that we do not have an energy policy in this country and not much in any other, and certainly we have nothing that looks like an energy policy on a world scale. We would be lucky indeed if we did not need one, if we could simply rely on change in the price structure, which energy shortages and exhaustion are going to bring about, to divert technical change into research and development processes that will solve the problem. A considerable number of very respectable economists on both sides of the Atlantic have issued comforting statements that all will be well and that the impact of the price system on technology will solve all our problems. I hope they are right, but I have grave doubts.

One of the most dangerous of all human illusions is to mistake good luck for good management. And we have had so much good luck in the last 100 years or so that it would be a little surprising if we did not have illusions about our good management. If there is to be a policy, therefore, it must take account of the possibility of bad luck. It must be preparing for the worst as well as hoping for the best and, indeed, preparing for the best as well. It may be that the search for good management has to go along with a tolerance for bad luck as well as a recognition of good luck when it happens. In the United States we were surprisingly tolerant of the Great Depression, which in retrospect was bad management rather than bad luck, but whether we will be equally tolerant of the bad luck that may come in the next 100 years, even under good management, is a critical question.

POLICIES FOR CERTAINTY AND UNCERTAINTY

Before we can have an energy policy perhaps we have to have a policy about what things we have policies about. The answer would seem to lie in the reduction of uncertainties where that is possible, and even perhaps in the organization of luck in the shape of a lottery for technological success. This in a sense the market provided. It is one of the great arguments for it. Where, however, the market is weak, which in this case it certainly is, we do need to think about how to provide a substitute for it. If all the certainties lead into anxiety, then perhaps we should cultivate the uncertainties. It has always puzzled the sober economists that what people buy with a lottery ticket is clearly not worth the price in statistical terms. The answer, of course, is that what they buy is dreams, hopes, and a little relief from the certain anxieties of life. Perhaps only a technological lottery will yield us the totally unexpected solar battery, the incredibly productive artificial algae, the cheap and efficient method of storing energy, or even a method of getting an enormous satisfaction out of a meager sustenance. It is indeed by hopes and dreams, as well as by sober plans and investments, that the shaky bridge of anxiety must be crossed, to the twenty-second century.

NOTES

1. Edison Electric Institute, *Economic Growth in the Future: The Growth Debate in National and Global Perspective* (New York: McGraw-Hill, 1976).

2. Barry Commoner, *The Poverty of Power: Energy and the Economic Crises,* (New York: Knopf, 1976).

7 | Future U.S. Growth and Leadership Assessed from Abroad

Norman Macrae

ANOTHER LOOK AT *AMERICA'S THIRD CENTURY*

In my book *America's Third Century* (published in 1976 but written in 1975)[1] I argued that

It is conventional to say that world economic growth will slow down in the next few decades, but it is in fact more likely to accelerate. Most of the shortages most feared by ecologists are of the particular things (such as energy) that will most probably go into glut.

There are bizarre dangers in the period of giddy economic advance that probably lies ahead. They include the dangers that the planet may be destroyed, and that the nature of man might be irreparably changed, both by mistake.

There will be a need for sophisticated and dynamic world leadership in this period. In the first two centuries of rapid economic advance—the British-led century from about 1776 to 1876, and the American-led century from 1876 to 1976—world leadership has been handled more sophisticatedly than it probably would have been under any other great power available at the time. But there are reasons for fearing that the Americans in the years around 1976 are showing some of the same signs of a drift from dynamism as the British showed when they started their decline round about 1876.

There will, in any event, need to be changes in North America's three main institutions, which are, in reverse order of importance, its business corporations, its governments, and its mechanisms for living together (by which I mean what takes over from church, family, pioneer spirit, small-town togetherness, the probably-failed experiment of suburbia, and so on).

In the two years since writing *America's Third Century,* I have grown even more confident that economic growth can continue; I have grown even more worried that bizarre dangers may lie ahead; and I have grown slightly more optimistic that the United States may recapture its dynamism, and that the necessary changes in its institutions are probably in train.

But let us begin with the forecasts of the ecologists.

PHYSICAL LIMITS TO GROWTH AND
THE "LAW OF OPPOSITES"

Ecologists tell us that the main barriers in the way of further growth will be shortages of energy, food, and raw materials, plus high birth rates and high pollution. These seem to me to be the five least likely barriers to growth in the next 20 years. Energy, food, and raw materials are each things of high elasticity of supply, each things whose production is now in a state of exploding technological innovation, each things in which the present selling price to advanced countries is well above even old-fashioned marginal cost of production. The same broad considerations apply to birth control devices and to antipollution techniques—that is, advancing technology and subsidized oversupply. If we do run into temporary shortages of supply, it is much more likely to be in things in which we do not allow a market mechanism to operate properly, such as water and sensible production-oriented education.

These forecasts in *America's Third Century* brought me the rudest letters —particularly about the forecast glut of energy—and it is appropriate that I should explain myself in this volume sponsored by the electric utility industry (which has, however, no responsibility for the wicked things I say).

Quite seriously, I believe it is nowadays rather easy to make one sort of correct medium-term economic forecast, and to become immensely unpopular thereby. The correct medium-term microeconomic forecast today is almost always the opposite of whatever is at any moment the most frenetically fashionable forecast.

During my 30 years as a journalist, there have been over 40 occasions when the great majority of decision-influencing people have united to say that some particular products are going to be in the most desperately short supply for the rest of this century. On almost every occasion the world has then sent that product within a measurable time limit into almost unsalable glut.

There are two reasons why this "law of opposites" is working with special force at the present time. The first reason is quite logical but rather technical, so forgive me for using one sentence of economic jargon. In modern conditions of high elasticity of both supply and substitution, plus surprisingly equal lead times for much investment, we now generally will create overproduction of whatever decision influencers a certain number of years earlier had said would be most desperately needed. This is because the well-advertised views of decision influencers tend by definition to influence the decisions of both profit-seeking private producers and consensus-following governments. And these two then combine to start the cycle of overproduction or overcorrection at exactly the same time.

Now it is of course nine-tenths a good thing that the greater elasticity of supply in post-1945 economics has managed to turn the old cruel short-term trade cycle into this far-less-damaging medium-term cycle of swinging from forecasts of shortage or "huge marketing opportunity" ineluctably to that particular glut. The one-tenth of nuisance is that (1) important prophets do not like looking silly, and (2) credulous investors lose their underpants. The forces of annoyance and of cover-up that are then set in train provide the second reason why the law of opposites now works with particular virulence, especially as they have become allied to the modern tool of—bow down and worship—the computer.

HELP FROM THE COMPUTER?

It is almost impossible to discuss modern computer forecasting models for particular microeconomic entities without sounding terribly rude and making people very cross with one. And I wonder if I can persuade you to believe that, belonging as I do to the well-known shrinking-violet profession of journalism, I don't want to be rude to anybody or to make anybody cross with me. I don't believe in being rude to people who make sheep forecasts; I believe in trying to help my readers make money out of them. But can I explain the difficulties I have as a journalist when asked to write weekly about such things as the computerized models for energy forecasting, explicitly believed in by so many prophets and governments today?

If you were asked if you could draw up a computerized model of world energy economics over the next dozen years, with any hope of being anywhere near as good as the model that will be worked out by market forces, your response should be "eh, no, of course not." Because you would add:

That would mean combining the thousands of possible ways of releasing energy from storage in matter and of changing distribution systems and consumption patterns for each, together with expectations of time lags for each, and their variations in accordance with all ranges of today's and tomorrow's relative prices for each, and then of guessed elasticities of supply and substitution and demand for each over different periods and of a few thousand other variables I won't bother you with into a multibillion factor equation.

Governments that produce "integrated energy policies" or "integrated transport policies" do not work with multibillion factor equations of this kind. In the bad old days they worked with the guesses of perhaps five experts and a secretary of state. In the worse new days they work with those six plus the propagandist efforts of a think tank with a computerized forecasting model.

Compared with a free market these models have no serious chance of proving right because they do not of course include multibillion factor equations. Typically, they include about 40 or 50 factors, of a rather special kind. Question: If you are employed by an ad hoc body to deal with a "grave" supposed "shortage," do you feed into the computer a choice of factors suggesting there is not a shortage and that you are doing a nonjob?

What these ad hoc bodies do I am afraid is to put into the computer the assumptions they want to come to—usually that there will be a great crisis unless they are given more power to order people about. And the computer then obediently prints back "there will be a great crisis unless you are given more power to order people about." Between the believers in a free market and the forecasters a weird communications gap then springs up. These forecasters say to us critics of their forecasts: "We think there is going to be a shortage of, say, energy. You say it is going into glut. Which of the 45 factors in my equation do you disagree with?" One replies that it is several billion to one that the main disagreement should not be with the 45 factors but with the multibillion left out. Then the forecasters say, "Ah, you're a science-fiction buff. What science-fiction invention are you expecting to break my forecasts within 5 to 12 years? Bioconversion or photovoltaic power or magnetohydrodynamics or what?"

And the *pons asinoram* across which you become a modern thinking man is when you realize, unlike governments, that the only proper answer to that question, on the level of inanity of the question itself, would begin, "Well, now, an improvement in magnetohydrodynamics would change the multibillion factors in the energy equation in the following multibillion ways." No economist can give that answer because no economist or computer forecaster is clever enough, and because the patient explainer would anyway be dead before he reached point multibillion-minus-one —and to take more than 100 years on answering a question about one possible factor determining policy in the next 12 years is not very useful, especially since I suspect that before the next 100 years are up the reader may want to slip out to lunch.

But what an economist can say, with absolute certainty, is that if a so-called energy crisis has been created because the Arabs have raised their asking price for oil to 100 times its marginal cost, then this event will cause the supply of energy to rise and the demand for it to fall—that is, will cause a glut relative to what would otherwise have happened. And when we get governments so often believing, in so many fields, that a shift in price will do the opposite, then we have some problems for public policy, but some interesting opportunities for private gain.

On longer-term energy prospects I think an economist can speak fairly clearly. There are many thousand possible ways of releasing energy from storage in matter. They range from very petty ways, like 25 BTUs per pound of matter by letting a pound of elastic bands untwist; through fairly petty ways, like 20,000 BTUs by burning a pound of petrol; through more sophisticated ways like 250 million BTUs from the fission of the U-235 isotope in one pound of natural uranium; up to 260 thousand billion BTUs from the fusion to helium of a pound of hydrogen. Note that this last system, in which the waters of the oceans could serve as a limitless reservoir of fuel, would be over 10 billion times more effective per pound of matter than burning a pound of the Arabs' oil.

The trend since 1776 has been for new technology to drive on in sudden bursts toward the cleaner power sources nearer the top of the range. The present "energy crisis" should make the next few bursts come a bit faster. The long-term prospect is that we are moving, however slowly, toward an age of abundant and very low marginal-cost energy—whether it be solar, geothermal, or fusion.

The short-term prospect is that the next energy advance in line, nuclear fission, is going to be held up by scares. Of course, it will be better if nuclear energy passes from infancy through teenagehood to maturity in responsible hands, because a situation in which the main market for it would be the less responsible countries would be a recipe for disaster. But at present the pressures are too heavy against nuclear energy in the responsible countries, and too slight in irresponsible countries, so we may be moving toward the generation of a plutonium glut in banana republics' hands. This is a gloomy prospect indeed. We come now to contemplation of the first of the bizarre dangers before the world.

NUCLEAR HORRORS

One thermonuclear explosion can now release more explosive power than was released by all the explosions of all the TNT in all the wars of history. And a thermonuclear bomb is soon going to be almost portable. Quite small groups of fanatics and terrorists and individual criminals may therefore have the capability of destroying the planet. We have not made the beginning of an advance toward thinking what we will do as that power of blackmail escalates.

It is probable that nuclear weapons technology will come into the hands of lunatic governments soon. Of the 158 governments in the world, about two-thirds are run by people who will go to bed tonight afraid they might be executed in a violent coup d'etat before breakfast tomorrow. This does not make for a calm and unexcitable mind in the lower two-thirds of what will become the nuclear trigger-minders' profession.

Among individuals we will—unfortunately, unwillingly, and illiberally —have to move to less freedom for people with mental illnesses and character defects, by which I don't mean incarceration, but they will probably have to carry electronic devices so that it will be known where they are. Among nations I think it is sensible to envisage before the end of the 1980s joint American-Soviet gunboat raids like Entebbe on the Amins or others who are threatening to blow up the world.

Another, and more civilized, policy for avoiding incineration of the planet will have to be changes in the international monetary system in order to pump much of the growth in the world's income into the poorest countries. One mechanism should run something like this. At present nearly all big industrial countries look forward to what their GNPs may be a year ahead, and they pump in extra spending power if it looks like there will be an underdemand. The rich countries should start instead to look forward to what gross world product may be a year ahead, and most often pump any desirable extra spending power initially into the hands of the poorer countries. The poor country's use of this would then mop up unwanted unemployment in the world's rich north.

One way in which the real GNPs of poor countries have been raised, though sometimes in the least essential fields, is by transfer of technology through multinational corporations. It is fine that Volkswagen Brazil and Coca-Cola in several countries have raised their productivity to levels commensurate with their plants back home, but the most urgent need in the poor countries is not necessarily to raise productivity in making cars and soft drinks. Aid schemes in the future will have to turn toward offering performance contracts whereby multinational service corporations can make a profit if they contract that they will raise nutrition standards, health care standards, educational attainments, provision of infrastructure in shanty towns, and so on. If the governments of any poor countries do not want such multinational service corporations, then they need not have them. But aid should be tied to projects that will raise real incomes in this way and in which performance contracts are open to bids in the marketplace.

The objective should be to raise ever more countries to the sort of income level where their governments will be composed of people who think of themselves and their political opponents as heading slowly toward comfortable retirement, instead of racing to get their brothers-in-law to the firing squad first. Probably the best definition of the sort of government that will not start nuclear fighting is: any government where the decision makers assume that they personally will end their lives in the local equivalent of Southern California, a dacha outside Moscow, or the House of Lords. This seems usual at GNPs per head over about $1,000 a year.

CHOOSE YOUR BABIES' INTELLIGENCE?

The next set of bizarre dangers may be connected with the nature and numbers of mankind. Because I believe in the law of opposites, I have never believed that the world was threatened by rising birth rates. To the extent that people began to believe in the 1960s that mankind was threatened by far too many births, food and raw material famines, and overwhelming pollution, this helped to set a short-term trend toward too few births, food and raw material gluts, and excessive fads against new investment projects on the grounds that they are pollutant. Some of those deleterious results have, in my view, in fact been put in train.

But although I personally think that the fall in birth rates, already a decade-and-a-half old in the rich countries, is going to dumbfound people by moving even more swiftly to the poor countries, I also think that a real though brief world population crisis may arise from the side for which people have not prepared. Some time in the next few decades some teams of doctors are likely to make breakthroughs in curing the main degenerative diseases, so that old people will start to exist longer. This will set the real population problem. As the death rate drops, mankind will probably have to move toward acceptance of euthanasia and even planned death (with a rousing going-away party on your 85th birthday?).

My guess is that mankind will accept this smoothly. Witness how abortion was a word you could not mention to auntie 15 years ago, but today any woman could get an abortion in most cities by next weekend. It will not be at all surprising if there is in some quite near decade-and-a-half a similarly swift and equally civilized dash to acceptance of killing off old codgers (by then, like me) as there has been, in so short a twinkling, toward the much more emotive act of killing unborn babies.

But, some time during this period, the most bizarre danger connected with population may arise. It will be the biophysical danger. The present orthodox way of creating a human being—namely by copulation between two individuals giving no thought to what the product will be—may quite soon change. Sex is already 99.9 percent for fun, and technology is bound to home in on the preplanned twice in a lifetime occasion when it will be for reproduction. Our children will probably "progressively" be able to order their babies with the shape and strength and level of intelligence that they choose as well as alter existing human beings so as to insert artificial intelligence, retune brains, change personality, modify moods, control behavior, enjoy artificial pleasure by stimulating the pleasure centers of the brain, and lots of even more horrid things like that.

The pace and sophistication with which some of these things are not done will hang on the world's leading nations whom other peoples will most wish to emulate or will most fear to fall behind.

ECONOMIC LEADERSHIP

It is fashionable to suppose that economic growth will slow from now on. I think it is much more likely to accelerate. The world's economic history is that, after a big surge when man stopped being a mainly migratory animal in about 8,000 B.C., real gross world product per head stood practically still for 10,000 years down to about 1776. Then it exploded. Real incomes have increased in 19 of the 20 decades since 1776 because of an increase in every decade in man's knowledge and control over energy and matter. To this has been added, in the last two decades, a breakthrough in the processing of information plus a nascent breakthrough in the distribution of information (that is, computers, telecommunications by satellite, the beginnings of packaged and computerized learning programs, maybe even at last a start toward understanding the learning process itself). Economic growth depends mainly on the advance of knowledge, plus the entrepreneurial drive to put that knowledge into productive effect. The computer revolution alone means that some mathematical and other logical calculations, which would have taken a month for any team to complete 25 years ago, can now be done in a nanosecond. This would be an odd prelude to a period when the world's advance in knowledge abruptly slowed down.

If my guess is right, man's main problem in the next few decades will be the same as in the last 20 decades; namely, that he is likely to be given some very dangerous toys to play with during another period of vertiginous economic advance and may use them unwisely unless political leadership in the world continues to be very sophisticated indeed.

The miracle is that world leadership has been sophisticated so far. Through some happy fluke, the two empires who through temporary dynamism led the two successive centuries of material advance—the British empire of 1776 to 1876, followed by the American empire of 1876 to 1976—have handled the task of world leadership rather surprisingly well. The right sides in these two centuries eventually won most of the big hot and especially cold wars—and their leaders were realistic enough to lie low after the few wars that they had rightly lost.

There was a moment of considerable danger for human freedom when British economic dynamism began to slither at around the stage which British economic history books will call the "great depression" of the 1870s. The main reason for Britain's entrepreneurial decay around 1876 was that a century's experience of being top dog had by then become debilitating. The British upper class was strengthening its gut feeling that new sorts of commerce were surely rather vulgar, while the British business-decision-making class had itself become bureaucratic and protectionist rather than entrepreneurial. As each new technological development appeared in the late nineteenth century there were interests in Britain (entrenched among the employers, the craft unions, and conservationists) who had prospered from or been less disturbed by the old technology which it would replace, so they sometimes united in pressure groups to wish that the new idea would please go away.

In *America's Third Century* I confessed to some fears that Americans in 1976 were showing the same symptoms of a drift from economic dynamism as the British did at the end of their century in 1876. I felt that the American people, with all their power for dynamism and good, might be about to desert what should be their manifest and now rather easy destiny of leading the rest of us toward a decent world society and an abundant cheap lunch. Two aristocratic trends in present-day America are very reminiscent of the early signs of British decay by the 1870s. First, the British intellectual class in about the 1870s joined the aristocracy in beginning to regard business as something rather vulgar, and to look upon new factories as things that were ecologically unfair to pheasants and wild ducks. That is exactly the mood of America's intellectual upper class now. Second, after about the 1870s a progressive person in British political life no longer meant a person who believed in progress, no longer a person who was eager to rout down to the roots of every way of doing things so as to cut and graft wherever an improvement in production or effectiveness or competitiveness or individual liberty could be secured. A progressive person began to mean a chap who did not like progress and change very much, but who was most decently eager to pass on in welfare benefits a larger part of the growth in national income which his own antigrowth attitudes now made it more difficult to attain. That is exactly the change that also happened in America in President Johnson's Great Society years, and that was very evident also in the Democratic majority in Congress during the Nixon and Ford administrations.

If these trends continue, world leadership is likely to pass into new hands quite early in the century 1976 to 2076. If one had been guessing in the 1870s who would take over world leadership from the British, one would have guessed Bismarck's Prussia and been quite wrong. If one is guessing in the 1970s who will take over from the Americans I would guess Japan and probably be quite wrong. The race will depend on what happens in each country to the three main institutions: the groups making business decisions (in capitalist countries this temporarily means big business corporations, and in socialist countries it means nothing that at present works), governments, and mechanisms for living together. Although the business decision-making group is least important for the long term, its success oddly matters most in the short term. America took over world leadership in 1876 to 1910 because its business system in those years allowed an extraordinary number of new entrepreneurs to come forward (Rockefeller, Morgan, Harriman, Carnegie, Ford) in order to seize a new age of technological opportunity. Another new age of technological opportunity is dawning now.

TELECOMMUTING TAKES OVER

Just as the first or British century of industrial advance from 1776 to 1876 was based on the transport revolution of the railways and on steam power, just as the second or American century of 1876 to 1976 was based on the transport revolution of the automobile and on manufacturers' assembly lines, so the third century of 1976 to 2076 is likely to be based on the third and by far the biggest transport revolution—that of telecommunications—allied to knowledge processing. This is likely to change the whole pattern of our lives because it probably means that an increasing number of us will no longer have to live near the places of our work. We will be able to live in Tahiti if we want to and be able to telecommute daily to our New York or Frankfurt or Tokyo office in order to have continuous contact with the computers and colleagues with whom we work. Sociologically, this makes it quite possible that the age of urbanization is about to end and the problems of reruralization are about to begin. Economically, it is one of several reasons why the nature of big business corporations is surely going to change.

Big business corporations were really created during the period 1875 to 1910. During the period 1975 to 2010 they will probably disappear, at least in their present form. The interesting question is what will replace them.

The modus operandi of a big business corporation is that each executive sits arranging what the man below him will do with his hands, down to the man turning a screw on the assembly line. Two rather fundamental things are now making this form of business organization archaic or impossible. First, we have begun to realize that educated workers in rich countries don't like working in such places. Second, the rich countries are moving out of the postmanufacturing age, but they still have great hierarchical corporations in which executives sit trying to arrange what the man below will do with his imagination. This doesn't work and can't work. New forms of business organization will have to be found, probably making big corporations into confederations of entrepreneurs. The firms and countries that will go bust in these circumstances are those that try to replace hierarchical corporations by even more ossified forms of hierarchical corporations: say, by deciding that you mustn't have a boss trying to arrange what free men do with their imaginations, but can have a trade union committee doing so instead. This last is a reason why socialism won't work; idealistic socialism means that a trade union committee tries to boss free men's imaginations, while actual socialism means that a government resists the recognition that it can't efficiently organize free men's imaginations either.

Another major development for capitalism is that it is gradually becoming clear that ownership is no longer a source of economic power and is probably increasingly a source of economic powerlessness. It is much easier to control subcontractors than direct employees. It is probably a good thing that the idea of multinational corporations—that is, U.S. corporations creating political bad blood by owning production facilities in foreign countries—reached its apogee in the 1960s and 1970s. Then, and to some degree now, the poor countries of the world were not very productive because more than half of their populations were below the age of 21 (so they were largely countries of schoolchildren who produce nothing and teenagers who produce riots). This age bulge will move through the most productive age groups (20 to 45 years old) over the next three decades, and a lot of manufacturing production will move down to those countries.

As a prototype for the most successful sort of firm in 30 or 40 years' time, it may be most sensible to visualize small groups of organizers of systems designers, all living in their own comfortable homes in pleasant parts of the world and communicating with others in the group (and with the systems designers) by picturephone, arranging for the telecommunication of the latest best computerized learning program on how to make a better mousetrap (or, more probably, how to make the next successor to integrated circuits). This would all be transmitted rooftop to rooftop to about 2,000 quickly trainable, even if only newly literate, workers assembled before their two-way teach-in computer terminals by some just tolerably efficient organizing subcontractor (also taught by long-distance telecommunicated computer lessons) in West Africa or Pakistan.

When I wrote *America's Third Century,* I thought (without being explicit) that Japan was probably the most likely country to sit at the center of the web, organizing the groups of organizers of systems designers. But it is possible that Japan has been the most dynamic country in the period 1950-75 because its government system was not unlike Britain's before 1876: politicians in Japan have not mattered much during these economic miracle years, and the country has really been ruled by cooperation and some creative tension between thrusting businessmen and a bureaucracy representing many interests. Two main hopes for those who want to see continued American leadership in the world (on the sophisticated grounds that the Americans can more safely be trusted with handling test-tube babies, nuclear-armed General Amins, and so on), are that (1) Japanese politicians may, to Japan's misfortune, become more important; and (2) American politicians may, to America's advantage, become less important. Let me explain what I mean.

GOVERNMENTS MUST DIMINISH

The American system of government has been to set up many competing governments—both in Washington (as between the Executive and Supreme Court and Congress and a shifting establishment) and at the local level (where the overlapping between the thousands of American local authorities is organized chaos). This system of government has one huge advantage, and one growing disadvantage. The advantage, as Madison saw when he created it, is that multigovernment saves America from being ruled by a "tyrannous majority," or indeed any tyranny (thus it would be impossible in America for trade unions to achieve the position of influence they hold over some sectors of British life, because one or other of the competing arms of government would not let them get away with it). The disadvantage of the Madisonian system is that it is the most inefficient system that could be conceived for spending a lot of money.

If you were an inquiring Martian and asked the normal questions to assess productivity in the American public sector over the past 20 years —By how much have crime rates gone down? How far has the legal system become more expeditious? By how much is the urban environment more beautiful and its infrastructure better fitted to meet changing demands? By how much has welfare spending strengthened the family structures of the urban poor and advanced the other aims most vital for making the poor happy, including especially making them more confident about the atmosphere in which their children are passing their teenagehood? How certain has America's multibillion spending on defense made it that you will win in less than Austerlitz's painless ten minutes any war threatened by ridiculous little countries such as North Vietnam?—the answer has to be that, over the last 20 years, each of those measures of productivity has, after vast expenditure of the taxpayer's dollar, grown worse.

In all the free industrial countries we now pick the purveyors of about three-fifths of our goods and services (such as soapsuds) through competitive consumer choice, and we pick the purveyors of the often-most-essential other two-fifths of our services and goods (like city management) through casting votes. At present the mechanism for picking purveyors of soapsuds (free market competition plus mendacious advertising plus independent assessments by consumers' associations) is plainly working better than the mechanism (known as the great democratic process) for picking President Nixons and Mayor Beames. Rich countries will have to reprivatize, recompetition, and denationalize a lot of present public-sector activities over the next few decades. We are going to have to move toward voter participation in defining what the community wants from a public service and then to extend new sorts of market competition to find who can most efficiently provide it.

When I wrote *America's Third Century,* I felt that Japan was more likely to seize these opportunities than America, partly because Japan has so much smaller a public sector than any other industrial country (that is a main reason why it has been growing fastest) and because its bureaucracy is used to moving out into competitive business at a relatively early age. Also I was very depressed at the failure of the American voting system. The choices of president in the three elections before 1976 (Johnson versus Goldwater, Nixon versus Humphrey, Nixon versus McGovern) had proffered five men whom I regarded as among the least suitable possible choices in all the 220 million Americans to hold the most powerful secular office on earth.

Since 1975 I have come to fear that Japan may increase its public spending too much. By contrast I am rather cheered by the fact that during the 1975 depression, Americans did not clamor for increased public works. The 1976 Carter versus Ford election seemed to be between two averagely decent and balanced men. Provided the hope holds that Mr. Carter is not an overambitious man (which it is at this time too early to judge), I am slightly more optimistic than before that America may start to reprivatize its excessive public expenditure.

THE PATTERN OF RERURALIZATION

A main reason for caution in making prophecies about America is that the country is obviously on the verge of another change in locations and thus life styles. The two previous runs of this drama had such unexpected results. First, there was the hugely successful decade a century ago between about the 1870s and 1880s. In one decade the Americans all seemed to be shooting each other at the OK Corral, and in the next decade Dwight Eisenhower was being born at Abilene. In one decade the per capita murder rate in the cow towns and mining settlements was between 10 and 20 times that in New York City today, and in the next decade these were the towns of the Bible Belt, as the homesteaders and madonnas of the plains moved west the settled family structures that produced just about the most decent as well as progressive small-town neighborhood system the world has seen.

Then in a single decade between the 1950s and 1960s so many things went hugely wrong, as the poor poured into the cities and the middle class moved out to the suburbs, unexpectedly making both more horrid. The influx into the cities proved to be of cowboys, not homesteaders, as family structures of the new immigrants there broke down, that is, suburbian mom went on tranquilizers, the kids on drugs, and the working father on martinis. American universities tend to blame this on the fact that planners were not ready for the urban crisis. Young lecturers castigate their predecessors for not recognizing that from the early 1950s the rural-to-urban migration had begun to reach 500,000 a year. However, they say that they've got professors of urban affairs and large urban departments all in place to study the problem now.

Meanwhile, it is unpopular to point out, the tide has already for the past six years been flowing the other way. In the first years of the 1970s there has been a population rise of just over 350,000 a year in America's nonmetropolitan areas. Telecommuting will surely cause this to rise fast. The new life styles associated with this will be the most interesting subjects for study.

NOTE

1. Macrae, Norman, *America's Third Century* (New York: Harcourt Brace Jovanovich, 1976).

PART THREE
Forecasts and Economic Analyses

8 | The Changing Metabolism of Growth

Ian Wilson

THE GROWTH DEBATE AS AN EXAMPLE
OF HEGEL'S DIALECTIC PROCESS

Hegel was right. There is a powerful logic to the flow from thesis to antithesis to synthesis. Indeed, in a broad historical sense, society often seems to move in the form of a Hegelian dialectic. Within the past ten years in the United States, for instance, we have witnessed such a pattern evolving in the area of individual and social value systems. Opposed to the established thesis of traditional values (patriotism, strict sexual taboos, Puritan work ethic, materialism, and so on), there appeared, with quite startling suddenness, the antithesis of the "counterculture" (flag burning, drugs and promiscuity, dropping out, antimaterialism, and so on). If there was, at the time (1969–71), one reasonable prediction as to the most probable future in this regard, it was (and still is) that the future lay with neither extreme, but with some synthesis of the old and the new, an eclectic blending of elements. Just where this new synthesis might lie was a reasonable topic for speculation; but that it would emerge could scarcely be doubted.

As with values, so with the "growth movement"—both the nature and scope of economic growth, and the attitudes (values) associated with it. Here, too, we can note the established thesis of "growth is good" (growth per se; careless, carefree growth), the spirit of Chamber-of-Commerce boosterism, epitomized as never before by the booming affluence of the United States in the 1960s; and then the sudden antithesis which propounded that "growth (like God) is dead." Neither the similarity in suddenness and polarization nor the coincidence in timing with the counterculture was purely accidental. In both cases the antithesis was a well-nigh inevitable reaction to past practices and attitudes, closely asso-

---

The opinions expressed in this chapter are purely personal ones and are not intended to reflect the views of General Electric, for whom Ian Wilson works.

ciated with the coming-of-age of the first wave of the post-World War II baby boom, and triggered by physical events (Vietnam, race riots, pollution crises, and so on) that were themselves interlinked by the cultural chain. Here, too, one might predict that the most probable future would be defined in terms of some synthesis of growth, restraint, and ecological consciousness.

In fact, that is the conclusion of the Edison Electric Institute in its study, *Economic Growth in the Future.*[1] Based on an extensive modeling effort, it was forecast that the future—at least for the next 25 years—will most probably take some middle way between growth of the 1960s and zero growth. Given the predictability of this conclusion, I always find it singularly unhelpful to have the debate on the growth issue set forth in highly polarized viewpoints. So much time and mental effort is wasted in debating generalities in which neither proponent fully believes (or which they have to qualify to such an extent that it becomes hard for the dispassionate and perplexed observer to determine where they really stand) that little attention is left over for specific policy issues of immediate concern.[2]

Such polarity was understandable, probably inevitable, back in 1971 (when Jay Forrester first published *World Dynamics*)[3] or in 1972 (when *The Limits to Growth*[4] appeared, based on the computer studies of Dennis Meadows and his associates). At that time the proponents of "growth is good"—better than 90 percent of the American public—basking in the euphoria of the 1960s' economy (if not its politics), reacted in shock and outrage against the doomsayers who dared to question the inalienable right of the United States to grow as if there were no tomorrow. The Club of Rome and its adherents, on the other hand, sought to drive home their psychological initiative and their message: equilibrium, or zero growth, *must* come, if not tomorrow (1985–90), then the next day (2010–25).

Clearly that was the time for knee-jerk reactions and polarized viewpoints—and for talking past one another. Nowhere is this better revealed than in the reviews of these two books. While some critics focused on legitimate criticisms (inadequate and highly aggregated data; little attention to the workings of the price mechanism; undue technological pessimism), most engaged in unscholarly debunking, if not in ungentlemanly conduct, reaching for the barbed witticism ("The Computer That Printed Out W*O*L*F*")[5] and delighting in the destruction of straw men.

Now, I hope, that unproductive phase of the debate is largely behind us. There is a greater willingness, on one side, to admit that some things must change, and, on the other, to concede that not everything will. There is even some convergence in the terminology. Mihajlo Mesarovic and Edward Pestel called their book *Mankind at the Turning Point;*[6] even that technological optimist, Herman Kahn, argues that mankind is at an "inflection point" on the global growth curve. The electorates in two states have chosen as their governors (Richard D. Lamm, in Colorado, and Edmund G. Brown, Jr. in California) men who subscribe to the tenets of E. F. Schumacher's *Small is Beautiful*. The Club of Rome, at its meeting in Philadelphia in April 1976, was prepared to subscribe to the necessity, even the desirability, of continued economic growth. But millions were starting to realize that (in the words of the Center for Growth Alternatives slogan) "We can't grow on like this."

THE CHANGING PERSPECTIVES ON GROWTH

The initial polarization of viewpoints has been overtaken by events, changes in attitudes, and a multitide of public and private policy decisions. For instance:

There is a developing recognition that there must be *limits to exponential growth,* that there is validity to the concept of the S-curve as it applies to the physical growth of human activities and institutions. Even critics of Forrester and Meadows are now prepared to concede that infinite growth is not possible on a finite planet, with finite resources and space. This recognition is a matter of philosophy, of values, not well articulated by many, and only subconsciously developed in most. But it is a new starting point, one which, however true, would not have been given even a grudging admission a decade ago. The argument, then, is over the *timing* of ultimate equilibrium; and, clearly, it makes a great deal of difference to policy makers whether that state is 50, 100, or 200 years away.

More immediately, at least in the United States, there has developed a de facto recognition of the need to impose *limits to population growth.* No doubt, the prime motivation for having smaller families is a good deal less cosmic and more personal than concern for the condition of mankind (though that is indeed *a* factor with a surprising number among the younger generation). No doubt, too, forecasting population growth is a highly inexact science: every Census Bureau forecast of the past 40 years has had to be revised within ten or so years of its promulgation. However, it is a fact that the overall fertility rate is holding at a level well below the replacement level (2.1); and this fact seems to be influenced as much by new "quality of life" choices by young married couples as by improved birth control technology. Significantly, too, population limitation is not merely a matter of personal and family decisions. It is also becoming a matter of public policy in many ways as, for instance, in questions about the use of U.S. aid abroad and Medicaid at home, and in decisions by communities such as Boca Raton, Florida, to impose a limit on their ultimate size.

We have already, as a nation, made a commitment to specifying *limits to pollution growth.* Little more needs to be said about this obvious point. The course has been set, and the laws have been passed. No doubt, as Russell Train observed on assuming his position as the head of the Environmental Protection Agency, "midcourse corrections will be made" as we gain better understanding of the costs and consequences of these statutes, or as we make new trade-off decisions in dealing with the development of new energy sources, at least on a short-term basis (for example, the Alaska Pipeline). But it is inconceivable that there would be a complete course reversal.

Both public policy makers and business executives are beginning to act on the need to put *limits to growth in resource consumption,* both energy and raw materials (particularly, of course, nonrenewable resources). Kenneth Boulding has written eloquently of our need to make the transition from a "cowboy economy" to a "spaceship economy"; and the progressive development (and financial attractiveness) of solid waste management technology surely heralds the end of a pure throughput system and the advent of a recycling system. As with private decisions regarding population growth, the motivating force is less a concern for global resources as such and more a pure economizing move, seeking to improve the productivity of inputs that had been historically cheap but registered dramatic cost increases in the early 1970s.

Finally, evidence is accumulating daily of widespread decisions to impose *limits to capital growth* in some segments of our society and economy. Many communities have followed the example of Petaluma, California, in setting limits to housing development, either by redrafting zoning ordinances or by controlling the rate of annual additions to the housing stock. New shopping centers are encountering a degree of local opposition that would have been unthinkable as recently as ten years ago. The power plant siting problems of electric utilities are well known, as are other dramatic examples of public and political opposition such as the supersonic transport, Florida International Airport, dams, canals, and highways.

I have chosen to phrase this "litany of limits" in terms of the major factors of the Forrester-Meadows model (population, resources, capital, pollution) simply to demonstrate that, while intellectual debate has been joined on these issues, a myriad of very pragmatic decisions is being taken —at the family, community and national levels—that are reshaping the terms and, in a sense, the arena of debate. As a wry aside, one can argue that these actual developments "prove":

either Forrester-Meadows to be wrong in their predictions of exponential growth followed by collapse, because society is already starting to make the necessary preventive adjustments in its growth mechanism;

or their critics to be wrong in their attacks on the model, because society can be said, in some sense, to believe in the fundamental validity of the model's concepts, and to be *acting* on that belief.

It is not, of course, that the limits referred to in this litany are limits in any absolute sense—population, capital, pollution, resource consumption are, after all, still growing—but they *are* indicators both of changing values and changing behavior.

WHAT IS THE NEW CONCEPT OF GROWTH?

The Edison Electric Institute report is assuredly correct in concluding that "a new concept of growth is called for."[7] I would argue that this new concept is already being formulated. Like the authors of the report, I am dissatisfied with the terms suggested to describe this concept—clean growth, quality growth, betterment. While these terms do attempt to reflect the shift in emphasis from purely quantitative growth, they suffer from a lack of precision and fail to come to grips with the essence of the change that is being sought. I suggest that we think and plan in terms of *ecologically compatible growth* as the goal toward which we must aim our public and private policies. At least this term has the considerable merit of underscoring the essential fact that for growth to be sustainable over the long haul it must be compatible with the carrying capacity of the earth's biosphere. It does not say a great deal, in itself, about the *type* of growth and *level* of growth that meets this criterion. And that is perhaps as it should be, for almost certainly the answers to these questions will evolve over time. Certainly this suggested term is *not* vulnerable to the charge made in the report that all such terms "tend to suggest a finality which does not exist in a world which is constantly changing and evolving."[8]

As a purely practical matter—as a result of factors that have little or nothing to do with "growth philosophies"—economic growth in the United States over the next 25 years is likely to average considerably below the rate in the 1960s (4 percent per year in real terms). Almost certainly it will be less than the 3.5 to 3.7 percent per year set forth in the "moderate growth scenario" contained in *Economic Growth in the Future.*[9] When one considers that the average annual growth rate in real GNP over the past 25 years (1950–75) was on the order of 3.2 percent —somewhat higher if you exclude the lean years of 1974–75—then it is difficult to assert that the *most probable* scenario for the next quarter century will include a growth rate 10–15 percent higher.[10]

This is because the key determinants of future economic growth will weaken over this period. Without engaging in a detailed economic forecast, one can say that future growth stems from two main factors:

increases in labor input, that is, growth of the civilian labor force *less* any prospective decrease in total hours worked;

improvement in productivity, reflecting increased quality of the labor force, new technology, increased efficiency in the use of capital, energy, materials.

In broad terms the sweep of the future growth trend becomes apparent from even a casual glance at Figure 8.1. Although the figure covers only the next 15 years, the basic momentum of these forces is likely to carry over into the final decade of this century:

Labor input: There will be a slowdown in labor force growth as the number of new entrants declines (reflecting the end of the post-World War II baby boom). In the 1990s, labor force growth will be reflecting the low birth rates of the early 1970s; and really the only uncertainty for the rest of the century so far as labor force growth is concerned is the birth rate for the next five years or so (1977–81). Overall, labor force growth will do well to average 1.1 percent per year (compared with 1.6 percent for 1950–75), even if one makes some optimistic assumptions concerning future increases in women's participation rates (which do appear to be approaching saturation levels).[11] Furthermore, even this growth rate would have to be discounted by whatever assumptions one cares to make about reductions in total hours worked (extra holidays, more vacation, shorter work week) to arrive at a net labor input growth rate. All told, then, the annual gain in labor input over the next 25 years will probably average 0.9–1.0 percent, higher in the first five years, but declining fairly steadily over the period.[12]

Productivity: Productivity gains have been weakening in recent years, and it is highly probable that this trend will continue. Among the more important factors contributing to this decline are:

a shift in the GNP mix from high-productivity sectors (agriculture, transportation, manufacturing) to low-productivity sectors (government, trade, services);

reduced benefits from innovation due to a weakening (already noticeable) in the nation's research and development (R&D) effort;

a decline in investment intensity (capital/output ratio);

diversion of funds from improving labor efficiency to "non-productive" investment (environmental protection, safety, and so on).[13]

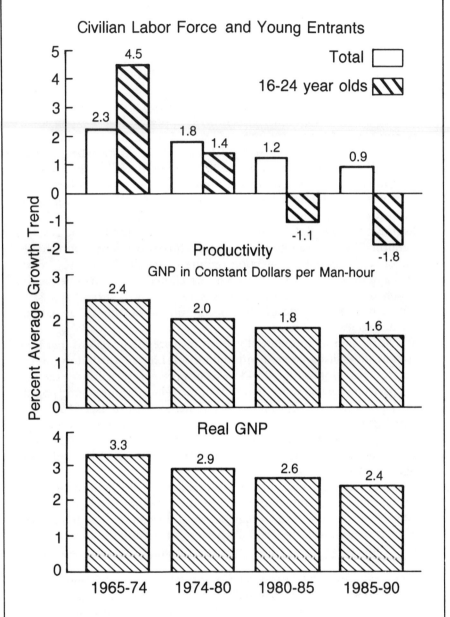

FIGURE 8.1: Some Determinants of Future Economic Growth

Civilian Labor Force and Young Entrants

Total

16-24 year olds

Productivity
GNP in Constant Dollars per Man-hour

Real GNP

1965-74   1974-80   1980-85   1985-90

Percent Average Growth Trend

Note: In order to avoid distortions due to cycles, all growth rates in these charts are trend-fitted values.
Source: General Electric Company, MAPCAST Economic Forecast, (Fairfield, Conn.: General Electric Company, March 1976).

The future of productivity improvement is necessarily less predictable than labor force growth, but it seems safe to say that it will probably follow a trajectory pretty much as indicated in Figure 8.1.

AN INFLECTION POINT ON THE GROWTH CURVES

If, then, real GNP growth is a factor of labor and productivity increases, the outlook for the next quarter century is appreciably less expansionary than the 3.5 to 3.7 percent forecast by the Edison Electric Institute report.[14] A growth rate closer to 2.9–3.1 percent per year can be expected. And this forecast, it is important to note, is *not* based on the effects of a conscious public policy decision to move as rapidly as possible toward a steady-state economy (that scenario would result in an even lower growth rate, approximately the 2.3 percent per year suggested by the Edison Electric Institute in its low-growth scenario).[15] It is the result of "traditional" demographic and economic forces combined with the impacts of environmental protection requirements and high energy costs.

It is apparent, therefore, that we in the United States shall be passing through some sort of inflection point on the growth curves, almost regardless of the outcome of any specific public debate about national growth policies.

It follows, almost automatically, from the foregoing analysis that I find myself in some disagreement with the Edison Electric Institute's forecast of energy growth (average 2.8–3 percent per year growth over the next 25 years). The past 50 years' history[16] of the relationships among population, labor force, GNP, and energy demand growth (see Table 8.1) strongly suggests that a real GNP growth rate of around 3 percent per year, combined with a resumption of the decline in the energy/GNP ratio, will produce an average annual growth in total energy demand in the range of 2.1–2.3 percent.[17]

Our national thinking, and to some extent both our public and private decision-making, is still conditioned by the economic experience of the 1960s. However unrealistic it may be, we still seem to hope for a return to the growth rates of the 1960–73 period. At least in the case of energy growth, the 1960s were a historical aberration:

> They exhibited the fastest energy growth rates (total, and per employed worker) of the past half-century but were followed in 1970–73 by appreciably slower growth, particularly in industrial consumption.
>
> They were the *only* period in which energy inputs increased faster than real GNP.

TABLE 8.1: U.S. Growth, 1920-73—Population, Labor Force, GNP, and Energy

Year	Population (000's)	Civilian Employment (000's)	GNP (1958 dollars)		Gross Energy Inputs (BTU's)			
			Total (billions)	Per Capita	Total (trillions)	Per Capita (millions)	Per Employed Worker (millions)	Per Dollars GNP (000's)
1920	106,466	41,497	140.0	1,315	19,782	186	477	141.3
1930	123,077	45,480	183.5	1,490	22,288	181	490	121.5
1940	132,594	47,520	227.2	1,720	23,908	181	503	105.2
1950	152,271	58,920	355.3	2,342	34,153	226	580	96.1
1960	180,671	65,778	487.7	2,699	44,816	249	681	91.9
1970	204,875	78,627	722.5	3,526	67,143	330	854	92.9
1973	210,396	84,409	839.2	3,989	75,561	360	895	90.0
Percent Average Annual Growth Rates								
1920-30	1.46	0.92	2.74	1.26	1.20	-0.27	0.27	-1.50
1930-40	0.75	0.44	2.16	1.45	0.70	0	0.26	-1.43
1940-50	1.39	2.17	4.57	3.13	3.63	2.25	1.43	-0.90
1950-60	1.72	1.11	3.22	1.43	2.75	0.97	1.62	-0.45
1960-70	1.27	1.80	4.01	2.71	4.13	2.86	2.29	+0.11
1970-73	0.89	2.39	5.12	4.20	4.02	2.94	1.58	-1.05

Source: Compiled by the author from data in the *Statistical Abstract of the United States: 1975* (96th ed.) (Washington, D.C.: U.S. Government Printing Office, 1976), pp. 718, 723.

It is particularly significant that there was some slowing of energy growth in the 1970–73 period—that is, *before* the Arab boycott and quadrupling of OPEC prices—despite the fact that GNP and employment exhibited the fastest growth of any period.

Assumptions about the future trend of the energy/GNP ratio are critical in making any generalized forecast of energy demand. As both Table 8.1 and Figure 8.2 make clear, the past trend has been persistently downward, with only a few interruptions.[18] Both history and analysis of future forces of conservation strongly indicate a further decline in the ratio to historical lows during the next ten years and beyond. The long-term trend toward greater technological efficiency will be augmented by price-induced and other forces for conservation so that energy consumption can increase at a lower rate than in previous years without causing a comparable reduction in GNP growth.

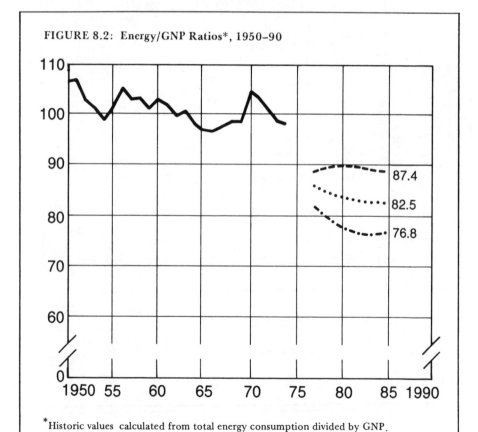

FIGURE 8.2: Energy/GNP Ratios*, 1950–90

*Historic values calculated from total energy consumption divided by GNP.
Source: Energy Environment Report, prepared by General Electric Company, Fairfield, Conn., December 1976.

Figure 8.2 displays plottings for three possible trend curves developed in a trend impact study conducted by General Electric and The Futures Group. On the basis of this analysis it would seem to be conservative to estimate a –0.8 percent growth rate in the energy/GNP ratio (less than the achievement of the early 1970s) to the point where the ratio would stand at around 82 in 1985, and between 70 and 75 in 2000. Such a decline would be consistent with a growth in energy demand of 2.1–2.3 percent per year, given an annual economic growth rate of 2.9–3.1 percent.

THE CHANGING METABOLISM OF GROWTH

These patterns suggest what I term "the changing metabolism of growth." The change is occuring for a whole complex of reasons and is *not* triggered solely by newly emerging constraints of energy, resources, and environment. Indeed, Jay Forrester has argued in his more recent writings that the social limits (crowding, conflict, crime, neuroses, and so on) may well be more constraining than the physical limits; that though we might optimistically hope to see technology overcome (or change our definition of) some of the physical limits, we would still be faced with these social constraints.[19]

That is almost certainly true; but even that is not the whole story. If we focus specifically on the future of growth in the United States, we can see that changes in the rate, the mix, the quality and "style" of growth will result from

Demographic factors: For example, a "ZPG-level" fertility rate; smaller families; much smaller increases (and ultimately stability) in both population and labor force.

Economic trends: For example, a slackening in R&D and productivity; the probability (at least over the near term) of sharper cyclical fluctuations; a rate of inflation approximately double that of the 1947–73 average.

Energy costs: Perhaps the most abrupt and significant change of any factor in the growth equation.

Resource problems: These are compounded by increasing worldwide competition for raw materials and increasing costs/difficulty in the mining and refining of (in many cases) less accessible, inferior-grade ores.

Value changes: For example, the new emphasis on "quality of life" (personal and societal), reexamination of the work-leisure mix, orientation to experiences rather than things.

Environmental constraints: That is, the limitations inherent in the carrying capacities of our land, water, and air (limitations that have already made themselves felt in crises or near-crisis situations).

Geopolitical factors: For example, the growing power of resource-rich developing countries; Third World demands for a "new economic order"; the role of food in trade—and diplomacy.

This is not an exhaustive list, but it should serve to drive home the infinite complexity of present and future developments. Above all, it should disabuse any lingering doubters of any complacent illusion that things will somehow "return to normal" (that is, the 1960s, in their minds); that we are not passing through an inflection point on the growth curve; that we can change things if only we can "win the debate" with the advocates of "no growth." We are, in fact, dealing not merely with matters of philosophy (though these are factors in the case—and important ones) but with a broad sweep of social forces and some very real physical imperatives.

No one should think that this transition period will be an easy one. Like an aircraft passing through the sound barrier, we shall be buffeted by shock waves for some time to come. In my earlier itemizing of beginning action to institutionalize some "limitations to growth," and in outlining my own lowered expectations as to the probable future growth rates for GNP and energy demand, I did not intend to suggest that the problem was already solved, or that we were on a problem-free, risk-free course. Clearly that is not the case. Much yet remains to be done; and it is all too easy to understate the need for new public policies designed to ease the transition, resolve trade-off problems, and reinforce trends that are on the right course.[20]

Population growth and distribution are a good case in point. There is a broad consensus that population must, and should, stabilize; and it is a fact that the fertility rate is already below the replacement level. But does this mean that "it is unnecessary to adopt *any* measures to control population size" (emphasis added)? or that "no measures to limit further concentrations are necessary"?[21] Scarcely, I think. As one possible agenda for future public policy actions, consider the following excerpts from the 1972 report of the Commission on Population Growth and the American Future:

The Commission recommends that:
sex education be available to all ... presented in a responsible manner through community organizations, the media and especially the schools.
states eliminate existing legal inhibitions and restrictions in access to contraceptive information, procedures and supplies.

federal, state and local governments make funds available to support abortion services in states with liberalized statutes.

federal expenditures for improved methods of fertility control be increased.

[there should be] increased and strengthened resources to deal with illegal immigration.

immigration policy be reviewed periodically to reflect demographic conditions and considerations.

the federal government develop a set of national population distribution guidelines to serve as a framework for regional, state and local plans and development.

Surely the strong message of even this partial agenda for public action is that much should still be done by way of public policy to reinforce and support "benign" trends that are already under way. If, in effect, we are in the process of establishing a "national goal" of ZPG, even though it is a goal arrived at by informal consensus rather than by political decision, is it not reasonable for public policy to be aimed at, and supportive of, such a goal?

Inevitably the question of population distribution leads into land use —and another area for further public policy development. This is an area where there have been many initiatives at the state level (for example, California, Washington, Oregon, Florida, Maine, Vermont) and the local level (for example, Ramapo, N.Y.; Petaluma, Calif.), but a federal land use planning bill to stimulate further state action has been stalled in Congress. Much of what has been done so far in this area smacks of "adhocracy" (for example, protecting particular kinds of land—wetlands, coastal lands, mountain lands) or else is locked in "the excessive geographic and functional labyrinth of governance that now so paralyzes equitable and efficient decision-making at local and regional levels."[22]

A more comprehensive and better-coordinated approach to land use planning remains an essential item on the public agenda. It is naive to believe that we can develop *and implement* "a new concept of growth" without such planning, for land use is at the heart of the growth issue. Without it the private sector will lack a clear and consistent development framework, jurisdictional disputes will proliferate, and trade-off decisions will be taken without relationship to one another and with inadequate appreciation of their long-term consequences. Of course, land use planning brings to a head the differences in viewpoint about priorities and balance among uses: But there can be no "ducking" of these differences —the only question is whether we shall face up to them as a piece or piecemeal.

Some of the principles on which land use policy should be based are:

The institutional framework for effective land use planning must be developed at *all* levels of government—federal, state, regional, and local.

The federal role should be one of granting incentives to states to encourage their planning activities, and of reviewing plans to ensure that national needs and goals are considered.

States should assume a major leadership role, *not* taking over land use planning now done at the local level, but to assign responsibilities to appropriate authorities (county, region, municipality), and to provide the framework and review mechanisms to protect the public interest and override local "exclusionary ordinances."

The base of the property tax should be shifted to heavier taxation of land as against buildings to promote better land use.

Governments must provide for both "windfall recapture" and "wipe-out avoidance" as a matter of equity between property owners affected by land use decisions.[23]

Many of these principles can, and should, be debated; but the need for public policy action, to help resolve some sharp trade-off dilemmas, can scarcely be questioned.

In yet another area, I doubt whether public policy should be as passive as the report seems to suggest on the whole question of recycling. If (as I have suggested) our long-term goal should be ecologically compatible growth, then a central aim of public growth policy must be conservation in the use of *both* renewable and (more particularly) nonrenewable resources and the *active* encouragement of recycling. No doubt rising prices and shortages of newly mined metals and forestry products will provide market-induced incentives to reuse the existing stock of resources. However, I would recommend a more activist role for public policy in fostering this trend.

For instance, it is at best anomalous—given such a national goal—for tax policy to foster resource depletion by the use of allowances. Some have suggested that we should substitute a depletion *tax* for a depletion allowance, and we may yet come to that. As a first step I would argue for a position of "tax neutrality" here, by a progressive phasing out over a number of years of such depletion allowances. A second step would involve adjusting Interstate Commerce Commission freight rates for secondary materials to make their transportation and re-use more competitive with primary materials. And a third would be an increase in federal research expenditures to advance recycling technology.

The Edison Electric Institute report leads off a set of recommendations with "a suggested approach to problem solving" in which two elements are goal setting and problem resolution. There can be no argument with the conceptual logic of such an approach; but many doubts linger as to how to implement it in a democratic society. Because this issue is so important, and because his remarks are addressed so precisely to this point, I want to offer the following lengthy quotation from "some observations on the national planning debate" by Charles E. Reed, Senior Vice President of General Electric. After observing that proponents and opponents in this debate agree on the need for improved coordination and foresight in public sector planning, Reed commented:

> A second point on which there is widespread agreement is the need to develop better information and clearer goals. . . .
>
> Today we face the grave threat of an effective disenfranchisement of large segments of the public through uncertainty and lack of information on the complex, highly technical issues that cry out for decisions. On energy, resources, the environment, land use, capital formation and many more, the situation is the same. The experts are divided. The public is confused and frustrated. Congress and the Administration, sensing this, tend to waffle and procrastinate on the needed decisions. . . .
>
> Obviously there are no easy ways out of this dilemma. However, it is clear that one need . . . is for more and better information on the key problems confronting us. You cannot have an active electorate, you cannot have a planful society, you cannot develop intelligent alternatives, in the absence of adequate, relevant information. . . .
>
> This suggests the possibility of a new institutional arrangement, at the national level, in which both the public and private sectors might participate. . . . Such an institute should derive its finances and its governing body from both the public and private sectors, and should be an independent entity, answerable to the public at large rather than to Congress or the Executive branch. . . .
>
> The purpose of this Institute would be to identify critical national issues, examine the policy options, disseminate information on the alternatives and catalyze debates. By focusing on forward-looking analyses, clarifying the relationships between ends and means and examining the trade-offs involved, it could do much to help our society clarify its goals and priorities, and make both public policies and private plans better informed and more in harmony with these goals.
>
> The third point on which agreement focuses is the need for improved economic problem-solving. . . .
>
> We should focus our data gathering, analyses and action programs on specific problems rather than diffuse our efforts over the whole field. This, after all, is a conclusion that European planners seem to be coming to.
>
> Certainly, we have no lack of agenda items. The nation is faced with severe problems in a number of key economic sectors, including energy, utilities, health care and construction, as well as in a number of issues that cut across industry sectors, such as inflation, capital formation, employment policy and urban revitalization. Each one of these problem areas calls for aggressive

joint business, labor and government action—to define the basic difficulties, to examine alternative futures and strategies, to develop possible programs, to inform the electorate, and to promote constructive action.

A model for such joint action is provided by the private labor-management group which meets under the chairmanship of former Secretary of Labor John Dunlop. . . .

However, the institutional format, though important, is secondary to the basic idea of agreement to pursue solutions to our problems on an incremental, problem-by-problem basis.[24]

Finally, because values (attitudes toward growth, the environment, resources, and future generations) must play such a key role in the decisions we shall make on these issues, I suggest that public policy can play its part in fostering the values that are consonant with ecologically compatible growth through the sort of "values clarification" that takes place in our public schools.

We need to develop more ecological/holistic/systemic thinking. Where better to start on this task than in the schools? Curriculum development should, for instance, focus on materials, courses, and projects that stress the interdependencies of our world, the interrelationship between man's works (economy) and nature (ecology), the interdisciplinary needs of solutions to so many problems. It is regrettable but true that scientific reductionism has proceeded so far that all too often we fail to see, or think of, the "wholes" for the "parts."

We need, too, to develop more competent futuristic thinking. I do not mean to imply that the past has lost its educational usefulness, even in an age of discontinuous change. I do mean to suggest that we must learn how to make decisions with a keener sense of futurity; and one way to start is to promote more "education in the future tense," to use Alvin Toffler's phrase. Systematic thinking about "alternative futures" is a comparatively recent arrival on the research scene, but already there are materials, techniques, methodologies that can be used by teachers to build a futures perspective into our educational system.

Education needs to break out of its value-free-mode lock in at least one major regard: It must help students explore and clarify the values that will determine the choices among "alternative futures" that they will be called upon to make in adult life.

In what would be a significant extension of their traditional "citizenship" and "socializing" functions, our schools could help lay the intellectual foundations on which a future society, more conscious of its interdependence with nature and the rest of the world, and so more viable in the long run, could be built.

NOTES

1. Edison Electric Institute, *Economic Growth in the Future: The Growth Debate in National and Global Perspective.* (New York: McGraw-Hill, 1976).

2. Interestingly, a similar time-and-effort wasting debate still occurs on the separate but somewhat related issue of "socialism versus free enterprise." So frequently corporate programs of economic education aim at the wrong target. They seek to educate the public to the merits of private enterprise as an ideology when, as Daniel Yankelovich points out, the great majority of the public already believes in that but *is* nevertheless seriously concerned about specific flaws in the system—about which many corporate communications programs are exasperatingly silent.

3. Jay W. Forrester, *World Dynamics* (Cambridge, Mass.: Wright-Allen Press, 1971).

4. Donella H. Meadows, Dennis L. Meadows, Jorgen Randers, and William H. Behrens III, *The Limits to Growth* (New York: Universe Books, 1972).

5. Karl Kaysen, "The Computer That Printed Out W*O*L*F*," *Foreign Affairs,* July 1972, pp. 660–68.

6. Mihajlo Mesarovic, and Edward Pestel, *Mankind at the Turning Point* (London: Hutchinson and Company, 1975).

7. EEI, *Economic Growth in the Future,* p. 254

8. Ibid., p. 254

9. Ibid., p. 173

10. As one who is dedicated to futures research, I subscribe wholeheartedly to the use of alternative scenarios in an attempt to bracket the actual future. In the final analysis, however, we have to place our main planning emphasis on what we believe to be the most probable scenario, and to develop contingency planning to deal with the other cases.

11. As noted in the figure, all growth rates cited here are trend-fitted values.

12. Admittedly, the "standard economic forecast" envisages a high rate of unemployment (over 6 percent) for at least the next five years, due largely to structural changes in the labor force. Public policy changes could reduce this figure (to, say, 4–4.5 percent) and so increase the labor input: but, when averaged out over the whole period, the net effect would not appreciably change the picture given here.

13. It must be noted here that "nonproductive" represents a matter of current definition and accounting. The Chamber of Commerce of the United States put it well in its report on *Economic Growth: New Views and Issues* (1975, p. 31):

Productivity is, by its simplest definition, useful output per unit of input. If society views environmental quality as important enough to expend resources on, then presumably it is a useful output. That it is not counted as an output in our national income accounting measures makes expenditures on environmental quality seem nonproductive, but this is an illusion created by the limitations of the statistic. To the extent that environmental expenditures on the one hand add to production costs and to product prices and on the other hand are not counted as adding to the value of goods and services, there is an illusion of price inflation. Prices have gone up without measured improvement in product quality. While this looks like inflation, it is more really another statistical artifact. In no case can it be "fought" like inflation.

14. EEI, *Economic Growth in the Future,* p. 173.

15. Ibid., p. 109.

16. 1973 has been selected as the terminal to avoid the confusing picture of 1974–75 when it was extremely difficult to disentangle the effects on energy consumption of a severe recession from those of a quadrupling of oil prices.

17. The fact that this plotting coincides with Data Resources Incorporated (DRI) statistical best-fit line (for the relationship between growth in energy and growth in GNP in the

post-World War II period) suggests that this may even be an exaggeration. The line is, after all, based upon a relationship that existed when energy was relatively cheap. With the dramatic increase in energy costs, one would expect a gradual "spread" in the relationship (that is, lower energy growth for any given GNP growth).

18. Temporary interruptions have resulted from recessions, increased use of petroleum, slowdown in utility technology advances, increased use of electric space heating and cooling, introduction of pollution control equipment, and the Vietnam war (especially during the 1966–70 period).

19. Jay W. Forrester, *World Dynamics*, 2d ed., Chapter 8, "Postscript—Physical Versus Social Limits" (Cambridge, Mass.: Wright-Allen Press, 1973).

20. By its omissions, *Economic Growth in the Future* does tend to understate the need for new public policies.

21. EEI, *Economic Growth in the Future*, p. 253.

22. Forty-Fifth American Assembly Report, *Land Use in America* (Harriman, N.Y.: Arden House, April 18–21, 1974).

23. For instance, the use of "transferable development rights" offers a possible redress to the landowner who is severely restricted by government action, permitting him to transfer development rights to other less restricted land or sell such rights to others for use on such land.

24. Charles E. Reed, "Toward a Planful Society," An address to the Fifth International Conference on Planning, Cleveland, Ohio, July 19, 1976.

9 | U. S. Energy Policy Options in the World Economic System

Barry B. Hughes and Mihajlo D. Mesarovic

There are three time horizons with which the United States should be concerned when pondering action in the energy field: (1) the status quo time horizon up to year 1985; (2) the economic options time horizon from 1985 up to year 2000; and (3) the era of technological innovations and period of adjustment beyond the year 2000. Each of these time periods is characterized by the degree of freedom the U.S. has with respect to the energy problem area and the options it can use to alleviate the problem. In the status quo era, that is up to year 1985, the United States actually has been left without any significant options of its own. The development of the energy picture is largely determined by the actions already taken on the national and international level over the last 15 to 25 years. The problem can be affected only by actions in the domain of international relations. The dependence of the nation on the world energy and economic system cannot be changed to any significant degree. However, energy supplies might be adequate and uninterrupted, depending on the skill of U.S. foreign policy. The dependence of the United States on the rest of the world has potentially peaked and hopefully will diminish in the years to come, depending, of course, on whether proper actions are taken.

The well-being and progress of the United States in the second period, from 1985 to the year 2000, depends on how well it uses its economic potential to regain control of the energy situation. The interdependence will still remain since the United States will rely to a considerable degree on other nations (in trade, oil, and so on), but economic rather than purely political measures could be used to deal with the problem. For example, in one extreme case, if nuclear development is slowed down, the United States will have to pay an import oil bill close to $100 billion annually. If food exports and food prices do not increase significantly and provide export earnings, such an oil bill would be impossible to finance. In another extreme case, when the United States relies maximally on nuclear sources, and under the assumption of reasonable economic prospects and progress, it would take almost 1,600 nuclear power plants or more than 30 on average in each state of the union to satisfy demand. The nation will almost certainly try to increase its degree of independence. Yet, whether it can really do so will depend not only on internal matters (such as favoring one type of supply over another) but also on its economic policy in the global context. Specifically, trade must be reasonably balanced to secure growth needed to generate capital for energy construction.

The problems in the third period cannot be solved either by political or economic means but represent a deep technological challenge as well as a challenge to our life style. This can best be seen by looking at the size of the nuclear establishment that will have to be built for further economic growth and progress. Without currently unforeseen changes in energy technology, by the year 2025 it would be necessary to have close to 5,000 nuclear power plants in the nation or on average almost 100 in each state. To provide security for such an effort it might well be necessary to have a police force in excess of 0.5 million (and possibly going up to 1 million) devoted exclusively to the job of securing nuclear facilities. (This estimate assumes 24-hour protection of generating facilities, enrichment and reprocessing plants, and fuel transportation lines.) Beyond the year 2025 the impact of energy consumption on climate and weather changes in different parts of the world might raise the prospects of global restrictions on energy use.

The assessment given here is based on factual and quantitative analysis of alternative likely developments using a second-generation regionalized world system model (the WIM-2 model). The analysis has been done so far primarily for the second, or medium-term, period. The results obtained and the numbers quoted in this summary are *indicative* rather than definitive; yet they are most certainly secure enough from major errors as to be a good basis for comparative evaluation of alternative policies.

It is perhaps not an exaggeration to say that the energy dilemma facing the United States is the most challenging and most fundamental dilemma since the birth of the nation. The life of the nation as far into the future as one can see will depend on what the United States and its federal government do about the energy problem over the next five or possibly ten years. These actions will have a most profound effect on the economic, social, and political life of the nation as well as on the lives of individual citizens and their children. There is no other challenge or peril facing the nation (except danger of nuclear holocaust) that is of the same magnitude and will have such a prolonged impact on the very existence of the society as we have it today.

The technique this report uses to investigate U.S. energy options is to look at the interaction of a variety of energy demand and supply strategies. First, it sketches the consequences in economic energy system terms of three alternative energy demand developments over the next 25 years: (1) no change in the ratio of energy demand to economic output, (2) moderate conservation (approximately 12.5 percent reduction in the ratio over 25 years), and (3) accelerated conservation (23 percent reduction). To facilitate comparison among the three demand patterns, a similar supply strategy was used in each. The conclusions were quite clear-cut. Accelerated conservation proved to have a market impact on the overall balance of payments situation and the pattern of economic growth. Economic growth in the no-change and moderate conservation demand scenarios proved to be both lower and more heavily skewed toward energy production. Thus conservation policies could be expected to result in more than $150 billion additional annual output by the year 2000, with a 10 percent reduction in total investment.

The report also looks at the impact of various possible shocks to the U.S. energy system over the next 25 years. These include dramatically reduced growth in the nuclear program, a delay in the implementation of rapid nuclear power growth, a two-year oil embargo, a two-year shutdown in nuclear plants as a result of an accident, and supply policies directed at energy independence. In each case the cost of the shock to the system for the gross national product was evaluated. In each case the resilience of the system proved considerably greater in the accelerated conservation demand scenarios than in the no-change demand scenarios. In fact, it proved possible to greatly delay or even to dramatically slow down the pattern of nuclear production without dramatic impact on gross national product in the accelerated conservation case. Naturally, costs in terms of greater import reliance would still exist. In neither the no-change energy demand scenario nor the accelerated conservation energy demand scenario did it prove possible to achieve energy independence by the year 1990 without significant economic costs.

Finally, the report examines the implications of alternative energy supply strategies. The examination is in the context of two energy demand scenarios: no change and accelerated conservation. It proves easier to pursue more flexible supply patterns in the case of accelerated conservation. The impact of the various energy supply policies on the economy also proves markedly less in the accelerated conservation case. This was the case for both the actual level of economic output and the structure of investment patterns within the economy.

Overall there are several major conclusions of this report. Most important, energy demand policies to be pursued over the next 25 years are critical because they have a direct impact upon economic developments, they greatly influence our ability to deal with surprises in the energy environment, and they greatly effect the flexibility with which we can pursue alternative supply policies. In fact, with what is a completely attainable goal for energy conservation, it is possible to evaluate energy supply policies not in purely economic terms, but in the more human and environmental terms that should frame the energy supply policy debate at the outset.

The computer model that has been used in this analysis is described elsewhere.[1] The reader should be aware, however, of some of its principal characteristics. The model is a global model in which 11 separate geographic regions are represented, including as separate countries the United States and Canada. The model contains economic, energy, capital goods, population, and agricultural submodels. The energy model represents supply, demand, trade, and pricing for oil, natural gas, coal, hydroelectric power, and nuclear power. The model is a dynamic simulation that is initiated in 1975 and can run scenarios either through the year 2000, as we are doing in this chapter, or further into the future. Although we will be examining demand and supply scenarios separately, it should be obvious that demand and supply portions of the model are interacting at all times in every scenario.

THREE ENERGY DEMAND SCENARIOS

The principal difference in the three scenarios we are examining in this section is the pattern of change in the relationship between energy demand and economic output of the economy. The first scenario is called the no-change scenario. This scenario is similar to the no-new-initiatives scenario of the Energy Research and Development Administration (ERDA) in that the unit energy demand per unit of economic output remains basically stable over time. The second demand scenario is called moderate conservation. In this scenario the energy demand per unit of economic output decreases over time. Specifically, between 1975 and the year 2000 there is a reduction of about 13 percent in the energy requirements of the economy in the production of every uninflated dollar's worth of output. The third scenario is one of accelerated conservation. In this scenario the unit demand requirements of economic output are reduced by approximately 23 percent over the period between 1975 and the year 2000. This scenario is slightly less optimistic than ERDA's Improved-efficiencies-in-end-use scenario and would result in total U.S. energy consumption of 133 quads in 2000.[2]

The ratio of energy demand to economic output can be seen in Figure 9.1 for all three scenarios. The units in Figure 9.1 are barrels of oil equivalent per $1,000 (1963) of economic output. It should be recog-

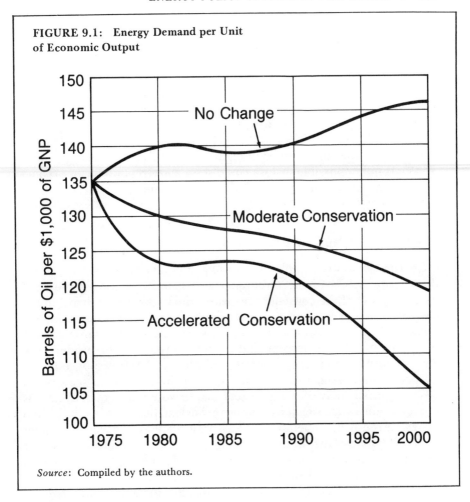

FIGURE 9.1: Energy Demand per Unit of Economic Output

Source: Compiled by the authors.

nized that the scenarios involving reduction of energy demand per unit of economic output in no way imply reduction of energy demand on a per capita basis. Energy demand per capita continues its historic increase in each of the three scenarios. In fact, even in the accelerated conservation scenario, energy demand per capita increases by nearly 50 percent in the period from 1975 to 2000 to approximately 540 million BTUs per capita. (The model is projecting U.S. population growth to 249 million in 2000, approximately a .6 percent annual rate of increase.)

It should be noted also that the accelerated conservation scenario is not at all an unlikely or impossible pattern of energy demand growth. In fact, the moderate conservation scenario is similar to the historic pattern of energy demand development, with some additional demand reduction, which could well result from recently higher energy prices. Thus the movement from the moderate conservation scenario to the accelerated conservation scenario would most likely require government initiative but would not be impossible to obtain. On the other hand, the no-change scenario cannot be ruled out either. Given increasing reliance upon relatively low efficiency energy types and electricity, higher levels of primary energy input are required in order to produce the same or reduced amounts of secondary energy delivered to the users. The energy demand per unit of output represented in Figure 9.1 is the primary energy input. Thus it is not impossible that we could see a pattern of no further reductions in energy demand per unit of economic output.

The Growth of Nuclear Production

Let us turn now to some of the consequences for the economy and for the energy system of the three energy demand scenarios. Figure 9.2 illustrates one of the consequences with primary impact perhaps on the environment, but also with economic implications. That figure shows the number of 1,000-megawatt nuclear plants operating with a capacity factor of approximately 65 percent that would be required to produce the amount of nuclear energy computed by the model in response to the energy demand scenarios. For instance, in the no-change scenario in 1975, approximately 36 such nuclear plants would be required. This is in fact a somewhat smaller number of nuclear plants than the United States currently has operating; the current plants are normally smaller than 1,000 megawatts. In the no-change scenario the number of nuclear plants grows to approximately 335 in 1985 and to nearly 1,600 in the year 2000. This number of nuclear plants is higher than that estimated by ERDA in its no-new-initiative scenario, and considerably higher than the Edison Electric Institute's high nuclear scenarios.[3] It is more like the earlier estimates of nuclear growth of the Atomic Energy Commission.[4]

There are several reasons for this. For instance, ERDA's scenario specifies a somewhat higher growth rate in other relatively capital-intensive energy sources such as solar and oil shale than has been used in our model runs. Most important, however, is the fact that this analysis uses an integrated and dynamic model. In ERDA's no-new-initiative scenario, oil imports in 2000 prove to be 10.6 billion barrels—at *today's* price that would cost over $130 billion. The world model used here cannot produce an increase to that level of imports at a price per barrel that would allow it financially. (It should also be noted that such heavy reliance on imports very near the time of maximum world oil production could be suicidal.)

In our moderate conservation scenario the number of nuclear plants

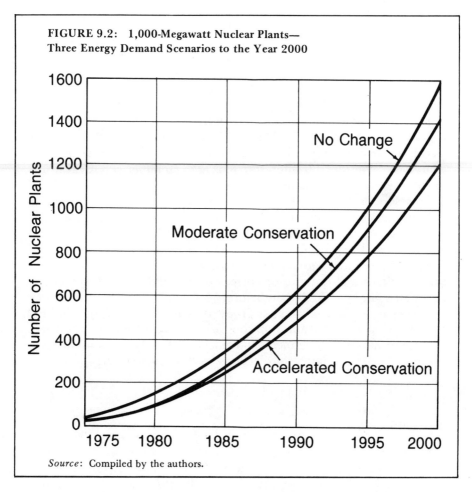

FIGURE 9.2: 1,000-Megawatt Nuclear Plants—
Three Energy Demand Scenarios to the Year 2000

Source: Compiled by the authors.

grows in much the same way in the first five years, obviously because investment patterns and decisions in the nuclear area have long lead times and cannot be changed quickly. But by the year 2000, at least 100 fewer nuclear plants are required in the moderate conservation scenario. Finally, in the accelerated conservation scenario, the number of nuclear plants grows to fewer than 300 in 1985 and to just over 1,200 in the year 2000. Again, these numbers are higher than many estimates, for the reasons noted above.

There can be little question that the numbers of nuclear plants we are talking about here are quite high. The reader should be aware, however, that even somewhat higher estimates of the number of nuclear plants than are shown in Figure 9.2 for the year 2000 would still produce less total energy than the United States currently consumes in the form of oil. Perhaps even more importantly, the total energy production from those nuclear plants, even in the no-change scenario, is less than half of the current total U.S. energy production. Most of that production, of course, is concentrated in oil and natural gas. Between 1975 and the year 2000 production patterns in those two fuels vary relatively little compared to historic variation. Moreover, they vary little compared to what is likely to occur after the year 2000 when domestic reserves and resources are largely exhausted and production in oil and gas decreases fairly rapidly. Thus it is of considerable interest to look at the number of nuclear plants in our three demand scenarios if we project forward past 2000 up to 2025. This is done in Figure 9.3.

In the no-change scenario the number of nuclear plants in the year 2000 reaches nearly 1,600; projecting to 2025 the number increases to nearly 4,500. The results are equally dramatic in the moderate conservation and accelerated conservation scenarios. In each case the number of nuclear plants and the rate of nuclear plant building have to increase faster after the year 2000 than before. Most energy studies that assume replacement of some oil and gas production between 1975 and the year 2000 by nuclear production stop short of drawing the full consequences of their scenarios' commitments to nuclear power. Those consequences can only be seen in longer projections such as those in Figure 9.3.

The Oil Import Bill

Moving to another result of our three scenarios, we can see in Figure 9.4 the dollar cost of oil imports in the United States in 1963 constant dollars. In the no-change scenario those dollar costs increase by approximately a factor of four over the 25-year period. In the moderate conservation scenario the increase is a factor of three and in the accelerated conservation scenario the increase is by approximately a factor of two. It should come as little surprise to us that such an increase in the oil import bill would have a considerable impact on the U.S. balance-of-payments situation. That impact is shown in Figure 9.5.

The indicator in Figure 9.5 is of the cumulative balance-of-payments surplus or deficit beginning in 1975 and carried through the year 2000. In the no-change scenario the United States begins by running a small balance-of-payments surplus but by 1985 has a cumulative deficit. That cumulative deficit accrues until the year 2000 when it reaches approximately $50 billion. In the moderate conservation scenario the United States again begins with a positive balance of payments, moves into deficit

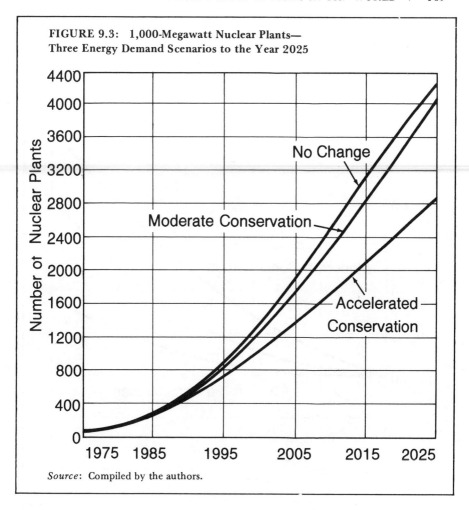

FIGURE 9.3: 1,000-Megawatt Nuclear Plants—
Three Energy Demand Scenarios to the Year 2025

Source: Compiled by the authors.

by 1985, but begins again to run a positive and relatively balanced pattern until the end of the century, culminating in a $77 billion cumulative surplus.

The balance-of-payments surplus and deficit pictures shown in Figure 9.5 also, of course, represent trade balances in nonoil commodities including food. This is important because in the runs of the world model used in this analysis, food exports and the price of food were increasing and contributing considerably on the positive side of the balance of payments. If for any reason prices fail to rise in real terms in the food area or exports do not continue to increase, the figures in Figure 9.5 would be commensurately reduced.

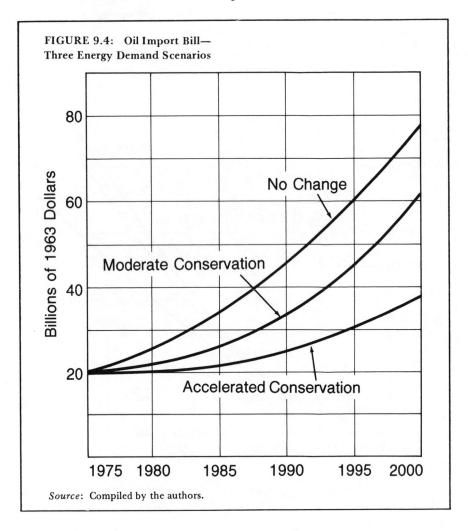

FIGURE 9.4: Oil Import Bill—
Three Energy Demand Scenarios

Source: Compiled by the authors.

The Economic Impact

Naturally, the cost of oil imports in the balance-of-payments situation does have an impact on the economy. In Figure 9.6, we see the gross national product of the United States in billions of constant 1963 dollars. In the no-change scenario the GNP grows from $980 billion in 1975 to $1,992 billion in the year 2000. In contrast, the GNP in the moderate conservation scenario grows to $2,149 billion, $150 billion higher (7.5 percent) than in the no-change scenario. Most of this difference is a direct result of the increased cost of oil imports and the cumulative balance-

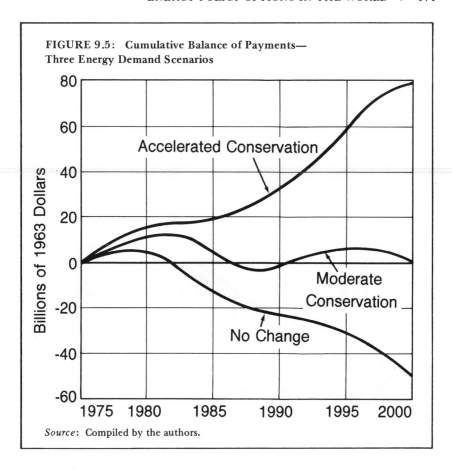

FIGURE 9.5: Cumulative Balance of Payments—
Three Energy Demand Scenarios

Source: Compiled by the authors.

of-payments surplus. In the accelerated conservation scenario the GNP grows even slightly higher than in the moderate conservation scenario, to $2,158 billion. The difference between the accelerated conservation scenario and the moderate conservation scenario is not that great because in both scenarios the balance of payments was positive or nearly balanced.

These differences in gross national product are not great considering the absolute magnitudes of GNP growth in all three cases. However, the differences in gross national product in the three cases underestimate the total impact of the three demand scenarios. Another consideration is the proportion of the economic capital and economic product that are concentrated in the energy sector and not producing for nonenergy consumption. Figure 9.7 gives us some indication of the pattern of investment in energy in response to the three demand scenarios. Specifi-

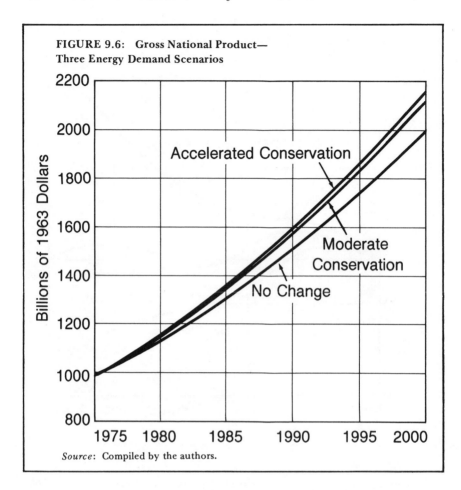

FIGURE 9.6: Gross National Product—
Three Energy Demand Scenarios

Source: Compiled by the authors.

cally, it shows the ratio of energy investment to total investment in the economy. Actually, the ratio somewhat underestimates the total energy investment demand because it does not include the energy transportation and distribution systems.

In the no-change scenario, energy investment grows from 19 percent of total investment to nearly 28 percent in the year 2000. In contrast, in the moderate conservation scenario, energy investment grows from 19 percent to 22 percent and in the accelerated conservation scenario, energy investment is relatively stable. The reason for the difference is in part the higher investment in nuclear energy required in the no-change and moderate conservation scenarios and at least equally a result of higher investment demands in the coal sector (including coal-fired gener-

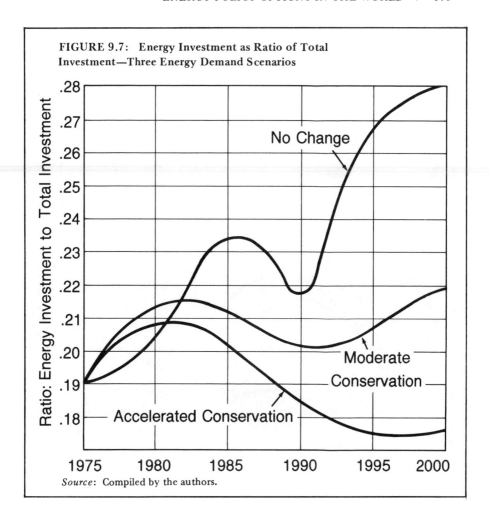

FIGURE 9.7: Energy Investment as Ratio of Total Investment—Three Energy Demand Scenarios

Source: Compiled by the authors.

ating plants). All three of these scenarios relied more heavily until 2000 on growth in coal than on nuclear energy. Thus to repeat, the reduction in gross national product resulting from failure to reduce consumption is part of the story and another part is the increased investment require-ment of the energy sector under such circumstances.

The Impact on Prices

Still another impact of the different energy demand scenarios can be seen in Figure 9.8. There the price of imported oil in 1963 dollars per

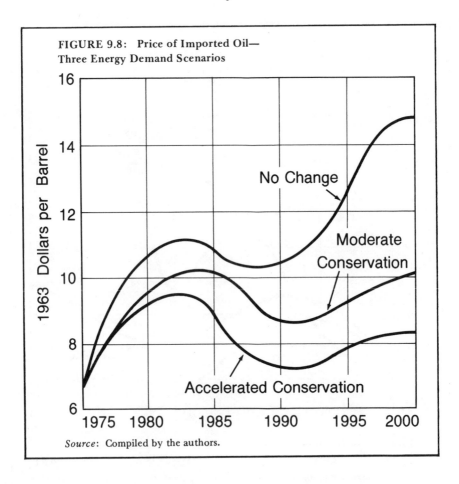

FIGURE 9.8: Price of Imported Oil—
Three Energy Demand Scenarios

Source: Compiled by the authors.

barrel is traced over time for each of the three scenarios. Obviously that price depends upon more than the energy demand policy in the United States. For the purposes of Figure 9.8 it was also assumed that other OECD (Organization for Economic Cooperation and Development) countries would follow the lead of the United States in adopting one of the three demand scenarios. In each scenario there is some further rise in the real price of oil between 1975 and 1980. The rise, however, is significantly less in the accelerated conservation scenario. In that scenario the subsequent erosion of oil prices in real terms is also considerably greater. In none of the scenarios was there any expectation that oil prices would fall to pre-1970 levels. Nor was there in any of the scenarios, with the possible exception of the no-change scenario, any indication of further dramatic oil price increases prior to the end of the century. Nevertheless, the increases suggested in both the no-change and the moderate conservation scenarios would be significant contributors to inflation and consumer discontent in all of the OECD countries.

This overview of the impact of three different patterns of demand has been relatively brief, and it has focused primarily on the United States. There is of course a great deal more detail from each of these scenarios that could be presented. Nevertheless, the general conclusion should be fairly obvious. As suggested earlier, energy demand policy is of critical importance. It is critical because the impact of different demand patterns is very substantial—on the overall pattern of economic growth, on the portion of that economic growth that contributes to the material well-being of U.S. citizens, and on the stability of prices. There is still another implication, however, of various demand scenarios. The vulnerability of the U.S. energy system and its economy to disruption from future surprise events (whether they be oil embargos, abrupt changes in oil prices, or changes in nuclear policy) is considerably greater in the no-change energy demand scenario than in the conservation scenarios. We shall see the differences in the next section.

THE EFFECTS OF POSSIBLE SHOCKS TO THE ENERGY SYSTEM

There are a number of developments that could quite dramatically affect patterns in the energy system. For instance, if a decision were made, perhaps on environmental grounds, to greatly retard the development of the nuclear program in this country, what would be the results?

Nuclear Program Retardation

In Figure 9.9 we see what such possible retardation of the nuclear program could mean. That figure shows four scenarios. It shows the no-change scenario that we saw earlier, relying in part on nuclear power, the accelerated conservation scenario that we saw earlier, also relying in part on a nuclear option, and the same two demand scenarios relying upon nonnuclear options. The figure shows some growth in the number of nuclear plants even with the nonnuclear options, since any scenario with no nuclear growth would be very unlikely. Yet in the no-change scenario the nonnuclear option holds nuclear growth to 250 one-thousand-megawatt plants by the year 2000. In the accelerated conservation scenario, nuclear plant growth is only to 130 plants by 2000.

Now let's turn to some of the implications of that scenario. In Figure 9.10 we see the oil import dollar cost in billions of 1963 constant dollars.

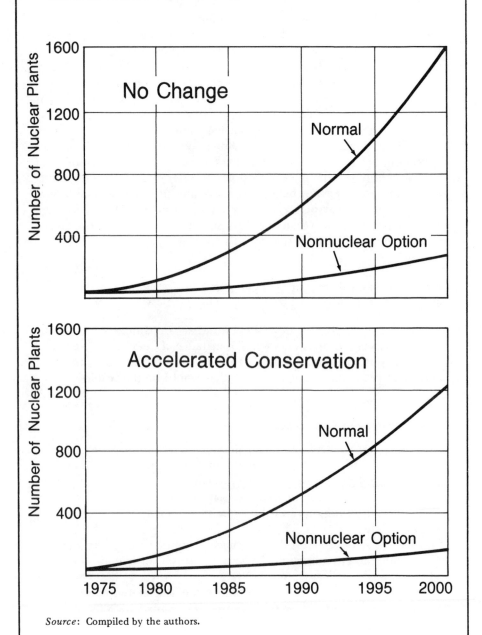

FIGURE 9.9: Nuclear Plants of 1,000-Megawatt
Size under Nuclear Program Retardation

No Change

Normal

Nonnuclear Option

Accelerated Conservation

Normal

Nonnuclear Option

Source: Compiled by the authors.

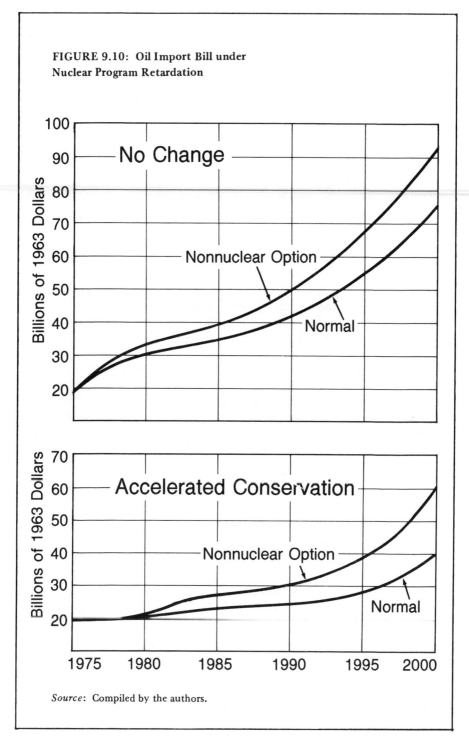

FIGURE 9.10: Oil Import Bill under
Nuclear Program Retardation

No Change

Billions of 1963 Dollars

Nonnuclear Option

Normal

Accelerated Conservation

Billions of 1963 Dollars

Nonnuclear Option

Normal

1975   1980   1985   1990   1995   2000

Source: Compiled by the authors.

In the no-change energy demand scenario annual oil imports grow from $20 billion to $94 billion with a nonnuclear option, in contrast to a growth culminating at $76 billion annually in the nuclear option scenario. The difference, $18 billion annually, is close to the current oil import bill. In the accelerated conservation scenarios the differences between the nuclear option and the nonnuclear option are relatively similar, with the difference in the year 2000 on an annual basis again being approximately $20 billion. An amount of $20 billion is not a great deal to an economy of over $1 trillion. But the cumulative impact on the balance-of-payments situation, particularly in the no-change scenario with an already very unsatisfactory balance-of-payment situation, is very large.

Balance of payments does affect economic growth, as we can see in Figure 9.11. In the no-change scenario, using a nuclear option as part of the overall energy supplied mix, GNP grew to just short of $2 trillion. Retarding greatly the growth of nuclear plants, the GNP grows to only $1,800 billion, less than a doubling of a current value and a relative loss of 10 percent. In the accelerated conservation scenarios there is a contrast. The difference in economic growth between the nuclear option and the nonnuclear option is relatively insignificant. There are a number of reasons for this. Among the most important is the fact that in the accelerated conservation scenario, with the nuclear option, there was an ongoing balance of payments of surplus. This contrasted quite sharply with a large balance of payments of deficits being run in the no-change scenario. Thus there was some economic slack in the system to facilitate a greater level of oil imports in the accelerated conservation scenario.

Nuclear Program Delay

It might be argued that the greatly retarded nuclear scenario is a very unlikely possibility. A delayed nuclear scenario is, however, much more feasible and may be developing. Increasingly, the pattern of nuclear plant growth by 1985 shown earlier looks difficult to obtain. In this scenario nuclear plant growth was slowed down considerably for ten years, keeping nuclear plants by 1985 under 100, and then allowed to proceed. In the no-change demand scenario, the number of nuclear plants in the delayed nuclear option still reaches 900 by the end of the century, a number well within the range of many nuclear scenarios currently being developed. In the accelerated conservation scenario, the number of nuclear plants under the delayed nuclear option reaches only 616 by the end of the century, a quite conservative estimate of the number likely to be built.

In both of the two delayed nuclear scenarios, the number of nuclear

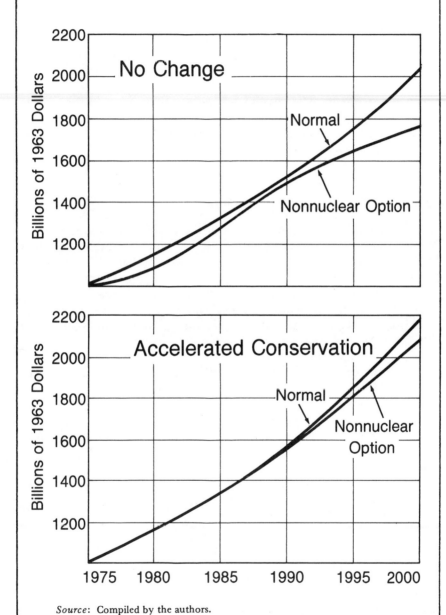

FIGURE 9.11: Gross National Product under
Nuclear Program Retardation

No Change

Normal

Nonnuclear Option

Accelerated Conservation

Normal

Nonnuclear
Option

Source: Compiled by the authors.

plants by the year 2000 is approximately 600 fewer than in the normal scenarios. Thus it is not too surprising that the bill for oil imports increases roughly the same amount for both of the delayed nuclear options. The two delayed nuclear options result in approximately $9 billion *annually* higher oil import costs by 2000 than the normal no-change and accelerated conservation scenarios. Again, the delayed nuclear option has relatively little economic impact in the accelerated conservation scenario. In contrast, the delayed nuclear option reduces total economic activity in the year 2000 by over $100 billion from its value in the normal no-change scenario. The reasons are much the same as in the greatly retarded nuclear scenarios, namely the relatively greater vulnerability to the increased oil bill in the no-change scenario than in the accelerated conservation scenario.

The Impact of a Second Oil Embargo

Another kind of shock to the system that could occur and that many fear is a repeated oil embargo of the kind the United States faced in 1973 and 1974. The next two scenarios introduce exactly that kind of embargo for the years 1990 and 1991 to see the impact. Again, the two scenarios with the embargo are contrasted with the normal accelerated conservation and no-change demand scenarios without an embargo. The results can be seen in Figure 9.12 where we see the oil import bill in billions of 1963 constant dollars over the next 25 years.

In the no-change demand scenario the embargo results in a decrease in oil import costs from a level of $40 billion in 1989 to a level of $11 billion in 1990. Obviously, the oil embargo being postulated here is more successful in reducing the level of oil imports into the United States than was the one we have already faced. This may be a reasonable assumption given the increased dependence of the United States on OPEC and particularly on Arab oil sources. We can see further that the disruption to the energy system and to the economic system results in a lower level of oil imports in 1995 in the embargo case than in the no-change and no-embargo case. By the year 2000 the system has largely recovered, but oil imports are still at a slightly lower level.

In the accelerated conservation scenarios the embargo results in a drop of oil imports from a level of $23 billion in 1989 again to a level of approximately $11 to 12 billion in 1990. The base level for continued oil imports in both embargo scenarios are similar because the alternative sources from which to import oil are much the same in both scenarios. Again in the accelerated conservation embargo scenario, the shock to the energy system of the oil embargo results in lower oil imports for the

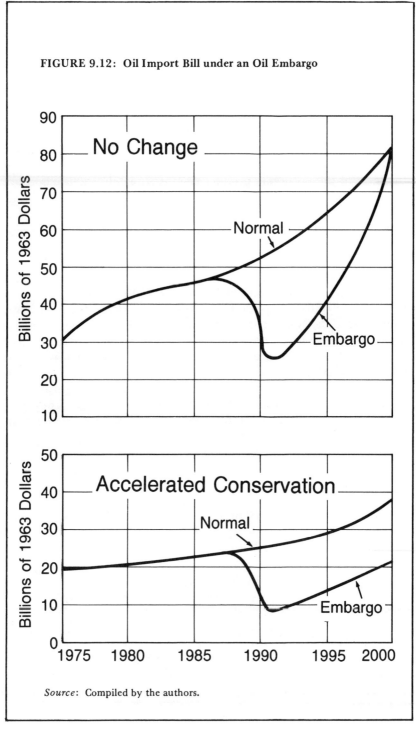

FIGURE 9.12: Oil Import Bill under an Oil Embargo

Source: Compiled by the authors.

period after the embargo to the end of the century when compared to the level of oil imports in the no-embargo case.

We can see the economic impact of these two embargo scenarios in Figure 9.13 showing the gross national product in billions of 1963 constant dollars for the four scenarios. In the no-change energy demand scenarios the embargo results in a drop of the economy from $1,522 billion in 1989 to $1,414 billion in 1990, somewhat over $100 billion or 7 percent. The economy does not recover in 1991 when the embargo continues and furthermore does not recover by 1995 or by 2000 when the level of the economic product is approximately $200 billion lower than in the comparable no-change energy demand scenario without an embargo.

In contrast to this, in the accelerated conservation scenarios the embargo results in a lower drop between 1989 and 1990, and the economy recovers by 1995 and is at the same level in the year 2000 in both embargo and no-embargo cases.

Again here we find a situation in which the economy is more robust and less susceptible to disruption from the energy system in the accelerated conservation demand scenario than in the no-change demand scenario. The reason here is not the balance-of-payments situation as in the nuclear scenarios discussed above. Instead the reason is primarily the lesser shock to the system initially because of a lower dependence on oil. Second, there is greater slack in the remaining energy system in the accelerated conservation scenario since that system is not producing at maximum capacity to fill the rapidly increasing demand of the no-change scenario.

The Impact of a Nuclear Accident

It would be interesting to compare the results of such a two-year-long oil embargo with the results of a nuclear accident resulting in the closing of nuclear plants for a similar period. This scenario has also been examined. Specifically, it was hypothesized that in 1990 some sort of nuclear accident occurred that resulted in the closing down for two years of nuclear plants in the United States after which time problems were resolved and nuclear production from the plants resumed. Other scenarios with different assumptions about the response to nuclear plants have also been run. For instance, it might be possible that nuclear plants would not close down for two years and then reopen, but would close down for a much longer period while alterations were being made to existing plants. It is also possible that the response to a major nuclear accident would be either complete closure indefinitely of nuclear plants or a ban on invest-

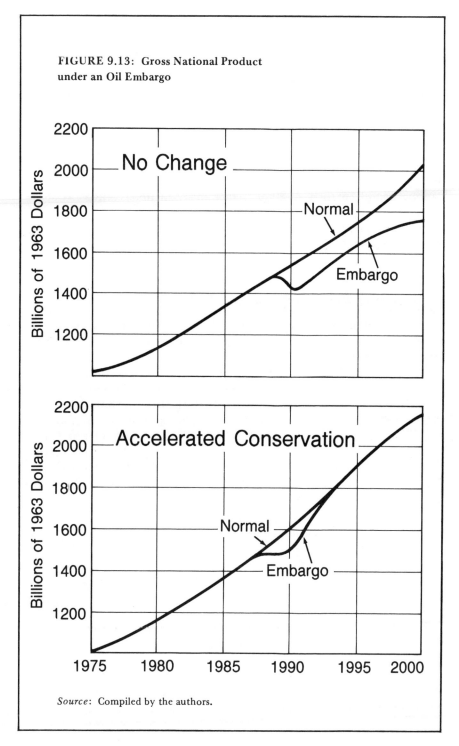

FIGURE 9.13: Gross National Product
under an Oil Embargo

No Change

Normal

Embargo

Accelerated Conservation

Normal

Embargo

1975   1980   1985   1990   1995   2000

Source: Compiled by the authors.

ment in the nuclear area and gradual deterioration of nuclear production levels from remaining and depreciating nuclear plants. The reason we are reporting on this particular nuclear scenario here is obviously because of its comparability with the oil embargo scenario just discussed.

In fact the economic impact of the two scenarios proved much the same. In the the no-change energy demand situation the nuclear accident results in a loss of economic product at the end of the century of $175 billion annually. In the accelerated conservation demand pattern the nuclear accident scenario results in much less reduction in the gross national product at the year 2000. In fact, the reduction is only $25 billion annually. Again the primary reasons for the greater robustness of the economy in the accelerated conservation scenarios include greater slack in the energy supply system as a result of slower energy demand growth.

The Impact of Energy Independence Policies

The final shock to the economic and energy system that we will be examining in this section is an effort to obtain energy independence by 1990. Although the possibility of obtaining energy independence for the United States by 1985, and even by the turn of the century, has been largely, if not totally, discredited, it would be interesting to ask what the cost to the economy might be of efforts to push ahead with such policies. Figure 9.14 suggests the impact on gross national product of gradually eliminating oil imports for both the no-change and the accelerated conservation energy demand scenarios. In the no-change demand scenario, achieving independence from foreign oil imports by 1990 through a gradual phasing out of those imports results in a loss of economic product in the year 2000 of $500 billion in comparison with the normal no-change scenario. In the accelerated conservation demand scenarios, the same movement to obtain independence by 1990 results in a slightly lower, but very comparable, loss in total economic product. Thus, in contrast to the previous shock scenarios that we have run, the movement toward independence would be such a severe shock to the overall energy and economic systems that it would disrupt those systems even with accelerated conservation.

The scenarios run in this section of the report have produced numbers that should be considered suggestive rather than definite. The object of this exercise has been to show relative impact of different types of shocks to the energy and economic systems and the relative impact of those shocks in the context of different energy demand policies. Although it has been said already in this report, it bears repeating that energy demand policies are critical to the development of the energy system.

FIGURE 9.14: Gross National Product under an Energy Independence Policy

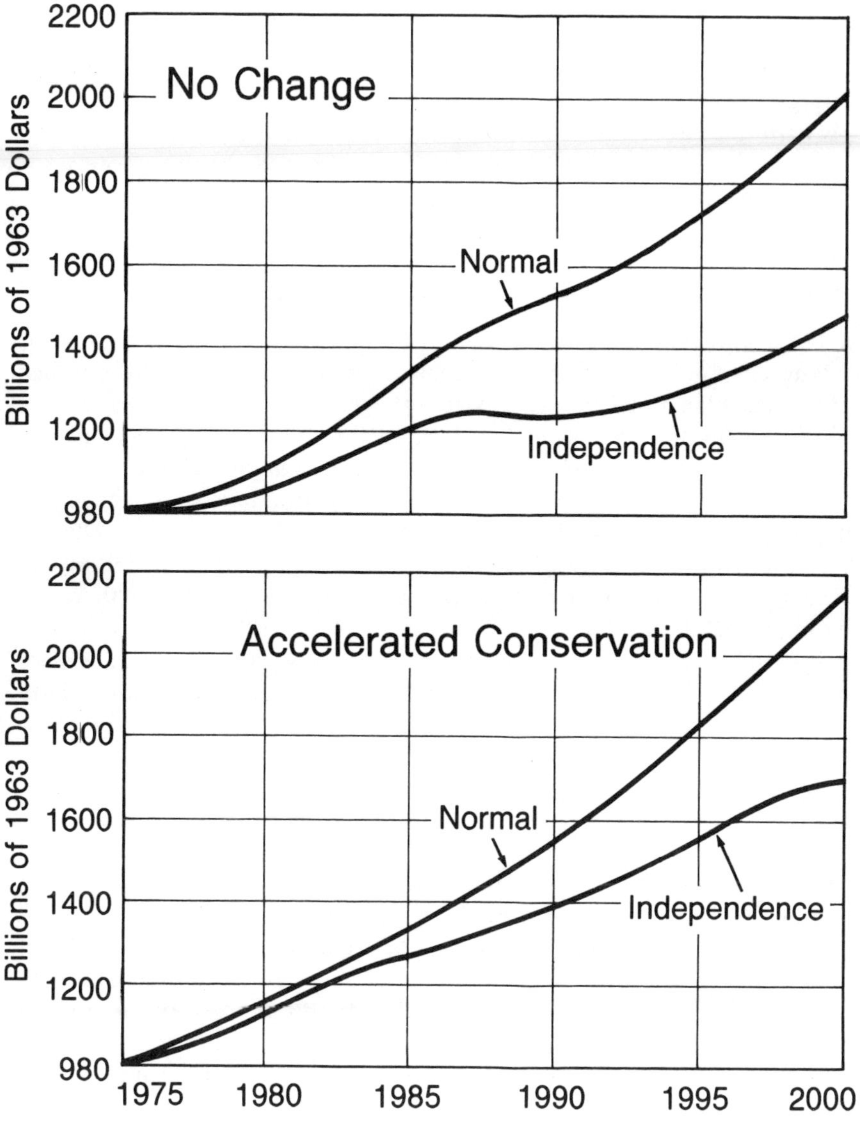

Source: Compiled by the authors.

ALTERNATIVE ENERGY SUPPLY SCENARIOS

In this section several alternative energy supply strategies are analyzed in light of the alternative demand patterns described above. Specifically, strategies are examined relying upon more rapid nuclear development, faster coal exploitation, and greater oil imports. Each of these is considered in the context of both the no-change energy demand scenario and the accelerated conservation energy demand scenario. The questions of interest concern the impact of alternative energy supply policies on supply patterns and on the economy. We are also interested in looking at the interaction between our policies regarding energy demand and our policies in the energy supply area.

Supply Policies and No-Change Energy Demand

Let us look first at alternative energy supply policies in the context of the no-change energy demand scenario. Figure 9.15 shows the number of nuclear plants of 1,000-megawatt size that would be required in each of four scenarios. We have already seen the number of nuclear plants (1,600) required in the normal or baseline no-change scenario. The figure shows that in the high nuclear scenario the number of nuclear plants by the year 2000 is nearly 200 greater than in the baseline no-change scenario. In the high coal scenario and especially in the high oil import scenario, the number of nuclear plants is considerably fewer than the baseline (1,360 in 2000).

If avoidance of nuclear waste problems and environmental impact problems were our primary criteria, we would obviously move toward the high import strategy. There are obviously costs in terms of trade associated with this course. Even in the no-change scenario the annual cost of oil imports increases by nearly a factor of four to a level of $76 billion (1963). High nuclear or high coal scenarios would reduce that somewhat (to as "little" as $62 billion), but the high oil import scenario would further increase the cost to an annual level of $88 billion.

Figure 9.16 shows the cost of the high coal scenario. The indicator in that figure is the number of coal cars that could be filled by the annual coal production (in millions). Coal production of the United States in 1975 would fill 21 million coal cars. That would increase in the normal no-change energy demand scenario to 73 billion coal cars in the year 2000. The high nuclear scenario and especially the high oil import scenario would reduce the number of coal cars that could be filled by annual production from the no-change baseline case, but in none of the scenarios would there be much less than a tripling of coal production by the end of the century. In the high coal scenario the production level increases nearly fivefold.

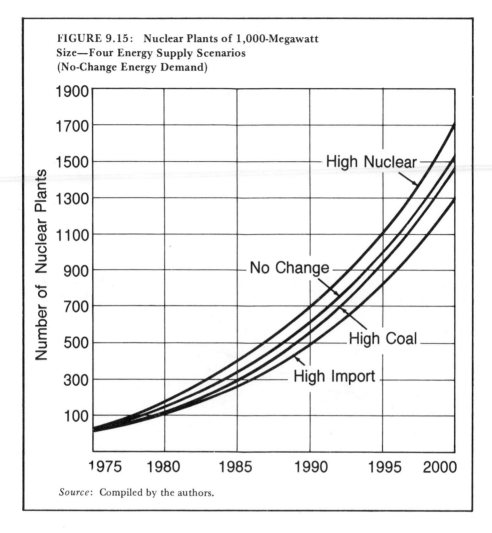

FIGURE 9.15: Nuclear Plants of 1,000-Megawatt Size—Four Energy Supply Scenarios (No-Change Energy Demand)

Source: Compiled by the authors.

Turning to Figure 9.17, we can see the economic impact of the various supply scenarios. Again we have already seen the baseline no-change economic growth pattern reaching $1,993 billion in the year 2000. In both the high nuclear and high coal scenario economic growth is somewhat greater, especially in the high coal scenario. The reasons for this lie in the U.S. balance-of-payments situation and its vulnerability to the greater oil import costs in the no-change energy demand scenario. Because the high nuclear coal scenarios both reduce that vulnerability, economic growth is somewhat greater than in the baseline no-change energy demand scenario. In contrast, the high oil import scenario leads to a level of economic output in the year 2000 that is nearly $150 billion

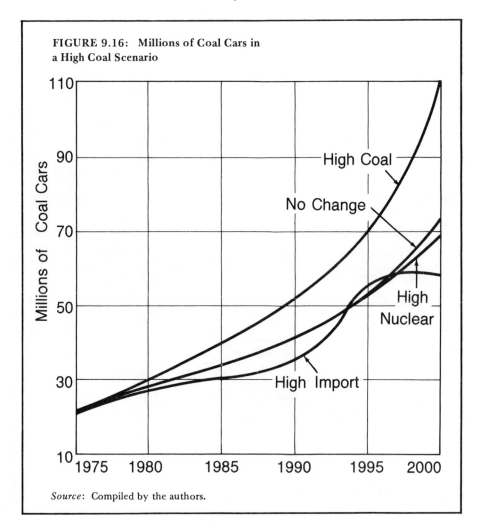

FIGURE 9.16: Millions of Coal Cars in a High Coal Scenario

Source: Compiled by the authors.

less (7.5 percent) on an annual basis than in the baseline case and nearly $400 billion less than in the high coal scenario.

If our only concern, or our primary concern, were the level of economic output, we would in this situation be likely to support either the high coal or a high nuclear scenario. Obviously environmental concerns must also be weighed. There is still another criterion for judgment. In both the high nuclear and the high coal scenarios there is even faster growth in the ratio of energy investment to total investment than in the no-change scenario, which in itself led to very considerable growth in the ratio (from 16 percent of investment in 1975 to 28 percent in 2000). Surprisingly, the high nuclear scenario only slightly increases the investment ratio, in part

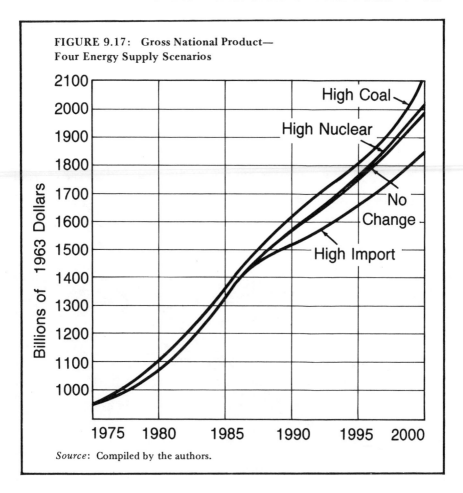

FIGURE 9.17: Gross National Product—
Four Energy Supply Scenarios

Source: Compiled by the authors.

because of the higher cost associated with the nuclear strategy, resulting in overall higher energy prices and thus some reduction in total energy demand. The high oil import strategy, to no one's surprise, leads to the least rapid rate of growth in the energy investment ratio, although it still increases considerably near the end of the century (reaching 25 percent). We can see, therefore, that at least in the light of a no-change energy demand scenario, energy supply policies have quite different consequences for the economy.

Supply Policies and Accelerated Conservation

The same energy supply scenarios show different results in the context of the accelerated conservation demand pattern. Figure 9.18 shows the

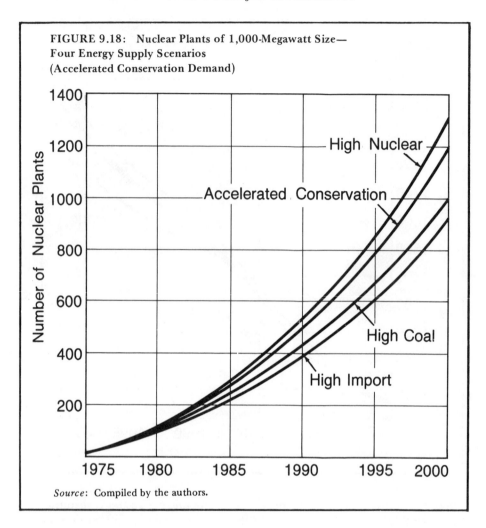

FIGURE 9.18: Nuclear Plants of 1,000-Megawatt Size—
Four Energy Supply Scenarios
(Accelerated Conservation Demand)

Source: Compiled by the authors.

number of nuclear plants in the four supply scenarios. These range from 941 by the year 2000 in the high oil import case to 1,328 in the high nuclear scenario. The difference of nearly 400 nuclear plants is only slightly less than the difference found in the supply scenarios for the no-change energy demand scenario. This is in itself meaningful, because proportionately that means the variability in our scenarios is greater in the accelerated conservation demand case than in the no-change demand case. It proved somewhat easier to develop more flexible energy supply scenarios with accelerated conservation than with no-change in demand patterns. The reason is fairly clear; it was necessary in the no-change energy demand scenario case to develop all energy supply options as rapidly as possible. There proved to be relatively little slack in the system allowing the option of switching fairly dramatically from one energy type to another energy type.

The same increased flexibility appears in the oil imports bill. The cost ranges in the year 2000 from $27 billion annually in the high coal supply scenario to $56 billion annually in the high oil import scenario—a total range of $29 billion. The range in the no-change energy demand scenario was $26 billion—absolutely and relatively a lesser amount. Most important, in the no-change demand scenario the lowest level of oil imports in 2000 (in the high coal scenario) was $62 billion.

Going still further with this point, the gross national product in billions of 1963 dollars for the four energy supply scenarios associated with the accelerated conservation demand case varies little. Gross national product level in the year 2000 ranges only from $2,137 billion in the high oil import scenario to $2,169 billion in the high coal scenario. Clearly, the supply scenarios in the accelerated conservation demand case show much less impact on the gross national product than the no-change demand case. Moreover, as we have indicated before, the relative variability in the supply scenarios is actually greater in the accelerated conservation case than in the no-change case. The strong conclusion is that accelerated conservation policies could afford much more flexibility in energy supply, without damage to the economy.

Figure 9.19 shows again the energy investment ratio to total investment in the four supply scenarios. Although there is considerable variation in the year 2000, the range is from 14 percent of total investment in the high oil import case to 19 percent in the high coal scenario. Not only is the variability less than in the no-change energy demand scenario, but the impact on U.S. citizens would be considerably less, because in no case is there a dramatic change from the current investment patterns. Examination of cumulative energy investment over the next 25 years in each of the supply scenarios makes clear the high cost of energy investment facing the nation but shows the possibility in all supply cases of savings approaching $300 billion (1963) over 25 years with accelerated conservation.

CONCLUSIONS

In the third section of this chapter the consequences in economic and energy system terms were sketched for three alternative energy demand developments over the next 25 years. To facilitate comparison among the three demand patterns, a similar supply pattern was used in each. The

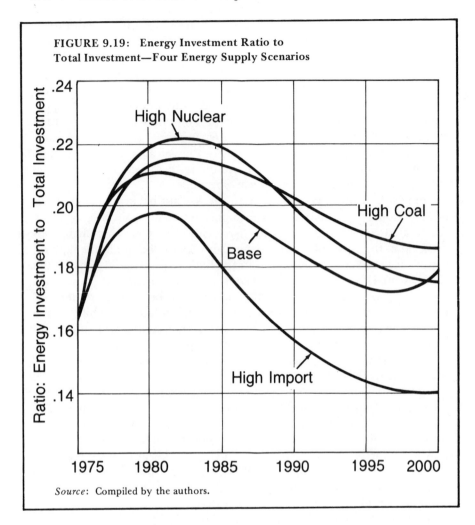

FIGURE 9.19: Energy Investment Ratio to
Total Investment—Four Energy Supply Scenarios

Source: Compiled by the authors.

conclusions were clear-cut. Accelerated conservation proved to have a
marked impact on the overall balance-of-payments situation and on the
rate of economic growth. Economic growth in the no-change and moderate conservation demand scenarios proved to be not only lower but much
more heavily skewed toward energy production. Thus conservation policies could be rewarded by more than $150 billion additional annual
output by the year 2000, by a per capita income $700 higher by the year
2000, and by energy investment requiring nearly 10 percent less of total
investment.

The fourth section looked at the potential impact of various shocks to the U.S. energy system over the next 25 years. Thcse included dramatically reduced growth in the nuclear program, a delay in the implementation of rapid nuclear power growth, a two-year oil embargo, a two-year shutdown in nuclear plants as a result of an accident, and energy independence supply policies. In each case the cost of the shock to the system for the gross national product was evaluated. In each case the resiliency of the system proved considerably greater in the accelerated conservation demand scenarios than in the no-change demand scenarios. In fact, it proved possible to delay greatly or even to slow down dramatically the pattern of nuclear production with minimal impact on gross national product in the accelerated conservation case. Naturally, there would be costs in terms of greater reliance on imports. In neither the no-change energy demand scenario nor the accelerated conservation energy demand scenario did it prove possible to pursue energy independence policies by the year 1990 without significant economic costs.

The fifth section examined the implications of alternative energy supply strategies. Again the examination was in the context of the two energy demand scenarios: no-change and accelerated conservation. It proved easier to pursue more flexible supply patterns in the case of accelerated conservation. The impact of the various energy supply policies on the economy also proved markedly less in the accelerated conservation case. This was the case for both the actual level of economic output and the structure of investment patterns within the economy.

Overall there are several major conclusions of this chapter. The first concerns the critical importance of energy demand policies to be pursued over the next 25 years. It bears repeating that demand policies are critical because they have a direct impact upon economic developments, they greatly influence our ability to deal with surprises in the energy environment, and they greatly affect the flexibility with which we can pursue alternative supply policies. In fact, with what is a completely attainable goal for energy conservation, it becomes possible to evaluate energy supply policies not in purely economic terms but in the more human and environmental terms that should frame the energy supply policy debate.

NOTES

1. Ram Dayal, *Description of the Structure of the Regionalized Multilevel World System Model* (Cleveland: Systems Research Center, 1977). Mimeographed.

2. ERDA, *A National Plan for Energy Research, Development and Demonstration* (Washington, D.C.: U.S. Government Printing Office, 1975), Vol. 1, p. IV-4.

3. Edison Electric Institute, *Economic Growth in the Future: The Growth Debate in National and Global Perspective* (New York: McGraw-Hill, 1976).

4. U.S. Atomic Energy Commission, *Nuclear Power Growth, 1974–2000* (Washington, D.C.: U.S. Government Printing Office, 1974), p. 2.

10 | Metering Economic Growth

William D. Nordhaus

It is widely believed that our economic future will *not* be simply an exponential blowup of the present: more people enjoying quantitatively more of the same goods and services. All techniques used to defend this belief—whether they are econometrics, thermodynamics, systems dynamics, or just plain good sense—agree that growth in human population will eventually cease and that the composition of consumption will undergo a transformation. What will turn out to be the ultimate stationary state—whether utopia, ecotopia, the Great Society, or the Malthusian treadmill—is the object of the current debate, as is the exact timing or transition to the stationary state.

In sorting out the issues concerning growth, the major confusion that arises is between the feasibility of future economic growth and its desirability. By and large, the Club of Rome school—Forrester, Meadows et al.—originally argued that economic growth is simply not possible, and that decline or collapse is highly plausible. Others, Mishan and Schumacher and before them Veblen and sometimes Galbraith, do not question the feasibility but find the fruits of growth quite bitter. The Edison Electric Institute report, *Economic Growth in the Future,* has attempted to examine both the normative and positive aspects of the debate, and that study is a welcome addition to the literature.[1] In what follows I will examine only the feasibility question, for it is both more central to the recent debate and logically prior to the desirability question.

THE GROWTH PROCESS

In broad brush, the process of economic growth refers to enhancement in the capability of the economy to produce goods and services. Putting aside for the moment the details of the economic tableau, as well as measurement problems, what are the sources of economic growth? Roughly speaking, there are four inputs into the growth engine: labor, capital, resources (such as energy), and technology. Of these four, it is clear that Western economic growth has been largely fueled by technological advances; recent studies estimate that at least half of the rise in measured per capita output is because of improvements in technology. Technical change has been so powerful a force that it has generally offset the diminishing returns to land and the increased scarcity of resources, such as oil or gas and certain minerals. Nor has this process been a recent phenomenon, as it extends as far back as reliable statistics go, about 100 years. It is clearly impossible to tell how long the trend will continue, but there is a great deal of technological change—some admittedly sounding a little like science fiction—in the pipeline between invention and full-scale adoption. These include computerized services and automation, microprocessing, communications, new pollution abatement equipment, new energy technologies like nuclear parks and solar farms, hydroponic agriculture. The momentum of in-the-pipeline technological change alone is probably enough to ensure substantial economic growth for 50 years without any fundamentally new discoveries. To make all this more precise, recall that over the last five decades (from 1929 to 1975) per capita potential output has grown about 2.1 percent annually with the second half showing a slightly more rapid growth than the first half. I would guess that over the next two or three decades the growth would be about this fast, perhaps a shade slower for environmental reasons. (The margin of uncertainty over the next 25 years is about one point either way, in the sense that I would take even odds that the growth rate will be in the range of 1.0 to 3.0 percent annually.) Subject to the reservations that follow, this pattern implies that the economic standard of living of the average consumer or household, or the ability to buy his or her chosen bundle of goods, doubles every 40 years or so.

The bird's-eye view of economic growth just described hides much of the economic terrain. Descending from the heights, we see several distortions making the picture of secular progress less sharp. The first is the superposition of irregular waves upon the more or less steady growth of output. Recall that the growth described above referred to *potential* output, or the potential that the economy would produce at a uniform potential rate of utilization of its productive capacity. Because of spurts or pauses of private and public spending, and more recently influenced by government stabilization policy, the path of actual output revolves around the potential path; a "gap" in which output is below potential brings with it unemployment, lower hours, low profits, and a higher share of wages in the national income; while a negative gap, with output above potential, brings with it balmy economic weather in the form of low unemployment but also generally high, sometimes accelerating, inflation.

There has been a great improvement in the ability of governments to control the business cycle over the last 40 years, and today fluctuations of major proportions can be forecasted and controlled. This being so, it is *prima facie* evidence that deep or prolonged recessions, such as the one experienced by the United States over the period from 1974 to present (summer 1976) are acts of government policy rather than acts of God or the devil. More important, however, it should be recognized that, within reason, the paths of potential and actual output are largely decoupled. Many defenders of the current economic system ring the unemployment alarum whenever significant or revolutionary reforms are proposed; surprisingly, they are often joined by the anxious reformers they criticize. For example, it is often heard that the environmental dilemma is jobs versus a clean environment. Sometimes the advocates of solar power argue that solar power is labor-intensive and, because it can create more jobs, it is socially more desirable than capital-intensive technologies like nuclear power. It must be emphasized in the strongest possible way that we can have whatever *aggregate* amount of employment we desire, up to the limits we are willing to tolerate with respect to the accompanying inflation, budget deficits, or other macroeconomic effects that are inherent in the particular policy that is used. In addition we can have whatever *distribution* of aggregate output we want, subject to our willingness to impose appropriate market or authoritarian policies that would be required to attain that distribution. It is often forgotten that after World War II there was a massive shift of employment from military to civilian industries, so that from the peak of 35 percent of GNP absorbed by the defense budget in 1945 the defense budget declined to 4 percent in 1947. It is inconceivable that such a rapid shift would be required by growth-directing policies.

YARDSTICKS FOR MEASURING GROWTH

The second qualification, and a much more serious one, concerns the measurement of economic progress. The customary yardstick for measuring economic growth is the Gross National Product. Several years ago James Tobin and I attempted to examine in some detail the extent to which the GNP was a reliable measure of economic progress. In doing so we found it useful to construct a welfare-oriented measure, one that was conceptually a measure of the consumption possibility of the country, rather than the production possibility. For example, a good part of the GNP really is double-counting in the sense that it simply represents replacement of worn-out equipment. Another part is "instrumental" expenditures that, although regrettable necessities to production, are not directly productive of consumer satisfactions—this group including national defense, police services, and sanitation services. In addition, we attempted in a very rough way to correct for the disamenities of urban life, such as noise and pollution, as well as to add in the uncounted services of the housespouse and fix-it-yourself types. Finally, we attempted to account for the depletion of our scarce natural resources.

When all the dust from this national accounts housecleaning had settled, we found a number of surprising things. The most important was that although GNP and other national income aggregates are imperfect measures of the economic standard of living, the broad picture of secular progress that they convey remains after correction of their most obvious deficiencies. Second, even from a scientific point of view purity has its price. In moving away from the conventional accounts, it was necessary to introduce concepts or data that have much greater imprecision and controversy than conventional accounts, such as the classification of defense as a regrettable necessity.

Beyond the crude attempt to construct more adequate measures of economic progress or decline, we must recognize that there are inherent limitations to making meaningful statements. For example, there are inherent index-number problems that arise because of the unbalanced nature of economic growth, a point to which we turn shortly. Also, the conventional (and unconventional) aggregates use market prices of a given year as weights to add together the horses, carriages, and automobiles of different years. While there are good theoretical reasons to suppose this is an appropriate procedure, it means that those whose relative values are not harmonious with the impartial but harsh verdict of the marketplace will have disagreements with the yardstick based on these marketplace values. Most important is the fact that even the purest of the economic measures is at best a measure of the consumption possibilities of a nation, or of the average household, rather than an estimate of the individual or collective "happiness" that consumption yields.

THE MICROECONOMIC TURBULENCE

The third and most serious way in which the bird's-eye view of economic growth omits the details of the growth process is in the inattention to the turmoil and convulsive structural change of the historical growth process—the rise and fall of products and communities, the joys and miseries of adaption to new technologies, occupations, and migration patterns, the differing fortunes of the various social, racial, and economic groups. In reckoning the net effects of economic growth, the most difficult dilemma posed by the recognition of structural change is that growth is inevitably a process of unbalanced structural change. The reason for the unbalanced growth is simply that the technological change referred to earlier as the source of the growth of per capita income strikes different industries or process at differential rates. Consider the illustrations of the growth of productivity presented in Table 10.1.

This informal and (for an academic) slightly embarrassing list of accomplishments of economic growth is illustrative of the way the invasion of technology into social and economic life leaves an uneven trail of results behind it. Yet behind these differential trends, and the economy's response to them, lies both the overall pattern and much of the discord of growth.

A more systematic and serious description is possible for the period from 1929 to 1973 for the United States. Table 10.2 shows the shares of eight important groups of the consumption bundle, with two durable

TABLE 10.1: Technological Change for Selected Products

	Percent Annual Growth Rate	Productivity Factor
Increase in computation speed, instruction per second 1953–75	73.3	10,000,000
Increase in speed of two-way transcontinental communication 1860–1976	7.0	112,320
Increase in copying speed 1953–76	27.0	1,200
Increase in transport speed, fastest conveyance 1860–1975	3.4	52
Increase in wheat yield per acre, U.S. agriculture 1900–75	1.3	2.6
Increase in bituminous coal mining output per employee 1901–72	1.3	2.5
Increase in haircut productivity 1939–63	.06	1.16
Increase in productivity of live performances, Mozart string quartets 1791–1975	0.0	0.0
Increase in B.A. per Yale professor 1901–75	−0.8	0.5

Source: Compiled by the author.

TABLE 10.2: Trends in Shares of Personal Consumption
Expenditures, 1929-73

Consumption	Share of Consumption Expenditures 1929	Constant Prices 1973	Change in Share[a]	Change in Price of Categories Relative to all Consumer Prices[b]
Motor vehicles	4.8	7.2	+2.4	1.08
Other durable goods	6.9	10.8	+3.9	.70
Food	26.2	19.5	-6.7	1.10
Apparel	13.0	7.9	-5.1	1.03
Energy	4.7	7.8	+2.9	.62
Other nondurable goods	6.4	9.0	+2.6	.89
Housing	10.1	16.0	+6.1	.62
Other services	27.8	21.8	-6.0	1.38
Total	100.0	100.0	0.0	—

[a] 1973 share less 1929 share.
[b] 1973 relative to 1929.

Source: Compiled by the author.

groups (motor vehicles and other), four nondurable groups (food, apparel, energy, and other), and two services (housing and other).

This table shows the rise of capital-intensive consumer goods (durable goods, housing, energy) along with the relative decline of food, apparel, and nontangible services. The last column shows the relative prices of different sectors (calculated from the national accounts deflators) for 1973 relative to 1929. Over this period the prices of "other services" rose 38 percent faster than consumer prices in general, while the prices of energy goods fell to 38 percent relative to consumer prices in general.

It is tempting to argue that the pattern of the consumption bundle has been overwhelmingly determined by differential technological change. With the exception of motor vehicles (for which the price figures are highly suspect), all sectors in the table that had higher shares showed relative price declines, while every sector that showed a decline had an increased price relative to the general consumer price level. Moreover, in as long a period as this, almost half a century, relative price movements have been dominated by productivity change. Although the broad aggregation masks much of the most dramatic changes, the general picture of rise and fall of sectors, following the evolution of technology, is clearly shown in the consumer expenditure pattern.

DE GUSTIBUS

The process of unbalanced growth of different industries, with some inevitably slow and others fast, means that the future course of economic growth is inextricably tied to the mix of future output. In the past few decades there has been no appreciable drag from slow-growth industries, like government and services, both because there has been at least some productivity in these and because (as Table 10.2 shows) the tastes of the average American have tended more toward high-productivity-growth industries like energy and consumer durables, more toward string quartets that are canned (in records and FM) than live. To put the point slightly melodramatically, *our economic future is up to our tastes.* If our tastes turn away from high-technology items like microcomputers, Sugar Pops, or touch-dial telephones toward the arts, homemade Granola, or backpacking in isolated wilderness areas, then it would appear that the possibilities for rapid economic growth are much more limited.

The unfortunate aspect of unbalanced growth, however, is that many traditions and patterns of living are shed like old skins because they are uneconomical. It is almost amusing to note that in many areas of the country, such as rural New England, the train is now the centerpiece of amusement parks—as if in a zoo for outmoded technologies. Many critics of the automobile, such as Barry Commoner in his recent book, *The Poverty of Power,* would have us believe that trains and trolleys were driven out by a wicked conspiracy of American automobile firms.[2] This would be plausible were it not quickly seen that the trend was global rather than peculiarly American. Further, almost everyone who has sat down and performed the calculations has concluded that, except in densely populated areas, automobiles drove out other forms of transportation for much the same reason that the telephone drove out the telegraph: because it performed desired services (whether transport or communication) more rapidly and cheaply than the alternative, at least by the private calculation of cost and time.

It is hard, however, not to mourn the passing of some of the old ways and technologies, as Ezra Mishan does with eloquence in his book *The Costs of Economic Growth.*[3] As we noted in Table 10.2, in the growth process the old technologies get relatively more expensive than the new, and consumers choose to spend their money on the cheaper technologies, however much they lament the passing of the old. There will be some real losses, in addition, as those few items whose prices get relatively more expensive than incomes—such as vacation land or domestic servants—become absolutely more difficult to buy. Those whose tastes tend toward the old technology may even suffer losses in real income.

RESOURCES AND THE METERING PROBLEM

A final question that must be raised in the discussion of future growth concerns the question of sheer resource adequacy: Are there sufficient energy, mineral, and environmental resources—along with the technology to use them—to allow continued expansion of the economy in both advanced and developing countries? Clearly neither mineral nor environmental resources—say, natural gas or clean air in our cities—are free goods, nor is there a strong presumption that they will become substantially cheaper than they are today. The important question, however, is whether the cost of squeezing out energy or maintaining a clean environment will become substantially more expensive in the future—so expensive, in fact, that the growth process is substantially slowed down. There is considerable evidence that, in an ideal world, if normal goods as well as environmental goods are efficiently allocated, there are ample resources to support considerable future growth. "If" is such a critical caveat, however, that the adequacy of current economic institutions is no longer clear. The reason for the difficulty is what we call the metering problem.

The major accomplishment of market economies is that they more or less automatically "meter" the production of goods and the accomplishments of people. In an efficient economy, metering occurs in such a way that firms and consumers have powerful incentives to increase the production of highly prized objects, such as food or automobiles, while economizing on the inputs of scarce resources, such as human labor. On a slightly more subtle level, human ingenuity is tapped if it can be metered, and many of our institutions, such as the patent system in the commercial sector or Nobel prizes in the scientific domain, are ways in which human ingenuity gets metered in terms of the quality of the engineering or intellectual contribution. There is, of course, no absolute way of judging how well or badly a particular set of institutions has performed, but judging by the values of the marketplace the mixed economies of the West have been enormously successful in focusing human ingenuity on market objectives.

The way that a market economy is able to focus and meter these talents is through the medium of prices. In an ideal setting, prices act as social signals: With high prices for goods like oil indicating that these are very scarce and therefore things on which consumers should try to economize, producers should try to produce more vigorously and inventors should try to invent substitute or synthetic products. In the idealization that would be both an efficient and a just economy, prices would reflect at all times both the social evaluation of what was the value of an additional unit of a good or service as well as the incremental cost of production.

Given the role of prices, it is natural to look at problems of misdirection of economic growth as ones where the price signals are incorrect. Put slightly differently, and this is the main point, *economic growth is misdirected because we are either unwilling or unable to meter the different goods and bads of economic growth and to price these goods or bads appropriately.* It is useful to illustrate this central proportion with some controversial examples from the energy sector.

First taking the case of oil, it has often been argued that if the market were allowed to allocate oil and gas by freely competitive prices over space and time, the allocation would be efficient. The reason for this is that (aside from some problems of reservoir ownership) oil and gas are already fully metered by markets in the sense that virtually all the costs and benefits of higher production are internalized to the owner and therefore he receives the proper signals for deciding when and how much to drill, how fast to produce, and so forth. An obvious exception to this is the possible influence of monopoly power, and there is little doubt that OPEC successfully exercised its monopoly power in 1973, resulting in higher prices, lower levels of production, and the ironic remark that monopoly is the conservationists' best friend. In the United States at the present time, there is a running debate between the Congress and the oil companies as to whether the domestic oil companies are abusing their market power sufficiently to warrant divestiture.

Notwithstanding the outcome of the debate about monopoly power, I have little doubt that today—taking as given the OPEC prices—price controls on oil and gas in the United States keep their prices at least temporarily below the efficient levels. If true, price controls serve to increase consumption and depletion of domestic reserves, and to increase the imports of oil and gas. The reasons for price controls are estimable. They are essentially designed to prevent the oil and gas companies from windfall gains, and to redistribute real income from these corporations to consumers. But the inescapable result is that we are pushed into a growth path that has more oil and gas consumption and greater transitional difficulties in the future.

Put differently, the social struggle over income distribution has led the United States to set the price meter on oil and gas at too low a setting. This too-low setting signals consumers that oil and gas are not really that scarce, and that no extraordinary efforts should be made to conserve them, while for producers the low setting indicates that there is no great rush to accelerate production.

EXTERNALITIES IN THE GROWTH PROCESS

The oil and gas industry is not, actually, terribly representative of the conditions under which American capitalism functions. With the exception of the period from 1971 to 1974, the private sector has set its prices and wages without any major constraints from the government. The metering problem is much more significant in areas where there are unintended consequences that are not included in market calculations. Economists have coined the term "externalities" for just those events, or parts of transactions, that are not included in market transactions. Because this concept is sometimes misunderstood or misrepresented, it is worthwhile to clarify the notion of externality before discussing its importance.

In considering environmental problems, it is useful to start with a transaction matrix for the economy. The activities of any economy consist of a very large number of transactions—a transaction being simply the exchange of a good or service from one economic agent to another. As a simple example, Figure 10.1 illustrates in a simplified way the process of air conditioning a house with electricity generated from stripmined coal. Each of the circles describes an activity or process (mining, transport, and so on); and each of the arrows and x_i processes describes a transaction (mining, acid runoff, knowledge, and so on).

Note that the 17 transactions in the figure fall into two general types: first, those that are *internal* to an individual or to the market system—that is, those for which arms-length transactions ensure that there is a more or less appropriate *quid pro quo* for the transaction. An arms-length transaction is one that certainly does not decrease the utility (or satisfaction) of either party and, on the margin, does not change utilities at all, as in, say, consumers who pay $4 per 100 kilowatt hour for purchases of electricity, x_{11}. All internal transactions in the figure (for example, the x_2, x_6, and x_{11}) are horizontal to indicate that on the margin they are not utility increasing or decreasing—that the consumer or producer just pays the marginal valuation of the transaction. A second class are those transactions that are *external* to the market and for which no appropriate *quid pro quo* is received. For these external transactions the receiver is not compensated and therefore the transaction is an external economy if the transaction increases utility, and an external diseconomy if the transaction decreases utility. These slope upward if they are on balance utility-increasing transactions, and downward if they are on balance utility-decreasing transactions.

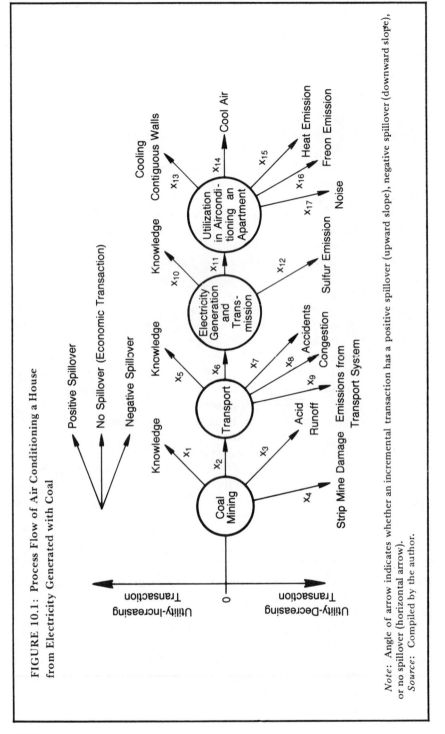

FIGURE 10.1: Process Flow of Air Conditioning a House from Electricity Generated with Coal

Note: Angle of arrow indicates whether an incremental transaction has a positive spillover (upward slope), negative spillover (downward slope), or no spillover (horizontal arrow).

Source: Compiled by the author.

In the transactional framework outlined here, the important points are that internal transactions are efficient because on the margin users just pay marginal costs, while external transactions are inefficient because users do not receive or pay compensation for all social costs or benefits. In the example shown in Figure 10.1 there are four external economies, while nine external diseconomies are listed.

Having identified the nature of externalities, we can ask briefly: *why* are externalities present? In general, they exist because transaction processes take place outside of markets. For example, the owner of a factory that is emiting sulfur into the air is "giving" polluted air to the neighbors rather than "selling" it. Were the factory forced to auction off the sulfur, it would command a nonzero *negative* price and the factory would pay those whose lungs or houses are so damaged. The nonexistence of markets generally arises from externalities because, legally, firms are not required (in the case of diseconomies) or able (in the case of economies) to bottle and sell knowledge or noise or acid runoff or automobile emission as they do oats or coal.

It is of course conceivable that air of different quality could be bought and sold in containers like different vintages of wine, but such an economy would experience such high production costs that it would have a very low standard of living. One of the functions of legislatures is just to determine legally what is and what is not appropriable by the process of internalization. Indeed, the environmental revolution arose because it was perceived that the absence of property rights in clean air or water or other risks—implicitly setting a zero price for these goods—was becoming "uneconomical." Or put differently it was thought that the high costs of metering the diseconomies (such as sulfur emissions) was worth paying because of the even higher costs in lives and property that would be paid if diseconomies were not metered but continued unabated. Another example of metering lies in the generation of knowledge, where patent systems allow the appropriation of mechanical inventions as property for 17 years to the first inventor; laws of nature cannot be monopolized but flow into the public domain immediately. Thus if the knowledge generated in mining (x_1) were patentable, this would become a horizontal line since the inventor could receive the value of the invention. Similarly, if the stack gases of the electrical generation plant were metered and priced at the proper rate for sulfur emissions (x_{12}), this diseconomy could be internalized and thereby the x_{12} activity would be efficiently supplied.

Although the idea of metering and marketing noxious by-products seems an elegant solution to the misdirection of economic growth, it must be recognized that especially in a dynamic economy there is a fundamental asymmetry in the economic incentives to meter. A profit-oriented firm will be attentive to metering and selling an effluent when it has positive

206 / WILLIAM D. NORDHAUS

value, and toward hiding or dispersing an effluent when it has negative value. Thus when the effluent has positive value, as in the case of by-product minerals or knowledge, firms will desire to separate out the mineral or patent the knowledge, thereby tending to internalize the externality. On the other hand, when the effluent is of negative value, no matter how large, as in the case of PCB in the Hudson River or asbestos in Lake Superior, there are no incentives short of scarce moral scruples to bottle and properly dispose of the effluent, and especially there are no incentives to set up the missing markets for disposal. This fundamental asymmetry in economic incentives, along with the enormous ingenuity of businessmen to invent new processes faster than bureaucrats can invent regulations, leads new inventions and processes to seek loopholes in regulations like wealthy taxpayers pouring over the tax code.

To summarize, the most important point about externalities is that when they are present, there are good *theoretical* reasons to think that markets will lead to incorrect levels of production. This is quite different from the case of nonexternality resources like oil and coal. For these nonexternality goods, a competitive market mechanism will lead to an efficient allocation over time. But if externalities are present, the system is implicitly setting a zero price on water supplies, or on health or on clean air or clean beaches. No one would be surprised if, after setting the price of labor at zero, labor were used wastefully in many situations. And it is perfectly natural that if the price of clean air is zero, it will be heavily used and abused. Thus there is a clear presumption that if there are externalities, there will be overuse and misuse of environmental resources.

I suspect, then, that the question of the cost of metering negative effluents or externalities may be a critical and up-to-now unidentified problem along future growth paths. This is not to suggest that metering costs are zero at the present: in the case of electrical or gas metering (where the name is not figurative) the metering costs of standard meters (without any fancy device like peak load or "smart" metering) is around 1 percent of the total cost. On the other hand, we see in many technologies in the chemical and energy industries that the metering costs are much higher.

TWO EXAMPLES OF UNMETERED GROWTH

In what follows we will consider two "global" metering problems, carbon dioxide and nuclear power. Although these are used primarily as illustrations of the way in which lack of metering distorts growth, they are also used because they are potentially very serious future problems. First consider the case of carbon dioxide. It is well known that continued combustion of carbon-based fuels is leading to increased atmospheric concentrations, which, by most reckonings, will lead to a substantial climatic change. For example, on a global scale the effect of carbon dioxide will be greater than the natural climatic variability within two decades, and within a century the increased temperatures will lead to a temperature outside the range of history for the last 100,000 years. The effects of this are almost impossible to calculate.

An efficient control strategy for carbon dioxide would call for metering and taxing carbon-based effluents on all sources throughout the entire globe for many years to come. This involves not only the distributional questions raised above about which countries would be most hurt, whether the losers should compensate the gainers, the level of the taxes; it also involves measuring the amount of carbon emissions, where the magnitudes will be in the order of tens of billions of tons annually.

Even more complicated than carbon dioxide is the problem of measuring and controlling the externality of diversion of nuclear materials from commercial power reactors. Much careful diplomacy went into prevention of the spread of nuclear weapons over the period from 1945, culminating in the Nuclear Nonproliferation Treaty in 1968. It is clear that with the spread of technology in peaceful power reactors the cost of a government's becoming a nuclear power is greatly and inadvertently reduced; enough weapons-grade material is created in a light-water reactor to make several dozen small bombs each year. In short, we are faced with a situation where the spread of a nuclear electrical generating industry around the world has a definite externality in the form of knowledge about and materials for construction of low-cost nuclear weapons, whether by official sources (as in the recent Indian case) or by unofficial terrorist groups (a case we have yet to witness).

There are at present quite imperfect techniques for metering the flows through the nuclear fuel cycle. These safeguards are under the aegis of the International Atomic Energy Agency in Vienna, which was formed as an adjunct to the Nuclear Nonproliferation Treaty. Many analysts feel that a more comprehensive metering system could reduce the amounts diverted to very small levels, if all countries agreed to take part in the inspection and if significantly more resources were allocated to inspection than at present. Unfortunately, both the high costs of metering these flows, as well as the strong incentives of individual countries to cheat, lead to a difficult political problem. For, while it would probably benefit all countries to set very strict inspection standards, it would pay any single country or group to cheat and develop a weapon while other countries were adhering to the agreement. This centrifugal tendency is particularly strong with a large number of countries. In the case of civilian nuclear power as well as carbon dioxide, then, the normal exonomic processes, throw off unmetered and unpaid-for by-products of enormous global significance.

In short, given the increased complexity and diversity of our future, as well as the fact that many of man's activities are beginning to affect his environment on a global level, we are faced with a dilemma. If we do not meter problems like carbon dioxide or flows of nuclear materials, we will find ourselves living in a world with unforeseen, unpredictable, and possibly catastrophic changes. Yet especially because the problems are becoming global, the political and social impediments to metering or internalizing the undesirable consequences of our activities are becoming unmanageably high. It should not be surprising, then, that many responsible analysts simply throw up their hands in despair and opt for a steady-state society, accepting the familiar ills of today in preference to the unforeseen consequences of continued economic evolution.

NOTES

1. Edison Electric Institute, *Economic Growth in the Future: The Growth Debate in National and Global Perspective* (New York: McGraw-Hill, 1976).

2. Barry Commoner, *The Poverty of Power* (New York: Knopf, 1976).

3. E. J. Mishan, *The Costs of Economic Growth* (Baltimore: Penguin, 1967).

11 | Growth in the Closed-Cycle Economy

S. Fred Singer

The nub of the matter is this: Will the price system keep us out of trouble? Will prices—as determined in a reasonably free market and representing the desires, interests, and actions of many participants—provide an adjustment mechanism, which will keep the economic machine on a path of continuing growth while avoiding going off the deep end? Will the "invisible hand" that Adam Smith so well described just 200 years ago keep us from falling off the precipice?

The free-market economist argues that the judgment of a few individuals, in government or outside it, should not be substituted for the collective wisdom of consumers and producers—all participants in the market. The neo-Malthusians, of course, tend to discount the price system. The economically more sophisticated ones point out that we don't have free markets, and that this flaw invalidates the conventional economic arguments. But they fail to point out how close markets are to being free, whether they are likely to become more free or less so, and, if they are imperfect, how they can be fixed. Well-elaborated statements of the pro-growth and no-growth views are contained in *Economic Growth in the Future*, the report of a large-scale study done by the Edison Electric Institute.[1]

The purposes of this chapter are to examine the question of whether even imperfect markets are adequate to assure a continued increase in the welfare of the population; forecast future market perfection; and examine whether markets can be or should be fixed and prognosticate whether they will be. Without being exhaustive, we will examine the operation of the price system, or equivalently of free markets, in these seven areas: (1) the formation and growth of capital; (2) the management of the physical environment; (3) the control of catastrophes, both natural and man-made; (4) the continued growth of science and technology, and the consequences in terms of productivity and economic growth; (5) natural resources, their finiteness, now and in the future, dealing with energy, mineral resources, and land; (6) population, its continued growth and distribution; (7) government, growth of complexity.

We will not be concerned with providing final and conclusive answers to the growth versus no-growth controversy. Rather we would like to move the debate into what we consider to be more fruitful channels— away from the rather indeterminate questions of whether we will run out of oil, whether pollution will become so great as to kill off the population, and so on. These specters, raised particularly in the Club of Rome study, *The Limits to Growth,* [2] have been adequately replied to and are no longer really very interesting. It is more important now to show to what extent automatic adjustments based on the price system can be relied on; and to what extent interventions are required that are not based on market forces.

CAPITAL FORMATION AND CAPITAL GROWTH

We start with capital because of all the seven items mentioned that could limit growth, capital growth should be most directly and naturally encompassed within the economic framework; therefore, in a sense, it is the simplest of the problems. Yet it is not quite so simple. Can we have a shortage of capital? Can we run out of capital in a situation of growth? The conventional economist will scoff at these questions. He will point out that when there is a scarcity of capital, that is, when there is an unwillingness of people to provide funds for capital formation, the interest rate will go up until enough capital is provided. The interest rate, therefore, takes the place of price in the usual supply-demand diagram. As the interest rate goes up, the demand for capital is decreased, but the supply is increased, and vice versa. But this is not the whole story.

The interest rate not only measures the return on capital investments, but is regarded by some as the equivalent of the social rate of discount, that is, the value that is placed on future consumption as against present consumption. But future consumption may be consumed by one's children or grandchildren, or by entirely different people, and this influences the value an individual or a group assigns to an interest rate.

Also, the interest rate embodies the expected rate of inflation. A high anticipated rate of inflation produces a high interest rate, simply because the money when returned to the investor will purchase fewer goods per dollar.

The problem of risk enters in. All things being equal, one would invest money in less risky ventures. Alternatively, more risky ventures would have to have higher interest rates in order to attract capital. Risks and uncertainty may be inherent in the venture, for example, when drilling for oil. But risks and uncertainty are also man-made: For example, if tax laws change, this will affect the profitability of certain investments and, therefore, the rate at which capital is attracted to them. Government has it within its power, therefore, to encourage or discourage investment activities, simply by reducing or introducing uncertainty. In the international sphere, there is the additional uncertainty of expropriation or nationalization.

Finally, we have the matter of the propensity to save. After all, the monies invested every year that go toward capital formation are equivalent to the goods and services that are *not* consumer that year, that is, to the fraction of GNP that does not go into consumption. Imagine a man who has no children, or equivalently one who has no concern for his children or his possible heirs. Imagine, also, that he has an adequate social security and pension program that insures him against any uncertainty. What he should do, of course, from a utility-maximizing point of view, is to consume all of his income, as well as his savings, so that when he dies his net worth will be exactly zero. His lack of interest in the future translates into an effectively higher interest rate. This makes it more difficult to raise money for private investments and puts a correspondingly greater burden on public investments financed not by voluntary savings but by taxes.

Overall, one would conclude that there would not be a "capital shortage" that could threaten an orderly long-run expansion of the economy. There is however the distinct possibility of short-run inadequacies, over a five- to ten-year span. Some of these are discussed by Henry C. Wallich and include misallocations between different sectors of the economy, and mismatches with respect to varying growth rates of the labor force.[3]

ENVIRONMENTAL MANAGEMENT

Environmental values, such as clean air and clean water, are just the opposite to capital in the sense that they are well known to be outside of the market rather than within it. Rather than being controlled by market forces, they are externalities, which have to be internalized—usually by governmental action. The reason for this, of course, is that air and, to some extent, water are public goods, available to all, and owned by no one in particular. Hence there is no incentive to conserve, protect, maintain, or clean-up, since the disbenefits can be passed along to others in the population.

Environmental amenities also are different from capital in other respects. Whereas capital is built up and thus benefits future generations, the initially available "stock of the environment" has been exploited, that is, used freely without payment, and the disbenefits have been passed along to future generations. The classic example is that of the eutrophication of lakes, and especially of Lake Erie. Whereas capital formation can be viewed as a decrease in consumption today for the purpose of increasing consumption in the future, the use of the environment is just the opposite. It is a kind of superconsumption. If the environment is overexploited today, it has to be paid for in the future and, therefore, will decrease consumption in the future.

It is a basic responsibility of government to recognize this failure of the market, which results from the fact that clean air and clean water generally enjoy no property rights. (Although courts can and do provide relief under the doctrine of "public nuisance" in cases where an individual is harmed by pollution.) With government intervention, owners would use public resources properly, so as to in some way maximize the owner's net return over a very long period of time, perhaps even spanning a generation or more. Again, the classical economist would argue that by internalizing the costs, the market imperfection is remedied. But this is only true after a fashion, and very approximately.

In the first place, how clean should the environment be? What should be the ambient standards for both air and water? And what should be the emissions from various polluting sources in order to achieve these standards? This is a very complicated question that can be settled in principle but requires much detailed work. In principle, the optimum amount of pollution is obtained when the marginal benefits derived by a further clean-up are just equal to the marginal costs involved in the cleaning up. But this statement ignores many important factors, such as: Who is receiving the benefits and who is paying the costs? What is the influence of the "dynamics," that is, of the time-path taken in achieving the "optimum" pollution standards? How is the optimum influenced by the technology and its continual evolution, by the continuing economic growth and, therefore, increasing level of effluents, and finally by the institutional methods whereby the pollution abatement is achieved? Most economists would prefer a pollution tax or effluent charge to the issuance of permits or to the imposition of strict regulatory limits.[4] In a sense, this is a detail, a market imperfection that can be fixed.

The matter of optimization over long time spans presents an additional problem. Any reasonable long-term interest rate on capital, like 3 or 4 percent a year (after correction for inflation), gives a doubling time of 20 years. This means that from an individual point of view anything that happens 50 to 100 years from now is of little consequence. This also happens to be the approximate life span of a human being—but that is coincidental. Society, however, does have a concern that spans generations. This fact can be expressed in terms of a lower societal interest rate or, equivalently, by investments in projects that would not be considered economic by accepted standards.

Among the more important scientific problems are the following: How can we recognize all of the adverse impacts on the environment produced by the emission of certain substances; how can we know the impact on, say, human health, of various levels of environmental standards for different pollutants? We need only to look at recent history to recognize that the discovery of various carcinogens in the environment has, if anything, accelerated; the recognition has been gained that freon gas from aerosol spray cans can affect stratospheric ozone. One can reasonably assume that more examples of this type will be discovered as our scientific knowledge increases.

It is in fact the global aspects of environmental pollution that cause great concern, particularly since they cannot be easily captured through market forces or internalized.[5] The classic problem is the creation of carbon dioxide through the burning of fossil fuels and the resultant well-documented increase in the carbon dioxide concentration of the atmosphere. The consensus among meteorologists and atmospheric scientists is that this will lead to a warming trend on the earth's surface. The degree of warming is hard to calculate; it involves a variety of effects that have not been put into the calculation, such as increased evaporation from the oceans with the resulting increase of cloud formation which, in turn, however, reduces the amount of solar energy reaching the earth's surface. One can calculate the effect without considering the water vapor, but it is clearly unrealistic, even though it gives some interesting and frightening upper limits. From this kind of calculation follow the horror stories about the melting of the icecaps, the rise in sea level, inundation of coastal cities, and so on. Actually there has been no warming trend; on the contrary, the major trend of the last decades has been a cooling trend. It is conventionally explained as being produced by increased turbidity of the atmosphere as a result of particulates that are only partly man-made and come mainly from volcanoes. Particulates, of course, will reflect light and thereby reduce the amount of solar radiation reaching the earth's surface.

This discussion illustrates the scientific difficulties surrounding even the best-known and best-explored of the man-made climatic effects. But even if the scientific conclusion were unambiguous, it would be impractical to stop the burning of fossil fuels or to impose a worldwide carbon dioxide pollution tax. In fact, no such proposals have been made, even by ardent environmentalists. (On the other hand, a production tax on freon would limit its use and protect the ozone layer.)

Climate is a good example to pursue further. We know from the studies of history, paleontology, geology, and such that climate has been quite unstable in the last 4 million years. There have been a series of ice ages, the last of which ended only 10,000 years ago. Little is known about the actual regions of stability of climate; therefore, the concern always exists that inadvertently we may enter a region of instability in the climatic regime, which could lead to irreversible change, irreversible on a time scale of hundreds or thousands of years.

Against this gloomy specter two things must be said. First, we don't know whether such instabilities will occur because we do something or because we *don't* do something. In other words, continuing as we are may lead to an instability with about the same probability. Second, there might be something we can do about the situation, provided we have adequate monitoring systems. Specifically, space satellites could be constructed that would intercept a small portion of the solar radiation. And this intercept could be made variable so as to regulate the climate on earth. While this may seem far out, it is scientifically straightforward and de- serves study.* Other more earth-bound schemes have been suggested, such as dropping carbon black on the polar icecap in order to melt it, or reversing the course of Arctic rivers, or similar schemes of planetary engineering. The great difficulty with those is that they are essentially irreversible, or lead to irreversible consequences. The polar cap once melted may never reestablish itself and may therefore lead to a rather permanent change in weather patterns and climate.

One can make a rather general statement about climate. Offhand, one would think that if a warming is bad, then a cooling must be good, or perhaps vice versa. Actually, any change may be bad. The simplest way to see this is to recall that we have over some thousands of years adapted ourselves to particular climatic regimes—not only human adaptation but, more importantly, adaptation of the soil. Soil formation has a time scale of hundreds or perhaps thousands of years. Therefore, any major climatic change that proceeds faster than this time scale can seriously upset agri- cultural patterns and productivity. Clearly, human adaptation by itself represents no fundamental problem—with air conditioning and heating —but an interruption of the world food supply could have more serious consequences.

Our conclusion is that the long-term effects of environmental changes are beyond the adjustment mechanism of the price system, and even beyond the ken of science. Shorter-term and more localized environmen- tal effects can be handled most efficiently by the price system, with gov- ernments performing certain essential roles without getting into details. One of the essential roles is to perform cost-benefit analyses to determine optimum levels of pollution and derive appropriate tax rates.

---

*A proposal to develop satellites to collect solar energy as an alternative source of energy is elaborated in detail in Chapter 12 by Gerard K. O'Neill.

CATASTROPHIC EVENTS

Catastrophic events are occurrences that have a very low probability, but when they happen have a very large impact. They are usually completely unanticipated. They can be divided into two categories: natural and man-made. Among the natural events are droughts, floods, volcanic eruptions, earthquakes, hurricanes, tornadoes, and even the possibility of the impact of a comet that might destroy life on a sizable portion of the earth. Among the man-made catastrophic events one would list warfare, now raised to the level of catastrophe by the use of nuclear weapons and long-range delivery systems. But one could also conceive of major accidents that are unpremeditated, such as the destruction of a large oil-loading facility, which could close down the economy of a part of the world; or the escape from the laboratory of a new virulent microorganism that could cause widespread damage and destruction. Some of these catastrophic events—for example, the impact of a comet—are not linked to the economic growth question in any way. Others, such as nuclear war, are probably linked but in ways that are latent and indefinite. One point that can be made is that the destructive potential of both natural and man-made events has increased because of growth, and particularly because of the increasing interdependence of various human activities, not only within a given country, but around the world. Therefore, an earthquake in the Persian Gulf might adversely affect the rest of the world if it destroys oil pipelines and shipping facilities. Fifty years ago this would have had impacts only in the immediate area of the earthquake.

It is not clear to what extent the price mechanism provides any adjustment potential in relation to such catastrophes. Clearly, however, governments and also private persons can and do protect themselves against uncertainties and risks—essentially by spending resources for insurance in one form or another. To the extent that the risk probability can be quantified, and to the extent that the damage can be estimated in advance, one can carry out the necessary benefit-risk analyses that will tell how much should be invested and where investments can be most cost-effective. What comes to mind are stockpiles of oil and other important commodities, both on a private basis and by governments, the provisions of underground nuclear shelters, hurricane shelters, earthquake-proof buildings, and so on. Clearly, there is an optimal investment program, as outlined above, which takes into account the probability of occurrence as well as the resultant damage and other impacts. Things being the way they are, it is likely that the allocations are badly mismatched to what they should be. A major imperfection is lack of information.

The situation is difficult to analyze also because of the "free-rider" problem and the role of government. Government stockpiles, for example, will tend to preempt private stockpiles. Everyone may feel that, in case of emergency, the government will provide. Worse still, those who do stockpile privately may bear the stigma of hoarders, when in fact they are being public-spirited by relieving some of the burden on the general taxpayer.

SCIENCE AND TECHNOLOGY

Scientific research and the technological advances resulting from science represent some of the most intriguing and most difficult items to analyze. Science and technology expenditures are affected by economic growth; in turn, technological progress also causes growth by increasing productivity. But the quantitative relationships are not clear.

Historically, science was supported by wealthy patrons, by princes and kings and by others who had surplus resources. It was valued both for its intellectual stimulus and for its practical attainments, be they in the construction of fortifications or in the development and practice of astronomy. The support of basic science has now become widely accepted as a governmental responsibility. But no prescription exists that allows one to judge whether the amounts spent are in any way optimal, either too much or too little. Applied science, or technology, is supported both by private industry and by government, which raises some additional problems. To the extent that a firm or industry can capture the benefits of the technological research through patents or through proprietary know-how, it will support such research. To the extent that the government is active in the area and makes the results widely available, it may preempt the conduct of privately funded research. The exact boundary is difficult to place and has been the subject of much discussion. It is generally agreed that government has an important role where the benefits of the research cannot be fully captured by the firm or by the industry, but where the benefits to the public at large, either directly or indirectly, exceed the costs.

Arguments are sometimes made that government ought to support research that is too risky for industry. It is not clear that the risks will be any less for the government, except where the government can in fact control the application of the research by its own regulatory actions, and thereby reduce the risk of regulation or the risk of acceptance of the technology.[6]

To the extent that scientific research and technological research produce public goods and are freely available to everyone in society, the absolute amount invested in research generally goes up with total GNP, which in turn depends also on the level of the population. But technological progress also causes an important multiplier effect on the GNP itself by increasing the productivity of capital and of labor; that is, more GNP can be produced by the same investment in capital and labor resources if a higher degree of technology is available. Conversely, the same goods can be produced with smaller resource inputs. It is even possible that there is a feedback taking place that increases GNP roughly exponentially —even if the population were to become stationary. In neoclassical growth theory, this in fact is the way in which GNP is modeled by assuming that technological progress increases exponentially with time and increases output exponentially. While this picture would seem to fit the available data over the last decades, there is no guarantee that it will be appropriate to the future. Technological progress may either increase faster or slower, since the relationship between technological progress and between expenditures on science and technological research is not empirically known. But since there are many negative aspects connected with growth, both population growth and economic growth, it is essential to have the technological progress factors present to overcome the negative factors. Some of the negative factors include the resources that must be spent on abating pollution or on extracting fuels and ores from locations that are further away or deeper in the earth or of lower quality.

Since we want to increase the net productivity of the nation, we want to know where to apply the research results in order to overcome a variety of factors that depress productivity and encourage technological progress, which increases productivity in agriculture, in industry, and the production of services, including government services.

To this end we ask the question whether the price mechanism provides the input incentives and the proper guidance. While far from perfect, the patent system does allow one to capture the benefits from expending efforts and resources on technical improvements and inventions. Financial rewards to entrepreneurs, farmers, workers, and managers serve to increase productivity in various ways. Competition works more or less to keep the services sector efficient, especially where measurable outputs are produced, for example, transportation or banking. This competition stimulates the adoption of more productive technology. But the application of competition to governmental services is less-well-developed; in fact, it is in the nature of governmental bureaus to eliminate competition and form monopolies, under the guise of "eliminating wasteful duplication."

We conclude, overall, that there are institutional barriers that in some ways impede the functioning of the price system in guiding science and technology.

NATURAL RESOURCES

There are really three kinds of natural resources: (1) energy resources, including primarily mineral fuels (such as oil, gas, coal and uranium); (2) minerals, including primarily metals but also nonmetallic substances and even gases (such as helium); and (3) land resources, for living space and for agriculture and timber. Ocean resources span all of these.[7]

The three resource classes have some common features. They involve ownership and therefore should, one would think, be subject to market mechanisms and be influenced by the price system. In other respects they are different. Fuels are strictly nonrenewable while minerals are somewhat renewable. Many minerals can be recycled and reused provided the economics are favorable. Helium gas may be an instance of a resource that is nonrenewable for all practical purposes.

Fuels and Energy

The public has been led to believe that there is an energy scarcity today and that we will run out of oil and even energy very soon. Both statements are misleading. There is not only a surplus of energy today, but more particularly a surplus of oil. Roughly 20 percent of the potential oil production of the world is not used, simply because at the current high price the world demand for oil is not great enough. If this additional oil were to come on the market, then the present cartel price of oil would drop considerably—which would have two consequences. It would eliminate some oil production from rather high-cost oil wells, such as those from far offshore or from uneconomic wells, such as stripper wells. The lower price would also increase the demand for oil and oil products. We should recognize, therefore, that however much we may dislike the existence of an oil cartel, set up by the Organization of Petroleum Exporting Countries, it does lead to a lower level of consumption because of the higher price and, therefore, to an essential measure of enforced conservation on a worldwide scale.

To know why we won't ever run out of oil, we need to consider the substitutability of energy resources. In the short run, of course, nothing can substitute for oil, say in the form of gasoline in cars. In the long run, however, not only coal but various forms of nuclear energy, including breeder reactors and fusion reactors can be substituted. Now the point about the new energy sources of breeder and fusion reactors, as well as solar and geothermal energy, is that they are essentially inexhaustible. We can manufacture synthetic fuels from oil shale or coal, or produce hydrogen from water, and then use these fuels as substitutes for gasoline.

Or we can develop electric automobiles, since after all the major purpose is to provide a transportation service rather than gasoline.

The argument about oil can now be easily constructed. As the already available supplies of oil become exhausted, the cost of finding and producing oil rises and, therefore, the price will increase. At a certain point it will be more economical to substitute other energy resources for oil, and gradually these will supplant oil. However, a certain amount of high-cost oil will always remain in the ground. It will be relatively too expensive to extract it.

This is the conventional economic argument that demonstrates that we will never run out of energy resources and, by implication, of resources generally.[8] Certainly this argument is preferable and more nearly correct than the simplistic *Limits to Growth* thesis that resources are strictly finite. This thesis completely neglects the adjustment mechanism provided by the price system. It considers fuel resources like a salami: slice, slice, slice —and then it is gone. Under the economic viewpoint, however, these slices become thinner and thinner as time goes on and the price rises, so that there is always some salami left. But at a certain point the hungry fellow starts to eat other kinds of sausages that up to now had not been available to him.

The economic argument has now been developed to a high level of sophistication in the theory of the optimum depletion of a nonrenewable resource. However, there are some problems that are not encompassed in the theory and, indeed, are not encompassed in the market. I mention three of them: (1) uncertainty regarding the size of the reserves and of undiscovered resources; (2) uncertainty regarding the date of commercial availability of backstop technology, such as breeder reactors, fusion reactors, solar energy, and so on; and (3) the problem of security of energy supply, for example, uncertainty regarding the availability of oil.

Some interesting points follow from this discussion of imperfections of the market. The uncertainty about reserves is essentially an imperfection relating to inadequate information. Information can be obtained, but at a cost. Exploration expenses can be very high. Presumably, the market can make allowance for the uncertainty about reserves and set a price that leads to optimum depletion, that is, optimum conservation. But at the same time, we are being urged to conserve even more. There are those who are prepared to ration fuel resources even now, and to lower the price. Others would raise the price artificially in order to decrease demand. Clearly, voluntary conservation is all to the good, since it eliminates waste and saves resources and money. Enforced conservation, on the other hand, can have damaging side effects and lead to severe distortions of the economy. Most economists would consider rationing to be a poor way to allocate resources, especially in a nonemergency situation.

Many would also consider that an artificially increased price in the form of a tax would have undesirable repercussions on the economy. (At the same time it must be pointed out that present government policies, principally the crude oil entitlement program and the regulation of well-head prices of natural gas, make fuels less costly for consumers [often at the expense of taxpayers] and thereby discourage conservation.) After all, the experience with the Arab oil embargo during the winter of 1973–74 demonstrated the effects of a quasi-rationing scheme plus a price increase.

The worst aspects of any price increase are the distributional ones: increased costs of heating and transportation fall especially heavily on the poorer segments of the population. (They also fall most heavily on the poor countries of the world.) Those who advocate enforced conservation measures should therefore think carefully about the side effects on the economy and about the distributional effects. One should also ask: How much conservation is justified, who should decide, how can one decide, what criteria can be used, and so on.

With respect to backstop technology, the discussion is somewhat different. Its timing is the most important factor. If, for example, fusion reactors can become commercially available within 25 years, then there would be little problem about effecting the transition from an oil economy, such as exists today, to one in which essentially inexhaustible sources of energy become available, although perhaps at a higher price. The vast coal resource of the world may not even be dented; even part of the oil and gas potential of Siberia might be bypassed. On the other hand, if commercial introduction of breeder and fusion reactors, or of solar energy, is delayed for another 50–100 years, then it seems likely that coal, and to a lesser extent oil shale and tar sands, will provide the necessary backstop. Finally, if some more permanent energy source cannot be developed within, say, 200 years, then the world is in for a terrible problem. There could be a dangerous hiatus between fossil fuels and the availability of other energy sources, when energy prices could become excessive and damage or imperil the world economy.

Since the success of an R&D program cannot be guaranteed in advance, and since the timing and phasing-in of a new technology is even less certain, we must ask whether prices for energy fuels are providing the right signals with regard to their optimum use. It is clear that if enough people felt that we would run out of oil and gas before other resources come into play, then the price for oil and gas would rise rapidly. In essence, higher prices would then enforce more conservation by dampening the demand. On the other hand, low prices for fuels are a signal that no shortages are expected.

But price signals are not reliable if markets are not free. We need only examine the experience of the last 25 years, when energy prices in the United States and throughout the world were dropping in real terms. As a result, it made sense to adopt energy-intensive agriculture, even to drive gas-guzzling automobiles, and to build houses and urban configurations that we now regard as wasteful of energy.

It is easy to say that in this case market forces misled us, that the price signals were not adequate; but that is not the whole story. We need to understand why it was that energy prices were falling, in spite of governmental policies, such as prorationing or import quotas, which were designed to prop up oil prices, while at the same time the controlled price of natural gas made energy cheaper for the consumer, at least in the short run. And it is evident that the 1973 escalation in the price of oil was also artificial, brought about by the operation of a cartel of oil-producing countries. (The sudden change is having a severe economic impact mainly because it came about within a time scale that was extremely short in comparison to the normal depreciation times of capital equipment, of cars, of houses, and of cities. This "nonadiabatic" change has made the adjustment process to the new prices quite painful.)

The correct answer may be that we have not really had a chance to see a proper free market in operation, and realistically we should not ever expect to see a completely free market. Nevertheless, it would be useful and instructive to analyze how energy prices would behave in a free market, how the gradual depletion of fuel resources will increase the price and thereby lead to energy conservation and elimination of waste, to the introduction of energy-saving devices, to process substitutions, materials recycling, and so on, and thereby achieve a kind of self-balancing situation.

Finally, one would like to see a discussion of a most fundamental problem: If a free market cannot adequately decide on the value of the future and on future consumption of resources, then is it preferable for politicians who are mere mortals to make such decisions? There is nothing to indicate that their time horizon is any longer than that of a private firm; on the contrary, their time horizon may only reach to the next election. How then should we decide on the optimum amount of conservation, beyond simply eliminating waste which is uneconomic? To what extent should we reduce the welfare of the present generation, and especially of its poorest segment? Those who would impose a "conservation ethic" that is not dictated by free markets and prices may have a case, but they have not made it a convincing one.

One point that has not been sufficiently appreciated is that conservation expenditures should be subsidized by society. Sound economic arguments dictate such a policy whenever the marginal cost of additional supplies (of energy or other materials) exceeds the average cost. Under these circumstances, conservation produces a positive externality. This externality is increased when at the same time it improves national security (as is the case when gasoline conservation reduces oil imports).

Minerals

With respect to mineral resources, the situation is not nearly as critical. True, we are rapidly depleting the higher-grade deposits of various ores, and it is likely that the rate of discovery of new high-grade deposits will slow down and eventually approach zero. But there are several factors that provide an adjustment mechanism—all in response to prices. In the first place, we are learning how to use lower-grade deposits; the taconite iron ore of Northern Minnesota is a case in point.* Advances in technology, plus the availability of energy, can take us down to the exploitation of ore bodies that are not considered economic today. Mine tailings provide another readily available source of low-grade minerals. And for certain materials the ocean and even sea water itself will provide an economic source. This fact is reflected in the prices of minerals and metals, which have remained reasonably constant over the last decades and in some cases have actually fallen. There have been fluctuations, of course, most recently the price increases following the oil increase. Whether this will lead to a more permanent increase in the long-term price level is hard to predict.

Two major features about mineral resources are that they are more readily substitutable than energy fuels and that they are recyclable (unlike oil or coal). Substitutability can be carried very far, as has been shown in an article by H. E. Goeller and A. M. Weinberg.[9] Advances in materials technology can substitute plastics and ceramics for scarce metals. It is safe to say that the limits of substitutability have not been reached or even approached.

It goes without saying that as the price of metals rises, their use will become more restricted. Conservation measures will be instituted in the design and manufacture of various products. In addition, recycling will become economically more attractive. Recycling of scrap actually means using a high-grade resource since the metal may be in almost pure form. With reuse, the stock of metals in use may become the important parameter, rather than the annual flow.[10]

The key to the long-term availability of minerals and metals and materials is the availability of energy. Ultimately, the cost of energy will determine the cost of various mineral resources, metals, and materials.

---

*The taconite industry experience in Northern Minnesota is discussed as a case study in Chapter 2 by Luther P. Gerlach.

Land Resources

Does the price mechanism influence the availability of land as a source of growth? Certainly land for living space may present an ultimate physical limit to population growth; but that point is far off. In the meantime, a scarcity of land for living space causes a rise in its value and makes it more economic for people to live in more crowded conditions. This is the reason for high-rise buildings in the central business areas of cities. While many decry the crowding that exists in cities, no one denies the fact that co-location of productive factors performs an important economic function. Many people find city life quite pleasant. The option of living in uncrowded areas still exists, although it may be difficult to combine that kind of living with the earning of an income. But within the political system of the United States, for example, there is reasonably free mobility of both capital and labor. It is therefore possible to find or establish various kinds of living conditions suitable to peoples' tastes. The options exist here more perhaps than they do in any other country. Certainly, in a planned economy a worker must live in an area where there are facilities that have been established by plan. On the contrary, in the United States many facilities have been set up in areas simply because they are pleasant to live in and will attract good people and talent. The adjustment mechanism here includes not just price, or the pecuniary rewards of the job, but also the unquantifiable amenities. A market economy, therefore, can even take into account factors that are not quantifiable, that is, that do not appear explicitly in the price system.

We can ask the question, however, whether land for recreation and, more particularly, open space, parks, wilderness areas, animal refuges, and so on, are adequately handled by the price mechanism. The answer may be that, as for environmental amenties, property rights must exist or be instituted. These can be either private or public, as appropriate—private for some recreation areas, public for wilderness areas.

In the discussion of food resources, one should distinguish between the idealized case and the real world. In the idealized case an increased demand for food will provide an incentive for increasing food acreage and increasing the yield, for example, through the use of more fertilizer. As land is brought into production that is less productive than the average, the cost of food will inevitably rise. If there are not further technical advances and the population keeps on increasing, then we will eventually reach the Malthusian dilemma. However, the actual experience has been otherwise. Particularly in the developed countries, the price of food has dropped, certainly in real terms; the fraction of population engaged in agriculture has fallen dramatically; and the amount of land under cultivation has stabilized or even decreased. Therefore it does not appear that food production will provide any kind of limit in the foreseeable future.[11]

The global situation, however, is somewhat different. There are many regions in the world where the population is undernourished or even close to starvation. However, this situation has existed since time immemorial. What has made it a world problem is the technical ability to communicate rapidly around the world, and the capability to transport food. Even granted the willingness of the richer countries to support the poorer countries on a long-term basis, without any *quid pro quo,* the technical problems of transportation and distribution may still impose a real limit to growth of population. That is why the commonly made projections about world population growth are rather unrealistic. It is difficult to see how the present rates of growth can be perpetuated over the next few decades. It is to be hoped that the limitation of population growth will be by the more humane methods of birth control rather than by the inhumane methods of starvation and disease.

POPULATION GROWTH

We need to ask the following questions: (1) Can we arrive at an optimal rate of population growth (which may be zero or even negative),[12] if we simply provide couples with the necessary information and with low-cost opportunities to control family size; that is, we make it possible for everyone to have exactly the number of children they want—no more, but also no less. (2) Does one need to go even further, that is, is it necessary to "internalize" the cost of children. Some argue that parents should be charged for the full cost, so that society is not saddled with the cost of bringing up children. If we view children as an economic good, then a societal subsidy results in an artificially low cost to parents and therefore in "overconsumption" of the good, that is, people would have too many children.

Assuming that the two conditions stated are satisfied, would we then automatically arrive at an optimum rate of fertility and therefore optimum rate of population growth? There are those who argue that the conditions stated are not sufficient, that the decisions that maximize private welfare do not necessarily maximize societal welfare, and that some governmental control on child bearing and family size may be required, either now or certainly eventually.[13]

A number of important questions require investigation. One is whether children are in fact an economic good, and whether families make their decisions on child bearing based on economic reasoning. Second is whether there is a divergence between optimum population as seen from a societal point of view and optimal size as seen from an individual point of view. Research and continuing discussions along these lines are in order.

Part of these discussions must include a careful accounting of the societal costs incurred by population growth, including the costs of congestion, pollution, the use of additional resources, and so on. Against this have to be balanced any benefits that come from population growth, such as possible economies of scale, the sharing in the provision of public goods, for example, scientific research, medical and space research, provision for defense, and so on.

We need to consider as well the possibility that higher levels of population and higher absolute spending on research also lead to a faster rate of technological progress. This hypothesis was discussed earlier in the section on "Science and Technology."

Overall, one would conclude that societal control of fertility is premature, at least in the United States. One should rather work on removing the two market imperfections described above: remove the lack of information, and internalize the cost of children more fully.

GOVERNMENT AND COMPLEXITY

It has been argued that as our society becomes larger and more complex, this complexity will result in additional layers of government. But this will also remove the individual even further from the level of decision making. Certainly, there is empirical evidence that would tend to support this extrapolation. In the United States we have gone from a frontier economy that relied on self-sufficiency to a complex society that is highly interdependent. The complexity of government and the size of all governmental bodies have increased accordingly.

On a world scale the same phenomenon has occurred. World trade has created a great level of interdependence, and world governmental bodies and world organizations have grown. Some antigrowth advocates have pointed to these phenomena as providing upper limits to the size of populations or economies; beyond these limits various instabilities are expected to develop.

However, the opposite point of view can also be put forward, namely, that as technologies become more and more complex, there will be not much point to centralized decision making, and local control will become important. This will become especially true if technology develops in such a way as to decentralize the extraction of resources. The argument runs as follows: High-grade resources are now distributed very unevenly in certain places around the world. As they become exhausted, we must go to lower-grade resources that are much more widespread and uniform. In fact, with energy based on fusion or solar power, each region can have its own power supply, its own food supply, a self-sufficient economy, and so on. With increasing autarky, the world becomes less interdependent rather than more interdependent. Therefore, government can be carried out at a much more local level.

In any case, the increasing cost of a more complex governmental structure, with increased regulation and other attendant manifestations, would eventually drive the political system and the economy into simpler and more efficient patterns of governance, as has been demonstrated many times in history.

CONCLUSION

To sum up, there are those who believe that Adam Smith's "invisible hand" will be good enough for the next 200 years. Free markets if given a chance to operate will solve our problems with environment, resources, and population. These people are ideologically opposed by another group that believes the problems facing us are so complex and far-reaching, and involve so many time delays between decision and impact, that even if markets were perfect, they could not adequately handle these matters; planning and centralized decision making must therefore take over to prevent disaster.[14]

From our exploratory analysis of the price system as an adjustment mechanism in dealing with a variety of potential problems, we conclude:

The price system now handles the bulk of decision making in the allocation of resources, both man-made and natural. It does this job efficiently and automatically, without requiring political intervention, therefore preserving a maximum of liberty to the individual. The price system provides an automatic and rapid adjustment and feedback mechanism and thereby tends to keep economic development "on track."

With some ingenuity, most additional decision making currently outside of markets can be brought within the market and then handled automatically. This may require government intervention by internalizing, by establishing property rights, by providing information, and by shortening lag times.

There remain a very few instances where markets are inappropriate and centralized decision making is required. By keeping their number very low, we can allow for the full political participation of the citizen.

In short, the growth versus no-growth controversy is largely a red herring. The real issue is whether the price system can do the job of guiding the necessary adjustments or whether centralized decision making is called for. From our examination so far we can find no instance where centralized decision making is superior to the dispersed decision making of a free-market system aided by judicious internalization in those areas that currently are not encompassed by the market. The price system, if free to operate, may well result in a reduced rate of future economic growth (measured in terms of GNP) while allowing an increase in "real income."[15]

NOTES

1. Edison Electric Institute, *Economic Growth in the Future, The Growth Debate in National and Global Perspective* (New York: McGraw-Hill, 1976). It is interesting to note that the "Electric Utility Industry View" presented in that volume reflects a more moderate posture; that is, "The economists' approach to pollution control of internalizing externalities is valid in principle but difficult in practice." (p. 65)

2. Donella H. Meadows et al., *The Limits to Growth* (New York: Universe Books, 1972).

3. Henry Wallich, "Is There a Capital Shortage?" A speech delivered at the International Monetary Conference, Amsterdam, June 11, 1975. For other views, see also B. Bosworth, J. S. Duesenberry, and A. S. Carron, *Capital Needs in the Seventies* (Washington, D.C.: The Brookings Institution, 1975).

4. This alternative is discussed in the EEI report, *Economic Growth in the Future*, p. 65. It is more fully discussed in A. V. Kneese and C. L. Schultze, *Pollution, Prices and Public Policy* (Washington, D.C.: The Brookings Institution, 1975). It should also be pointed out that the pollution tax approach has problems. See, for example, W. J. Baumol and W. E. Oates, *The Theory of Environmental Policy* (Englewood Cliffs, N.J.: Prentice-Hall, 1975).

5. S. F. Singer, ed., *The Changing Global Environment* (Boston and Dordrecht: Reidel Publishing Company, 1975).

6. J. Herbert Hollomon and Michel Grenon, *Energy Research and Development* (Cambridge, Mass.: Ballinger, 1975).

7. Ocean resources include energy resources such as offshore oil; mineral resources such as manganese nodules, as well as magnesium extracted from sea water; and even the possibility of living space. Certainly the margins of the ocean are used for recreation and commerce very intensively, while the analog of agriculture is the harvest of fish. An important distinction between land resources and ocean resources is that the ownership of ocean resources is not as clear as it is for land resources. The ownership of deep sea bed minerals is now under intensive discussion, and the ownership of coastal fisheries is undergoing a change in concept. The unilateral declaration of 200-mile limits by a number of coastal nations is bringing these fisheries under their jurisdiction and ownership.

8. This argument is more fully developed in a chapter presenting "the pro-growth view" contained in *Economic Growth in the Future*, p. 34. This source summarizes the classical treatment and includes references on optimum depletion over time of a nonrenewable resource and the corresponding optimum increase of price.

9. H. E. Goeller and A. M. Weinberg, "The Age of Substitutability," *Science* 191 (1976): 683.

10. One controversial and vexing question relates to the obsolescence of equipment, and especially consumer goods. For example, if cars were to last 30 years instead of 10 years, the stock of metals would not be affected; only the flow would be reduced by a factor of 3. Granted that advertising stimulates demand, an equilibrium of sorts is reached when the new plus used car market is saturated. In favor of obsolescence one must cite the improved services resulting from technological advance; for example, color TV gives more pleasure than black-and-white TV.

11. Yet the adequacy of the price mechanism is constantly questioned when, for example, prime agricultural land is turned over to housing projects or covered by highways—simply because the developer can buy out the farmer. Does the price of agricultural land then represent fully its real value, including its future value? Economists would argue that it does; although the rapid price increase of energy, fertilizer, and labor costs will make farm land scarcer and more valuable.

12. S. F. Singer, ed., *Is There An Optimum Level of Population?* (New York: McGraw-Hill, 1971). See also S. F. Singer, an article on "Optimum Population Levels and Growth Rates" to be published in *Scientific American.*

13. One method of control that preserves some features of a free market would be a system of transferable birth licenses. This is described in a chapter presenting "the no-growth view" contained in the EEI report *Economic Growth in the Future,* p. 49. An alternative method would be a societal subsidy paid to families who forego having children. Again, as for conservation, this method is based on sound economic precepts. If having the extra child produces an externality, then foregoing the opportunity produces a positive externality. From a practical standpoint, if it is determined that fertility should be reduced, then a semiannual fee could be paid for each female in the fertile age range who is found to be not pregnant.

14. R. L. Heilbroner, "National Economic Planning," New York *Times Magazine,* January 25, 1976.

15. For a discussion of real income, welfare indexes, and projections into the future, see S. F. Singer and B. W. Perry, *The Economic Effects of Demographic Changes,* Vol. 10 of *U.S. Economic Growth from 1976 to 1986: Prospects, Problems, and Patterns,* Studies prepared for the Joint Economic Committee of the U.S. Congress (Washington, D.C.: U.S. Government Printing Office, 1977).

12 | Space: The New Energy Frontier

Gerard K. O'Neill

The early 1970s have been remarkable. For the first time, new problems of growth on a global scale have become apparent to us, while at the same time new solutions, as different fundamentally from the old as three dimensions are different from two, have become possible. The radically new ideas concern the practical use of the material and energy resources of space, in such a way as to benefit profoundly the lives of people on earth, and to make of the space environment a new frontier for human activity.

The industrial revolution has been the mechanism by which our physical power has increased and by which, for the first time, a substantial fraction of the human population has reached a high living standard. Comfort, a reasonable life expectancy, freedom of travel, and the easy availability of news and education have all come to the advanced countries as benefits of industrialization. Yet the same process has brought environmental damage; and far more serious, the population increase that has exploded as a consequence of control over pandemic disease confronts us with sharp limits on food, energy, and materials—these limits appearing at a time when most of the human race is still poor and much of it is on the edge of starvation.

POPULATION GROWTH

The United Nations Department of Economic and Social Affairs has forecast population growth on the assumption that population control programs will be relatively successful.[1] As a consequence of the present skewed age structure in the developing nations, the world population is forecast to rise to 6.5 billion by the year 2000; at that time the population within South and East Asia alone will be larger than the entire population of the world in the year 1977. This is the overriding statistic concerning population, and it will generate social forces of explosive intensity. A detailed breakdown of these numbers can be found in the Edison Electric

Institute's *Economic Growth in the Future.*[2] In comparison with these numbers, the data on population growth rates within the United States represent almost a condition of stasis.[3] Logically, the conclusion can be drawn that the major growth-induced social and political pressures that can be anticipated over the next decades will be externally applied to the United States, rather than internally generated. Although the United Nations does not forecast more than 25 years into the future, its graphs extrapolate to a total population of 8.5 billion in 2020 and to about 10 billion in 2035; by 2050 the population, if not reduced by disease or war, is predicted to reach approximately 12 billion, some three times its present level. I should emphasize that these figures are "best case" values, based on the assumption that population control programs will be relatively successful.

ENERGY AND THE STANDARD OF LIVING

In the developed nations the comfort, abundance, and freedom of choice enjoyed by most people are achieved only by a high rate of energy use. The correlation between energy usage and per capita income has been so well established by now that there is little point in arguing it. In *Economic Growth in the Future,* that correlation is documented with almost chilling exactness by the Case Western Reserve World Model.[4] According to that evidence, if the standard of living in the poor nations is to rise to match our own, it can only do so if their use of energy rises correspondingly. As Robert Heilbroner has pointed out,

> [I]mpassioned polemics against growth are exercises in futility today. Worse, they may even point in the wrong direction. . . . In the backward areas, the acute misery that is the potential source of so much international disruption can be remedied only to the extent that rapid improvements are introduced, including . . . health services, education, transportation, fertilizer production and the like.[5]

As Heilbroner and others have emphasized, the alternatives of a rapid transition towards zero growth, or a massive redistribution of wealth between the nations of the world, on a time scale of significance when viewed in the context of rapid population growth rates, could hardly be realized without a substantial assault on individual freedom. Dennis Gabor observes: "What we have to lose, what we have at stake, is the most precious thing our civilization has given us, in addition to material satisfaction—an unusual degree of freedom. No other civilization before us has allowed so much individual freedom. This freedom is now in very, very considerable danger."[6]

In sum, our hopes for improvement of the standard of living in our own country, and for the spread of wealth to underdeveloped nations, depend on our finding a cheap, inexhaustible, universally available energy source. If we continue to care about the environment in which we live, that energy source should be pollution-free and should be obtainable without stripping the earth. In terms of the practical, political world in which we live, it is also becoming clear that the acceptability of that energy source to the public is no small issue.

In that regard, I cannot draw from the public response I see reported every day conclusions as sanguine as those in *Economic Growth in the Future* in regard to public acceptance of nuclear power: "The recent Rasmussen report will be very helpful in reducing the remaining uncertainty about the possibility of serious accidents. . . . Only when such concerns are dispelled from the mind of the average citizen can the electric utility industry and the nation proceed to develop nuclear power at the pace needed."[7] As a physicist who by choice carried out his Ph.D. thesis experiment in nuclear physics, using the deuterium-tritium reaction, I have no reason to consider the Rasmussen report other than as a carefully prepared document, representing a great deal of serious research and analysis. Yet that is not the issue: Such reports are too sophisticated mathematically to be understood by the average citizen. He can listen for their interpretation to government or industry, both of which he regards as biased observers, or he can listen to independent scientists.

But in the United States, highly intellectual authorities are not usually considered as more worth listening to than other people; in fact, a sizable fraction of the public regards the intellectual as incapable of making any worthwhile judgment about practical issues. We have no equivalent in significance to the French term *Savant*. In the United States, nuclear energy is not an intellectual but an emotional issue, and I see no substantial grounds for optimism that such emotionalism is going to change noticeably over the crucially short time that we have available to us.

The utility industry sees itself as located at a unique position in regard to the growth issue, and in my opinion that self-image is justified. With relatively optimistic assumptions about population growth rates, it is still going to be necessary to increase energy production very rapidly: according to *Economic Growth in the Future*, by roughly a factor of ten over the next half-century.[8]

Even more disquieting from the viewpoint of the responsibility of the utilities is the fact that in only 20 years, from 1980 to 2000, the supply of energy from nuclear or other nonfossil-fuels energy sources must rise by almost a factor of ten.[9] If indeed the major element of that rise is to be nuclear energy, it seems to me very likely that it will entail great controversy within countries such as the United States, and that it will have consequences involving nuclear proliferation in the rest of the world, generating substantial political pressures on this country. As the principal element of new energy growth apparently must be electrical,[10] it appears to me to be no more than an accurate assessment of the facts to state, as has *Economic Growth in the Future:*

> Electric utility companies have been thrust into the center of the growth debate by a combination of circumstances. The rate of growth of electricity usage makes the industry a conspicuous element of economic growth. Present means of producing electricity have environmental impacts and consume limited resources. Also, the physical facilities required for generating and distributing electricity are highly visible.[11]

THE DISPOSAL OF HEAT

We have, then, one clear-cut problem that can be stated numerically in terms of the parameters of physics. Is there a second problem of the same nature? How real is the "heat barrier" to the use of energy within the biosphere of the earth? In the most optimistic case, the world population will be "only" 12.8 billion in the year 2060 and growing at an average of only 1 percent per year. We can assess the reality of the heat barrier by setting the condition that artificial generation of energy not exceed the amount that would raise the temperature of the earth by one degree centigrade. If by 2060 the present great disparities in the wealth of nations have been reduced, so that all are using energy at about the same per capita rate, that maximum tolerable rate turns out to be greater than our own by only 3 percent per year of per capital growth. The heat barrier is therefore a real one and cannot be delayed for long: Another 55 years and we would be putting into the biosphere 10 percent as much heat as is received from the sun. A continual growth of energy usage on the surface of the earth is therefore an absurdity, even if that growth is quite moderate, on a time scale of 85 to 140 years.

AN ALTERNATIVE

In 1969 considerations of this kind prompted my raising, within an academic context, the question: "Is a planetary surface really the right place, in the long run, for an expanding technological civilization?" After reviewing the numbers in detail over a period of years, it became apparent that the proper answer was, "No, it is not." In space there is a clean, reliable, virtually inexhaustible energy source: the sun, a well-shielded thermonuclear reactor thoughtfully provided for us at a distance of 160 million kilometers. Without the blanket of the biosphere, any amount of waste heat can be radiated away from a manufacturing facility in space, into the permanent four-degree-Kelvin cold of outer space. The materials available to us within the asteroids (a point no more distant from lunar orbit than is geosynchronous orbit from the earth, when viewed in energy terms) are so abundant that they far surpass what we could obtain locally without stripping the earth. For example, even if we were to excavate the entire land area of the earth to a depth of half a mile, and to honeycomb the terrain to remove a tenth of its total volume, we would obtain only 1 percent of the materials contained in just the three largest asteroids.

In the long term, therefore, on a time scale of 50 years or more, it is clear that we have a frontier on which continued growth could occur, if desired, even for many centuries. Yet we must acquire a time sense: For us to attempt to design for the year 2027, 50 years away, would be as pointless as it would have been for the Wright brothers in the year 1902, before the first powered flight, to have attempted the design of aircraft for the year 1952—by which time in fact transcontinental air travel and supersonic flight were commonplace. What is the time scale over which we can usefully plan? Not more than one or two decades, because beyond that time our plans fall far short of the scientific and engineering possibilities that will exist. We should recall that in September 1957 even Sputnik 1, the first artificial satellite, had not yet flown; less than 12 years later, two men had made a safe and successful round trip to the moon. That rapid schedule was possible precisely because the rocketry of the 1960s required no new basic science but rather the scaling up by large factors of engineering principles already well known. Thereby lies a lesson for us, which I would like to raise to the status of a guiding principle: "If we wish to solve our most serious problems, we must do so within the limits of engineering already well-understood; in practical terms we must also do so within the ground rules of our existing governmental and social institutions, imperfect as they are."

To say "First we must solve all our earthly problems within the confines of the earth, and then look to space" would be futile for two reasons: First, the technological methods that stand ready to give us the greatest payback and quickest return are usable in space, not on earth; second, humankind changes only very slowly, on a time scale of millennia at best, and a decade or a century from now is quite unlikely to be more rational, more cooperative, less combative, or less driven by unworthy motives than it is now.

The concept originally called "space colonization," now generally referred to as the "humanization of space," was formulated in a manner partly philosophical and was found to have many precursors especially in the works of Tsiolkowsky, Bernal, Goddard, and Stroud. In speculative form, many of the relevant ideas were described as long ago as 1920 in a remarkably prophetic novel, *Beyond the Planet Earth,* by Konstantin Tsiolkowsky.[12] In practical form, though, it would have been impossible to consider these possibilities before the Apollo project returned to us the lunar soil samples, giving us the first hard data on material resources available to us from a nonterrestrial source.

The relative percentages of metals vary depending on the Apollo landing sites which were distributed between the lunar mare and highland areas. All the Apollo sites, though, shared in common the abundances 20–30 percent metals, 20 percent silcon, and 40 percent oxygen. These abundances are of importance to us in considering a special class of tasks: those that result in end-products whose points of use are to be in free space or in high orbit. The barrier in potential energy between the lunar surface and free space is only one-twentieth as high as between the earth and free space; the ratio for a final location in geosynchronous orbit is slightly less spectacular but comparable. The vacuum environment of the moon makes it an ideal site for the location of ground-based machinery, capable of launching raw materials into space efficiently and precisely.

Estimates for the lift cost per kilogram to low-earth-orbit by advanced vehicles 20 times the size of the Space Shuttle, made by the designers of such vehicles, are in the range $22 per kilogram (kg).[13] That corresponds to $60–80/kg to geosynchronous orbit. For any product whose end-use is to be in geosynchronous orbit or beyond, a space manufacturing facility processing lunar-derived material begins with that advantage of at least $60/kg, and the cost of establishing such a facility and setting up a materials supply line can be offset in part by the saving in the development cost for the large rocket vehicles, estimated by Boeing, their designer, as $11.4 billion.[14]

Similarly fundamental energy considerations rule out of consideration, at least in any early time frame, the return of material objects from nonterrestrial sources to the surface of the earth. For all such tasks the potential energy advantage just referred to, equivalent to a minimum of $60/kg, would be thrown away at the start, and the total of all costs of recovery and return would have to compete in a much tougher market, that of materials alone, typically $1/kg.

FOUR KEYS TO PRODUCTIVITY IN SPACE

Guided by considerations of the availability of energy and materials, the four essential features of space manufacturing can be identified as these:

1. The location of manufacturing in free space, for full-time solar power, zero gravity for the assembly of large structures, and low gravitational field to permit low-thrust transport.

2. Obtaining nearly all the necessary raw materials from the lunar surface, where there is a great reserve of metals, glass, and oxygen already placed for us 95 percent of the way up the gravitational mountain at whose feet we now stand.

3. Use of the "bootstrap process." That is, lifting from the earth only a relatively small quantity of equipment, in the form of extraction and processing machinery, with which the first productive facilities of small size can be built. With these as nuclei, then building larger facilities capable of producing not only products for use in high orbit, but additional manufacturing facilities of the same kind. In that way, the growth of productivity and of payback can be exponential with time rather than linear.

4. Dependence only on near-term technology, that is, on engineering which can be planned and carried out without great technological risk.

The fourth point is of great importance, because speculation based on hopes for basic science breakthroughs can never be sufficiently risk-free to attract investment capital. For example, although the scientific research aimed toward fusion power is quite worthwhile, it has already been in progress for a quarter-century without reaching the level of scientific certainty that would allow practical engineering and detailed cost-estimating to be carried out. In contrast, for the space-manufacturing option we must be careful to plan on no vehicles more advanced than the space shuttle, no techniques not already thoroughly understood and no materials that do not already exist. The space-manufacturing concept is in fact a systems-design approach, in which existing building blocks of technology, each individually understood, are combined to produce a whole far greater than any of its parts.

The space-manufacturing method is clearly applicable to a broad range of output products; many of these are primarily scientific in nature: radio and optical telescopes of large size and great resolution, for use in high orbit where nearly full-time observation is possible without interference from the electromagnetic radiation generated on earth; ships of exploration, capable of carrying scientific expeditions to orbits around all the planets of the solar system, just as Darwin's H.M.S. *Beagle* explored the Pacific islands a century ago; permanent laboratories to be used in deep space. Yet the fraction of our interest and attention devoted to pure science has always been relatively small, and that is but proper.

The largest-scale application of space manufacturing is to those tasks that yield products directly and vitally affecting the lives of most or all human beings. At present we see one such task as deserving of detailed study: the construction of satellite solar power stations, for location in geosynchronous orbit above the earth, to supply us with clean, full-time reliable solar energy in the electrical form.

To quote again from *Economic Growth in the Future*, "In the moderate-growth-policy climate assumed for Case B, electric energy demand would grow at an average rate of 5.3 to 5.8 percent over the 25 year period. Even under low-growth conditions, electric energy demand would grow an average 3.7 percent per year."[15]

Taking the median value of 5.5 percent annually, the generating capacity of this country will be called upon to grow from its present value of approximately 500,000 megawatts to about 2 million megawatts by the turn of the century, and at that time the annual need for the new generating capacity will be in the neighborhood of 100,000 megawatts per year, requiring an investment of some $50 to 100 billion per year. The low-growth scenario would be lower than those estimates only by approximately a factor of two. Our further discussion should be carried out with those numbers in mind, to provide a relevant scale for reasonable investment.

Readers who have studied the issue of new energy sources are familiar with the various alternatives so far considered most seriously: fission breeder reactors, fusion power, coal, geothermal, hydroelectric, ocean thermal, terrestrial solar, wind power, and so on. Similarly, readers with that background are familiar with the arguments for and against each of these sources. In the United States we now spend approximately $700 million per year in research on nuclear power (fission and fusion) alone.

SOLAR ENERGY CONVERSION IN SPACE

The concept of Satellite Solar Power Stations (SPS) originated in the 1960s; its most active champion has been Peter Glaser of Arthur D. Little, Inc. in Cambridge, Mass. The plan consists of locating in geosynchronous orbit, above a fixed point on the earth's surface, large solar power stations either photovoltaic or turbogenerator. At each station solar electric power would be converted to microwave energy, which would then be directed in a narrow beam to a fixed antenna on the ground. At first glance this scheme appears impractical. Without calculation, most engineers would assume that the inefficiencies of conversion, transmission, and reconversion would be so low that no such power station could be economically viable. Curiously, the transmission problem seems to be soluble. Research on high-power microwave transmission has demonstrated experimentally that power can be transmitted to an overall efficiency of at least 55 percent.[16] The target figure for economic viability is only about 63 percent, so with moderate development one would expect that the target will be attained. The environmental problems of microwave power transmission will have to be studied carefully, but so far they seem to be much less severe than those of radioactive waste generation from fission or fusion nuclear plants. The microwave beam would be nonionizing and would leave the orbiting antenna with a diameter of about 1 kilometer; it would arrive at the earth with a beam width of about 7 kilometers. Its intensity would be modest, less than that of sunlight. In contrast to sunlight, though, it would be there all the time, even at night or in clouds or rain, and it would be in a form ready for conversion to DC current with a loss of only 10 or 20 percent. The antenna region on earth would be fenced, and outside the fence the intensity of microwave radiation would be no higher than outside a microwave oven with the door closed.

Clearly it will be essential to conduct research into possible adverse environmental effects of microwave power transmission at the earliest possible opportunity. It appears that such research may be carried on within the next few years. Already a group at the Los Alamos Scientific Laboratory (ERDA-supported), interested in supporting research into satellite power, has proposed a microwave generator that would permit conducting tests high in the inosphere on possible chemical reactions promoted by microwave radiation. The tests would be carried on in conjunction with a three-meter optical telescope already proposed for ERDA support and intended for the laser detection of trace components in the atmosphere.

OVERCOMING THE ECONOMIC CATCH

Although satellite solar power as a concept has been with us for nearly a decade, it has been slow to win substantial support. The reason can be summed up in one phrase: lift costs. For vehicles of the Space Shuttle era, using Space Shuttle main engines but optimized for freight transport, lift costs are estimated in the range $230/kg to low orbit, corresponding to some $950/kg to geosynchronous orbit. So far, the specific masses of photovoltaic solar-cell arrays in operational satellites have been in the range of 70–100 tons per megawatt.[17] One operational satellite designed as a short-life test vehicle achieved 29 tons per megawatt. Taking that lower figure together with a 63 percent transmission efficiency, the establishment of an SPS, even if it costs nothing to manufacture, would require the investment of some $44,000 per kilowatt in lift costs alone, which would render such a plant uncompetitive by a factor somewhere between 20 and 100.

To reduce that large factor, the proponents of earth-launched satellite power have had to presuppose developments that would reduce lift costs by an order of magnitude beyond those of the Space Shuttle era, and that would reduce power-plant mass by about a factor of four, while holding plant construction costs to low values. Even so, economic projections for SPS have generally relied on the assumption that base-load power would be competitive at 25 mils per kilowatt hour (kwh) in the time range of interest and that interest rates on capital would be relatively low during SPS construction and development. Because the failure of any one of these assumptions would be sufficient to remove satellite power from a possible competitive position, observers have generally followed a wait-and-see policy in regard to that option.

Late in 1974 it became apparent that a space manufacturing facility, processing lunar surface materials, might greatly improve the economics of satellite solar power; a paper on that subject appeared in *Science*.[18] Testimony concerning space manufacturing has been published by sub-committees of both the House and the Senate.[19]

The economics of SPS construction at a high orbital facility requires a fresh viewpoint. In that construction relatively little material from the earth will be required. A space manufacturing facility with a workforce in long residence will be growing its own food and will be in most respects self-sustaining; its residents will be paid mainly in goods and services produced at the space facility. The generation of wealth, it has been pointed out, requires three things: energy, materials, and organization (intelligence). Given an active, well-educated workforce in space, the last condition will be present; the first two are already there.

To analyze the economics of SPS construction in space, we must consider all the investments that must be provided in order to establish the space facility to the point where it can be self-sustaining and can replicate itself. The economic input to a combined space community/satellite power program will be the sum of the development and construction costs for the first community, the cost of lifting the material needed from the earth for subsequent communities and for those SPS components that cannot be made in space economically, a payment on the earth annually to the credit of each member of the workforce, representing that portion of salaries convertible to goods and services on the earth (for subsequent use on trips or, if desired, on retirement) and a carrying charge of interest paid on the outstanding balance in every year of the program.

Such an analysis, in rudimentary form, was carried out for the *Science* article previously referred to and has been validated substantially by later more detailed work.[20] The earlier calculation was based on relatively cautious assumptions: high lift costs of $950/kg for components lifted from the earth, high interest rates (10 percent interest in constant dollars, corresponding approximately to a 17 percent discount rate), a relatively low productivity assumed in space, and an assumed necessity to sell base-load power at 15 mils per kwh in order to be competitive, even a quarter-century from now. Even so, the simplified economic analysis indicated a benefit/cost ratio substantially above one and bracketed the necessary investment at between $100 and 200 billion, some 12 to 25 percent of the investment capital already considered to be necessary for conventional generator installations during the same time period.

The space-manufacturing concept has developed quite rapidly during the past two years; before giving the present status it is perhaps worthwhile to point out that the first conference on "Space Colonization" occurred at Princeton in May 1974, following more than four years of my own work carried out on a part-time basis.[21] The first publication of the technical nature appeared in September of the same year.[22] A conference on space manufacturing, supported by NASA and the National Science Foundation and cosponsored by the American Institute of Aeronautics and Astronautics (AIAA), was held at Princeton in May 1975. The *Proceedings* of both conferences are available from the AIAA as a single volume.[23]

By the end of 1975 it had become apparent that the space-manufacturing concept was surviving detailed review and criticism, and that its characteristic numbers were continuing to appear very attractive. At the same time, it was also clear that three fundamental problems would have to be solved if space manufacturing were to become a reality. These were the transfer at low cost of lunar material into space, the processing of that material into pure metals—glass, ceramics, and oxygen—and the evolution within cosmic-ray shielding constraints of an initial construction station into a productive space-manufacturing facility. Although conceptual solutions to all three problems had been available for some time, none had been examined in detail by scientists and engineers with sufficient specialized education and experience.

Recognizing these facts, NASA headquarters through its Office of Aeronautics and Space Technology (OAST) founded a special 1976 Summer Study on Space Manufacturing, to be held at the NASA Ames Research Center at Moffett Field, California. I was asked to direct that study, from which as a corollary the OAST division of NASA requested an extensive list of research topics, for consideration should space manufacturing be chosen as a major NASA theme. The study participants were senior aerospace professionals, aided by a selected group of students. The conclusions were presented in the form of a collection of papers signed by the individual research teams.[24] In the opinion of the participants the 1976 study was extremely successful, and much of the remainder of this chapter summarizes the results. Still later research on the subject will be contained in the *Proceedings* of the 1977 Princeton University Conference on Space Manufacturing, which will be brought out by the AIAA. Both in the study and in the conference, as in the case of all previous work on this topic, we ruled out of consideration any method requiring new basic science or technological development with materials or techniques not presently available.

RECENT PROGRESS IN RESEARCH

The first essential for the practical utilization of nonterrestrial material resources is a system for their transport in large quantities from their source to a precise point in space. Eventually, it may well be that the Apollo-Amor class of asteroids, from which the velocity interval to the region near the earth is only about 15 percent as much as from the main asteroidal belt, will become the favored source for materials.[25] They have been ruled out of consideration so far on the basis that we presently lack experience in conducting operations in space at distances farther than the lunar orbit.

The lunar surface is relatively well-known to us, at least at a few isolated sites, and the available information includes not only chemical compositions but the depths of the lunar regolith (the layer of soil above the rock). For lowest cost of shipment, several independent analyses have confirmed that ground-based launch is to be preferred to rocketry. Ideally, a launcher should have high values of all the following parameters: throughput in tons per year; efficiency of energy conversion from electric to kinetic form; ratio of throughput to system mass; accuracy of placement; reliability; ease of maintenance; growth potential.

A possible solution to this problem had been suggested earlier in an article on magnetic flight.[26] In magnetic flight a vehicle containing superconducting coils is supported near a passive, conducting guideway by the interaction of the coil currents with their magnetic images. The lift-to-drag ratio can reach 50 to 100 and improves the faster the vehicle flies. Acceleration forces can be applied by currents in stationary windings; in effect the vehicle becomes the armature of a linear electric motor. More than 300 references exist on these concepts, which go back more than 60 years. One further idea, the recirculation of the vehicles so that nothing expensive would be thrown away, was added to form the concept of the mass-driver, originally called the "Transport Linear Accelerator"[27] (see Figure 12.1).

In the mass-driver design, payloads of lunar soil in glass-fiber canisters produced on the moon are placed in small magnetic-flight vehicles called "buckets." Each bucket is then accelerated to the desired final velocity (close to the escape velocity from the moon), releases its payload, is decelerated and returned.

FIGURE 12.1: Mass-Driver (0.6–6.0 Million Tons per Year Throughput)

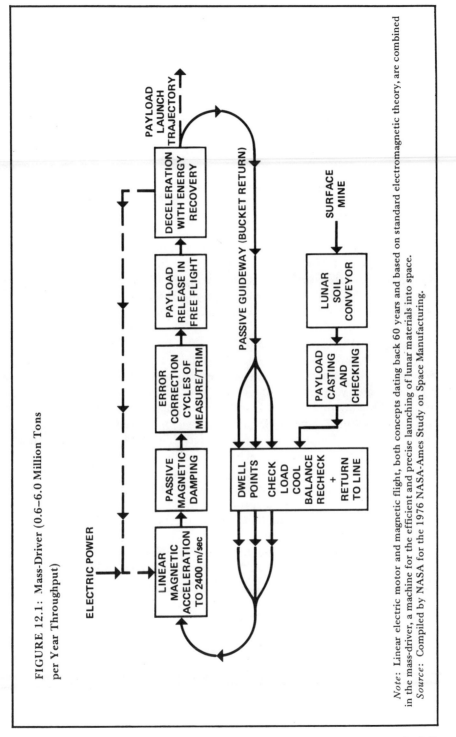

Note: Linear electric motor and magnetic flight, both concepts dating back 60 years and based on standard electromagnetic theory, are combined in the mass-driver, a machine for the efficient and precise launching of lunar materials into space.

Source: Compiled by NASA for the 1976 NASA-Ames Study on Space Manufacturing.

The 1976 mass-driver design employed a symmetric three-phase drive, with capacitors and silicon-controlled rectifiers that were cataloged shelf items at that time. The superconducting wire specified for the bucket was of a type that had already been used commercially for several years in much larger magnets. For simplicity the bucket was designed and stressed to be a totally sealed system containing superfluid helium. A bucket taken out of service could therefore be stored at room temperature without the necessity of refilling with liquid helium again when needed.

At the present time there are programs, each at the level of more than $100 million per year, in Germany and Japan aimed at magnetic flight /synchronous motor interurban transit systems that are intended to be operational by the early 1980s. Canada has a program that is similar though smaller in scale. Until early 1975 the United States also was active in this field, but at that time, by action of the Office of Management and Budget and the Department of Transportation, U.S. efforts on this subject were cut off. We draw now upon the research being conducted rapidly and successfully in what one might call the "more advanced" nations.

During the 1976 Ames Summer Study the acceleration forces on the moving bucket were calculated in four different ways, one of which was a computer calculation previously carried out by Raytheon for an identical coil geometry. Within small factors depending on the approximations used, the four methods agreed, and the final number is estimated to be accurate to within 2–3 percent. Participants experienced in the construction of magnetic-flight systems considered that 1,000 (earth) gravities (g's) of acceleration could be achieved in the mass-driver, but in the nominal design a limit of 102 g's was set arbitrarily. For power-plant mass, quite high figures of 45 tons per megawatt (mw) for nuclear power and 14 tons/mw for the solar-power option were taken. These correspond to near-term systems and are about the highest (that is, most cautious) figures now circulating within the aerospace field. Indeed, a recently completed study done at the Johnson Space Center concluded that in space, rather than on the lunar surface, a figure of 2.6 tons/mw should be achievable during the 1980s for solar power as a median estimate. With these input numbers, the optimized masses and other parameters for a mass-driver with a throughput of 600,000 tons per year are given in Table 12.1.

As the bucket "flies" within the guideway, which is itself little more than a pair of aluminum extrusions, it experiences strong centering forces by the interaction of the coil currents with their images. For a displacement of the bucket by 1 centimeter from its central position in the guideway, a restoring-force acceleration of about 32 gravities is devel-

TABLE 12.1: Parameters for a Mass-Driver To Be Used at the Lunar Surface

Power Supply	Nuclear (tons)	Solar (tons)
DC lines	100	150
Feeder lines	70	100
Silicone controlled rectifiers (SCRs)	30	50
Capacitors	140	200
Drive windings	200	300
Structural members	200	230
Maintenance enclosure	100	100
Pipes and radiators	220	330
300 buckets	6	6
Mass-driver subtotal	1,066	1,466
Electric power plant	3,000	1,600
Total mass	4,066	3,066

Common parameters

Throughput	600,000	tons/year
Acceleration	1,000	meters/s^2
Acceleration length	2,900	meters
Efficiency (electric → kinetic)	92	percent
Payload	20	kilograms
Winding current	60,000	amperes
Thrust per bucket	40,000	newtons
		(9,000 pounds)

Source: Compiled by the author.

oped. In consequence the dynamic stability of the bucket can be characterized by six oscillation frequencies (three in x,y,z translation plus roll, pitch, and yaw). They were calculated and all were found to be in the range 20–50 hertz.

Following acceleration, during free flight beyond the guideway, the position and attitude of the bucket is to be measured by flying spotlight beams scanning a precision test pattern on the bucket. For an accuracy of ± 10^{-6} $\Delta\theta$ and $\Delta v/v$, obtained by scans at intervals of 30 meters, the precision required is ± 0.02 millimeteres (mm). Because the light level is high and the test pattern on the bucket can be very precise, the accuracy is limited mainly by the precision with which laser light can be focused. The depth of field needed is only ± 2 centimeters, over which laser light can be focused much more finely than required.

Ten to twenty cycles of measure/calculate/magnetic trim are planned, only the last of which need be more than 100 meters in length. The bucket payload canister is to be released after all fine-trim corrections have been carried out, while the bucket is not being accelerated.

The bucket is to reenter the guideway and then is to be "snapped out" away from the payload canister to a distance of 2 meters in 50 milliseconds by passive guideway magnetic-flight forces that are calculated to produce 170 gravities of transverse acceleration. The lunar soils contain sufficient iron so they are to some degree paramagnetic, and in consequence magnetic interaction with the bucket fields will produce some velocity errors during snapout. These have been calculated and although not large are sufficient to require further correction. Additional guidance is therefore provided, at points 3 and 150 kilometers (km) downrange, by sequences of payload-charging/electrostatic deflection and acceleration/payload discharge, each sequence requiring 100 meters (see Figure 12.2). Optical flying-spot scanner measurements to an accuracy of ± 0.6 mm, made 63 seconds into the flight at a distance of 150 km from the launch point, should give the velocity to errors of about 10^{-2} mm/sec, corresponding to a targeting accuracy of ± 1 meter at the collection point in space. That is about 500 times better than the accuracy required for a passive collector of tolerable mass.

If space manufacturing becomes as significant as its potential now seems to indicate, there will be many occasions on which it will be convenient to be able to transport very large payloads, of the order of 50,000 to 100,000 tons, through velocity intervals of several km/second. The most economical reaction engine for such tasks may be another mass-driver, using as reaction mass liquid oxygen. The lunar surface is 40 percent oxygen, as mentioned previously, so in the course of chemical processing in space liquid oxygen will almost surely be a waste product. It has the further advantage of being rather benign, so that if introduced into the earth's biosphere in substantial quantities little if any harm will be done by it.

In a mass-driver reaction engine using oxygen as the reaction mass, the buckets will not require moving parts, and as they will not contact the guideway the system can approach the ideal of a mechanical machine without contacting surfaces.

The rocket equation tells us that the ratio of initial to final masses during the operation of one stage of a rocket vehicle is given by

$$M_{initial}/M_{final} = \exp{(\Delta v/v_{exhaust})}$$

FIGURE 12.2: Launch Trajectory for Firing Angle of –1.176°

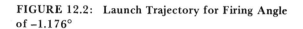

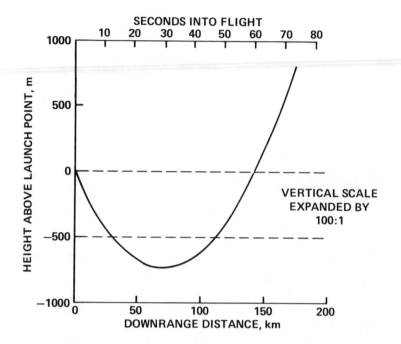

HEIGHT ABOVE LAUNCH POINT, m

DOWNRANGE DISTANCE, km

VERTICAL SCALE EXPANDED BY 100:1

Note: Launch at a slight negative angle permits convenient location of a downrange station at which payload trajectories can receive final correction after one minute of flight.

Source: Compiled by NASA for the 1976 NASA-Ames Study on Space Manufacturing.

Where Δv is the velocity interval through which the payload must be moved, and $v_{exhaust}$ is the exhaust velocity of the rocket's reaction mass. For minimum expenditure of reaction mass, therefore, it is desirable to have a high value for the exhaust velocity. On the other hand, for a given thrust the amount of kinetic energy that must be put into the reaction mass in linearly proportional to $v_{exhaust}$. For any given task an optimum value of $v_{exhaust}$ can therefore be defined, and the optimum depends on the relative cost of the reaction mass and the amortization of the power plant supplying energy to it. Table 12.2 illustrates this trade-off by listing the parameters for a reaction engine suitable for moving payloads of

TABLE 12.2: Mass-Driver as Reaction-Engine for Low Earth Orbit (LEO) to Geosynchronous Orbit (GSO) Transfer

Exhaust velocity	6,200	meters/sec (i_{sp} = 633)
Thrust	198,000	newtons (45,000 pounds)
Exhaust rate	20 × 1.6	kg/sec
Efficiency	89	percent (electric → kinetic)
Solar electric power	4,800	tons (at 7 tons/megawatt)
Mass-driver	4,200	tons (with structure + radiators)
Payload	100,000	tons
Velocity intervals	4,300 + 4,300	meters/sec (inbound/outbound)
Reaction mass	223,000	tons (liquid oxygen)
Outbound transfer time	40	days
Round-trip time	83	days
Engine cycle time	90	days (with 7 days maintenance)
Payload transfer cost	60	cents/kilogram ($0.60/kg)

Source: Compiled by the author.

100,000 tons each from low earth orbit to geosynchronous or higher orbit, the reaction mass being obtained in high orbit.

The remarkable point about Table 12.2 is that it refers to a machine that requires no high-strength or exotic materials, and that could be designed to the same level of accuracy and cost-accounting as could an electric motor. Table 12.2, payload transfer cost has been derived assuming that the 9,000-ton engine/power plant combination is built at the space facility, at an effective cost of $100/kw for the power plant plus $400/kg for the mass-driver itself; the latter figure is approximately three times the cost per kilogram of commercial aircraft. The amortization is based on a total write-off over 40 trips, or alternatively on paying 10 percent interest continually on a machine of indefinitely long life.

ORBITS AND TRAJECTORIES

Planning for space manufacturing has now reached the level of detail at which optimizations are beginning to be carried out. Some of these concern locations in space for particular operations. In the 1976 study a trajectory analysis team brought into working form a computer program for the three-body gravitational problem of a third object in the earth-moon system and applied it first to the mass-driver payloads on their climbout from the surface of the moon to a collection point. Sensitivities to launch errors were minimized by particular siting of the mass-driver, at a specified longitude on the near side of the moon, and by location of the collector near L2, the second Lagrange libration point, located about 63,000 km beyond the moon and the earth-moon line.

The collection point was chosen so that the steady force on the collector due to stopping the arriving payloads would be balanced to a first approximation by a location slightly away from the L2 gravitational saddle point. The situation is analogous to the case of a cylinder maintained in equilibrium partway up an incline by directing on it a steady stream of water from the foot of the slope. The collector must be station-kept, possibly by a small mass-driver, during the lunar month in consequence of lunar libration. In order to compensate for libration of the moon both in latitude and longitude, there must also be a small programmed variation (some tens of meters per second) in forward velocity at launch. Within the limits of the three-body approximation, the launch site was chosen to provide approximately achromatic trajectories (collection point independent of forward velocity at launch). Arbitrarily it was assumed that this special siting would gain only a factor of 20 in error reduction, although theoretical predictions are much higher.

The siting of the manufacturing facility is not yet final. Ultimately there may be several sites, each optimized for a particular specialized output product; a manufacturing facility producing large spacecraft, for example, may optimally be sited quite differently from a facility whose products are power satellites. The study identified as quite promising a location on a 1:2 resonant orbit in the earth-moon system. Transfers to this orbit from the L2 collection point appear to require velocity changes of only some tens of meters per second. For completed manufactured products, the velocity interval from that orbit to geosynchronous is slightly less than from stable orbits around L4 or L5, which have also been discussed as possible sites for such facilities. Perturbations by the sun have been considered to first order, but the generalization of all of these results to the four-body case is an obvious candidate for further research. The trajectory analysis problem is equivalent to charting the "valleys" within the complicated gravitational mountain range of the earth-moon-sun system, and the optimum trajectories are those that follow the valleys rather than attempting to scale the heights (see Figure 12.3).

PROCESSING AND MANUFACTURE

A chemical processing group analyzed a multistage process for the lunar material. Reduction and separation of iron is to be followed by carbothermic reduction of metals (silicon, aluminum, magnesium, and so

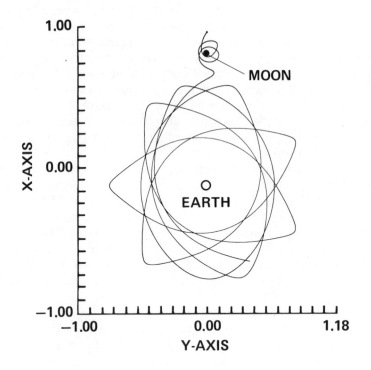

FIGURE 12.3: Transfer Trajectory
(L2 to 2:1 resonant orbit)

Note: With a velocity interval of less than 40 meters per second, lunar materials accumulated near L2 can be transferred to a 2:1 resonant orbit, possibly a good location for a space manufacturing facility.

Source: Compiled by NASA for the 1976 NASA-Ames Study on Space Manufacturing.

on), then by the separation of those metals. The iron reduction section, for example, reduces oxide to iron in separably large grains by the reaction

$$2 \text{ FeO} + \text{Si} = 2 \text{ Fe} + \text{SiO}_2$$

Diffusivities, optimum reaction temperatures, and grain size have been considered. The process plant makes use of vibratory ball-mills operating in zero gravity, with materials transfer by gas entrainment. Magnetic separation followed by a heated centrifuge gives an output of molten iron with SiO_2 as an overlying separated slag (see Figure 12.4).

Several of the processes used in the chemical separation system were tested at the pilot-plant stage during World War II, when research on noncommercial ore types was last carried on at a substantial level. Some, though, are presently known only in terms of equilibrium states, and bench-level chemistry will be required to verify their reaction rates and the degree of purity that can be reached by them under practical operating conditions.

In cooperation with the processing group, a team working on construction and scheduling detailed mass estimates for the chemical processing plant on the basis of production machinery used on earth. The layout (see Figure 12.5) is within a modular assembly 15m X 140m. It is designed to process up to 1.5 megatons per year, the capacity anticipating eventual upgrading of the lunar mass-drive by the addition of external power supplies. At full rate its output would be 450,000 tons per year of iron, aluminum, and silicon, 450,000 tons per year of oxygen, and 600,000 tons per year of slag. A conservative plant design yields its own mass in oxygen, silicon, and structural metals in less than six days. Production efficiency in terms of energy required is quite good, 600 tons per year-megawatt.

Establishment of an initial facility and of the lunar mass-driver installation is, in our plan, based on conventional chemical rockets using engines that have already been designed and tested (for example, the Space Shuttle main engines.) Typically these engines burn a fuel-rich mixture, with a ratio of about six parts oxygen to one part hydrogen by weight, rather than the stoichiometric ratio of 8:1. It had long been anticipated that great savings in lift costs from low earth orbit to the manufacturing site and to the lunar surface could be achieved by providing the oxygen component, 86 percent by weight, from a nonterrestrial source. This was verified by transportation studies, which resulted in a recommendation that a processing plant for oxygen be set up at the earliest opportunity, so as to reduce drastically the requirement for the lift of propellants to low earth orbit from the earth.

HABITATS

An initial construction station for up to 6,500 people was designed (see Figure 12.6). It would be capable of slow rotation for fractional gravity

FIGURE 12.4: Processing of Lunar Soil

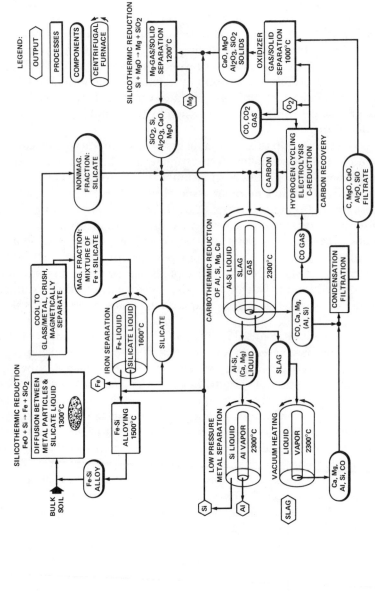

LEGEND:

OUTPUT

PROCESSES

COMPONENTS

CENTRIFUGAL FURNACE

SILICOTHERMIC REDUCTION
$FeO + Si \rightarrow Fe + SiO_2$

DIFFUSION BETWEEN METAL PARTICLES & SILICATE LIQUID 1300°C

BULK SOIL

Fe-Si ALLOY

Fe-Si ALLOYING 1500°C

COOL TO GLASS/METAL, CRUSH, MAGNETICALLY SEPARATE

NONMAG. FRACTION: SILICATE

MAG. FRACTION: MIXTURE OF Fe + SILICATE

IRON SEPARATION

Fe-LIQUID

SILICATE LIQUID 1600°C

SILICATE

Fe

SILICOTHERMIC REDUCTION
Si + MgO $\rightarrow$ Mg + SiO$_2$

Mg-GAS/SOLID SEPARATION 1200°C

SiO$_2$, Si, Al$_2$O$_3$, CaO, MgO

Mg

CaO, MgO Al$_2$O$_3$, SiO$_2$ SOLIDS

OXIDIZER

GAS/SOLID SEPARATION 1000°C

CO, CO2 GAS

O$_2$

CARBOTHERMIC REDUCTION OF Al, Si, Mg, Ca

Al-Si LIQUID

SLAG

GAS

2300°C

CARBON

HYDROGEN CYCLING ELECTROLYSIS C-REDUCTION

CARBON RECOVERY

CO GAS

C, MgO, CaO, Al$_2$O, SiO FILTRATE

CONDENSATION FILTRATION

CO, Ca, Mg, (Al, Si)

Al-Si, (Ca, Mg) LIQUID

SLAG

LOW PRESSURE METAL SEPARATION

Si LIQUID

Al VAPOR

2300°C

Si

Al

VACUUM HEATING

LIQUID

VAPOR

2300°C

Ca, Mg, Al, Si, CO

SLAG

Note: Chemical processing is based on carbothermic reduction of metals with recycling of carbon. Metals, glass, silicon, and oxygen are the output products. The calculated productivity indicates that the plant can yield its own total mass in output products within less than six days.
Source: Compiled by NASA for the 1976 NASA-Ames Study on Space Manufacturing.

FIGURE 12.5: Chemical Process Plant Concept
(Approximately to scale)

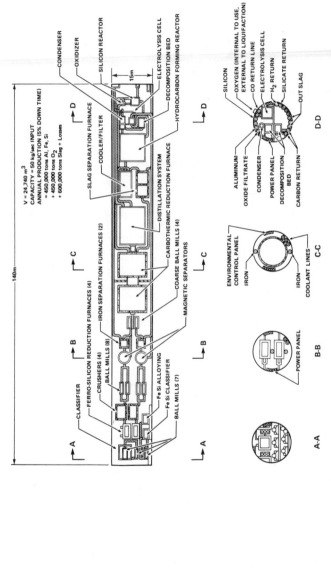

Note: The processing plant, launched for earth, is designed in modules of 15-meter diameter. Throughput is 20 grams per second per megawatt or 600 tons per year-megawatt.

Source: Compiled by NASA for the 1976 NASA-Ames Study on Space Manufacturing.

FIGURE 12.6: Initial Zero G Habitat for Crew

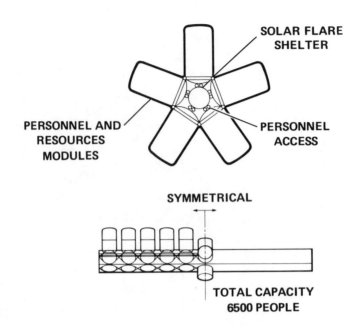

SOLAR FLARE
SHELTER

PERSONNEL AND
RESOURCES
MODULES

PERSONNEL
ACCESS

SYMMETRICAL

TOTAL CAPACITY
6500 PEOPLE

Note: Modular initial habitat could be spun at a low rate for simulated partial gravity. Minimal shielding could be provided by an external shell of hydrocarbons, later to stock the first habitat with food-growing capability.

Source: Compiled by NASA for the 1976 NASA-Ames Study on Space Manufacturing.

and could be shielded partially by using chemicals containing carbon, nitrogen, and hydrogen, which would be reused to stock a later habitat based on agricultural food supply.

Analyses of the trade-off between frequent crew exchange to earth and three-year or longer tours of duty accompanied by family members (see Figure 12.7) showed the urgency of setting up long-term comfortable habitation at the space manufacturing facility. As the details of chemical processing were worked out, it also became clear that industrial slag for shielding will be at a premium.

It became necessary therefore to consider space habitats of minimum structural and shielding mass. One such design, already being further improved, is shown in Figure 12.8. It is about as efficient in its use of

FIGURE 12.7: Comparison of Cumulative Mass in Low
Earth Orbit (LEO) for Various Crew Exchange Periods

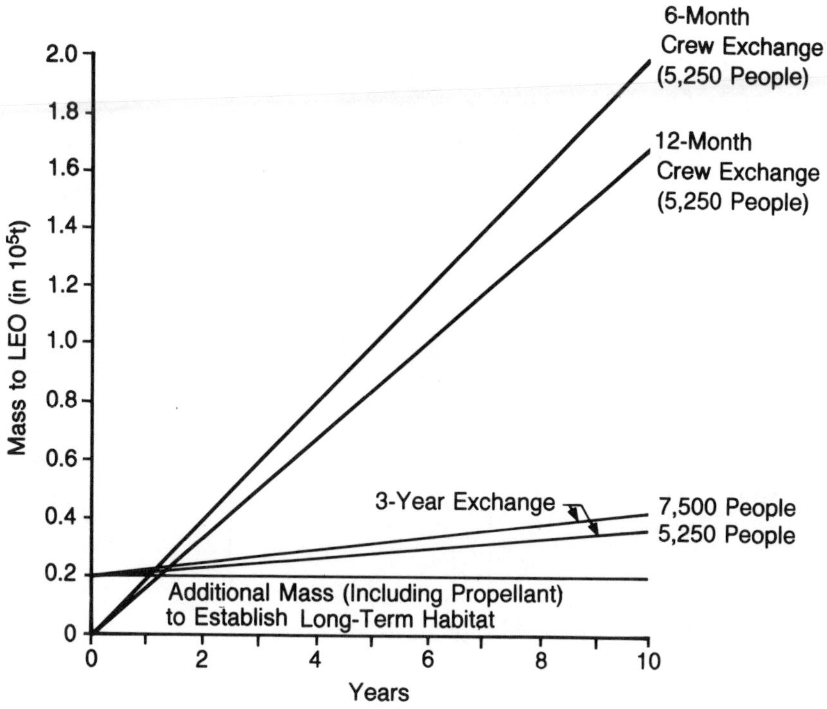

Note: Exchange of crews to the earth is sufficiently costly that economics favor setting up long-term habitation as soon as possible.

Source: Compiled by NASA for the 1976 NASA-Ames Study on Space Manufacturing.

shielding mass as a sphere of equal usable area and is about three times
as efficient (that is, requires about one-third the total shielding mass) as
a toroidal design worked on during a previous Ames Laboratory study of
which I had been technical director. For the new design the structural
mass would be only 50,000 tons, in the form of multiple wheels, with the
gravitational load taken by radial cables. The structure would be very stiff,
using metal in cable form where the working stress can be highest. An

FIGURE 12.8: Habitat and Manufacturing Facility with Shielding in Place

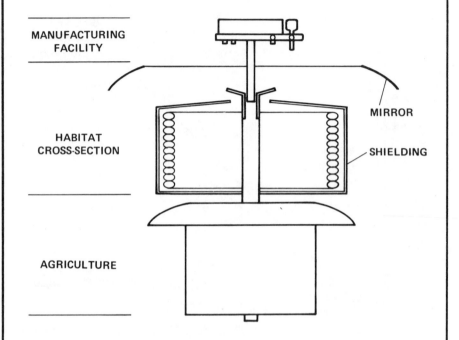

MANUFACTURING FACILITY

MIRROR

HABITAT CROSS-SECTION

SHIELDING

AGRICULTURE

Note: Schematic of an early habitat of minimum mass consistent with full cosmic-ray shielding, normal gravity strength, use of natural sunshine, and adequate land area. Pressure loads are taken over the minor diameters of multiple wheels; gravitational loads are taken and stiffness provided by cables like the spokes of a bicycle wheel.

Source: Compiled by NASA for the 1976 NASA-Ames Study on Space Manufacturing.

experienced structures engineer, John Blume of Blume Associates, whose working history extends as far back as the construction of the San Francisco-Oakland Bay Bridge, reviewed the design in some detail to verify its practicality.

After the initial habitat, progress toward more luxurious and earthlike space communities must be made within the constraints of productivity and of shielding mass. A spherical design would be as efficient in its use of shielding mass as the earliest geometry. A sphere nearly a mile in

circumference would require approximately 125,000 tons of basic structure. Total mass including shielding would be almost the same as for the
more utilitarian structure of Figure 12.8. The cost of obtaining the extra
75,000 tons can be estimated from the productivity achievable during
construction.

Productivity on earth for large objects ranges between 26 tons per
person-year for tankers and mass-produced cars, and 218 tons per person-year for construction steel (see Figure 12.9). Analyses made so far by
the aerospace industry and by NASA centers average an intermediate
value of 64 tons per person-year for operations in space. Clearly, such
values can only be achieved if practically all operations are done under
comfortable and efficient conditions, for example, within large pressur-
ized assembly bays, where workmen can take advantage of the zero-
gravity (or a deliberately very low-gravity) environment but remain in
normal clothing. Any operation that requires a spacesuit will be less
productive by several orders of magnitude. The increment in effort nec-

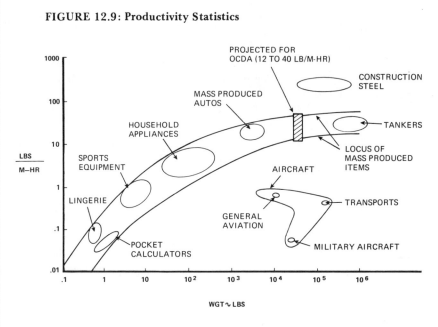

FIGURE 12.9: Productivity Statistics

Note: Productivity for specific industries on earth, as analyzed by Grumman Aerospace Corp. as of the mid-1970s.

Source: Grumman Aerospace Corporation.

essary to produce the quite spacious, earthlike habitat of the spherical design, rather than another of the minimal facilities such as Figure 12.8, will be about 1.5 months of calendar time, at the 64 tons per person-year figure. I suspect that many members of the construction workforce would be willing to work some extra shifts to obtain for themselves the more comfortable living conditions.

Existing designs for satellite power stations, optimized for earth-launch rather than for construction in space, were found to be largely constructable from lunar materials (see Figure 12.10). A reoptimization for construction in space would presumably raise these percentages considerably.

SCHEDULES AND COSTING

Cost estimates based on lift by near-term (Space Shuttle derived) vehicles indicated that a total investment of $31 billion ($63 billion with 100 percent escalation) could yield a minimal complete system, with a workforce of a few hundred people, producing 11,000 to 22,000 tons per year of finished products from lunar materials. The principal task of such a facility would be to build a larger one, of the size shown in Figure 12.8. It was assumed that the principal task of the larger facility would be to produce satellite power stations (SPS), and that a subsidiary task would be to further expand the beachhead in space, to increase the manufacturing capability and therefore the rate of construction of power stations. At a total investment of $103 billion ($207 billion with 100 percent escalation) there would be 20 SPS on-line, supplying a total of 200,000 megawatts at the busbars on earth. At that level the production rate would be five SPS per year, but a very short time later, given the exponential growth of the bootstrap process, the production rate could be as high as the market could absorb.

The 1976 study group prepared three schedules, with decision points and times for development and construction, based on the experience from previous space programs. A low-concurrency, step-by-step schedule indicated substantial production rate by the late 1990s. Maintaining low risk but permitting some concurrency, considerable productivity could be reached as early as 1992. The latter schedule is comparable in its degree of concurrency to the Apollo project, but it is far slower than what would be achieved if the conditions were military rather than peaceful.

The economic and political implications of space manufacturing are substantial. Its resources would be nonterrestrial, so their utilization would enrich rather than impoverish the earth. By the same token, as space manufacturing approaches realization the issue of the ownership of

FIGURE 12.10: Space Constructability—Fraction of Satellite Power Station (SPS) Mass from Space Manufacturing Facility (SMF) Lunar Materials

BRAYTON SYSTEM*		SILICON PHOTOVOLAIC SYSTEM**	
– CONCENTRATORS 98% CONSTRUCTABLE	= 13% OF SPS	– SOLAR ARRAY 98% CONSTRUCTABLE	= 61% OF SPS
– ENERGY CONVERSION 28% CONSTRUCTABLE	= 9% OF SPS	STRUCTURE/POWER DISTRIBUTION 98% CONSTRUCTABLE	= 8% OF SPS
– RADIATION 80% CONSTRUCTABLE	= 27% OF SPS	– TRANSMITTER 78% CONSTRUCTABLE	= 22% OF SPS
– POWER DISTRIBUTION 26%	= 2% OF SPS		
– TRANSMITTER 78%	= 7% OF SPS		
TOTAL SPACE CONSTRUCTABLE FRACTION	= 58% OF SPS	TOTAL SPACE CONSTRUCTABLE FRACTION	= 91% OF SPS
*BOEING		**MSFC	

Note: Existing designs for satellite power stations are analyzed for their constructability from lunar materials. Solar-thermal system designed for minimal mass is 25 percent sodium-potassium liquid metal alloy, therefore is poorly matched to construction in space.

Source: Compiled by NASA for the 1976 NASA-Ames Study on Space Manufacturing.

nonterrestrial materials will be debated and may raise controversy. That issue was addressed during the 1975 Princeton University Conference on Space Manufacturing.[28] At that time the best legal opinion was that nonterrestrial resources could be used freely, without violating existing treaties if three conditions were met: One, the space facilities would have to be nonmilitary; two, research results would have to be made available on request to member nations of the United Nations; and three, clear-cut responsibility for each space facility would have to rest with a sponsoring nation or group of nations. Already meetings of the International Bar Association have been held on the topic of communities in space, and every effort should be made to develop the space manufacturing program in such a way that roadblocks are anticipated and avoided rather than being met without preparation.

Discussion and activity within the federal government on this topic is now so frequent that a status summary would be seriously out of date before this chapter could appear. My own view, though, is that a space manufacturing program, given its potential for profits running into the hundreds of billions of dollars per year, should be private or multinational rather than governmental. It is particularly important that the necessary research and engineering be carried out in the most careful and responsible manner, and that no unjustified claims be made. So far we are fortunate that every number presented in the earliest publications on this subject has been substantiated by the later reviews. That record must be maintained if this concept is to realize its potential.

As the engineering reaches greater depth and the estimates of investment and payback are verified and improved with all possible independent checks and reviews, the real test of the validity of our work will be at the attraction of private capital. If our line of research makes sense, at a certain point it will become clear that the technological risks it entails have been reduced to low enough levels to justify substantial private investment, in the expectation of profit. In my view, our every effort should be devoted to conducting the research in such a way that the voluntary-investment point is reached as soon as possible, on the basis of full and careful information transfer, and with a studious avoidance of sensationalism or unjustified commentary.

Although our day-to-day work is necessarily of a practical nature, we should not lose sight of the fact that the long-term effect of our efforts is of more than economic or material significance.[29] Within the past decade it has been a cruel blow to us to discover, as we thought, that there were no more frontiers, and that freedom and individuality were necessarily to decrease in an ever more hostile world. If we are successful, our work will be remembered for its effect on our view of ourselves in a world of three rather than two dimensions. Through all of history we have been flatlanders, limited except for brief moments to a two-dimensional world. We need remain so no longer.[30]

NOTES

1. UN Department of Economic and Social Affairs, *World Population Prospects as Assessed in 1968,* Population Studies #53, Code ST/SOA/SER.A/53 (New York: United Nations, 1973).

2. Edison Electric Institute, *Economic Growth in the Future: The Growth Debate in National and Global Perspective* (New York: McGraw-Hill, 1976), Table 7.1, p. 203.

3. Ibid., Chart 5.3, p. 78.

4. Ibid., Chart 7.10, p. 221.

5. Robert Heilbroner, *An Inquiry into the Human Prospect* (New York: Norton, 1974), pp. 133 and 134.

6. As quoted in EEI, *Economic Growth in the Future,* p. 72.

7. Ibid., p. 250.

8. Ibid., Table 7.16, p. 226.

9. Ibid., Table 7.17, p. 227.

10. Ibid., Table 7.16 and Chart 5.12, pp. 226 and 89.

11. Ibid., p. 3.

12. Konstantin Tsiolkowsky, *Beyond the Planet Earth*, trans. Kenneth Syers (London: Pergamon Press, 1960).

13. G. E. Woodcock, E. E. Davis, and J. J. Olson, *Future Space Transportation Systems Analysis Study*, Phase II, Midterm Briefing, D180–19800–1 (Seattle: Boeing Aerospace Co., 1976) p. 223.

14. Ibid.

15. EEI, *Economic Growth in the Future*, p. 15.

16. News Release, Office of Public Information, Jet Propulsion Laboratory (Pasadena, Calif.: California Institute of Technology, May 1, 1975).

17. R. E. Austin and R. Brantley, Presentation at NASA Headquarters, Washington, D.C., April 17, 1975 (unpublished).

18. Gerard K. O'Neill, "Space Colonies and Energly Supply to the Earth," *Science*, December 5, 1975.

19. Gerard K. O'Neill, *Space Colonization and Energy Supply to the Earth.* Testimony before the Subcommittee on Space Science and Applications of the Committee on Science and Technology, U.S. House of Representatives (Washington, D.C.: U.S. Government Printing Office, July 23, 1975); and *Power Satellite Construction from Lunar Surface Materials.* Testimony before the Subcommittee on Aerospace Technology and National Needs of the Committee on Aeronautical and Space Sciences, U.S. Senate (Washington, D.C.: U.S. Government Printing Office, January 19, 1976).

20. O'Neill, "Space Colonies and Energy Supply to the Earth."

21. Jerry Grey, ed. Space Manufacturing Facilities: *Proceedings of the Princeton/AIAA/NASA Conference May 7–9, 1975* (including the *Proceedings of 1974 Princeton Conference on Space Colonization*) (New York: American Institute of Aeronautics and Astronautics, March 1, 1977).

22. Gerard K. O'Neill, "The Colonization of Space," *Physics Today*, September 1974.

23. *Proceedings of the 1974 and 1975 Princeton Conferences on Space Manufacturing.*

24. Gerard K. O'Neill, ed., "The 1976 NASA Ames Study of Space Manufacturing from Nonterrestrial Materials," collected papers to be printed in 1977 in *Progress in Aeronautics and Astronautics* series, ed. Martin Summerfield.

25. B. O'Leary, "Apollo/Amor Asteroids as Sources of Materials for Space Manufacturing," mimeo.

26. H. H. Kolm and R. D. Thornton, "Electromagnetic Flight," *Scientific American* 229, no. 4, October 1973.

27. O'Neill, "The Colonization of Space."

28. *Proceedings of the 1974 and 1975 Princeton Conferences on Space Manufacturing.*

29. Tsiolkowsky, *Beyond the Planet Earth.*

30. Gerard K. O'Neill, *The High Frontier; Human Colonies in Space* (New York: Morrow, 1977).

PART FOUR
Analyzing the Steady State and the Entropy Argument

13 | The Steady-State Economy

Herman E. Daly

"All the rivers run into the sea: yet the sea is not full."

Ecclesiastes 1:7

As readers of *Economic Growth in the Future*[1] will be aware, the growth debate involves two related questions: (1) Is there a feasible alternative economic strategy that is not based on an assumption of continual growth? and (2) Is continual growth itself a feasible economic strategy? The answer here given to question 1 is "yes." The alternative strategy is called a "steady-state economy" and is defined and elaborated in the first section of this chapter. The answer given to question 2 is "no." The reasons why continual growth is neither possible nor desirable are discussed in the second section. If these two answers prove convincing, then the obvious third question is: What policies will best allow us to make the transition from a growth economy to a steady-state economy? The third section offers some policy suggestions that, though they will appear radical to some, are nevertheless firmly rooted in our basic institutions of private property and the price system. The suggested policies seek to avoid the romantic fallacy of assuming a "clean slate," while not falling prey to the crackpot realism of "business-as-usual."

THE CONCEPT OF A STEADY-STATE ECONOMY

The steady-state economy (SSE) is defined by four characteristics:

A constant population of human bodies,
A constant population or stock of artifacts (exosomatic capital or extentions of human bodies),
The levels at which the two populations are held constant are sufficient for a good life and sustainable for a long future,
The rate of throughput of matter-energy by which the two stocks are

/ *263*

maintained is reduced to the lowest feasible level. For the population this means that birth rates are equal to death rates at low levels so that life expectancy is high. For artifacts it means that production equals depreciation at low levels so that artifacts are long lasting, and depletion and pollution are kept low.

Only two things are held constant: the stock of human bodies and the total stock or inventory of artifacts. Technology, information, wisdom, goodness, genetic characteristics, distribution of wealth and income, product mix, and so on, are *not* held constant.

Three magnitudes are basic to the concept of an SSE:

Stock is the total inventory of producers' goods, consumers' goods, and human bodies. It corresponds to Irving Fisher's (1906)[2] definition of capital and may be thought of as the set of all physical things capable of satisfying human wants and subject to ownership.

Service is the satisfaction experienced when wants are satisfied, or "psychic income" in Irving Fisher's sense. Service is yielded by the stock. The quantity and quality of the stock determine the intensity of service. There is no unit for measuring service, so it may be stretching words a bit to call it a "magnitude." Nevertheless we all experience service or satisfaction and recognize differing intensities of the experience. Service is yielded over a period of time and thus appears to be a flow magnitude. But unlike flows, service cannot be accumulated. It is probably more accurate to think of service as a "psychic flux."[3]

Throughput is the entropic physical flow of matter-energy from nature's sources, through the human economy, and back to nature's sinks, and it is necessary for maintenance and renewal of the constant stocks.[4]

The relationship among these three magnitudes can best be understood in terms of the following simple identity.

$$\frac{\text{Service}}{\text{Throughput}} = \frac{\text{Service}}{\text{Stock}} \times \frac{\text{Stock}}{\text{Throughput}}$$

The final benefit of all economic activity is service. The original useful stuff required for yielding service, and which cannot be produced by man, but only used up, is low-entropy matter-energy—that is, the throughput. But throughput is not itself capable of directly yielding service. It must first be accumulated into a stock of artifacts. It is the stock that directly yields service. We can ride to town only in a member of the existing stock of automobiles. We cannot ride to town on the annual flow of automotive maintenance expenditures, nor on the flow of newly mined iron ore destined to be embodied in a new chassis, nor on the flow of worn rusting hulks into junkyards and auto graveyards. Stocks may be thought of as throughput that has been accumulated and frozen in structured forms capable of satisfying human wants. Eventually the frozen structures are "melted" by entropy, and what flowed into the accumulated stocks from nature then flows back to nature in equal quantity, but in entropically degraded quality. Stocks are intermediate magnitudes that belong at the center of analysis and provide a clean separation between the cost flow and the benefit flux. On the one hand stocks yield service, on the other hand stocks require throughput for maintenance. Service yielded is benefit; throughput required is cost.

In the SSE a different behavior mode is adopted with respect to each of the three basic magnitudes. Stock is to be satisficed—that is, maintained at a level that is sufficient for an abundant life for the present generation and ecologically sustainable for a long future. Service is to be maximized, given the constant stock. Throughput is to be minimized, given the constant stock. In terms of the two ratios on the right-hand side of the identity this means that the ratio, Service/Stock is to be maximized by maximizing the numerator, denominator constant, while the ratio Stock/Throughput is maximized by minimizing the denominator, with numerator constant. These two ratios measure two kinds of efficiency. Service efficiency (Service/Stock) depends on allocative efficiency (does the stock consist of artifacts that people most want, and are they allocated to the most important uses), and on distributive efficiency (is the distribution of the stock among alternative people such that the trivial wants of some people do not take precedence over the basic needs of others). Standard economics has much of value to say about allocative efficiency but treats distribution under the heading of social justice rather than efficiency, thus putting it on the sidelines of disciplinary concern. Maintenance efficiency (Stock/Throughput) depends on durability (how long an individual artifact lasts), and on replaceability (how easily the artifact can be replaced when it finally does wear out). Maintenance efficiency measures the number of units of time over which a population of artifacts yields its service, while efficiency measures the intensity of that service per unit of time. Maintenance efficiency is limited by the second law of thermodynamics (nothing lasts forever, everything wears out). Service efficiency may conceivably increase forever, since the growing "magnitude," service, is nonphysical. There may, however, be physical limits to the capacity of human beings to experience service. But the definition of the SSE is in terms of physical stocks and throughput and is not affected by whether or not service could increase indefinitely.

Conceptually it is easier to think of stock as the operational policy variable to be directly controlled. Practically, however, as will be seen in the third section, it would be easier to control or limit throughput directly and allow the stock to reach the maximum level sustainable by the fixed throughput. This presents no problems.

The above concepts allow us to make an important distinction between growth and development. Growth refers to an increase in service that results from an increase in stock and throughput, with the two efficiency ratios constant. Development refers to an increase in the efficiency ratios, with stock constant (or, alternatively, an increase in service with throughput constant). Using these definitions we may say that an SSE develops but does not grow, just as the planet earth, of which it is a subsystem, develops without growing.

How do these concepts relate to GNP, the most conventional index of "growth"? GNP makes no distinction among the three basic magnitudes. It simply adds up value estimates of some services (the service of those assets that are rented rather than purchased, including human bodies, and omitting the services of all owned assets not rented during the current year), plus the value of the throughput flow (maintenance and replacement expenditures required to maintain the total stock intact), plus the value of current additions to stock (net investment). What sense does it make to add up benefits, costs, and change in inventory? The concept of an SSE is independent of GNP, and what happens to GNP in the SSE simply does not matter. It could go up or down. The behavior modes of satisficing stock and minimizing throughput would tend to lower GNP, while maximizing service would tend to raise it. On balance GNP would probably fall. So what? The best thing to do with GNP is to forget it and replace it with two separate social accounts, one measuring the value of service (benefit) and the other measuring the value of throughput (cost). In this way costs and benefits could be compared, although this aggregate macro-level comparison is not at all essential, since regardless of how it turns out the behavior modes remain the same with respect to each of the three basic magnitudes. Aggregate economic indexes should be treated with caution, since there are always some kinds of stupid behavior that would raise the index and thus become "justified." The amount of waste that has been justified in the name of increasing GNP is surely astronomical. Maximizing a sum whose principal component (throughput) is a cost just cannot be good economics.

Neither the concept nor the reality of an SSE is new. John Stuart Mill (1881) discussed the concept in his famous chapter "on the stationary state."[5] Historically man has lived for 99 percent of his tenure on earth in conditions very closely approximating a steady state. Economic growth is essentially a phenomenon of the last 200 years, and only in the last 50 years has it become the dominant goal of nations. The SSE of the future can be much more comfortable than those of the past, thanks to development (but not to growth).

THE NECESSITY AND DESIRABILITY OF THE SSE

It is one thing to define a concept and something else to show that its realization is possible, necessary, and desirable. A good starting point for this effort is provided by the conventional textbook definition of economics as "the study of the allocation of scarce means among competing ends, where the object of the allocation is the maximization of the attainment of those ends." This rather ponderous definition at least has the virtue of emphasizing that economics' fundamental concern is with ends and means. GNP, prices, elasticities, and so on, are all secondary and instrumental to the basic task of using means to satisfy ends. The growth debate and arguments for the necessity and desirability of the SSE can be much illuminated by a consideration of the total ends-means hierarchy as shown in Figure 13.1.

At the top of the hierarchy is the ultimate end—that which is intrinsically good and does not derive its goodness from any instrumental relation to some higher good. At the bottom is ultimate means—the useful stuff of the universe, low-entropy matter-energy, which cannot be made by man, and hence cannot be the end of any human activity. Each intermediate category in the hierarchy is an end with respect to lower categories and a means with respect to higher categories. Below the ultimate end we have intermediate ends, which are in a sense means in the service of the ultimate end. Intermediate ends are ranked with reference to the ultimate end. The mere fact that we speak of priorities among our goals presumes a first place, an ordering principle, an ultimate end. We may not be able to define it very well, but logically we are forced to recognize its existence. Above ultimate means are intermediate means (essentially stocks), which can be viewed as ends directly served by the use of ultimate means (throughput of low-entropy matter-energy).

On the left of the line are listed the traditional disciplines of study that correspond to each segment of the hierarchy. The central, intermediate, position of economics is highly significant. In looking only at the middle range, economics has naturally not dealt with ultimates or absolutes, found only at the extremes, and has falsely assumed that the middle-range pluralities, relativities, and substitutabilities among competing ends and scarce means were representative of the whole hierarchy. Absolute limits are absent from the economists' paradigm because absolutes are encountered only in confrontation with the ultimate poles of the

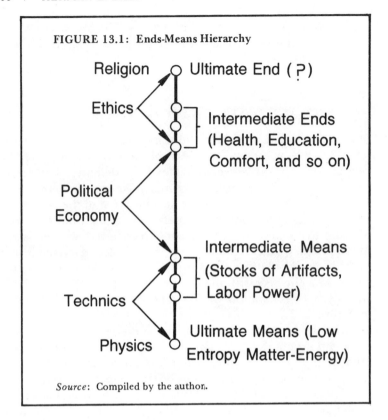

FIGURE 13.1: Ends-Means Hierarchy

Religion — Ultimate End (?)

Ethics

Intermediate Ends
(Health, Education,
Comfort, and so on)

Political
Economy

Intermediate Means
(Stocks of Artifacts,
Labor Power)

Technics

Ultimate Means (Low
Physics — Entropy Matter-Energy)

Source: Compiled by the author.

hierarchy, which have been excluded from the focus of our attention. Even ethics and technics exist for the economist only at the very periphery of his awareness.

In terms of this diagram economic growth implies the creation of ever more intermediate means (stocks) for the purpose of satisfying ever more intermediate ends. Orthodox growth economics recognizes that particular resources might be limited, but does not recognize any general scarcity of all resources together.[6] The orthodox dogma is that technology can always substitute new resources for old, without limit. Growth economists also recognize that any single intermediate end or want can be satisfied for any given individual. But new wants keep emerging (and new people as well), so the aggregate of all intermediate ends is held to be insatiable, or infinite in number if not in intensity. The growth economist's vision is one of continuous growth in intermediate means (unconstrained by any scarcity of ultimate means) in order to satisfy ever more intermediate ends (unconstrained by any impositions from the ultimate end). Infinite means plus infinite ends equals growth forever.

A consideration of the ultimate poles of the spectrum, however, gives us a very different perspective. It forces us to raise two questions: (1) What, precisely, are our ultimate means, and are they limited in ways that cannot be overcome by technology? (2) What is the nature of the ultimate end, and is it such that, beyond a certain point, further accumulation of intermediate means (people and artifacts) not only fails to serve the ultimate end, but actually renders a disservice? It will be argued below that the answer to both sets of questions is yes. The nature of the ultimate means limits the possibility of growth. The nature of the ultimate end limits the desirability of growth. Moreover, the interaction of desirability and possibility provides the economic limit to growth, which is the most stringent and should be the governing limit.

Paradoxically, growth economics has been both too materialistic and not materialistic enough. In ignoring the ultimate means and the laws of thermodynamics it has been insufficiently materialistic. In ignoring the ultimate end and ethics it has been too materialistic. Let us consider in more detail the implications of paying due attention to these ultimate poles. Since the subject of ultimate means is more concrete we will consider it first.

From a basic branch of physics, thermodynamics, we learn that for man's purposes the ultimate usable stuff of the universe is low-entropy matter-energy. To answer the question, "What is low entropy?" we can draw on the pioneering work of Nicholas Georgescu-Roegen.[7] In terms of materials, low entropy means structure, organization, concentration, order. Dispersed, randomly scattered molecules of any material are useless (high entropy). In terms of energy low entropy means capacity to do work, or concentrated, relatively high-temperature energy. Energy dispersed in equilibrium temperature with the general environment is useless (high entropy).

We have two sources of low entropy: terrestrial stocks of concentrated minerals, and the solar flow of radiant energy. The terrestrial source (minerals in the earth's crust) is obviously limited in total amount, though the rate at which we use it up is largely subject to our choice. The solar source is practically unlimited in total amount, but strictly limited in its rate of arrival to earth for use. Both sources of ultimate means are limited —one in total amount, the other in rate of use. Ultimate means are finite. Furthermore there is an enormous disproportion in the total amounts of the two sources: if all the world's fossil fuels could be burned up, they would provide the energy equivalent of only a few weeks of sunlight. The sun is expected to last for another 5 or 6 billion years.

This raises a cosmically embarrassing economic question: If the solar source is so vastly more abundant, why have we over the last 150 years shifted the physical base of our economy from overwhelming dependence on solar energy and renewable resources to overwhelming dependence on nonrenewable terrestrial minerals? An important part of the answer is that terrestrial stocks can, for a while at least, be used at a rate of man's own choosing—that is, rapidly. Solar energy and renewable resource usage is limited by the fixed solar flux and the natural rhythms of growth of plants and animals, which in turn provide a natural constraint on economic growth. But growth can be speeded beyond this income constraint, for a time at least, by consuming geological capital—by running down the reserves of terrestrial low entropy. If the object is high growth rates now, then it can be more easily attained by using up terrestrial sources rapidly. As growth results in population and per capita consumption levels that are beyond the capacity of renewable resources alone to support, then we face even greater pressure to continue consuming geological capital.

The difficulty is twofold. First, we will run out of terrestrial sources eventually. Second, even if we never ran out we would still face problems of ecological breakdown caused by a growing throughput of matter-energy. Even if technology were able to double the flow of solar energy (by far the cleanest source), the millions of years of past evolutionary adaptation to the usual rate would make a doubling of that rate totally catastrophic. The whole biosphere has evolved as a complex system around the fixed point of a given solar flux. Modern man is the only species that has broken the solar income budget. The fact that man has supplemented his fixed solar income by consuming terrestrial capital has thrown him out of balance with the rest of the biosphere. As stocks of artifacts and people have grown, the throughput necessary for their maintenance has had to grow also, implying more depletion and more pollution. Natural biogeochemical cycles become overloaded. Exotic substances are produced and thrown wholesale into the biosphere—substances with which the world has had no adaptive evolutionary experience, and which are consequently nearly always disruptive.

But are we not giving insufficient credit to technology in claiming that ultimate means are limited? Is not technology itself a limitless resource? No, it is not. All technologies, nature's as well as man's, run on an entropy gradient—that is, the total entropy of all outputs taken together is always greater than the total entropy of all inputs taken together. No organism can eat its own outputs and live, and no engine can run on its own exhaust. If the outputs of a process were of lower entropy than the inputs, once all inputs and outputs were accounted for, we would have a process that violates the second law of thermodynamics, and so far no such process has ever been observed. Technology itself depends on the ultimate means of low entropy. If low-entropy sources are not unlimited, then neither is technology.

It is especially ironic to be told by growth boosters that technology is freeing man from dependence on resources.[8] It has in fact done the opposite. Modern technology has made us *more* dependent on the *scarcer* of the two sources of ultimate means. In view of the popular belief in the omnipotence of technology, it is even more ironic to recall that the most basic laws of science are statements of impossibility: it is impossible to create or destroy matter-energy; it is impossible to have perpetual motion; it is impossible to exceed the speed of light; it is impossible to measure momentum and position simultaneously with greater accuracy; and so on. The remarkable success of physical science has been in no small measure due to its intelligent recognition of impossibilities and its refusal to attempt them. Paradoxically this success has, in the popular mind, been taken as "proof" that nothing is impossible.

The entropy law tells us that when technology increases order in one part of the universe it must produce an even greater amount of disorder somewhere else. If that "somewhere else" is the sun (as it is for nature's technology and for man's traditional preindustrial technology) then we need not worry. If "somewhere else" is here on earth, as it is for technologies based on terrestrial mineral deposits, then we had better pay close attention. The throughput flow maintains or increases the order within the human economy, but at the cost of creating greater disorder in the rest of the natural world, as a result of depletion and pollution. There is a limit to how much disorder can be produced in the rest of the biosphere and still allow it to function well enough to continue supporting the human subsystem. There is a limit to how much of the ecosphere can be converted into technosphere.

Although technology cannot overcome the limits here discussed, it could achieve a much better accommodation to them, and could work more in harmony with nature's technology than it has in the past. But an improved technological accommodation to limits, while certainly possible and desirable, is not likely to be forthcoming in a growth context, in an economy that would rather maximize throughput than reduce it. Such improvement is much more likely within the framework of an SSE, where profits would be made from development, not growth.

Let us now leave the issue of ultimate means and turn to a discussion of the ultimate end and the ways in which it limits the desirability of growth. The temper of the modern age resists any discussion of the ultimate end. Teleology and purpose, the dominant concepts of an earlier time, were banished from the mechanistic, reductionistic, positivistic mode of thought that came to be identified with the most recent phase of the evolution of science. Economics followed suit by reducing ethics to the level of personal tastes. Economics became the "mechanics of utility and self-interest," in Jevons' phrase. No questions are asked about whether individual priorities are right or wrong, or even about how they are formed. Whatever happens to interest the public is assumed to be in the public interest.

Our modern refusal to reason about the ultimate end merely assures the incoherence of our priorities, both individually and collectively. It leads to the tragedy of Herman Melville's Captain Ahab, whose means were all rational but whose purpose was insane. One cannot lend rationality to the reckless pursuit of a white whale by pointing to the sophisticated techniques of whaling that are being employed. To do more efficiently that which should not be done in the first place is a very perverse form of progress.

What is the ultimate end? The question is logically unavoidable. But only a minimum answer to such a maximum question is likely to command much consensus. As a minimum answer let me suggest that whatever the ultimate end is, it presupposes a respect for and continuation of creation and the evolutionary process through which god has bestowed upon us the gift of self-conscious life. Whatever values are put in first place, their further realization requires the continuation of life—the survival of biosphere and its evolutionary processes. This minimum answer begs many important questions: Survival and evolution in what direction? To what extent should evolution be influenced by man and to what extent should it be left spontaneous? For now, however, the only point is that survival must rank very high in the ends-means hierarchy, and consequently any type of growth that requires the creation of means that threaten survival should be forbidden. Nuclear power and the "plutonium economy" is a prime example of the kind of growth that must be halted.

But what about other kinds of growth? Are *all* kinds of physical growth subject to desirability limits? Is there such a thing as *enough* in the material realm, and is enough better than "more than enough"? Is "more than enough" inimical to survival? Certainly all organic needs can be satisfied and to go beyond enough is usually harmful. The only want that seems insatiable is the want for distinction, the desire to be in some way superior to one's neighbors. Even the want for distinction need not cause problems except when the main avenue of distinction in society is to have a larger income than the next fellow and to consume more. The only way for everyone to earn more is to have aggregate growth. But that is precisely the rub. If everyone earns more, then where is the distinction? It is possible for everyone to earn more is to have aggregate growth. But that is precisely the rub. If everyone earns more, then where is the distinction? It is possible for everyone's *absolute* income to increase, but not for everyone's *relative* income to increase. To the extent that it is higher relative income that is important, growth becomes impotent. As British economist E. J. Mishan put it,

In an affluent society, people's satisfactions, as Thorstein Veblen observed, depend not only on the innate or perceived utility of the goods they buy, but also on the status value of such goods. Thus to a person in a high income society, it is not only his absolute income that counts but also his relative income, his position in the structure of relative incomes. In its extreme form —and as affluence rises we draw closer to it—only relative income matters. A man would then prefer a 5 per cent reduction in his own income accompanied by a 10 per cent reduction in the incomes of others to a 25 per cent increase in both his income and the incomes of others.

The more this attitude prevails—and the ethos of our society actively promote it—the more futile is the objective of economic growth for society as a whole. For it is obvious that over time everyone cannot become relatively better off.[9]

Aggregate growth can no more satisfy the relative wants of distinction than the arms race can increase security. The only way this self-cancelling effect and its resulting futility can be avoided is if growth is allowed to make the relatively well-off relatively better-off. But then the price of continuing growth would be ever-increasing inequality, and all the pious talk about "growth for the poor" would be seen as the evasion that it really is. When society has reached a level of affluence such that at the margin it is relative wants that are dominant, then aggregate growth becomes either futile or the source of increasing inequality. At some point growth becomes undesirable, even if still possible.

The effective limit to growth, however, is neither the desirability nor the possibility limit, but the interaction of desirability and possibility, that is, the *economic* limit. It is not necessary that the marginal benefits of growth should fall all the way to zero, nor that the marginal costs of growth should rise to infinity, but only that the two should become equal. As growth continues we know that marginal benefits fall and marginal costs rise and at some point they will become equal. We do not satisfy our ends in any random order, but strive always to satisfy our most pressing needs first. Likewise we do not use our low-entropy means in any order, but we exploit the highest-grade and most accessible resources first. This elementary rule of sensible behavior underlies both the law of diminishing marginal benefit and the law of increasing marginal costs, which are the very keystones of economic theory.

The possibility, desirability, and economic limits are depicted in Figure 13.2.

As growth increases the total stock, total benefits rise at a diminishing rate, while total costs rise at an increasing rate. At point A the slope of the two curves are equal (marginal cost equals marginal benefit) and the vertical distance between the curves (net benefit) is a maximum. Point A is the economic limit and, though not easily recognized, is the relevant limit. If we overshoot point A we will meet either the possibility or

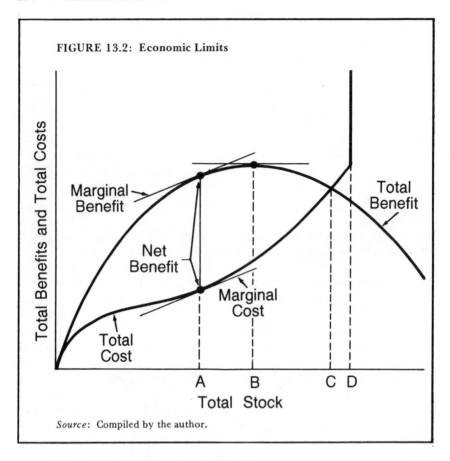

FIGURE 13.2: Economic Limits

Source: Compiled by the author.

desirability limit, though not necessarily in the order shown. (In fact, it is possible that marginal costs could discontinuously rise to infinity somewhere to the left of point A, and that the possibility limit would occur before the economic limit.) At point B the marginal benefit of growth (slope of total benefit curve) has fallen to zero (horizontal). Even if the costs of growth were zero we should not grow beyond B. At point D the marginal costs of growth become infinite (vertical slope) and growth would perforce end, regardles of benefits. Once we have passed point A, further growth makes us worse off, not better off. But it seems that the experience of reduced well-being is attributed to the heavy hand of commodity scarcity, and the call is for more growth, which makes us still worse off, leading to the call for still more growth, and so on. Like Alice on the other side of the looking glass, our image of reality becomes inverted and the faster we run the behinder we get. Our journalists and pundits defend growth by arguing that the total cumulative benefits of past growth still outweigh the total costs—"Thanks to growth the average man of today is better off than the average man of 300 years ago, therefore further growth must be good." They argue as if point C rather than point A were the economic limit and are guilty of confusing totals with marginals.

But the growth economist will rightly point out that our diagram is too static. Technical progress and the emergence of new wants shift the cost curve down and the benefits curve up, and point A will move ever to the right, and growth in stocks will always be called for. There are two replies to this objection. First, even though the curves shift apart, point A need not move to the right. It could remain fixed or move to the left. It all depends on how the curves shift, because the location of point A is determined by the *slopes* of the two curves, not their positions. To assume that point A will always move to the right as the curves shift seems to overspecify the kind of dynamic change permitted. The second reply is that, even assuming the necessary rightward shift of point A, there are limits to how far apart the curves can be shifted. Our discussion of ultimate means and the second law assures us that there are limits to the efficiency increase represented by a downward shift of the total cost curve. Likewise our discussion of the ultimate end leads to the presumption that there is such a thing as enough in the material realm. Time sets a limit to how many artifacts can be serviceably used in a day. Perhaps the intensity of enjoyment of a given stock can increase forever (a doubtful proposition), but that would not contradict the SSE, which is defined in terms of constant stocks, not constant service. But in a growing economy service efficiency is likely to fall. As the growing throughput pushes against biophysical limits it provokes a decline in service efficiency. More of the stock must be devoted to the defensive use of repairing life-support systems that formerly provided their services gratis. Also, in our economy billions are spent to push up artifically the marginal benefits of growth by stimulating new wants through commercial propaganda. In a sense, these billions measure the degree to which our natural recognition of "enoughness" or sufficiency must be overcome by artful cajolery. Whether these expenditures really raise the benefit curve is. debatable, since the stimulated wants are often meretricious. Likewise, billions are spent on research and development to lower the cost curve. The net result of these expenditures may be to raise the true cost curve as a result of irresponsible technical razzle-dazzle (for example, fission power and the supersonic transport), and the lavish use of resources induced by low prices that fail to reflect the full dimensions of scarcity.

But such diagrams, though of heuristic value, are not operational because we have no national accounts measuring either the costs or benefits of growth. We have only GNP, which is merely a measure of activity and lumps together costs, benefits, and changes in stock. As previously noted, an SSE would seek to measure the value of service (benefit) in one account and the value of throughput (cost) in a separate account. Only then would we have even a remote change of getting an operational estimate of where point A lies.

But there are many sensible policies that can be taken in the absence of an operational estimate of the optimum level of stocks, which may in any case be a will-o'-the-wisp. Once the optimum level is reached it follows that the optimum growth rate is zero. But it is not necessary to know the optimum level in order to argue for a zero growth rate. Even if we have not yet reached the optimum we should still learn to live in an SSE so that we could remain at the optimum once we got there rather than grow through it. We can achieve an SSE at existing, historically given levels without being forever frozen there. If we later discover that a larger or smaller stock would be better, then we could always grow or decline to the preferred level, at which we would again be stable. Growth, or decline, would then be a temporary adjustment process, not a norm.

My own belief is that we have passed the optimum and in the future will have to reduce both population and per capita consumption. But the issue of the optimum level for a nation is enormously difficult because four related questions must be answered simultaneously: (1) What size population do we want, (2) living at what standard of stocks (and throughput) per capita, (3) for how long, (4) on the basis of what kinds of technology? The answer given to each of these questions affects the answers given to the others. Also, we should ask whether the level we choose for the United States can be generalized to the world as a whole. Currently, the 6 percent of the world's population in the United States consumes around 30 percent of the world's annual production of non-renewable resources. To generalize this standard to 100 percent of the world's people would require, at minimum, a sixfold increase in current resource flows. In addition, to supply the world with the "standing crop" of industrial metals embodied in the existing artifacts in the ten richest nations would require more than 60 years' world production of these metals at 1970 rates.[10] The ecological disruption caused by the next sixfold increase would be greater per unit of resource produced because of diminishing returns. If world energy use continues to grow at 5 percent annually, then in 200 years man would be producing as much energy as he receives from the sun. Before then global climatological limits will restrict energy use, and these limits may be felt within 30 to 50 years.[11] In fact, we may already be experiencing climatological changes provoked by man's energy use. In any event it is sobering to recognize that man's energy requirements are now as great as those of all other terrestrial organisms put together.

These considerations do not constitute proof, but they are sufficient to induce strong doubt that U.S. levels are generalizable, either to the world as a whole or to very many future generations, much less to both. High and increasing levels of population and per capita consumption have been bought by sacrificing the possibility of extending such a condition either to the future or to poor nations of the present. Attempts to generalize the ungeneralizable are leading to technological adventurism of the most fanatical kind. Space, the green revolution, and atomic power are recent promises of a technical solution that have proven empty and are threatening much worse.

The SSE would stop mindless growth in stocks of artifacts and people and would allow a less driven and more judicious choice of technology, as well as the possibility of sparing more resources for use both by future generations and present people in poor countries. The SSE is not a panacea. Even an SSE will not last forever, nor will it overcome the entropy law and the law of diminishing returns. But it would permit our economy to die gracefully of old age rather than prematurely from the cancer of growth mania.

POLICIES FOR AN SSE

How can we achieve an SSE without enormous disruption? The difficult part is mustering the moral resources and political will to do it. The technical problems are small by comparison. People often overestimate the technical problems because they mistakenly identify an SSE with a failed growth economy. A situation of nongrowth can come about in two ways: As the success of steady-state policies or as the failure of growth policies. Nongrowth resulting from the failure of a growth economy to grow is chaotic beyond repair. But the fact that airplanes fall from the air if they try to stand still does not mean that a helicopter cannot stand still.

In an effort to stimulate discussion on policies for attaining an SSE, I have suggested three institutions that seem to me to provide the necessary social control with a minimum sacrifice of individual freedom. They build on the existing bases of private property and the price system and are thus fundamentally conservative, though they will appear radical to some. The kinds of institutions needed follow straight from the definition of an SSE: "constant stocks of people and artifacts maintained at chosen levels that are sufficient for a good life and sustainable for a long future, by the lowest feasible rate of throughput."

Let us leave population issues to one side. Of all the population control schemes suggested, I prefer the transferrable birth license plan, first advocated by Kenneth Boulding,[12] then elaborated by Herman Daly[13] and by Heer.[14] For purposes of this discussion, however, I will invite the reader to substitute his own favorite population control scheme if he does not like that one.

A constant aggregate stock of artifacts will result from holding the throughput flow constant by means of a depletion quota auction, to be discussed below. Since aggregate growth can no longer be appealed to as the "solution" to poverty, we must face the distribution issue directly by setting up a distributist institution, which would limit the range of inequality to some justifiable and functional degree. This could be accomplished by setting minimum income and maximum income and wealth limits for individuals and families, and a maximum size for corporations. The maximum and minimum would define a range within which inequality is legitimate and beyond which it is not. The exact numbers are of secondary importance, but just suppose a minimum of $7,000 and a maximum of $70,000 on family income. The idea of a minimum income is familiar, but the notion of a maximum is not, because in the growth paradigm it is not necessary. But in the steady-state paradigm the total is constant and this implicity sets a maximum on individual income. Some limits on inequality are essential, though we may debate just how much inequality is legitimate.

The key institution would be the depletion quota auction by which the annual amount extracted of each basic resource would be set and the quota rights auctioned by the government in conveniently divisible units. The resource market would become two-tiered. First, the government, as monopolist, would auction the limited quota rights to many resource buyers, who, having purchased their quota rights, would enter the second tier of the market where they would confront many resource sellers in a competitive market. Buyers would pay the resource producers the market price and surrender the requisite quota rights to the producer at the time of purchase. The firms in the extraction industry would be audited to make sure that production plus change in inventories balanced with quota certificates collected.

Figure 13.3 illustrates more clearly how things would work. DD' is the market demand curve for the resource in question, and SS' is the industry supply curve. A depletion quota in the aggregate amount Q is imposed, shown by the vertical line QQ'. The total price paid per unit of the resource (unit price paid to resource producer plus unit price of the quota right paid to the government) is OC. Of the total price OC the amount OB is the price paid to resource producers, and BC is the price paid to the government for the quota right. Of the total amount paid, OQAC, the amount OSEQ is cost, reflecting necessary supply price (extraction costs). the remainder, SEAC is surplus, or rent. Rent is defined as payment in excess of supply price. Of the total rent area the amount BES is

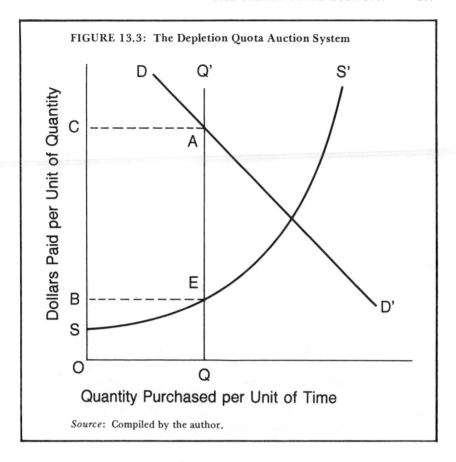

FIGURE 13.3: The Depletion Quota Auction System

Quantity Purchased per Unit of Time

Source: Compiled by the author.

differential rent and accrues to the resource producers as profit. The remainder, the amount CAEB, is pure scarcity rent and accrues to the government. As a monopolist in the sale of quota rights the government is able to extract the full amount of pure scarcity rent that results from lower quantity and higher price.

Let us review what is achieved by the depletion quota auction. First, the throughput of basic resources is physically limited, and with it the rate of depletion and pollution associated with that resource. Allocation of the fixed resource aggregate among competing uses and firms is done by the market. The price of the resource increases; inducing greater efficiency of use, both in production and in consumption. Resource-saving technical improvement is induced, and so is recycling. The monopoly profits resulting from the higher prices are captured by the government, while resource producers earn normal competitive profits. The government revenues could be used to finance the minimum income part of the distributist institution. Efficiency is served by high resource prices, equity is served by redistributing the proceeds of the higher prices to the poor, and by a maximum limit on incomes of the rich.

What criteria are there for setting the "proper" aggregate quota amounts for each resource? For renewable resources there is the fairly objective criterion of maximum sustainable yield. For nonrenewables there is, of course, no sustainable yield. But economist John Ise suggested 50 years ago that nonrenewables should be priced equal to or more than their nearest renewable substitute.[15] Thus virgin timber should be priced at least as much per board foot as replanted timber; petroleum should be priced at its BTU equivalent in terms of sugar or wood alcohol, assuming that is in fact the closest renewable substitute. For nonrenewables with no reasonably close renewable substitute, the matter is simply a question of how fast should we use it up, that is, an ethical weighing of present versus future wants. One further criterion might be added: Even if a resource is in no danger of depletion, its use may produce considerable pollution (for example, coal), and depletion quotas may be imposed with the objective of limiting pollution, the other end of the throughput pipeline.

The combination of these three institutions presents a nice reconciliation of equity and efficiency and provides the ecologically necessary macro control with the least sacrifice of micro freedom and variability. The market is relied upon to allocate resources and distribute incomes within imposed ecological and ethical boundaries. The market is not allowed to set its own boundaries but is free within the boundaries imposed. Setting the boundaries externally is necessary. It is absurd to expect that market equilibria will automatically coincide with ecological or demographic equilibria, or with a reasonably just distribution of wealth and income. The very notions of "equilibrium" in economics and ecology are antithetical. In macroeconomics equilibrium refers not to physical magnitudes at all, but to a balance of desires between savers and investers—equilibrium means full employment at a stable price level. This implies, under current institutions, a positive flow of net investment to offset positive savings. Net investment implies increasing stocks and a growing throughput, that is, a biophysical disequilibrium. Physical boundaries guaranteeing reasonable ecological equilibrium must be imposed on the market in quantitative terms.

How do these proposals differ from the orthodox economists' prescription of "internalizing externalities via pollution taxes"? Pollution taxes are price controls on the output end of the throughput, while depletion quotas are quantitative controls on the input end. Depletion is spatially far more concentrated than pollution, and consequently much easier to monitor. Quantity should be the control variable rather than price because prices cannot limit aggregate throughput. Higher relative prices on resources would induce substitution and bring the resource content per unit of output down to some minimum. But prices cannot limit the number of units of output produced, and therefore cannot limit the total volume of resource throughput. For every increase in price there is an equal increase in someone's income, or in the government revenue. Aggregate income is always sufficient to purchase the growing aggregate supply, regardless of prices. In the famous words of Say's Law, "Supply creates its own demand." Taxes, by raising relative prices, could provide a one-shot reduction in aggregate throughput by reducing throughput per dollar's worth of output down to some feasible minimum, but the number of units of output could keep growing, unless the government ran an ever-growing budget surplus. Finally, it is quantity that affects the biosphere, not price. It is safer to set ecological limits in terms of fixed quantities, and to let errors and unexpected changes work themselves out in price changes, than to set prices and let errors and omissions cause quantity changes.

The "internalization of externalities" is a good strategy for fine-tuning the allocation of resources by making relative prices better measures of relative marginal costs. But it does not enable the market to set its own absolute physical bounds. To give an analogy: proper allocation arranges the weight in a boat optimally, so as to maximize the load that can be carried. But there is still an absolute limit to how much weight a boat can carry, even if optimally arranged. The price system can spread the weight evenly, but unless supplemented by an external absolute limit it will just keep on spreading the increasing weight evenly until the evenly loaded boat sinks. No doubt the boat would sink evenly, ceteris paribus, but that is little comfort.

Two distinct questions must be asked about these proposed institutions for achieving an SSE. First, would they work if people accepted the need for an SSE and, say, voted these institutions into effect? Second, would people ever accept the goal of an SSE? In this last section I have argued that the answer to the first question is "yes." Although the answer to the second question would surely be "no" if a vote were held today; that is because the growth paradigm is still dominant. With time the concepts and arguments sketched out in the first two sections will look more and more appealing and will themselves be sharpened, as the real facts of life push the growth paradigm into ever greater anomalies, contradictions, and practical failures.

NOTES

1. Edison Electric Institute, *Economic Growth in the Future: The Growth Debate in National and Global Perspective* (New York: McGraw-Hill, 1976).

2. Irving Fisher, *The Nature of Capital and Income* (London: Macmillan, 1906).

3. Nicholas Georgescu-Roegen, *The Entropy Law and the Economic Process* (Cambridge, Mass.: Harvard University Press, 1971).

4. Kenneth Boulding, "The Economics of the Coming Spaceship Earth," in *Environmental Quality in a Growing Economy,* ed. Henry Jarrett (Baltimore: Johns Hopkins University Press, 1966); and Georgescu-Roegen, *The Entropy Law.*

5. John Stuart Mill, *Principles of Political Economy* (New York: Appleton-Century-Crofts, 1881).

6. Harold Barnett and Chandler Morse, *Scarcity and Growth* (Baltimore: Johns Hopkins University Press for Resources for the Future, 1963), p. 11.

7. Georgescu-Roegen, *The Entropy Law.*

8. Barnett *Scarcity and Growth,* p. 11.

9. E. J. Mishan, "Growth and Anti-Growth: What are the Issues?" *Challenge,* May/June 1973, p. 30.

10. Harrison Brown, "Human Materials Production as a Process in the Biosphere," *Scientific American,* September 1970, pp. 194–208.

11. Alvin Weinberg, Editorial, "Global Effects of Man's Production of Energy," *Science,* October 18, 1974, p. 205.

12. Kenneth Boulding, *The Meaning of the Twentieth Century* (New York: Harper and Row, 1964).

13. Herman Daly, *Toward a Steady-State Economy* (San Francisco: Freeman, 1973). See Reading no. seven.

14. David Heer, "Marketable Licenses for Babies: Boulding's Proposal Revisited," *Social Biology,* Spring 1975, pp. 1–16.

15. John Ise, "The Theory of Value as Applied to Natural Resources," *American Economic Review,* June 1925, pp. 284–91.

14 | Extending the Growth Debate

E. J. Mishan

COMMENTS ON *ECONOMIC GROWTH IN THE FUTURE*

The Edison Electric Institute's report, *Economic Growth in the Future,* is another extension of the growth debate.[1] My first reaction on reading the report was that it is well-organized and stimulating, but that possibly a tactical misjudgment had been made. Bound together in a large volume, comprising an uneasy *menage à trois,* are three separate studies; one on the growth/anti-growth debate, one on economic growth patterns over the future, and one on the growth pattern of the electricity industry. To be sure, they are linked by a common theme, and their order is sensible enough; the forecasts of the electricity industry building, as they should, on the forecasts of GNP. Yet the juxtaposition of Part I, on the economic growth debate, with Parts II and III, on growth forecasts, does seem to me to weaken the authority of each.

The skeptical reader is apt to think that the electricity industry has an uneasy conscience about its plans for future expansion and seeks to quieten it by a little public relations stratagem in the form of a sponsored tournament between growth and no-growth teams. And this same skeptical reader can have no doubt of the sort of conclusions that the industry will reach: after ceremonial recognition of the legitimate apprehensions of the no-growth party, it will, unavoidably, find in favor of a more judicious and discriminating economic growth—one which, by definition, is devoutly to be desired.

This gratuitous impression would, I think, be erased if the report had been split into at least two separate volumes; one on the debate and one on forecasting. Each alone would be taken more seriously as a study in its own right. But if this course were adopted, the volume on the growth debate would need to be revised and amplified. For though the industry's judgment of the debate is the very soul of prudence, it lacks sinew and definition. Not only is its interest in the outcome of such a debate transparent, an impartial synthesis can hardly be fashioned from a debate in which the contestants seldom come to grips with each other.

THE LIMITS OF FORECASTING

Part II of *Economic Growth in the Future* includes the results of a major modeling and forecasting effort. This bears some general observations and a specific criticism.

No matter how sophisticated the forecasting techniques incorporated into a model, the plausibility of the figures generated depend, in the last resort, first on the factual assumptions with respect to economic behavior, to institutions and public policies, and to international developments. Second, they depend upon the tacit assumptions that inhere in the mathematical properties of the forms of the equations adopted, and, third, upon the appropriateness of these expressions as interpretations of the underlying reality. Since I am not conversant with the relevant details of the Data Resources Incorporated (DRI) model used in the Edison Electric Institute effort, I restrict my remarks to the set of factual assumptions.

For short-term forecasting, say three to five years, reliance upon the economist's conventional parameters—for example, measures of the reaction of market demand to prices and income—is likely to produce good results. The longer the period of time, however, the greater is the scope for "exogenous" forces to reshape these parameters in an unpredictable manner, as a result of institutional and policy changes, some of which take place in response to international developments or to the political initiatives of foreign governments. Even known international factors have to be left out of these models if their magnitudes are highly speculative. The postwar growth in the scale of illegal immigration, with the United States a particularly favored destination, is likely to make a significant difference to the resulting population and income pattern over the future, to touch only on the barest of economic aggregates. But there is nothing for it but simply to point out the possibilities.

My specific criticism of *Economic Growth in the Future* is related to switches in public policy that follow, with a lag, the formation of public opinion. True, Parts II and III of the report touch on the opportunities for economizing on energy through greater use of public transport, through reductions in speed limits, and generally through alterations in life styles. But it does not face the possibility that, for a number of reasons, the country might want to seek far more radical ways of cutting down on its energy consumption. It could, for example, seek to implement policies designed to maintain per capita energy consumption at the existing level, or even to reduce it.

Thus, it might need only a single serious nuclear accident to precipitate public opinion into a posture of unyielding opposition to the nuclear fission industry. Whether, in fact, one or two serious nuclear accidents, say every ten years, should be regarded as being costly enough on strictly economic grounds to warrant the prohibition of nuclear energy production is an issue that will have little bearing on the public's reaction, and the political consequences following therefrom. Anyone who has been reading the popular environmental literature on the hazards of breeder reactors, or anyone who has read John Fuller's description of a number of nuclear mishaps in his recent book, *We Nearly Lost Detroit,* may be excused for thinking that a nuclear catastrophe of respectable dimensions is in the offing.[2]

I am suggesting that a fuel policy designed to give expression to a public demand for zero energy growth, one that excludes nuclear fission, should have been given more serious consideration. Such a policy would require for its success higher taxes on fuels, or electricity, and also, perhaps, on the range of electric and gasoline gadgetry. Yet so radical a fuel-economizing policy is not necessarily inconsistent with the continuation of fairly high rates of economic growth. True, the calculation in this report would require a "low-growth scenario," one averaging about 2.3 percent per annum growth of GNP between 1975 and 2000, if energy consumption is to grow from 77 quadrillion BTUs (QB) in 1975 to no more than 117 QB by the year 2000. But it is possible to do much better than this. In a recent fuel study, *A Time to Choose* (1975), one also claiming, incidentally, to use the DRI model, a "zero energy growth scenario" is generated which produces no more than 99.6 QB of energy by the year 2000—withal the average growth of GNP is about 3.2 percent per annum.[3] If this 1975 study is acceptable, one must infer that the connections in this report between GNP growth and energy growth are not flexible enough: For a given level of "real" product, there must be opportunities for substituting against the use of energy that have not been fully investigated.

THE GROWTH/ANTI-GROWTH DEBATE

Turning now to the growth/anti-growth debate, my overall impression is that most of the pro-growth arguments are rather worn and flimsy; whereas most of the no-growth arguments are too terse or ambiguous. It would require a far more searching debate than that presented in *Economic Growth in the Future* to attract the impartial reader toward either camp.

The Pro-Growth Arguments

Having said so much by way of preface, I shall now voice a number of strictures on the contribution of the pro-growth writers undeterred by apprehension that I will be accused of bias.

First, the crucial issue in this sort of debate is not what some "purified" economic growth could offer humanity, were it attainable. It is what economic growth is in fact likely to offer us, judging by its past and present performance, and by expected developments over the future. I hasten to add that included among the expected developments are the political ones also. For even where the noxious side effects of an industrial process are manifest and tangible, and the remedy technically simple, political opposition to the remedy is common enough and, alas, frequently decisive. Any number of economists have testified to the efficiency of the effluent tax. Yet its very efficacy, as pointed out by M. Freeman and R. Haveman (1972), has attracted opposition enough from the industry as to render it politically impracticable.[4]

At all events, this invocation of the *potential* of economic growth for doing us all proud is one of the less interesting propositions that keeps popping up in *Economic Growth in the Future*, both in the pro-growth view and the industry's view. With terms like "clean" growth, "purified" growth proliferating, what begins as a conjectural possibility is apt to be interpreted by the unwary as a feasible program.

Certainly a high-growth, high-consumption society can also be a low-quality and low-spirited society. It can be a degenerate society even though it produces more leisure and more medicine for the masses and as much "education" as they can stomach. The really interesting question, I should have thought, is whether this possibility is not in fact in the process of realizing itself. Be that as it may, the no-growth economist is concerned not with definitions of beneficial growth, but with the actual growth process. And he bases his case on the premise that the more important of these adverse "externalities," environmental and social, are inherent in the process of economic growth as commonly understood. No defense of economic growth can hope to be effective if it ignores this basic form of attack.

Second, questions about whether a worker today would prefer to be employed in America or in India, or whether a person prefers to be rich or poor, are nonissues. If anyone had the slightest doubt of the answers, he could always conduct a survey. The question being asked by the no-growth advocate is whether it is prudent for an already affluent society to continue to strive for economic growth.

Third, allegations that continued economic growth is needed in the United States in order to remove poverty or to maintain employment are little more than bits of effrontery. The merest fraction of America's annual expenditure on neogarbage—on expendables, inimicals, and on inane trivia—would suffice to remove all the remnants of hard-core poverty in the land. And if we must be chary of passing judgment on the public's taste in a democracy, we can have recourse to the Chicago School proposals for alleviating poverty: a switch from wholesale and indiscriminate welfarism to selective and discriminating welfare measures that, it is believed, would benefit both the taxpayer and the really poor.

As for the maintenance of high levels of employment, what is wanted from the growth proponents is at least one convincing reason why a high level of employment is incompatible with a steady-state economy. I can think of no reason, deriving from standard economic analysis, why it should be so.

Fourth, with all respect to the ingenuity of William Nordhaus and James Tobin, they did not, as alleged, "test the argument" that the supposed gains from economic growth are nonexistent. (It is only fair to say, however, that these deservedly respected authors were far more qualified in their conclusions, and far more reticent about their figures, than the pro-growth men who continue triumphantly to quote them.) Even if they did, some of their measurements would not stand up to scrutiny. In particular, their idea of using the wage differential between urban and rural labor as an index of the growth of disamenity over time was an inspired piece of audacity. A moment's reflection will suggest quite a number of reasons why this wage differential can widen over time, both in rich and poor countries. Another moment's reflection on the heavy costs of movement suggests that substantial changes in pollution can take place with little effect on the price of property or labor.

More important, even if costs of movement were nil, and if the disamenities in question were the only factor influencing population movements as between rural and urban areas: the wage differential would be useless as an index of increasing disamenity—unless it could be assumed that rural amenity remained constant over time. In fact, such things as noise levels and crime levels have been rising everywhere in America, even though they are rising faster in urban areas.

Finally, a market measure of disamenity can be regarded as being a lower bound to the true cost inasmuch as it is based, generally, on what a person is willing to pay to escape a particular environmental nuisance. Wherever the impact of this environmental nuisance on a person's welfare is large, this sum that he is willing to pay can be but a fraction of the sum he would be ready to accept for bearing with the nuisance. As revealed in the Report of Britain's Roskill Commission (1971), quite a number of people were unwilling to be put to the trouble required, however large the compensation offered them. Yet they could pay very little actually to prevent it.

It is reasonable to conclude that a more widely acceptable method of evaluating the growth of disamenities over time would produce figures that would reverse the Nordhaus-Tobin tentative conclusions.

The No-Growth Arguments

Turning, finally, to the no-growth view, a rereading of the section reveals the ecological discussion to be insufficiently explicit. Admittedly, it serves to place economics in a broader perspective. But there can be reasonable doubt about the relevance of the second law of thermodynamics for the time scale we have in mind when thinking in terms of "the foreseeable future."

However, the section does have the merit of raising a "moral issue": asking questions about the social purpose of continuing economic growth in the United States—assuming, always, that poverty has been eradicated and the income distribution is satisfactory. At one level of the debate we might be asking whether it is worth incurring the sorts of risks currently being associated with technological growth simply to be able to stuff our lives with more goods than we shall, in any case, have time to ingest.

And for just how long could we expect to grow at present rates? Suppose that by some miracle we survive the gauntlet of hazards produced by our technical ingenuity. Five hundred years of economic growth, in the United States, at a per capita rate averaging 3 percent would generate a per capita real income (measured in conventional "real" terms) that would be 1 million times as great as it is today.

A statistician does not flinch at a figure of 1 million, even if it is a multiplicative factor. But a factor of ten in this context would be enough to strain most people's imaginations. I confess to difficulties in picturing the extent of the drain on the earth's finite resources (despite the treasures of an Aladdin's cave we have now begun to believe lie just below the earth's surface, patiently awaiting our ransack), in disposing of the heat generated by such a colossal output (even if most of it is "services"), to say nothing of the space needed by each individual in order simply to accumulate his quantum of property and machines, or of the frenzy with which this superenriched individual would have to move in order to cram his quotidian $10 million's worth of goods and recreations into the space of a woefully inadequate 24-hour day.

Rather than continue to expatiate on the wonders of the price mechanism in providing incentives and inducing factor and product substitution, or on the opportunities for further engorgement by ripping through the earth's crust, or on technological marvels yet to come that will whip us about the world and into outer space, and bloat us with euphoric drugs, we should seek to remove the scales from our eyes and, remarking the sense of purposelessness and disorder gathering about us, face the critical question: whether further economic growth in the already prosperous countries of the world is more likely or not to improve the human condition.

In this connection, I find a number of observations in the no-growth section of *Economic Growth in the Future*[5] that look as if they could bear elaborating. I confine myself to one of the more topical: the thesis that continued economic growth in the West will unerringly erode the area of personal liberty there.

EXTENDING THE ARGUMENTS AGAINST GROWTH

This thesis can be stated briefly as follows: rapid technological change creates social problems, the response to which is cumulative and detailed legislation. More importantly, the particular direction taken by technological progress extends the reach of governments and also, by creating social conflicts and hazards, increases the need for more government. Recent examples arising from familiar technological innovations serve to illustrate these points.

1. The increasing use over the last two decades of computers to control the operations of chemical plants, telephone exchanges, and such public utilities as sewage disposal and electricity, gas, and water supply. Since a single plant can be made to serve a vast metropolitan area, a breakdown of these public utilities, or their sabotage, is exceedingly costly and could be disastrous. In consequence, there is a need for closer check and tighter controls on the personnel involved in the day-to-day management, maintenance, and repair of computers and other critical bits of apparatus. The more intimate personal knowledge required to implement these precautions is coming to be provided by specialized agencies with highly developed methods of prying into the private lives of citizens. The distaste in which they are held by liberals cannot prevent their future growth, which, in fact, is facilitated by the cooperation of a growing number of citizens whose job opportunities comes to depend upon the availability of such information.

2. The postwar expansion of motorized pastimes, involving the use today of motorcycles, speed boats, private planes, snowmobiles, and the like, has started a reaction among the more amenity-conscious citizenry, one that is manifestly on the increase. As a result, restrictions on the freedoms hitherto enjoyed by the motorized multitude have begun to spread within all the industrialized countries.

Again, the promotion of mass tourism, arising from the spread of air travel, has begun to run into the incipient resentment of populations in the host country or region. The pressures are growing on legislatures to limit the freedom of people to travel when and where they wish. Within rich and highly populated countries, for instance, motorized travel to national parks, wilderness areas, and lake districts will soon have to be rationed, whether by price or by more direct measures, if the scenic areas are to be preserved for the future.

In view of their excessive mobility and enterprise, it is not surprising that Americans are more conscious of these problems than other nationals. In the introduction to a recent report commissioned by Congress, economist Ronald Ridker wrote:

> Conservation of our water resources, preservation of wilderness areas, protection of animal life threatened by man, restrictions on pollutant emissions, and limitations on fertilizer and pesticide-use, all require public regulation ... It appears inevitable that a larger proportion of our lives will be devoted to filling forms, arguing with the computer or its representative, appealing decisions, waiting for our case to be handled, finding ways to evade or move ahead in the queue. In many small ways, everyday life will become more contrived.[6]

3. Ridker's remarks above, therefore, have reference also to the mounting concern over the past decade with air, soil, and water pollution, arising from new industrial processes, from the wanton use of chemical pesticides and chemical fertilizers, and from the dumping of sewage in estuaries and oil on the high seas. The increase in controls in Britain seem to have excited little attention as yet. In the United States, however, the environmental interest has been vociferous enough to precipitate a rash of restrictive legislation at all levels of government. In 1970, for instance, the powerful Environmental Protection Agency was set up by the federal government. Today, American businessmen no longer have the freedom to choose their most profitable type or scale of plant, or its most profitable location.

4. It is by now abundantly evident that continued scientific research produces not only more powerful missile systems, but also deadly gases and bacteria. It produces also critical simplifications in the design of missiles or bacteriological bombs that place them within the capacity of the smaller and, often, the less politically stable nation-states. As this situation becomes more dangerous, the temptation exerted on the larger powers to intervene, singly or jointly, in the internal affairs of the smaller countries will become stronger.

Weapons innovations and simplifications, however, also increase the power of the modern criminal organization and of guerrilla fanatics, and they do so at a time when such outlaw groups are active in intimidating the public by the kidnapping and killing of hostages. As people in towns and cities come to realize how vulnerable they have become—both singly, through terrorist victimization, and collectively, through a disruption of vital services—they will become increasingly amenable to proposals for closer monitoring of internal and international travel and, consequently, less resistant to the idea of surrendering to the police more arbitrary powers of search and arrest.

This trend toward a more repressive internal security system is reinforced by two other developments:

5. The arms race among the great powers, which no longer takes the form simply of expanding military personnel. The more significant form it takes today is that of massive investment in research and development, in the continuing effort to produce more deadly weapons. For every new weapon of offensive capability, there is soon a weapon of defensive capability, the response to which is yet a more destructive offensive weapon, and so on. This spiral of self-sustaining research inevitably proliferates scientific secrets of value to enemy agents.

The resulting fears, real and imaginary, of ubiquitous enemy intelligence go far to sanction the use of special powers for counterespionage activities. There is precious little a government, even a democratic government, cannot do today in the name of national defense or military necessity.

6. The breeder reactor program, believed, until recently, to be the answer to the world's impending oil shortage, has begun to arouse apprehension and controversy. Yet such is the momentum of modern technology, and such the fears among the industrial powers of slipping behind, that only a miracle can prevent the expansion of the nuclear fission industry.

In order to appreciate the magnitude of only one of the major risks associated with a nuclear economy, that of plutonium poisoning, the following facts must be borne in mind: (1) that a fully developed U.S. nuclear industry would be producing some 200,000 pounds of plutonium a year; (2) that the half life of this substance is 24,000 years; and (3) that a mere half pound of it, dispersed as fine particles into the atmosphere, would be enough to inflict every living mortal with lung cancer. It follows that a containment level even as high as 99.9 percent would be unacceptable. Yet, since plutonium is a necessary material for the fabrication of nuclear weapons, and is expected to be a lucrative item of illicit traffic, a containment level of 99.9 percent is hardly feasible—at least, not without an extraordinary and sustained security program.

The measures required by such a program will involve armed defense of all nuclear establishments, armed protection of the transport network along which move the containers of atomic materials, and a surrender to specially trained forces of power of entry, arrest, interrogation, and detention if, as they will claim, they are to move fast enough to prevent gangs of criminals, fanatics, or psychopaths from capturing position from which they can effectively blackmail a nation or cause irreparable disaster.

In sum, and contrary to the beliefs of liberal economists such as Milton Friedman, the return to a more competitive economy cannot of itself suffice to shore up traditional freedoms against the expanding encroachment of the modern state. As we move into a world of increasing conflict and increasing hazard, the unforeseen by-products of scientific and technical progress, men can come reluctantly but inevitably to surrender to governments far greater powers of surveillance, control, and repression than are compatible with contemporary notions of personal liberty.

NOTES

1. Edison Electric Institute, *Economic Growth in the Future: The Growth Debate in National and Global Perspective* (New York: McGraw-Hill, 1976).

2. John G. Fuller, *We Nearly Lost Detroit* (New York: Reader's Digest Press, 1975).

3. The Energy Policy Project of the Ford Foundation, *A Time To Choose: America's Energy Future* (Cambridge, Mass.: Ballings Publishing Co., 1975).

4. M. Freeman and R. Haveman, "Clean Rhetoric, Dirty Water," *The Public Interest,* Summer 1972.

5. EEI, *Economic Growth in the Future,* Chapter 3.

6. R. C. Ridker, ed., *Commission on Population Growth and the American Future,* Vol. III (Washington, D.C.: U.S. Government Printing Office, 1972), p. 31.

15 | Matter Matters, Too
Nicholas Georgescu-Roegen

THE CARNOTIAN REVOLUTION

Mechanics was the first science to reach a level of analytical development as perfect as that to which Euclid had brought the old art of land
measurement—the *geometria*. But still more significant is that mechanics
reached the same level of accuracy in prediction. By the turn of the
eighteenth century, scientists and scholars no longer entertained any
doubt about the notion that mechanics is *the* science, that the world is
ruled by it. Laplace was thus able to claim in his famous apotheosis of
mechanics (1814) that every happening in the universe, past or future, is
determined by a system of mechanical equations. He conceded that only
a demiurgic mind, a mathematical demon, could obtain all the necessary
data of the parameters and solve the vast system.[1] One can hardly imagine the elation felt by all scientific circles when, in 1846, Urbain Leverrier
discovered the planet Neptune, not by scanning the firmament with a
powerful telescope, but at the tip of his pencil after a series of calculations
based on the equations of mechanics. Laplace's position seemed vindicated beyond any right of appeal.

Yet, during the same period, something happened that was to constitute soon the first blow inflicted to the mechanistic dogma and to cause
the first important revolution in physics. While Laplace and almost all his
peers were interested only in celestial affairs—then a long tradition with
the students of the physical world—a few people devoted their attention
to some pedestrian problems, nearer to man's everyday life. By the end
of the eighteenth century, with the improvements brought by James Watt,
the old steam engine was already operational. In 1807 Albany became
connected with New York by a steamboat. Most important of all events,
in 1824 Sadi Carnot, a young officer in the French Engineer Corps,
published a memoir on "the motive power of fire" in which the process
of a steam engine was theoretically analyzed.[2] In it he proved that no
conversion of heat energy into mechanical work by a cyclical engine can

be complete: some definite amount of heat energy must be transformed from the boiler to the cooler without being converted into mechanical work. This means that the boiler must be hotter than the cooler. No matter how hot the boiler may be, if the outside is just as hot, the engine cannot possibly work. Although Carnot's findings may appear surprising to many even nowadays, they were mundanely dull for the analytical minds of the epoch. The memoir remained completely unnoticed until Emile Clapeyron unearthened it ten years later for further contributions to the theory of heat.[3] From then on, nothing could stop the march of ideas that ultimately led to that peculiar and extremely complex branch of physics known now as thermodynamics.

It is a peculiar discipline, because of its pronounced anthropomorphic web (as I shall explain presently). But the unique complexity of thermodynamics as it exists today does not prevent us from telling its story in some simple terms.

WHAT THERMODYNAMICS TEACHES US

What we read first in the conventional literature of thermodynamics is that energy can neither be destroyed nor created. The internal energy of a partial process, therefore, can vary with the import and export of energy.[4] For a process that constitutes a *closed* system—that is, a system that can exchange only energy, but not matter, with the rest of the universe —the balance is expressed by the ultrafamiliar formula

$$dU = \Delta Q - \Delta W \tag{1}$$

where dU is the change in the internal energy of the system, ΔQ is the heat received by the system (if $\Delta Q > 0$) or released by the system (if $\Delta Q < 0$), and ΔW is the work performed by the system (if $\Delta W > 0$) or on the system (if $\Delta W < 0$).

A curious aspect of this layout is that we are never told what energy actually is. And even when we read something on this point—such that energy is "a 'capacity' to do work"—the instruction is misleading, notwithstanding the high authority of some of its sources.[5] True, for a thermally insulated process (an adiabatic system), relation 1 yields

$$dU = -\Delta W \tag{2}$$

However, as is the case with many relations in thermodynamics and some other fields, relation 2 is often valid only on paper. For there are energies, such as those contained in coolers or sea waters, that normally cannot be converted into work. We must, therefore, recognize that energy—just like time and space, for example—is an intuitive notion that can be turned into an analytical entity only concomitantly with a few other similar notions (temperature, pressure, and mechanical work, in particular).

Relation 1, which represents the first law of thermodynamics, does teach us some important lessons not intuitively or immediately obvious. First, mechanical work, just like heat or any other more common kind of energy, is a form of energy. And just as heat can be transformed into mechanical work, mechanical work can be converted into heat—as Benjamin Thompson (Count Rumford) had observed long before Carnot's memoir and as J. P. Joule was to endow the fact with an exact formula some years later.

Second, and highly important for our understanding of the entropic predicament of mankind, is one obvious consequence of relation 2. There can be no mechanical work without an equivalent expenditure of energy. This rules out completely the possibility of perpetual motion of the first kind—a dream surrounded for a long time by sanguine hopes.

We should note, however, that both heat and mechanical work are energies *in transit* only. For, contrary to the position adopted by Carnot, heat is no longer thought of as the immutable fluid he called "caloric."[6] We cannot say, therefore, that such and such a partial system contains so much heat or so much mechanical work. A definite partial system contains only so much internal energy, or so much thermal or chemical energy, and so on.[7] This is why in 1, following a very few authors, I have used the notations ΔQ and ΔW, instead of dQ and dW, in order to indicate that these elements are not integrable separately. In other words, there is no sense in speaking of the difference in the amounts of heat or mechanical work between two systems. Only the difference in internal energy has a definite meaning.

Nevertheless, Carnot has left an indelible mark on thermodynamics. Although heat is no longer viewed as a fluid, energy is viewed so—a general jelly, as it were, that may acquire diverse concrete forms. That is not all. Just as Carnot spoke only of the perfect engine and only of the caloric passing through it, the theoretical framework of thermodynamics deals only with ideal gases, ideal apparatuses, and totally ignores the effect suffered by the material scaffolds of the engines or of the apparatuses. Briefly, matter is completely left out of the basic picture. This omission is regrettable even for the most elementary considerations.

In the real world every process involves both energy *and* matter. Radiation of massless particles, such as the photon, have as a rule a material emitter and a material receptor. It is puzzling, therefore, that the material transformation associated to any material process could possibly be ignored, given that all the demonstrations used by thermodynamics involve the use of material contraptions.

When any energy is converted into mechanical work, part of this work is always work against friction, a fact just as elemental as the spontaneous and inevitable run of heat from the hotter to the colder body. Only the latter has been incorporated in thermodynamics as one of its cornerstones, while the former is still wholly ignored. Equally important (and equally overlooked by the recognized body of thermodynamics) is the fact that any work against friction produces not only heat but also the dissipation of matter from at least one of the bodies moving against each other.[8]

For the omission of friction and its material consequences from the basic framework of thermodynamics, there are, however, some attenuating circumstances. We may recall that it was the impossibility of getting rid of friction that troubled Galileo and, at the same time, galvanized his experimental imagination. But surprising as it may appear at first blush, friction is still the most poorly understood phenomenon of the physical domain. Should one study more and more closely the various aspects of that phenomenon, one would soon discover that the laws of friction grow "*more* complicated, not *less*." Any law of which we may think to have gotten hold at one stage or another appears falser and falser under further probings.[9] A minimum of force is required to overcome the force of friction between solids, which in some cases is roughly proportional to the force normal to the friction surface. However, even this law is not valid for all speeds or for fluids. Think further that friction is not only when automobile tires roll against the road surface, but also when the kinetic energy of the wind blows against the paint of a house or when that of rain water washes away part of the topsoil. Yet even the engineering tables of friction *coefficients* between commonly used materials say nothing about the material erosion that goes with friction.

It is not hard, therefore, to understand why the students of thermodynamics have felt no attraction for entering into such a complicated domain. They have not gone beyond paying attention to Joule's famous discovery "that the quantity of heat produced by the friction of bodies, whether solid or liquid, is always proportional to the quantity of force extended."[10] Actually, even this express reference to friction has gradually fallen into oblivion. Only few works speak now of friction and only in passing. No one, to my knowledge, makes even a marginal remark about its diffusing effect on matter.

The full truth is that theoretical thermodynamics is erected on the notion of frictionless processes, even though the restriction is not expressed openly in this form. Instead, the axiomatic foundation speaks of processes that proceed with an infinitely slow motion. The justification offered for this condition is that thermodynamic theory must build on systems in thermodynamic equilibrium with their surroundings, the only ones for which the theoretical state functions have an operational meaning. The traditional argument is that, if the speed is infinitely slow, there is no time for the equilibrium to be disturbed. By rote, and without much ado, it concludes that if the differences between pressures or temperatures are infinitesimal, the process may move in *either* direction, just as the mechanical or electromagnetic ones do.[11]

This friction may reflect the mechanistic complex mentioned in the previous section, but that would be no reason for denying its substantial analytical merits. The thermodynamicist's sin is that he failed to move away from a high abstraction and nearer the real phenomenon, away from "clean thermodynamics" (of fluids) to a "dirty thermodynamics" (of matter as well). For the issue at hand is not that reversible processes of thermodynamics are only ideal approximations of reality, but that they abstract entirely from "dirt"—that is, matter.

There are other ways of showing the factual impossibility of reversible processes, but the most direct one is to point out that even the smallest motion of a process proceeding with an infinitely slow speed would require an infinite time. This point (which should be retained for later use) reveals the actual way by which friction has been blocked out from pure thermodynamics. If the motion is infinitely slow, friction is infinitely slow; hence, there is no need to include it in the picture.

A point to be borne in mind without fail is that since the reversibility of a system implies a continuous thermodynamic equilibrium with its surroundings, the surroundings, too, must undergo a reversible process. To use a striking fable, reversibility does not only mean to bring a 70-year-old back to the newborn he once was but also to bring the whole world, the entire universe, back to what they were 70 years earlier. For this reason the conventional theory is based on still another fiction, the *isolated* system. This is a system that can exchange neither matter nor energy with the outside; it is meant as a cosmos in miniature.[12]

For the theoretical development, an isolated system is generally divided into several (ordinarily, two or three) nonisolated subsystems so as to suit each individual purpose.

The simplest case is that in which the isolated system contains two homogeneous subsystems capable of exchanging only heat with each other. An experience as old as the dawn of the human culture vouches that, if the temperatures of the two subsystems are different, heat will flow *by itself* from the hotter to the colder body, never in reverse. The inevitable outcome is the everlasting thermal equilibrium, when both systems have reached the same temperature.[13] Nothing, absolutely nothing, *within the system itself*, can reverse the direction of the heat flow and alter its irrevocable outcome.

Here we see the irreducible conflict between thermodynamic phenomenon and the laws of classical mechanics. For if these phenomena were
governed by the laws of classical mechanics—as statistical thermodynamics sustains—the ice cubes melted in an isolated glass of warm water
should reappear again and again. And the rub is that no one has ever
witnessed a spontaneous formation of ice cubes, not even of a mere speck
of ice, in a glass of water.[14] Actuality consists only of irreversible processes such as that of the heat flow. In fact, the first formulation of the
second law of thermodynamics, alias the entropy law, merely asserted the
unidirectionality of the heat flow.[15]

Still, descriptions of how one could construct a reversible mechanism
are a constant feature of all thermodynamic manuals. But the details
generally concern only the perennial piston acted by the pressure of an
ideal gas in a cylinder. If the subsystem cannot exchange any heat with
its surroundings (which is said to be an adiabatic process), and if the
external pressure is allowed to decrease so slowly that its difference from
the internal pressure is at all times just sufficient for the piston to move
out, the piston performs on its surroundings a certain amount of work
that—we are instructed—just suffices to bring *everything* back to its initial
position.[16] But just as, over a finite interval, infinitely small amounts of
work accumulate into a finite amount, so must infinitely small friction, the
accumulated useful work will not suffice to bring the piston back. One
cannot invoke the miracle of infinitesimal integration, only for work, but
not for friction. Therefore, to make any sense even of the ideal blueprint,
we must deny the existence of friction completely.

The case of a heat transfer is even more telling—which probably is the
reason why it is not usually detailed in the literature. A possible blueprint,
the simplest of its kind, is as follows. An isolated system consists of a
practically infinite number of lamellae of, say, copper, arranged in a
uniform series, at first thermally isolated from each other. Let the temperature between each lamella and its neighbor grow by an infinitely small
amount (the temperature difference between the first and the last lamella
being finite). The logical foundation of thermodynamics claims that when
the insulation between the lamellae is removed, each lamella is in thermal
equilibrium with its neighbors and hence heat may move slowly from the
coldest to the hottest lamella. If such a contraption could be made to
work, the entropy law would be defeated. Indeed, the contraption would
allow us to run the boiler of a steamer with the heat sucked in from the
sea waters, nay, even from the ice caps, and use these as coolers. This
would constitute a perpetual motion of the second kind. This is a system
that needs energy, only it can operate on a finite amount of energy in a
perpetual cycle by converting that energy into work and then the work
back into the exact initial amount of energy, and so on *ad infinitum*.

One cannot possibly overstress the point that the impossibility of a perpetual motion of the second kind is not justified by the ubiquitous presence of friction. Friction simply transforms part of energy into heat. It is only because this conversion is one instance of the irreversible degradation of energy that goes on continuously in actuality that a perpetual motion of the second kind is not feasible. This degradation constitutes the most significant object lesson of thermodynamics for the economy of natural resources.

The story is easily told. Even though energy can neither increase nor decrease, it continuously changes qualitatively from the *available* into the *unavailable* form. The universe (or any other isolated system) may thus be portrayed plastically as an hourglass in which the available energy from the upper half changes into unavailable energy as it continuously pours down into the lower half (Figure 15.1). the only difference between the hourglass of the universe and an ordinary one is that the former can never be turned upside down. So the qualitative change of energy is both continuous and irrevocable—which is a more telling expression of the entropy law.[17]

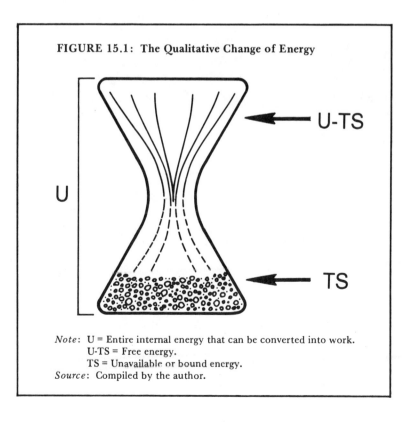

FIGURE 15.1: The Qualitative Change of Energy

Note: U = Entire internal energy that can be converted into work.
U-TS = Free energy.
TS = Unavailable or bound energy.
Source: Compiled by the author.

But the most relevant aspect of this statement concerns the two quali-ties of energy. The distinction between them has its roots in man's spe-cific interests (although subsequently it proved to be of great help in all domains of life). Available energy is the energy that can be used by man for obtaining mechanical work. Actually, it is the form of energy that supports every bit of life on this planet. Unavailable energy, on the other hand, cannot be useful in any of these processes.[18]

This anthropomorphic distinction, which presided over the genesis of thermodynamics, acquired specific analytical formulations at the hands, first, of Hermann Helmholtz and, later, of J. Willard Gibbs. From these definitions (which are not identical), it is seen that in fact entropy is a relative index of the unavailable energy in the hourglass of a system. To recall, entropy is defined by the formula

$$\Delta S = \frac{\Delta Q}{T} \tag{3}$$

for a reversible process. (T is the absolute temperature.) Irreversible processes are characterized by

$$\Delta S > \frac{\Delta Q}{T} = \frac{dU + \Delta W}{T} \tag{4}$$

For an isolated irreversible process, this yields the famous formulation of the entropy law

$$\Delta S > 0 \tag{5}$$

that is, the entropy of such a process continuously increases.[19]

The important fact brought to light by Helmholtz is that not the entire internal energy U can be converted into work—as relation 2 would make us believe. The maximum amount of work that can be derived from a system depends on the entropy of the system as well; it is equal only to the available energy—Helmholtz called it "free energy":

$$F = U - TS \tag{6}$$

The remainder, TS, is unavailable (or bound) energy. The expression of the entropy law by relation 5 is therefore tantamount to saying that the relative importance of unavailable energy of an isothermal system contin-uously and irrevocably increases.[20]

SOME DIRTY THERMODYNAMICS

One issue raised by matter was brought within the visual field of the thermodynamicist by J. Willard Gibbs, 100 years ago.[21] Gibbs asked himself what happens to the entropy of two different ideal gases of the same temperature if they were allowed to interdiffuse. Using the Dalton law concerning the mixture of gases, and the well-known formula for the entropy of ideal gases, he arrived at the conclusion that the entropy of the two subsystems increases by

$$-R(n_1 \ln c_1 + n_2 \ln c_2) \tag{7}$$

where R is the gas constant and $c_i = n_i/(n_1 + n_2)$ is the concentration of the moles n_i of gas i. The result proved an old commonplace; namely, that gases mix spontaneously—that is, the mixing process is irreversible. As Gibbs saw it, it also raised a paradox. Certainly, if the gases are identical, their mixture does not change in any way the initial state, hence, neither its entropy. This fact contradicts Gibb's result (relation 7), which is always a positive number.

The paradox has ordinarily been explained on the basis of either the statistical interpretation of thermodynamics or of the so-called information theory.[22] Gibbs himself observed that relation 7 must not be interpreted as a continuous function, because a qualitative difference is not a continuous variable: Two gases are either different or identical. But still more important is that with the aid of an apparatus of the same imaginary nature as the mechanisms capable of reversing the energy flow the mixture can be undone. The blueprint has two pistons within the same cylinder, each piston consisting of a semipermeable membrane—one membrane permeable only to gas 1, the other only to gas 2. Moving the pistons forth and back the gases are mixed and separated again. The blueprint also allows us to calculate the necessary work to achieve the separation of the mixed gases; it is found that this work is equal to ST.[23]

There is, I submit, one snag in this unified picture of diffusion of energy and diffusion of matter. One would hardly quarrel with the fact that whenever different gases (or any other substances, for that matter) are mixed there is *a loss of availability* as far as our own interests are concerned —just as there is one whenever energy becomes diffused. It also is perfectly reasonable to accept formula 7 as a measure of this loss, especially since, as we have just seen, it is intimately related to the cost in mechanical work for removing the loss. Yet one objection seems equally reasonable: On what *operational* basis can the loss of matter availability be treated as being of the same essence as the loss of energy availability? In other words, why should the sum of the two entropies

Entropy of Energy Diffusion + Entropy of Matter Mixing (8)

have one and the same meaning regardless of its distribution among the two terms? Let us assume, for example, that while we allow two different gases to interfuse we cool the container to just the necessary level so as to compensate for the increase of the mixture entropy. Which is the operational sense in which the initial and final states may be *qualitatively* identical (since this is precisely what entropy is supposed to express)?

More recently, the material coordinate was introduced in thermodynamics from a different direction than that used by Gibbs. A new branch, called the thermodynamics of irreversible systems, grew out from some momentous results obtained in 1931 by L. Onsager for an *open* thermodynamic system, that is, for a system that may exchange not only energy but also matter with its surroundings. The relevance of this new endeavor derives mainly from the fact that living organisms—and, we should add, the economic process—are open systems. The basic idea is elementary. The change in the entropy of an open system breaks down into to components:

$$\Delta S = \Delta S_e + \Delta S_i, \tag{9}$$

where $\Delta S_i > 0$ is the entropy "produced" within the system by its irreversible processes, and ΔS_e is the entropy imported from the surroundings. In this case, ΔS may have any sign. However, living organisms strive to maintain themselves as steady states, that is, they strive to compensate for their increase of entropy by trading it for low entropy from the environment. The steady state, which is characterized by the condition

$$\Delta S_e + \Delta S_i = 0 \tag{10}$$

thus constitutes the salient preoccupation of the new thermodynamics.[24]

However, even this discipline is still "clean." In its conception, the low entropy of energy is a perfect substitute for the high entropy of matter. In other words, it still subscribes to the idea hatched by Gibbs's paradox that even though the spontaneous transformations of matter cause matter to become less available, they can be *completely* reversed at a cost in mechanical work, hence, at a cost in available energy.

In support of this notion, which now seems to dominate all thoughts on mankind's entropic problem, one may also invoke relation 2. This relation seems, indeed, to assure us that even in a *closed* system any task can be accomplished if enough available energy is forthcoming for the necessary work. We need not, therfore, worry about the scarcity of matter at all, in spite of the fact that, for all practical purposes, the earth is a closed system.[25] The direct harnessing of solar energy will suffice in principle to undo the material mixing, should all other energy sources become exhausted.

The entropy law of any clean thermodynamics tells us that certain operations are not possible, not because of the "dirt" produced by friction, but because even clean, ideally abstract apparatuses cannot be operated with unavailable energy. For each such apparatus, the law sets a maximum limit (much lower than 100 percent efficiency) to the theoretical efficiency. It behooves dirty thermodynamics to add, ordinarily from the back row, that friction prevents us from attaining this limit—a truth as inexorable as any other well-established scientific proposition. Still, this new limitation does not refute the position about the *complete* reversal of the material entropy. It only makes it more expensive in entropy terms.

The key word in this issue is "complete." The rub is, as I hope to prove now, that in actuality no reversal of material entropy can be complete. This proposition may be considered as the first law of dirty thermodynamics—alternatively, as the fourth law of a unified thermodynamics. Like the other four laws of clean thermodynamics,[26] this new law expresses a denial: "Perpetual motion of the third kind is not possible in actuality." By perpetual motion of the third kind it is meant a closed system that can perform *forever* work between its subsystems.

The logic of the proof begins with the truth, already emphasized, that any work, of absolutely any kind, is carried out by some material structure, and that matter is inevitably dissipated by the friction. But—one may perhaps interject from the outset—matter is granular and with enough energy we ought to be able to reassemble it again. Undoubtedly, we can reassemble the pearls of a broken necklace scattered all over the floor of an auditorium or even over a football stadium. It will necessarily take some energy *and some time*, but the job ultimately can be done.

Several observations are called for by this argument. First, the argument unwarrantedly extrapolates phenomena of the macrolevel, that is, of the level of our direct senses, to the microlevel of molecules and atoms. The bridge between these two levels constitutes one of the most challenging problems in science and philosophy. From all we know, it cannot be built so as to do away with the numberless gaps present at all turns. In the domain in which we are now dwelling, entropy, temperature, and pressure have no sense whatsoever for a single molecule, much less for a single elementary particle. There are no nanotweezers with which we may pick up *all* the scattered molecules of copper, for example, in the same way in which we can pick up *all* the scattered pearls with our fingers. By their own assumed role, such nanotweezers are unthinkable. Besides, the true setting is far more staggering: The pearls should first be dis-solved into some acid and the solution be spread over the oceans. Even if we accept the possibility of completely reassembling *all* the pearls by using some physical-chemical procedure, the operation will take a *practically infinite* time. This conclusion alone should suffice to place the mate-rial reversal beyond actual reach. As we may remember, the feasibility of completely reversible processes involving only energy transfers is denied in the most direct way because such procedures require an infinite time even for a finite advance.

The second observation concerns the very apparatus presumed to un-mix two different gases with the help of two semipermeable membranes. Semipermeable membranes do exist in actuality; any living organism is full of them. Yet the undeniable fact is that no actual membrane fulfills the ideal function required by the theoretical blueprint anymore than an actual process can operate without friction. Semipermeable membranes —any membrane, for that matter-gradually and inevitably clog up through use. The most crushing evidence I wish to adduce is the fact that all organisms age and ultimately die precisely because of this clogging up of their semipermeable membranes. But the truth, mentioned only ex-ceptionally, is still stronger. "Neither a gas nor a liquid nor a solid body can ever be completely freed from the last traces of foreign contaminat-ing substances."[27] This means that even if we start with some absolutely pure substance—the highest form of available matter—the thermody-namic whirlpool will transform it after a while in *irreducible* dissipated matter. This residual, which may not amount to too much in a single laboratory experiment, accumulates through repeated cycles and at the scale of the whole planet will ultimately reach considerable proportions. This is probably the right moment to remind us of an important fact: laboratory experiments generally share with the paper-and-pencil dem-onstration the faculty of eluding us into believing that their results are equally applicable to the larger scale of actual phenomena. Thus an isolated pilot experiment may not reveal all the difficulties of a proper operation *in vivo*.

Third, even to pick up a few pearls we must use not only some energy and spend some time, but we must also use some material structures— the bodies of the searchers, their apparel, and (perhaps) some flashlights. And since there are no eternally durable material structures any more than externally moving mechanisms, these material structures will wear out through the operation. (They will wear out in any case, even if left "idle"). An additional dissipation of matter is, therefore, part of the cost of reassembling just the macropearls. We are thus drawn into an infinite regress, the result of which can be analyzed only within a completely comprehensive framework of the entire system. An analysis piece by piece, as those which now make the rounds of the expert circles on energy and conservation, is fraught with dangers; it may greatly deceive us.[28]

THE GENERAL FLOW MATRIX OF MATTER-ENERGY

For the reasons expounded in the foregoing section, from the first moment in which I came to realize the entropic nature of the economic process—alternatively, the intimate relation between this process and the entropy law—I have continuously spoken of low entropy of energy *and* matter.[29] My position is that the concept of *net* energy, of which Fred Cottrell spoke some time ago as "surplus" energy and which has recently been rekindled by Howard T. Odum,[30] is amiss. If in mining ten tons of coal we use the equivalent energy of one ton of coal, there is, we are told, a *net energy* of nine tons of coal. But by the same token we should say that the mining of copper yields a *net matter* as well as some *negative net energy*. On the other hand, any power plant yields some negative net matter of some sort or other.

One may submit that the roundabout process of production may be nevertheless reduced to a single primary environmental input, available energy, by a step-by-step telescoping. So that even the cost of mining of copper, for example, can be reduced to energy alone. But even this admission would not clear the tables for the net energy. One must further find a common denominator for matter (copper, or aluminum, or lumber) and energy. Notwithstanding the well-known Einsteinian equivalence between energy and mass, $E = mc^2$, a common denominator between matter and energy meaningful for our economic activity (or even for the biological activity at large) is not available. There simply is no way by which we can produce matter from energy alone operationally. Furthermore, not even all chemical elements can be reduced to a meaningful common denominator. We should not overlook the important fact that the Einsteinian equivalence works mainly from matter to energy. And this goes not only for the various sources of available energy accessible to us —the point is true even if we get energy from burning a match—but also for the transformations going on in the stars. Our sun, for example, burns each second 4 million tons of matter into energy. We know that at very high temperature two photons—which are massless particles, hence pure energy—may produce an electron-position pair. But the creation of matter (mass) from energy alone is extremely rare as well as marginal even in whole universe. The elements in the universe have not been produced from energy alone, but from an original fund of hydrogen and, possibly, helium.[31] These alchemical reactions still go on in many stars, and for all our own purposes only there.

On the earth, radioactive elements have decayed into lighter elements, releasing energy according to the Einsteinian formula. One the basis of the same formula, we now produce heavier from lighter elements by converting energy into matter (mass). Yet we cannot produce any element from scratch, that is, from energy alone. As I have just pointed out, such a conversion is rare even in the greatest concentration of energy in the universe. With the exception of the elements produced by radioactive decay, the number of atoms of any stable chemical element within the planet is nowadays the same as at the birth of the earth.[32]

It is utterly impercipient to say that we cannot possibly run out of matter—as cornucopians of all strains insist. The ecological issue does not concern matter, pure and simple, but available matter. And since available matter irrevocably degrades, the inevitable conclusion is that in some indefinite future available matter may prove to be a more crucial item than energy in this closed abode of ours.[33] Some particular items—such as helium, mercury, and tin (which are the most frequently mentioned)—are already becoming increasingly scarce.

The clean thermodynamics of closed systems has accustomed us to think only of efficiency in converting energy, of considering only net energy. Dirty thermodynamics teaches us that, even though the economic process (actually, any actual process) is entropic, there is no way of reducing it to a single material coordinate, be it net energy or net matter. All that counts is *global accessibility*.[34]

And since matter and energy cannot be reduced to a common denominator, one of the popular illusions has to go by the wayside. We cannot decide on purely technical grounds which of the two processes producing the same product is more efficient—that which uses more energy and less matter or that which uses less energy and more matter. This decision requires considerations of the relative supplies; hence it belongs to the economic science, but to one that would not take into consideration only the present generation. For, unwilling though we may be to accept and live by it, the harsh truth is that every Cadillac, or Rolls-Royce, or Volvo means fewer plowshares for some future generations. What we are now doing is contrary to the traditional call to beat our swords into plowshares: We are beating future plowshares into present swords of all kinds and of all dimensions.

The ideas developed in this section may acquire a sharper and also more instructive contour if we try to construct a general flow matrix of the circulation of matter and energy (figure 15.2). In doing so, I shall bypass all the technical aspects that not only are irrelevant but also hide the crucial articulations.

The relation of the economic process with the environment boils down to five fundamental categories: the inflows of environmental energy and

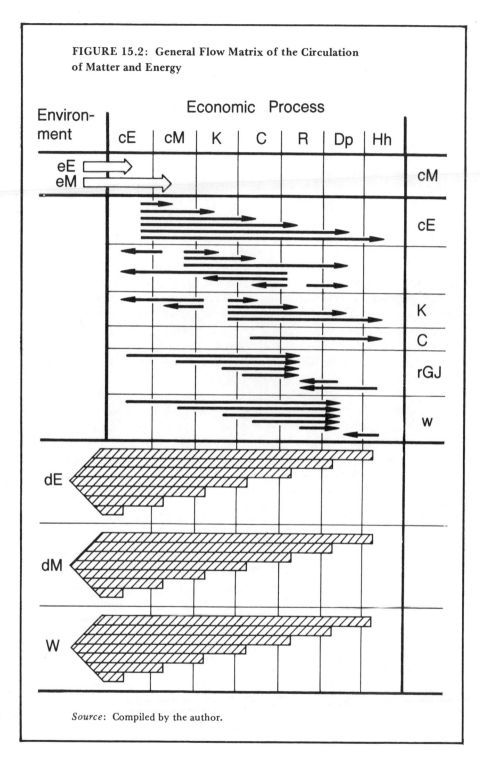

FIGURE 15.2: General Flow Matrix of the Circulation
of Matter and Energy

Source: Compiled by the author.

matter, eE and eM, and three outflows consisting of dissipated energy, dE, dissipated matter, dM, and waste,W. The last flow represents that matter-energy which, although not necessarily completely dissipated, is no longer useful ecnomically in any known way. Typical examples are supplied by crushed rock or nuclear garbage.

Inside the economic process, I shall distinguish seven basic sectors. The first two processes transform environmental energy and environmental matter into controlled energy, cE, and controlled matter, cM, respectively. Each of these two elements then circulates through every other sector. Two other sectors represent production proper: K produces capital goods, and C, consumer goods. Hh, the households, is the consumption sector. All these sectors produce, in addition to dE and dM, three other material flows: "garbojunk," denoted by rGJ, depollutable waste, denoted by w, and just waste, W. By "garbojunk" I mean any material object that can be recycled: It does not include dissipated matter, which by definition is irretrievably lost as far as the economic or any other life process is concerned. The point that deserves unparsimonious emphasis here is that we can recycle only worn-out objects—pennies, motors, bottles, and so on—that still consist of available matter but are no longer in a *shape* beneficial to us. We cannot recycle, for example, the copper molecules scattered from a worn-out penny to the four corners of the world.

The process R recycles everything recyclable, so that itself it does not produce any garbojunk. This, it should be noted, does not mean that recycling is complete; R produces not only cM but also dM and W. Hence, not all matter in the garbojunk is recuperated.[35] Similarly, since the sector Dp depollutes all depollutable w, it does not produce such waste.

A glance at the general flow diagram tells us that neither recycling nor depolluting is free. They both require that some *flow* factors—namely, cE, cM, and K—as well as some *fund* factors—namely, physical production capacity, labor power, and Ricardian land—be diverted from other uses.[36] It also tells a rather surprising fact: All that the economic process produces is unavailable matter—energy and waste. However, this is only the matter-energy side of the story. The full story is that the true product of the economic process is not a material effluent but an inmaterial flux —the enjoyment of life.

For the human species, the enjoyment of life implies not only the maintenance of biological bodies with all their organs in good functioning order but also the maintenance of the capital fund (tools and installations of all sorts) in the same order. Indeed, the evolution of the human species has long since transgressed the biological domain, as it began producing detachable limbs—exosomatic organs, as they may also be called—such as knives, boats, automobiles, guns, airplanes, and so on.

The point is that for mankind these exosomatic organs are just as vital as the endosomatic organs (the organs with which the human body is endowed by its genetic make up). It would be a real amputation to suddenly deprive mankind of some of these detachable limbs, probably an even more painful amputation than a biological one. Consider the specter that is looming largely over the Western world ever since the oil embargo. Very probably, mankind will prefer to die in penthouses rather than return to the cave, where it could live with much fewer detachable limbs and survive longer by squandering less of its terrestrial dowry of matter-energy.

The picture is now clear. Terrestrial available matter-energy, as well as the solar radiation reaching earth, would gradually degrade, whether life were present or not. But the presence of consumer species speeds up this degradation. And man's contribution to this degradation is of unique dimensions, not only as regards energy but also as regards matter. When a tree dies, rots, or is burned by a thunderbolt, entropy is increased by the simple working of the entropy law. But when man fells the tree, transports it to a far-away city, and burns it in his fireplace, an additional entropy is produced that is not the direct working of that law. It is the working of man's existence. A still weightier example is the nitrogen contained in the food produced in some distant countryside and consumed in the cities of the world.

It is because matter matters, too—as I have endeavored to prove in this chapter and as the general flow matrix plainly shows—that we must stop talking of forests that can be exploited without end or of prairies and farm lands that can be grazed and cultivated forever. Jonathan Swift's observation that "whoever could make two ears of corn, or two blades of grass, to grow upon a spot of ground where one grew, before would deserve better of mankind . . . than the whole race of politicians" appears well off the mark in retrospect. From what we know today, we cannot hope to make even one single blade of grass grow on the same spot of ground year after year for as long as the sun will shine.[37] To do so would mean to make a perpetual motion of the third order work.

That matter may matter in still another way is just now becoming obvious for whoever stops to look at some evidence. The direct use of solar energy and the development on a large scale of fission or fusion reactors seems now to be the only hope, given the patent dwindling of fossil fuels supply. However, solar energy reaches us as an extremely fine mist whose density is a cosmological constant—one langley per square centimeter—completely beyond our control. Moreover, because solar radiation, in contrast with a rain mist, does not accumulate by itself so as to ultimately form a Niagara of energy, we must catch it by a "net" of some sort. And the inexorable rub is that to catch enough solar radiation for a Niagara of energy, we need a plate of an enormous size, which means an immense amount of matter. I do not share the view that prices may serve as reliable entropic indexes; yet the fact that the recent solar installation sponsored by ERDA as a model of technological achievement at an Atlanta elementary school cost $1 million, but supplies only 60 percent of the needs, tells enough about how much matter may matter in the effective use of other energies than fossil fuels. No one has any idea what a fusion power plant will look like when and if fusion will be successfully controlled. But we may get some fair idea about its dimensions by observing that the accelerator at Fermilab is 2 kilometers (1.25 mile) wide and contains no less than 1,000 magnets.

Some writers like to belittle the idea that matter may ever become scarce by talking about the possibility of infinite material substitutability. Undoubtedly, substitution has been greatly advantageous at times. But this does not mean that it can be so indefinitely. Besides, most illustrations used to support the idea of endless substitution sin by considering only the local impact of the change.

As our general flow matrix indicates, any technological innovation must diffuse itself through the entire economic process, thus bringing about changes in every individual sector. *Ex post* it is a simple matter to recognize a successful innovation: Anything that has succeeded is a success. *Ex ante*, however, the same question must be projected against the flow matrix, not like that represented in very broad lines in Figure 15.2, but one in which every sector is divided into relevant subsectors and the corresponding flow rates are specified. Without such a matrix we cannot be sure that suggested innovation will prove successful in the end, for it is what will happen through its diffusion in the end that matters. The problem is even more complicated than is currently realized, not only because matter matters, too, but also because concrete matter (in contrast with energy) consists of different forms irreducible to each other.

Unfortunately, to fill in the significant boxes of a detailed flow matrix is a titanic task. Moves in this direction are now scattered in several works —*Economic Growth in the Future*, the report of the Edison Electric Institute, is a good example.[38] But these efforts have been so far quite timid. I hope that the argument of this chapter will show not only the proper way to understanding of mankind's economic problem, but also that to arrive at some quantitative expression of the general flow matrix must be the first order of the day for all those concerned with mankind's future, in the short and in the long run.

NOTES

1. Pierre Simon de Laplace, *A Philosophical Essay on Probability* (New York: John Wiley, 1902). (The original French edition appeared in 1814).

2. E. Mendoza, ed., *Reflection on the Motive Power of Fire, by Sadi Carnot; and Other Papers on the Second Law of Thermodynamics, by E. Clapeyron and R. Clausius* (New York: Dover, 1960).

3. Ibid.

4. Naturally, the internal energy of the total process (the entire universe) remains constant throughout.

5. For example, Max Planck, *Theory of Heat* (London: Macmillan, 1932), p. 28.

6. There is no more glaring example of the truth that correct conclusions may very well be based on wrong premises than Carnot's work. His conclusions are just as valid in the new analytical framework as they were with the caloric. This proves it unavailing to argue that the probabilistic interpretation of thermodynamic phenomena is necessarily vindicated by the similarity of its results with those measured in the laboratory. On the logical and epistemological difficulties of the probabilistic interpretation of phenomena perfectly determined by the system of equations of classical mechanics, see Nicholas Georgescu-Roegen, *The Entropy Law and The Economic Process* (Cambridge, Mass.: Harvard University Press, 1971), Chapters II.7, VI, Appendixes C, D, E, F.

7. A partial process must be understood as a slice of the entire actuality, well defined by a boundary that separates it from its so-called surrounding (that is, from the rest of actuality). The boundary—and this is the point of paramount importance—is a vacuous entity. Everything during the duration of the process belongs either to the partial process or to its surroundings but not to the boundary. Thus, the surface of a fluid must be carefully included either in the process or in the outside. Only in this way may we avoid bookkeeping errors related to surface tension. On these issues, see Georgescu-Roegen, *The Entropy Law*, Chapter IX, and *Energy and Economic Myths* (New York: Pergamon Press, 1976), Chapter 5.

8. Probably the only exception in this respect—R. S. Silver, *An Introduction to Thermodynamics* (Cambridge: The University Press, 1971), pp. 29–31—distinguishes between *useful* work and work *against friction* in equation 1. Yet even that author fails to connect friction with the dissipation of matter.

9. *The Feynman Lectures on Physics*, 2 vols. (Reading, Mass.: Addison-Wesley, 1963), Vol. I, pp. 10.5, 12.3–12.5.

10. James Prescott Joule, "On the Mechanical Equivalent of Heat," *Philosophical Transactions* (1850).

11. For example, Planck, *Theory of Heat*, pp. 37–38.

12. Of course, isolated systems can be realized only in laboratories and, even there, only with a very gross approximation. No actual system on this planet can be isolated from the influence of the gravitation force. Think also of the copious flux of neutrinos that are supposed to go right through the earth.

13. We should not ignore, however, that the brute fact consists only of the temperature changes. As P. W. Bridgman warned us, "No physical significance can be directly given to flow of heat, and there are no operations [as opposed to set-up calculations] for measuring it." P. W. Bridgman, *The Logic of Modern Physics* (New York: Macmillan, 1928), p. 130.

14. On this point, see references cited in note 6.

15. By Rudolph Clausius, in 1850, see Mendoza, *Reflection on the Motive Power of Fire*.

16. The instruction provides that a weight of fine sand supported by the piston be displaced grain by grain and then put back in reverse order (never mind how or by whom).

17. The above icon was introduced by the author in his papers, "Economics or Bioeconomics," read at the American Economic Association Meeting' (Dallas, December 1975) and "A Different Economic Perspective," read at the AAAS (Boston, February 1976). See also "The Steady State and Ecological Salvation: A Thermodynamic Analysis," *Bioscience* 27, no. 4 (April 1977):266–70.

18. Whether other forms of life than that found on earth may use unavailable energy has been and still is a moot question. The issue is deeply anchored in the famous paradox of the Maxwellian demon that is assumed to be able to *use* unavailable energy.

19. Planck, *Theory of Heat*, pp. 74–75. We need to add an essential point that is generally ignored by the conventional literature. To speak of an increase we must specify which of the two quantities involved is the *later* in time. For relation 5, the order is that of our stream of consciousness. The march of entropy, portrayed by our hourglass, not a mechanical clock, imparts to the physical world a definite temporal direction.

20. Planck, *Theory of Heat*, pp. 80–83. The simplest illustration of this truth is provided by the two subsystems at different temperatures mentioned earlier. As long as they are not allowed to reach thermal equilibrium, they can be used to derive work through a heat engine. As they approach equilibrium, entropy increases and the work than can be derived decreases.

21. *The Collected Works of J. Willard Gibbs*, 2 vols. (New Haven, Conn.; Yale University Press, 1948), Vol. I, pp. 165–68. The point was made in a path-breaking article, "On the Equilibrium of Heterogeneous Substances," published in two installments, between 1875 and 1878.

22. For example, Richard C. Tolman, *The Principles of Statistical Mechanics* (London: Oxford University Press, 1938), pp. 626–29; and D. ter Harr and H. Wergeland, *Elements of Thermodynamics* (Reading, Mass.: Addison-Wesley, 1966), pp. 85–89.

23. See the blueprint and the calculation in Haar and Wergeland, *Elements of Thermodynamics*.

24. An instructive presentation of the results along this new line is offered by A. K. Katchalsky and Peter F. Curran, *Nonequilibrium Thermodynamics in Biophysics* (Cambridge, Mass.: Harvard University Press, 1965).

25. To be sure, there is the meteorite fall, which is substantial—150,000 tons per year. But it consists mainly of dust, of highly unavailable matter. One should not overlook the existence of particles that occasionally may escape the gravitation pull. However, they count even less in the balance.

26. We may recall that the last of these four laws is the third law (Nernst's law), because one law is the *zeroth law*, of transitivity of thermal equilibrium. As Planck, *Theory of Heat*, pp. 5–6, instructively explains, this law is not an idle tantology.

27. Ibid., p. 125.

28. Some examples will be cited later. But for a start, I may mention the recent elation in Washington circles over the feasibility of extracting aluminum from flyash.

29. See Nicholas Georgescu-Roegen, *Analytical Economics: Issues and Problems* (Cambridge, Mass.: Harvard University Press, 1966), pp. 92–97; also *The Entropy Law and The Economic Process*, pp. 276–283, and *Energy and Economic Myths*, Chapters 1 and 3.

30. Fred Cottrell, *Energy and Society* (New York: McGraw-Hill, 1955), pp. 11-14; Howard T. Odum "Energy, Ecology, and Economics," *Ambio* 2 (1973):220–27.

31. R. J. Tayler, *The Origin of the Chemical Elements* (London: Wykeham Publications, 1972).

32. With the saving clauses mentioned in note 25.

33. The remark brings to mind the idea of interplanetary sources, which makes itself heard from time to time. To be able to work there, those planets should present conditions adequate for life. The nearest such planets may probably exist at about ten light-years from us. (Su-Shu Haung, "Life Outside the Solar System," *Scientific American*, April 1970, pp. 55–63). By space rockets, they may be reached in just 100,000 years.

34. See references cited in note 17, and Georgescu-Roegen's lecture at Yale University, reprinted as Chapter 1 in *Energy and Economic Myths*.

35. The assumption that R produces no garbojunk can be elucidated by the manner in which Achilles, with each step, reduced the distance that separates him from the tortoise and finally catches it. Yet the assumption is that the successive recycling percentages, r_n, shall not tend to zero. If s_n is the quantity recycled after n steps from an initial quantity a, then $r_{n+1} (a - s_n) = s_{n+1} - s_n$; in the limit, $\lim(a - s_n) \times \lim r = 0$. Hence, if $\lim r_{n+1} = 0$, $\lim s_n$ may not be a.

36. On the necessity of distinguishing between flow and fund factors of production, see Georgescu-Roegen, *Entropy Law and The Economic Process*, Chapter IX, and *Energy and Economic Myths*, Chapters 4 and 5. It is only for the sake of simplification that the fund elements are not represented in Figure 15.2.

37. Georgescu-Reogen, *The Entropy Law and The Economic Process*, p. 302.

38. Edison Electric Institute, *Economic Growth in the Future: The Growth Debate in National and Global Perspective* (New York: McGraw-Hill, 1976).

16 | Does Entropy Production Limit Economic Growth?

Peter L. Auer

In this chapter the pro-growth/anti-growth controversy is reexamined in the framework of Georgescu-Roegen's thesis that the principle of entropy production has a central role in economic theory. It is concluded that while many valuable lessons can be drawn from this line of thought, it is difficult to extract useful guiding principles by this procedure. Resorting to more standard methods of analysis, one can infer that there are possible paths along which humankind could sustain a high level of economic activity for indefinite periods of time.

And yet, the growth debate goes on, and at first glance it appears the anti-growth forces have the upper hand when it comes to providing arguments in support of their position. After all, they have so many "minuses" at their disposal. Growth leads to pollution, foul air, putrid water, and an environment contaminated with various chemical poisons as well as radioactivity. In addition, growth produces indelible scars on the land. Inevitably, growth will create more congestion, dehumanization as labor is replaced by machines, pride in workmanship is lost, and social amenities become even more scarce. The essential and nonrenewable resources of planet earth are finite and becoming rapidly exhausted as a result of continued growth. Future generations are not only being deprived of these riches but are also destined to inherit an environment with less capacity to absorb the insults to it that result from human activity. Finally, there comes the ominous Malthusian warning of impending catastrophe and doom from any of a variety of factors, only dimly perceivable at this time, as a consequence of humankind's persistence in not living at harmony with nature.

It is not a simple matter for the pro-growth advocate to respond to these accusations, for there is considerable merit to them. It would be easy enough to try and dispose of the anti-growth arguments as being elitist, born of the rich who are simply trying to protect their priviliged station. But this does not give full justice to their position. No intelligent student of society would wish to claim that growth is good for the sake of growth itself. Economic growth can be justified only as a means toward some other end. But to what end, what ultimate purpose? There are perhaps two fundamental driving forces at play: the strive for affluence and the growth in population.

Affluence in simple terms means a high level of personal consumption. Many might claim that there is no particular intrinsic value or fundamental virtue in increasing per capita consumption; nevertheless, Western society appears to have adopted it as a desirable social goal. How are we to convince our own poor and the greater multitude in the poorer nations that this is an aspiration they would be ill advised to follow? The question comes down to redistribution of wealth and reallocation of resources. The present inequities among the people of one nation and among the peoples of the many nations are just too large to be tolerable. As long as the rich adhere to the notion that redistribution can only be achieved through a "trickle down" principle, it would seem that the necessity of growth is a foregone conclusion.

While it appears that the problem of achieving stability, both domestically and internationally, is difficult enough with a stable population, the persistent growth in population can only serve to exacerbate the situation. The continuing inability of the developing nations to catch up with the more prosperous ones is often blamed on their unabated rise in population. Here we might expect to find a common meeting ground between the growth and anti-growth camps. How can anyone of reasonable intellect be in favor of continued population growth? Obviously the problem is not as simply stated as that, for in the foreign political forums we can not obtain unanimous opposition to rises in population; the Vatican continues to favor it, the Soviet Union endorses it as a matter of national policy, and the peoples of Latin America, South Asia, and Africa continue to practice it. Clearly we have some distance to go before those conditions that demographers believe will lead to a stable population size can be expected to prevail globally. So, if our planet appears overcrowded to some with 4 billion people on its face, our grandchildren can look forward to sharing it with 10 billion and perhaps even more.

As long as the rise in world population continues, it becomes all the more difficult to envision a transition to a no-growth mode of economic practice; unless, that is, the Western societies can find some means to isolate themselves from the pressures of the developing nations. But, one may well ask, how long can economic growth persist? Are there unavoidable limits to growth? In much of what follows we shall be interested in pursuing these questions, and in particular we wish to ask how certain fundamental laws of nature, revealed through the science of thermodynamics, affect the pro-growth/anti-growth debate.

TRACING THE GROWTH CONTROVERSY

In a world of finite resources, one must eventually come to grips with the tyranny of exponential growth and the irrefutable law of diminishing returns. These were the guiding principles laid down for us by the pioneering works of the Reverend Malthus[1] and David Ricardo.[2] Although their warnings have yet to be heeded and their predictions so far have not come true, their theme has been revived in modern dress by a number of authors.[3] A reexamination of the controversy over growth has been sparked more by the activities of the Club of Rome than perhaps any other recent effort.[4] The most recent and most exhaustive work on the subject is an Edison Electric Institute report entitled *Economic Growth in the Future.*[5] Because of its depth and scope, this volume deserves further comment.

The Edison Electric Institute report sets out to consider this extremely difficult subject in an objective manner. In this respect it provides a valuable service. The arguments for both the pro-growth and antigrowth sides are given in some detail, although it is possible to find more extensive scholarly treatments of this matter elsewhere.[6] This exposé is then followed by a reasoned statement of the electric utility industry's view, along with a very detailed analysis of potential future growth patterns. While the report treats both the domestic and the international scene, the principal focus is, understandably, on the United States.

The forecasting time scales in the Edison Electric Institute report are only moderately long term, with detailed projections to the year 2000, and in a few instances there are extrapolations beyond that date. The approach adopted is similar to that used by a number of other forecasters viewing the same time period. Population growth is specified and from this one deduces the growth in the labor force. The growth in national income and product accounts, or simply the GNP instead, follows from the size of the labor force once a figure for labor productivity is given. This, in turn, will be a function of assumptions made about the distribution of the labor force over the several production and service sectors and the respective changes in productivity with time. Short-term business cycles are not reflected by this approach, instead one deduces an annual average growth rate for the economy. The forecast can then be completed by invoking some relationship between the level of economic activity and the demand for energy or electricity or yet some other commodity. At the same time, some form of judgmental analysis can be made of to what extent the various demands will be met by supply sources of a particular kind.

The analyses presented in *Economic Growth in the Future* seem to have been prepared with a high degree of professional skill. There should be little cause to quarrel with their results. The high growth case that is given has a small likelihood of happening, given the realities of today's rather drastic changes in energy prices, the regard for environmental care, and the drop in the U.S. fertility rate. Some analyses, sensitive to post-oil-embargo developments, giving greater attention to rising energy prices, long-term price elasticities in demand, and the advantages of energy conservation, would probably argue that the Edison Electric Institute moderate growth rate case is still too high and that their low growth case might be closer to the situation most likely to develop in the future. In any event, the report would appear to have placed realistic bounds on future trends, particularly when one reflects on the magnitude of uncertainties involved in any forecast.

WHAT DOES THE FUTURE HOLD?

Our task here is not so much concerned with what is the most likely course the next 25 years will take, but rather to ask what fundamental facts of nature are destined to intervene and bring growth to a halt. Thus, we return to the theme of humanity existing in a world of finite resources, living off of nature's limited endowment. Clearly, we can pretend to be neither comprehensive nor infallible in addressing such a sweeping topic. As a start, however, let us describe economic activity, at the risk of oversimplification, by one of three possible characteristics: exponential growth at one extreme, decline or negative growth at the other, and steady state at the division line between the two extremes. Historically, one might note that throughout the world exponential growth has persisted for most of the past 200 years, while close to steady state and even declines have occurred according to recorded history during earlier periods.

Exponential Growth

It is unnecessary to belabor the obvious, that unchecked exponential growth will lead to catastrophic effects in any finite system. A simple, well-worn illustration should suffice to make the point. Consider a fish pond free of any water lilies; now introduce one into the pond and assume that each month the number of lilies will double. After some length of time their numbers will have multiplied until the lilies cover exactly one-half of the pond. Regardless of how many months it took to achieve this sorry state, in the very next month all of the pond will be covered by lily pads and become useless. So much for exponential growth.

Steady State

An alternative to growth, whether exponential or otherwise, is the steady-state society. Many anti-growth advocates argue that the sooner we transform to a steady-state pattern the better. First and foremost, a steady-state society requires that the population level become frozen. This implies that at some earlier period of time the fertility rate on a worldwide basis will have reached the replacement value (nominally 2.1 births per female in the child-bearing span) and that the fertility rate will remain at that level. Next, it becomes necessary to stabilize production and consumption so that the rate at which nonrenewable resources are depleted remains constant or diminishes with time. Recycling of materials becomes common practice so as to reduce depletion rates. Pollution is carefully maintained low enough so that the environment can readily tolerate it and irreparable damage is avoided. Life styles change and human aspirations find outlets other than a craving for increasing consumption. In such a fashion humankind should find a relatively harmonious means for coexisting with nature.

Decline or Reversed Growth

The perceptive reader will have already noted the fallacy in the above argument. In a world of finite resources, steady state can only prolong the final day of doom. The following illustration is taken from Nicholas Georgescu-Roegen.[7] Let p_k denote the world's population in year "k" and let q_k denote the per capita quantity of some vital resource of limited extent that is consumed in that year. The total amount of this resource that can be made available ultimately is represented by Q. Then, summing over all years, past, present and future, one can write

$$\sum_{k=0}^{\infty} p_k q_k \leq Q.$$

Since the q_k must be positive quantities by definition, it follows that the value of p_k must vanish after "k" reaches some upper bound. If the intent is to prolong humanity's existence on this earth, then it is not sufficient to let the p_k reach an asymptotic value, as the steady-state models would have us do, instead it becomes necessary to let them decrease with them. That is to say, the world's population would have to decrease if human existence is to be extended. Substitution, a favorite stratagem of the technologists can not circumvent this argument unless it can be shown that there are no bounded Q that are essential to the life support of humankind. Of course, the argument is based on a sweeping assumption that there are commodities of limited extent on which organized society must depend and for which no substitute can be found. Let us for the time being accept this and return to question it subsequently.

Thus, we are led to believe that our days on this planet are numbered. This, in itself, is not particularly useful information, unless more specific time scales can be deduced. For example, on the basis of current understanding of how stars evolve, we expect that in the course of the next 5 to 10 billion years the earth will become a very inhospitable place to live, the sun will grow to giant proportions, prior to its own collapse, and life will become extinct in this part of the solar system. That is a datum point of sorts we might take comfort in, since time spans of billions of years seem far too large to merit serious concern.

There are plenty of other natural phenomena, however, with shorter time spans that might give one cause for concern. The motion of the continents resulting from plate tectonics should lead to very drastic changes in the face of the earth in the course of only millions of years. Large-scale climatic changes, periods of ice ages, and relative warming trends in between occur at intervals measured in only tens of thousands of years. One might wish to worry about as yet little-understood processes in the sun that might affect in some cyclical fashion the rate at which it burns hydrogen and gives off energy. Geological evidence seems to indicate that the sense of the earth's magnetic field has reversed several times in the past. If this flip is to occur again at some unknown future date, it may be accompanied by a sudden dumping of the energetic charged particles trapped in the geomagnetic field above the earth's atmosphere (the Van Allen belts). The resulting burst of cosmic radiation could lead to severe genetic effects. I should think there is plenty of ammunition afoot for any willing Cassandra to seize upon within the incompletely understood domain of large-scale natural disturbances.

The above is not meant to detract from the severity of the problem created by the depletion of nonrenewable resources. It is meant to emphasize, however, that any discussion revolving around the exhaustion of some essential resource, which could conceivably limit growth, must be phrased in terms of the corresponding time scales. One should also try to agree on some ground rules regarding the relative importance of possible future events. Are the consequences of some process that may be perceivable only centuries hence to be given equal weight with ones whose consequences might be observable within merely decades? As long as we are making no more than educated guesses about rather long-term effects, should we attempt to discount the future? One should give the answer cautiously. A catastrophe is a catastrophe, even if it's destined to occur at some distant future time, providing we are convinced it is unavoidable. No amount of discounting can remove its shadow while we continue to live underneath it.

.

ENTER THERMODYNAMICS

One might readily conceive that the precious resource whose threatened depletion will lead to the end of human activity could be fertile land, fresh water, clean air, or perhaps some essential fuel (coal or uranium), or some all-important mineral, such as the iron-bearing ores. But no, none of these is quite important enough to occupy center stage in Nicholas Georgescu-Roegen's unconventional outlook on humanity's future. Even before the current rash of writings on growth versus no growth, Georgescu-Roegen sought to draw attention to what he claimed was a fundamental flaw in economic thought in that it did not reflect properly the dictates of thermodynamics.[8]

We are told by him that much of modern economics is based, erroneously, on the mechanistic principles of classical physics, a concept Georgescu-Roegen likes to term locomotion. Presumbaly, by this is meant Newtonian mechanics, which, but for the modifications due to Einstein, continues to serve today as a foundation to the physical sciences. Among other things, Newtonian mechanics holds that the laws which govern the motion of bodies are time reversible. That is to say, a pendulum, mounted on frictionless bearings and enclosed in a vacuum chamber, will continue to swing along whatever arc it was started on, returning to its initial position, *ad infinitum.*

In the real world, however, we know that a pendulum will not behave this way. It will eventually come to rest, for there is no such thing as a frictionless bearing or a perfect vacuum. Have any fundamental laws been violated by damping the pendulum's motion and bringing it to rest? What, for example, happened to all the energy represented by the pendulum's motion? The laws of physics do not allow energy to be either created or destroyed; it is conserved (except insofar as on the subatomic scale energy and mass can be interchanged according to Einstein's famous formula).

What happens in the above example is that through the dissipative action of friction, the energy associated with the pendulum's motion is transformed into heat, the energy originally stored in the pendulum turns up as heat in the pendulum itself and in its surroundings. One can establish this with any degree of precision that may be required for a convincing proof. More important, perhaps, admitting dissipative effects into the mechanical system of pendulum *and* its surroundings destroys the time reversibility of the laws of motion. Common experience tells us that even if all the energy in the form of heat is trapped and held to within the close proximity of the pendulum, its original motion will not be restored after this has been allowed to decay.

Heat and the processes by which it and such other forms of energy as mechanical, chemical, electrical, or radiative, for example, are transformed, one into the other, is the subject of a branch of physics known as thermodynamics. Thermodynamics tell us that all *natural* processes on a *macroscopic* scale are irreversible, just as the winding down of the pendulum's swing. In part, this is certainly due to the fact that macroscopic processes are invariably accompanied by dissipation. But there are more subtle aspects; for example, we observe that heat will flow *spontaneously* only from a hotter body to a colder one.

Georgescu-Roegen spends considerable effort in telling his readers that there is a fundamental conflict between the reversible concepts of classical mechanics and the irreversible ones of thermodynamics. In this he is just plain wrong. There isn't any conflict, and we have Ludwig Boltzmann, J. Willard Gibbs, and David Hilbert, among others, to thank for having laid the issue to rest. It would take us too far afield to enter into this fruitless argument in any detail. Suffice it to say for the moment there is ample evidence that the irreversible laws of thermodynamics on the *macroscopic* scale follow from the reversible laws of mechanics on the *microscopic* scale. When one plows through the appropriate steps, irreversibility can be associated with the loss of detailed information, a loss necessitated by the overwhelmingly large number of microscopic entities present in any representative macroscopic system. The consistency between mechanics and thermodynamics, as derivable with the aid of certain statistical formulations, does *not* mean that we are likely to see the pendulum return to its swinging once it has stopped and all its energy has turned to heat, yet Georgescu-Roegen would have us think so.

It's difficult to understand why Georgescu-Roegen spends so much time setting up a fallacious straw man. His argument is with economic theory and here, for all I know, he may have a valid point. Economic theory, after all, appears to be concerned largely with equilibria, departures from it, and the return to it. For example, demand and supply for some given commodity may be functions of several economic factors, at any given time an imbalance may develop between the two, but under the forces of the marketplace (or astute state planning if that is your game) demand and supply will come to equilibrium or at least proceed in that direction. Does this imply reversibility and a conflict with the thoughts of thermodynamics? A thermodynamicist might describe such undulations in an economy as fluctuations about an equilibrium state. As such, the trend to equilibrium is neither unique to reversible nor irreversible processes. We need more details in order to distinguish.

At this point it becomes necessary to make a further excursion into the realm of thermodynamics. It is a very precise and axiomatic science, somewhat divorced from the rest of physics. Strictly speaking, thermodynamics treats only systems that are in equilibrium. It is possible to discuss what happens to a system if work is done on it or by it on its surroundings, or if the system exchanges heat or matter with its surroundings, or if some chemical reactions are allowed to take place within the system. But, in order to use thermodynamic arguments, it is necessary to imagine that the system starts from equilibrium and ends up in equilibrium. Thermodynamics can then say something about the changes that occur between the initial and final states, but it can never pretend to say anything precise about the system while it is in a process of change. That is, thermodynamics does not describe dynamic systems. Perhaps it would have been less confusing if the name given to this branch of physics had been thermostatics. (The word, as derived from the Greek, was meant to denote the relationship between heat and mechanical work.)

Reversibility and irreversibility are concepts used frequently in thermodynamics. A reversible process is an idealized abstraction, since all natural processes are held to be irreversible. But the terms refer to the manner by which a process takes place, taking into account both the system chosen for observation *and* its surroundings. Thus, if a system goes from some initial state to a final state by an irreversible process, it *does not* mean that the system can not be restored to its initial state. It simply means that if it is to be restored to its initial state, its surroundings cannot assume its original state simultaneously. Reversible processes, on the other hand, allow both the system and its surroundings to be restored to their original state without change. Reversible processes also represent optimum paths, in the sense of energy required or work performed, for example. One might insert an economic concept here and claim that the economic value of some given process can never be greater than if it could be performed in a thermodynamically reversible manner.

A rather common popular misconception is that the irreversibility discussed in a thermodynamic sense is somehow related to the inevitable death of living organisms. Nothing could be further from the truth. A prime example of systems not amenable to the laws of classical thermodynamics are living systems, that is until they do die, when in fact they can begin to come to equilibrium.

Georgescu-Roegen believes that thermodynamics is the proper guide for economics, insofar as both sciences were born from human experience. It is not our role to argue that economics should follow one or another or any branch of the physical sciences, but one may inquire that similarities or discrepancies do exist between the one science and the other. Consider the earlier example of supply and demand. Elementary economic theory assumes that both supply and demand are responsive to prices—a concept that can be quantified further in terms of what economists call elasticities. As the price of some commodity relative to other goods increases, producers are inclined to supply more of it, just as consumers are inclined to purchase less of it. One imagines that as the state of an economy changes and so do the prices, it is possible to move up and down these curves, appropriately shifted to account for the changes, freely to find the new equilibrium point. Normally, time does not appear explicitly in these economic formulations, and neither does it appear explicitly in the body of thermodynamics. Time does have an implicit role in thermodynamics and I would assume it does so in economics. Certainly the economist is well aware of time lags in reaching equilibria and the effect of secular variations on his demand and supply curves. Whether reversibility or irreversibility is inherent to these traversals along equilibrium paths is very much a function of what is assumed to be happening outside the boundaries of the system per se, its surroundings, that is. Thermodynamics is careful in how it draws the boundaries around whatever system is being examined and pays attention to what thermodynamic quantities are exchanged through the boundaries between the system and its surroundings. Georgescu-Roegen seems to feel that this aspect of analysis has not received the rigorous attention it deserves from economists. Both thermodynamics and economics are concerned with transformations; the system we've selected may be where the transformations take place; but in general there will be flows both in and out of the system through the boundaries. And it is often at the boundaries where the issue between reversibility and irreversibility must be settled.

An economist, for example, who sets out to project the long-term supply of crude oil without taking into account that future discovery rates will decline as this resource becomes depleted, is certainly open not only to Georgescu-Roegen's criticism but to ours, as well. Anyone so negligent would be at fault for not having included properly the boundaries of his system, where for the sake of argument we might assume the boundary lies somewhere between proven oil reserves and undiscovered resources in this instance. I have the impression, however, that few if any economists would be so negligent.

Of the various axioms that appear in thermodynamics, two have particular prominence and may be termed "laws." The first states that both work and heat are forms of energy, a quantity that can be neither created nor destroyed. (It may be useful to distinguish work and heat by noting that when energy is transferred by work, some form of organized motion must be invoked, whereas this is not true when energy is transferred by heat.) The second is a statement of inequality and may be given in a variety of forms. I choose to put it as follows: One can always find a natural process by which work can be transformed entirely to heat without producing any other effects; the converse of this statement is never true. (The astute reader may suspect that this discrepancy is somehow related to the fact that the energy of work has an organized component while the energy of heat does not.)

ENTROPY

If work is done or heat is exchanged in the process of a thermodynamic system going from its initial state to its final state, the amount of work and/or heat will be a function of the process and not a function of the initial and final states. The bookkeeping among thermodynamic functions can be done much more conveniently in terms of state variables, that is, quantities that depend only on what state the system is in and not on the manner by which it reached that state. Entropy is one such variable. The second of the preceding axions regarding the asymmetry between work and heat can be restated in terms of the entropy function as follows: Within an isolated system any natural process is accompanied by an increase in entropy. Georgescu-Roegen has seized upon the irreversible production of entropy as the centerpiece to his argument that conventional economics errs in the way it treats a world of limited resources. We continuously need a source to replenish our stock of low entropy, for nature requires our activities be accompanied by entropy production. Ultimately, only the sun can serve as such a source, and Georgescu-Roegen would have us recognize this fundamental limitation. The concept of entropy and its relation to economics deserves some further discussion.

Georgescu-Roegen is fond of citing the piece of coal burning in the grate and turning to smoke and ash as an illustration of nature's irreversibility, and incidentally of irreversible entropy increase. The point is well taken, but it is worth making a distinction. Systems of chemically reacting species can, in principle, always be restored to their original state. Granted that in practice one would find relatively little economic value in reconstituting coal from its combustion products, we do wish to stress the difference between reversibility and restorability. Perhaps another example can illustrate the nature of entropy better. Suppose we have a bomb, a vessel capable of withstanding explosive forces, and we place into this bomb an explosive mixture of hydrogen and oxygen, seal it and cover it with a perfect thermally insulating material. Inside the bomb there is a mechanism for igniting the mixture, an electrical spark, for example. After ignition there is a violent chemical reaction and the hydrogen combines with the oxygen to form water vapor. We have an example of an adiabatic process here, and one that proceeds at constant volume. As far as the system in the bomb is concerned, no work has been done and no heat has been exchanged through the boundaries. The energy content of the system is the same after the reaction is complete as it was at the start. The chemical elements, hydrogen and oxygen, have been preserved, but they are now combined in the form of water molecules. The entropy of the system, however, has increased considerably, as may be inferred from the rise in pressure and temperature within the bomb. Since the process leading to the formation of water was irreversible, the original state of the system can not be reconstituted via a similar (that is, any adiabatic) process. Instead, the thermal insulation must be removed from the bomb, additional heat has to be supplied from the outside in order to raise the temperature to the point where water will dissociate into hydrogen and oxygen, and then the system must be cooled, with the temperature reduced rapidly through heat removal. After all this is done, the system within the bomb will have returned to its original state, containing a mixture of hydrogen and oxygen. In the course of the second series of steps, the entropy of the system within the bomb will have been reduced at the expense of increasing the entropy of its surroundings by a greater amount. As far as system and surroundings are concerned, entropy was increased in both the process leading to the formation of water and the process leading to the dissociation of water. As far as the system within the bomb is concerned, its entropy is the same after reconstitution as it was in the beginning. In the process that reconstituted the system, negative entropy was fed to it. Hydrogen and oxygen are potentially valuable fuels from which useful work can be extracted. If we wish to produce them from abundantly available supplies of water, we must have a source of not only energy but also negative entropy. (As to the latter, remember that it was essential to cool rapidly.)

Entropy is a useful unit of account in thermodynamics, but it leaves something to be desired. It can not be measured directly. Its value can be inferred indirectly through the measurement of other thermodynamic properties of a system and the use of thermodynamic relationships between entropy and other variables. Entropy can be calculated directly from the fundamental properties of matter, providing one uses the laws of statistical mechanics. This, in turn, requires using the concept of probabilities to describe the most likely state of a macroscopic system consisting of many entities at the atomic or molecular level. It then becomes evident that entropy is a measure of randomness. One can now begin to appreciate more fully why it is that in a process where entropy must increase it may be possible to convert all work to heat but not vice versa.

Entropy, as a measure of randomness or disorder, is a concept that applies to phenomena other than just heat flow. Consider the following example. Suppose I have two piles of small glass beads, one pile contains transparent beads and the other pile contains beads that are all colored red. I now mix the two piles together so that the red and transparent beads are more or less uniformly distributed. The entropy content of the single pile containing the mixture of beads is said to be greater than the sum of the entropy contents of the original two separate piles. Unfortunately, there is no direct means for measuring the change in entropy, but it can be readily calculated using the rules of statistical mechanics. If I now take a pair of tweezers and separate the red beads from the transparent ones so that I can restore the system to its original state in two separate piles, I will have done some work, but more important, I have supplied negative entropy to the system. The negative entropy factor enters because I was able to distinguish between the red and the transparent beads with the aid of my intellectual powers. Had the original two piles contained beads of identical color and I mixed them up, no entropy change would have resulted. Separating them into two piles would have involved essentially the same amount of work as before, but no entropy exchange. Analogous mixing and unmixing processes at the molecular level also can be envisioned.

The notion of probability and the science of statistical mechanics are anathema to Georgescu-Roegen, and that's a pity. Thermodynamics is a self-contained discipline, capable of standing on its own two legs. It's even more useful, however, with the complement of statistical mechanics. Thermodynamics is incapable of predicting the properties of matter, it can only supply the relationships that must be obeyed by certain sets of macroscopic variables. In order to manipulate these variables in some constructive fashion, it becomes necessary to have additional information. Somebody must tell us, for example, what is the compressibility of the fluid we might be working with, or the heat capacity of some pure substance that has caught our fancy. Thermodynamics cannot supply this information, but statistical mechanics can. Of course, one can be pragmatic about such affairs and measure the compressibility or heat capacity in the laboratory. The advantage of statistical mechanics is that it permits us to calculate a whole host of such desirable quantities in terms of the atomic and molecular properties of matter, often with greater precision than measurements can give.

ENTROPY AND THE LIMITS TO GROWTH

Having noted that entropy is a measure of randomness or degree of disorder and observing that in a sense the entropy principle of thermodynamics says that natural processes tend to move in a direction from order to chaos, one can begin to appreciate Georgescu-Roegen's view that the entropy principle must underlie economic processes. After all, the economic activities of organized society, in one way or another, are constantly promoting order out of chaos. A skyscraper or bridge or jet airliner is an enormously more ordered structure than the pieces of sand, dirt, and rock from which they were fashioned. Economic activity, therefore, has to be constantly infused with negative entropy in order to sustain the entropy balances required by nature. As stated earlier, the sun is a prodigious supplier of low entropy and in the ultimate scheme of things is the sustainer of all organic processes on earth. Human intellect, however, is a powerful tool for transforming systems from states of high entropy to low entropy, and Georgescu-Roegen is concerned that the rate of such activities is growing so rapidly that they will soon reach the limits set by nature. There are really two central points to Georgescu-Roegen's argument that must be examined further. Most important perhaps is the point that thermodynamic principles will limit growth—if so, are these limits within sight or so remote as to be essentially of no interest? Second, does economic theory properly reflect thermodynamic principles—and if not, is it for justifiable reasons?

Let us examine in slightly greater detail how the flow of low entropy enters into economic activities. Consider, for example, the various steps involved, starting from the extraction of minerals from the ground, to the refining and manufacture of metals and alloys, to the forming of structural material, such as steel rods, cables, and so on, all of which must precede the design and construction of a bridge. By the time we get to the bridge, in this sequence of events, a considerable amount of negative entropy will have been invested in the project, accompanied by a large increase in the entropy of the rest of the world.

By good fortune the earth is not an isolated system; it is in radiative contact with the sun. Each day the earth receives enormous amounts of energy from the sun, a tiny fraction of this is absorbed and retained to support life, the rest is ultimately reradiated to the rest of the universe. To put matters into a little more quantitative perspective, the amount of solar energy reaching the earth's surface each day is approximately ten times greater than the total energy used by the world's present population in an entire year.

It is not simply energy that we need, of course, but high-grade energy with low-entropy content. Then it becomes the useful source needed by humankind to carry out its organized activities. In simple words, what we want is useful, manipulatable energy. For example, it is often stated that the large amounts of waste heat rejected by a thermal plant in the course of generating electricity should be put to some useful purpose, rather than be thrown away as a thermal pollutant. It is true that for each unit of electrical energy that is produced, approximately two units of waste heat are produced. Unfortunately, the waste heat is rejected at a low temperature, it's not even warm enough for a comfortable shower. We would say it's not very usable, and all things considered it is probably best to just throw it away, though some will argue the point. In order to determine just how useful energy is, it must be indexed somehow in terms of its entropy content. This was recognized by the famous nine-teenth-century American physicist J. Willard Gibbs, who introduced the thermodynamic variable "availability" as a measure of how much useful work could be obtained from a system with a given amount of energy, entropy, and volume.[9]

The use of "availability," or, as some prefer to call it, available work, has come into vogue recently. Fundamentally, this is because of increased interest in energy conservation and in more efficient utilization of energy. Consumers are usually not so much interested in energy per se as in the task it accomplishes. Conventionally one measures the efficiency with which the task is accomplished by comparing, for example, the work output of a device with the heat input. This mode of calculation relies on the first law of thermodynamics, which establishes the equivalence be-tween work and heat. On this basis a typical home hot-water heater, burning gas, might be 50 percent efficient.

This manner of computation, however, concentrates on the specific device and not the task, that is, the production of hot water. It also neglects the second law, which cautions that both the system and its surroundings, effectively the ambient atmosphere in this case, must be considered in order to keep track of the entropy flows. A more unified way to compute efficiencies and take into account limitations arising from second-law considerations and entropy production is to use availabilities. On this basis one finds that the very same hot-water heater is only 3 percent efficient in supplying hot water, where the comparison is made with respect to the most efficient way hot water could be provided from the combustion of a unit amount of gas.

The use of availability and second-law efficiencies has been stressed by Barry Commoner in a series of articles first appearing in *The New Yorker* magazine and now available in book form.[10] Some of Commoner's argu-ments, however, are sufficiently misleading so anyone wishing to pursue this matter would be well advised to consult the original source.[11]

AN OPTIMISTIC VIEW OF
THE IMPORTANT MATTER
OF TIMING

Let us rephrase our earlier question as follows: To what extent will economic growth be limited because of finite energy sources of high availability? The theoretical, or speculative, answer to this is that in these terms there are no practical limits. The high availability supplied by the sun's energy, or that could be produced from the uranium- and thorium-containing minerals on earth through fission, or that might be supplied from the waters of the earth through fusion, is sufficient to support the current level of organized human activity for time durations longer than the anticipated lifetime of the earth. Even if the world's population were to increase tenfold and its appetite for useful energy increased by a similar amount, we would conclude that solar energy, fission energy, or fusion energy each represent virtually inexhaustible sources. (The earth's heat that can be tapped from the upper layers of its crust, geothermal energy, is yet another source, but not as large as the other three.)

PLUS SOME RESERVATIONS

There are practical problems, of course. Sunlight is a diffuse form of energy and we have yet to learn how to use it economically to furnish all the energy needs of a highly industrialized society. Nuclear fission reactors work very well, but it is the nuclear fission breeder that we need in order to extend the utility of uranium or thorium in limitless fashion. The breeder is not yet a commercial entity; and, if some critics of nuclear energy had their way, it would never come into being. Fusion works, we know, but not in the way we need it for commercial purposes. Controlled fusion reactors have been under development for nearly 25 years, both in this country and elsewhere. It is a difficult problem on which steady progress is being made. Virtually everyone working on the problem is quite optimistic about the prospects of fusion. Some who are close to it, but on the outside, as well as some who are not very close to it, have become skeptical that fusion can ever be made practical. Having devoted the better part of my adult life to this pursuit, I must confess to being on the optimistic side of this issue.

One or another of these potentially unlimited energy sources will have to be placed at the disposal of society within the next century, for the popular sources of energy today—hydropower, organic fuels, and all the fossil fuels—are too limited in extent. If we are to contemplate the continued existence of civilization, it becomes axiomatic that its energy supplies will be assured, and we should look elsewhere for fundamental limitations to growth.

Human activity is unavoidably accompanied by environmental impact, some of it is not benign. One might wish to equate the unavoidable discharge of waste products resulting from economic activities with the principle of entropy production, since "waste" is a consequence of creating disorder. This is not the place, however, to enter into a debate on whether technology can or cannot control the release of undesirable pollutants to the environment faster than they are generated, for I believe this is inherently a near-term problem. Either we learn to control it or we shall soon begin to choke on it. I do not believe that catastrophic events will ensue from unabated pollution, since long before that happens we will be forced to curb it by one means or another. If we are to worry about long-term effects, we should focus on impacts that can lead to irreparable damage and global consequences. In this respect I would cite climatic effects as deserving high-priority attention. As stated earlier, our knowledge of long-term climatic variations due to natural causes is very imperfect; for this plus other reasons it becomes difficult to say with any precision how humankind's activities are likely to cause significant climatic changes.[12] One worries, however, about additional heat, dust, and carbon dioxide released to the atmosphere through human activity. Each of these, in sufficient amount, could change the mean temperature of the earth so that the effect would be noticeable, and probably found to be unpleasant. Rather than continue speculating here on these unknowns, let it be agreed that the subject of climatic modification through human intervention must be studied seriously by all nations.[13]

While not a climatic issue, the proper disposal of long-lived radioactive waste resulting from nuclear reactors is another long-term issue of major consequence. We believe today that such material must be isolated effectively from the biosphere for periods ranging up to 240,000 years. Again, I'm of the opinion that such matters must be resolved satisfactorily in the relatively near term, otherwise society will not tolerate the use of nuclear energy.

In addition to a benign climate, humanity needs land and water for its survival. While these are not exhaustible resources, they are limited in extent. On a global basis, not quite 10 percent of the total runoff of rainfall is used by present levels of human activity, and of this amount, about 80 percent is used for irrigation. Particularly due to regional variations, it is unlikely that significantly larger amounts of land cultivation can occur without desalination. This, in turn, requires energy. Once again, on a global basis, land use would seem to be less restricted. About 3 percent of the land mass is cultivated today, and it has been estimated that as much as 20 percent could be cultivated ultimately, given enough water for irrigation. Food production today is not particularly efficient, insofar as human taste prefers to invest large amounts of grain crops on feeding animals. It's not for me to say that a world without T-bone steaks or mutton chops is one to contemplate with pleasure, but tastes can change. Suffice it to say, that given enough energy at a cheap enough price, it should be possible to feed and sustain a significantly larger population than the one currently occupying our globe. The fact that today large masses of the population subsist at well below nutritional norms does not necessarily reinforce one's confidence in the rosy picture of the future painted above. The limitations, however, are not caused by some ultimate scarcity and could be alleviated, in principle, by better management of the existing resources. Unforeseen changes in climate or inability to find cheap forms of energy in timely fashion, while the world's population continues to increase, could easily turn this picture to one with tragic dimensions.

Humanity requires not only replenishable resources to carry out its organized activities, but also a large variety of seemingly essential and depletable resources. A variety of views can be found in this subject, ranging from hopeless abandon to wild optimism. In general I view the school that would have us mine the oceans and dig up the earth's crust to depths of many kilometers with a certain amount of skepticism. On the other hand, it seems to me that the recent analysis given by H. E. Goeller and Alvin Weinberg is essentially sound.[14]

These authors conclude that those materials in common use today that are in some danger of eventual depletion can be substituted for by materials that are essentially inexhaustible (for example, aluminum substituting for copper in electrical conductors). One has to pay a price for this in terms of going from today's high-grade materials to tomorrow's low-grade materials, but the price they estimate is well within acceptable bounds, providing only that the requisite energy can be supplied. So, although Georgescu-Roegen is quite correct in stating that the equivalence between energy and matter is a physical principle of interest only in the realm of particle physics, he has not stressed sufficiently, in my opinion, that with abundant energy (availability) one can continue for a very long period of time to transform the earth's resources into the capital stock and materials required by a high level of economic activity. Put in other terms, the Qs in Georgescu-Roegen's paradigm are so large as to be nearly irrelevant.

CONCLUDING REMARKS

As to the original question of does entropy production imply a limit to growth, I find the question not particularly useful. Presumably we are seeking physical limitations to economic growth. The concept of entropy production is so broad and inclusive that in itself it can offer very little constructive guidance. Instead, I believe one must search for a detailed list of potential physical limitations, as I have attempted to do above in part, and examine each such limit carefully. That is what Goeller and Weinberg have done for depletable resources and that is the type of analysis we must continue to pursue in searching for the proper answer.

Economic theory has always paid close attention to scarcity, but perhaps until recently it has not given sufficient attention to resource exhaustion and the diseconomies associated with waste production. Here one can draw valuable lessons from Georgescu-Roegen, although well before his writings appeared other economists had addressed these issues.[15] The question of whether conventional economics, if there is such a beast, is fundamentally unsound because it does not take into proper account the teachings of thermodynamics, and in particular the irrevocable increase of entropy, is a matter I would just as soon leave to other economists to debate.

One can certainly have sympathy for Georgescu-Roegen's criticism that many current economic formulations are static (time independent), while the real world (to which the model is meant to apply) is always in a state of evolution. How can economics speak of closed cycles when there's no returning to the original starting point? We may suspect, along with Georgescu-Roegen, that the boundaries around the systems the economists are concerned with are not always treated with sufficient care. Criticisms of a similar nature can also be made of models used by physical scientists, even in the realm of thermodynamics. The greatest gift an analyst can have is to know how far he can simplify his model and still obtain a result that is informative about the behavior of the real system.

It is possible to construct a line of argument, following some of Georgescu-Roegen's observations on values, that spells out a rationale for a halt to economic growth. As the richer grades and types of nonrenewable resources become exhausted and as waste products continue to accumulate, the transformation processes on which economic activity depends reach a state where the net economic, social, and political value of the outputs no longer exceeds that of the inputs. But, such a course of affairs depends in fact on how much or little faith one places on technology and innovation. One would like to think that the case against growth is not an open and shut case, but one that deserves careful scrutiny, along with a critical appraisal of the adequacy of the analysis that is being applied.

When the potentially limiting physical factors are examined in detail, one notes the rather central role that energy must play in all future considerations. To this extent, then, the entropy principle reenters along the lines mentioned earlier. Why the entropy principle should spell the downfall of conventional economic thought is a little more difficult to comprehend. Economics seems to be a fairly adaptable discipline, it speaks of externalities and diseconomies, even more so now that environmental protection is in vogue. In the same breath one hears much more discussion these days about economic rent, seeing as how depletable resources and OPEC cartel action have become current events topics, although Ricardo wrote on economic rent more than 100 years ago.

In the past, economics has been closely allied with politics, and politics is not noted for its long-range outlook. If economics is to become an important tool for long-range planning, and presumably that's what the pro-growth/antigrowth argument is all about, then it had better become thoroughly conversant with the immense technological challenges we face under either a continued growth or zero growth policy. The nature of the challenges may be quite different, but, nevertheless, they will be severe in both instances. It has been remarked that since no one can really say what will happen over the next 25-year period, a lot of people are spending their time talking about the next 200 years, instead. Well, in all seriousness, talking about the next 200 years is not without some virtue, just so long as we bear in mind that there won't be any next 200 years unless we manage to get through the next 25.

This brings me to a final point, that the next 25 or perhaps even the next 50 years will probably continue to provide for a troubled world: one with pockets of turbulence and regions of political unrest. The inequities mentioned earlier are destined to remain with us for some time. Charting a stable course through these troubled waters will require unusual amounts of political, economic, and technical skills. It seems to me that under these conditions it is not particularly instructive to take the no-growth talk very seriously at this time. I would be inclined to pay much more attention to a course that was destined to bring the world to a state of self-limiting growth through a process of gradual evolution.

NOTES

1. Thomas Robert Malthus, *Essay on Principles of Population* (1798) (Reprinted by the Royal Economic Society, London, 1926).

2. David Ricardo, "Principles of Political Economy and Taxation" (1817) in *The Works and Correspondence of David Ricardo,* Piero Sraffa, ed. (Cambridge: Cambridge University Press, 1953).

3. See, for example, Paul R. Ehrlich and Anne H. Ehrlich, *Population, Resources and Environment: Issues in Human Ecology* (San Francisco: Freeman, 1972); and Barry Commoner, *The Closing Circle* (New York: Knopf, 1971).

4. Donella H. Meadows et al., *The Limits to Growth* (New York: Universe Books. 1972).

5. Edison Electric Institute, *Economic Growth in the Future: The Growth Debate in National and Global Perspective* (New York: McGraw-Hill, 1976).

6. See, for example, "The No-Growth Society," *Daedalus,* Fall 1973.

7. Nicholas Georgescu-Roegen, "Energy and Economic Myths," *Southern Economic Journal* 41 (1975):347–81.

8. Nicholas Georgescu-Roegen, *Analytical Economics: Issues and Problems* (Cambridge, Mass.: Harvard University Press, 1966); and *The Entropy Law and the Economic Process* (Cambridge, Mass.: Harvard University Press, 1971).

9. *The Collected Works of J. Willard Gibbs* (London: Longmans, Green, 1931), p. 39.

10. Barry Commoner, *The Poverty of Power* (New York: Knopf, 1976).

11. American Institute of Physics, *Efficient Use of Energy, The APS Studies on the Technical Aspects of the More Efficient Use of Energy* (New York, 1976).

12. "Man's Impact on the Global Environment," Report of the Study of Critical Environmental Problems (Cambridge, Mass.: MIT Press, 1970); and "Inadvertant Climate Modification," Report of the Study of Man's Impact on Climate (Cambridge, Mass.: MIT Press, 1971).

13. It is possible to sound a guarded but somewhat cheery note, however. Of all the pollution variants, the one that is unavoidable is thermal pollution or waste heat rejection. Recalling the axioms of thermodynamics, it should be apparent that all the energy used in organized human activity must eventually turn to heat. We must, then, compare heat caused by the transformations originating in economic activity with the amount of radiation received from the sun. As the two figures become comparable, watch out! The average solar flux received on earth is about 160 watts per square meter. The per capita rate of energy consumption in the United States is about 10 kilowatts on an annual average basis, and considerably higher than in other countries. Suppose the earth were populated with 10 billion people, each enjoying the energy-intensive affluence of the current U.S. population. If the 10 billion were spread over 10 percent of the continental land mass (about 150 million square kilometers) the resulting mean waste heat rejection would be 4 percent of the solar flux. When congestion and economic activity begin to approach these levels, one should begin to worry.

14. H. E. Goeller and Alvin M. Weinberg, "The Age of Substitutability—What Do We Do When the Mercury Runs Out?" *Science* 191, no. 4228 (February 20, 1976): 683.

15. H. Hotelling, "The Economics of Exhaustible Resources," *Journal of Political Economy* 39 (April 1931); and A. C. Pigou, *The Economics of Welfare*, 4th ed. (London: Macmillan, 1932).

| Index |

action patterns, inability to control others', 80

Aeronautics and Space Technology, Office of (OAST), 239

affirmative hiring, 28

AIAA (*see*, American Institute of Aeronautics and Astronautics)

Alaska Pipeline, 146

American Governments, need to reduce spending by, 138–39

American Institute of Aeronautics and Astronautics (AIAA), 239, 240

America's Third Century, 127–28, 135, 137, 139

Ames Research Center, Moffet Field, Calif., 239, 253

"amondie," 78–79, 85; changes needed to cure, 79–80

Animal Farm, 79

anomie, 78

Apollo project, 234, 256

Apollo-Amor asteroids, 240

Aquinas, Thomas, 63

armaments, investments in, 291

Atomic Energy Commission, 166

Augustine, 62

availabilities, 328, 331

balance of payments, 163, 168–71, 178, 182, 187

basic value systems, need to reconstitute, 80

Beagle, H.M.S., 235

Beame, Mayor Abraham, 139

Beard, Charles, 65

Bell, Daniel, 108, 109

Belle Epoque, La, 65

Beyond Despair, 81

Beyond the Planet Earth, 234

big business corporations, impending demise of, 136–37

biophysical planning, 133–34

birth and death rates, 133

Biscayne Aquifer, 31, 32

Blume, John, 254

Boeing, 234

Boltzmann, Ludwig, 321

Boulding, Kenneth, 146, 277

Boundary Waters Canoe Area (BWCA), 36

Brave New World, 64, 76

Britain's Roskill Commission, Report of (1971), 287

Brooks, Harvey, 20–21

Brothers Karamazov, The, 62

Brown, Edmund G., Jr., 145

Bushmen, 43

business cycle, controlling the, 195–96

BWCA (*see*, Boundary Waters Canoe Area)

Callahan, Daniel, 66

Canada, 242

capital, formation of, 210–11, 212

carbon dioxide, 206–07, 213

Carnegie, Andrew, 136

Carnot, Sadi, 293

Carter, President Jimmy, 139

Case Western Reserve World Model, 230

Census Bureau, 145

Chicago School, 287

Chinese, classical, cyclical life of, 44–45

citizen participation activities, models of, 87–88

City of God, 62

Civilization and Its Discontents, 69

Clapeyron, Emile, 294

Clerk-Maxwell, James, 119

climatic effects, concerns for, 330

Club of Rome, 13, 14–15, 17, 42, 57, 58, 68, 74, 75, 76, 144, 145, 194, 210, 316

| About the Editor and Contributors |

Kenneth D. Wilson is Executive Assistant for Corporate Planning and Policy Analysis at Southern California Edison Company. He received his Doctor of Public Administration degree from the University of Southern California School of Public Administration where he teaches a core seminar in Public Administration. He also teaches at the Center for Public Policy and Administration, California State University, Long Beach, and for the UCLA Extension Department. Prior to undertaking work on this volume, Dr. Wilson served as the co-staff member (along with William Thompson of Philadelphia Electric Company) on a large-scale study of the growth issue sponsored by the Edison Electric Institute. The results of that project were reported in *Economic Growth in the Future: The Growth Debate in National and Global Perspective* (1976).

Peter L. Auer is Professor of Mechanical and Aerospace Engineering in the Sibley School of Mechanical and Aerospace Engineering at Cornell University. His Ph.D. in chemistry and physics was awarded by the California Institute of Technology. From 1970 to 1974 he served as Co-Director of the Cornell Energy Project. He was a special consultant to the Chairman of the Atomic Energy Commission from 1973–74. Subsequently, he served with the Federal Energy Office and then the Federal Energy Agency. He continues active consultation on various committees of the National Academies of Sciences and Engineering, as well as with the Electric Power Research Institute and other organizations, both public and private. He serves as an editor of *Plasma Physics* and as an associate editor of *Energy—The International Journal*.

Daniel Bell is a Professor of Sociology at Harvard University. He received his Ph.D. from Columbia University. Dr. Bell has served as a member of the President's Commission on Technology, Automation and Economic Progress, 1964–66; and was coauthor of the report, *Technology and the American Economy*, 1966. He was also cochairman of the Panel on Social Indicators, Department of Health, Education and Welfare, 1966–68. His writings in the areas of sociology are considered among the most important in that field.

Kenneth E. Boulding is Professor of Economics at the University of Colorado, and he is a Director of the Program of Research on General Social and Economic Dynamics at the University's Institute of Behavioral Science. Mr. Boulding (M.A. Oxford) is an internationally renowned economist, social theorist, and writer. From 1949 to 1967 Boulding was Professor of Economics at the University of Michigan, where he was also Co-Director of the Center for Research on Conflict Resolution. A prolific writer, Boulding has authored more than 25 books. His articles appear in numerous professional journals and periodicals.

Richard Carlson is an economist at the Stanford Research Institute (SRI). He attended Harvard College, the University of Maryland (M.A., Economics), and Stanford University, where he is completing his Ph.D. in economics. Carlson was economist and chief analyst for the recent SRI publication *Solar Energy in America's Future.* Before joining SRI, Carlson was Assistant Director of the Illinois Budget Bureau (Office of the Governor). He has worked at the Office of Management and Budget and in the U.S. Office of Education.

Herman E. Daly is Professor of Economics at Louisiana State University. He graduated from Rice University before taking his Ph.D. at Vanderbilt. Dr. Daly has also taught at Vanderbilt University, and was Ford Foundation Visiting Professor at the University of Ceará in Brazil during 1967–68. In 1970 he was a Research Associate at Yale University. In 1972 Daly was appointed to a three-year term on the Committee on Mineral Resources and the Environment of the National Academy of Sciences. He edited the book *Toward a Steady-State Economy.*

Nicholas Georgescu-Roegen is Visiting Bendum Professor of Energy Economics, Regional Research Institute, West Virginia University, and Professeur Associé, Louis Pasteur University, Strasbourg. He studied mathematics at the University of Bucharest, then statistics at the Sorbonne, and as a postgraduate fellow with Karl Pearson at University College, London. After serving as Professor of Statistics at the University of Bucharest (1948–49), Georgescu-Roegen joined Vanderbilt University where he retired as Distinguished Professor of Economics in 1976. His most recent books include *Analytical Economics, The Entropy Law and The Economic Process,* and *Energy and Economic Association.* He is currently working on a new volume, *Bioeconomics.*

Luther P. Gerlach is Professor of Anthropology at the University of Minnesota. He received his Ph.D. from the University of London. He has served as a member of the Energy Resources Lecture Team sponsored by the U.S. Information Agency lecturing in Far and Mid-East cities. He has also been a visiting Associate in Anthropology and Environmental Studies at the California Institute of Technology and Senior Consultant at the Aspen Institute for Humanistic Studies. Dr. Gerlach has written numerous articles and coauthored two books: *People, Power, Change: Movements of Social Transformation,* and *Lifeway, Leap: The Dynamics of Change in America.*

Willis W. Harman is Associate Director of the Center for the Study of Social Policy, Stanford Research Institute (SRI), and Professor of Engineering-Economic Systems at Stanford University. He received his B.S. in Electrical Engineering from the University of Washington, and an M.S. in Physics and his Ph.D. in Electrical Engineering from Stanford University. He has been a consultant to the National Goals Research Staff of the White House and to the Conference Board in New York. He is a member of the Commerce Technical Advisory Board serving the U.S. Department of Commerce. He is the author of *An Incomplete Guide To The Future.*

Barry B. Hughes is Associate Professor of Political Science at Case Western Reserve University in Cleveland, Ohio. He earned a B.S. in Mathematics at Stanford University, an M.A. and a Ph.D. in Political Science at the University of Minnesota. Since 1972 he has been affiliated with the Systems Research Center at Case Western Reserve University and has worked on the Club of Rome's World Model Project. Dr. Hughes has publications in the areas of European integration, global cooperation and conflict, American foreign policy, energy modeling, and world modeling.

Norman Macrae is Deputy Editor and leading economic writer for *The Economist,* published in London. He was educated and did postgraduate research at Cambridge University. In 1973 he was the recipient of the Wincott Award as British Financial Journalist of the Year. In addition to over 3,000 articles, mostly for *The Economist,* he has written two books on the United States: *The Neurotic Trillionaire* and *America's Third Century.* He has also written books on Britain and Japan: *The London Capital Market, Sunshades in October, Consider Japan,* and *The Risen Sun.*

Mihajlo D. Mesarovic is Professor of Engineering and Mathematics and Director of the Systems Research Center at Case Western Reserve University, Cleveland, Ohio. He received his Ph.D. in technical science at the Serbian Academy of Sciences. He is President, Systems Applications Co. of Cleveland. Dr. Mesarovic is the author of ten books and more than 60 papers in scientific, professional, and technical journals and proceedings. He is the founder and editor of *Mathematical Systems Theory Journal.*

E. J. Mishan is Professor of Economics at the London School of Economics and Political Science where he has taught for 20 years. Dr. Mishan's articles have been published extensively in the top professional journals. He is also the author of *Cost Benefit Analysis; Economics for Social Decisions: Elements of Cost-Benefit Analysis; Cost-Benefit Analysis: An Informal Introduction; Technology and Growth: The Price We Pay; Twenty-One Popular Economic Fallacies;* and *Welfare Economics.*

William D. Nordhaus is a Member of the President's Council of Economic Advisers. He is on leave from Yale University where he is Professor of Economics and a member of the Cowles Foundation for Research in Economics. He received his B.A. from Yale University and his Ph.D. in economics from MIT. Dr. Nordhaus' economic research has concentrated on macroeconomics, growth economics, and resource and energy economics. Many of these studies will be forthcoming in a book, *The Efficient Use of Energy Resources.* His writings have included numerous books and articles in the professional and general literature.

Gerard K. O'Neill is Professor of Physics at Princeton University, where he has taught since 1954. He received his Ph.D. in Physics from Cornell University. In 1976–77 Dr. O'Neill served a year as Jerome Clarke Hunsaker Professor of Aerospace at MIT. Dr. O'Neill's main research area is high-energy particle Physics. In 1956 he invented the storage-ring technique for colliding particle beams, a method which is now the basis for nearly every new high-energy machine. He is a member of the Advisory Board of the National Air and Space Museum of the Smithsonian Institution, and serves regularly on advisory boards and panels related to advanced developments in space. Dr. O'Neill is the author of *The High Frontier: Human Colonies in Space.*

S. Fred Singer is Professor of Environmental Sciences and a member of the Center for Advanced Studies at the University of Virginia. He leads a multidisciplinary study and educational program on energy resources, environmental science, and public policy, with particular reference to the effects of a growing population. His degrees include a B.E.E. degree from Ohio State University, plus an A.M. and a Ph.D. in Physics from Princeton. A geophysicist, Dr. Singer has held academic posts as professor, research scientist, and university dean. He has served as advisor to Congress, General Accounting Office, Treasury, and other governmental agencies as well as major industrial concerns. Dr. Singer writes extensively for newspapers and magazines on public policy problems and he has published numerous technical and general articles on the physics of the earth and solar system and on the physical environment with special emphasis on water resources, the atmosphere, oceans, and space. His books include *Is There an Optimum Level of Population?; The Changing Global Environment;* and *Arid Zone Development: Potentialities and Problems.*

Robert Theobald is an author, consultant, and speaker. He is a consultant working with Control Data Corporation helping them to understand the ways in which their computer/telecommunications-based PLATO system can work for education and management. He is also working with the state-based "Hawaii Commission on the Year 2000" to discover how citizens can be more involved in creating their own future. Mr. Theobald's books include *Beyond Despair; An Alternative Future for America's Third Century; Futures Conditional; Teg's 1994;* and *The Guaranteed Income.*

Anthony J. Wiener is Professor of Management and Director of Policy Studies at the Polytechnic Institute of New York. He is also Director of the Program to Plan and Establish a School of Technology Management and Policy Studies under a grant from the Alfred P. Sloan Foundation. He received an A.B. degree in sociology and psychology from Harvard College and a J.D. from Harvard Law School. Wiener joined the full-time staff of the Hudson Institute at its founding in July 1961, where he remains as consultant while he is on leave of absence from the full-time staff. In 1969 Dr. Wiener served as Chairman of the White House Urban Affairs Research Committee. Dr. Wiener is coauthor with Herman Kahn of *The Year 2000: A Framework for Speculation,* prepared for the Commission on the Year 2000 of the American Academy of Arts and Sciences, and has written widely in such areas as social science, law, and education.

Ian Wilson is a member of General Electric Company's Public Issues Research staff. He is a graduate of Oxford University, England. Wilson came to the United States in 1954 following six years' work with Imperial Chemical Industries in London. An articulate and insightful writer, Wilson has had numerous articles and papers published in business and academic periodicals. He coauthored *The Business Environment of the Seventies,* and authored *Corporate Environments of the Future.*

RELATED TITLES
Published by
Praeger Special Studies

ALTERNATIVE ENERGY STRATEGIES:
Constraints and Opportunities
                        John Hagel III

*COST-BENEFIT ANALYSIS
                        E. J. Mishan

THE ENERGY CRISIS AND THE ENVIRONMENT:
An International Perspective
                        edited by *Donald R. Kelley*

*PLANNING AND CONSERVATION:
The Emergence of the Frugal Society
                        Peter W. House
                        and *Edward R. Williams*

*SOCIAL SCIENCE AND PUBLIC POLICY
IN THE UNITED STATES
                        Irving Louis Horowitz
                        and *James Everett Katz*

*THE SUSTAINABLE SOCIETY:
Implications for Limited Growth
                        edited by *Dennis Clark Pirages*

*Also published in paperback as a Praeger Special Studies Student Edition